Praise for *Nothing Is Impossible*

"This is a lot more than a first-rate memoir. It is a brilliantly organized account of a decades-long struggle towards reconciliation, not just on the part of two governments but on the part of two nations bearing the physical and emotional scars of a protracted war. As U.S. ambassador to Vietnam, Ted was far more than merely diligent. He was intensely creative in finding ways, both moral and material, to soften bitter memories with new hope. In the process, he served the strategic interests of the United States by stressing common interests and building mutual respect. His work in Vietnam is a reminder of something often overlooked in our country: the extraordinary value of its professional Foreign Service—which I personally saw every day as Vice President, and which is clear as day on the pages of this book."

—Al Gore, former U.S. vice president

"America's reconciliation with Vietnam is one of the most remarkable diplomatic stories of the past three decades, and Ambassador Ted Osius was at the center of it all. In his new book, Ambassador Osius takes readers behind the scenes of this initiative, helping them understand how two old enemies came together to forge a better future for their people. *Nothing Is Impossible* is an absorbing memoir from one of America's finest diplomats."

—Madeleine K. Albright, former U.S. secretary of state

"In the great tradition of Dean Acheson's *Present at the Creation*, Ambassador Osius has provided us with a thoughtful and gripping diplomatic history of the critical moments in the reconciliation and the rebuilding of relations between the United States and Vietnam. This book provides important historical context but is also deeply personal, reminding us just how valuable diplomacy and the creative diplomats who toil tirelessly, often behind the scenes, are. This is a must-read not just for those interested in the role of the United States in Asia, but for anyone who seeks to understand what contribution an individual can make to addressing the complexities of international relations."

—Ambassador Michael Froman, former U.S. trade representative

"The title of this book tells you a lot about Ted Osius, and about the instrumental role he played in building trust and cooperation between the United States and Vietnam. Forty years after a war that caused incalculable suffering and loss for the people of both countries, Ted's story of how an openly gay American ambassador won the hearts of the Vietnamese people contains priceless lessons for every aspiring diplomat, and for people everywhere who believe in the power of listening and of staying true to one's convictions in pursuit of a larger goal in a foreign land."

—Patrick Leahy, U.S. senator

"Ambassador Ted Osius tells a remarkable story of how the United States and Vietnam overcame the tragedy of war to build an enduring new relationship. My husband John played a part, along with so many Americans, including principled Democrats and Republicans in Congress, successive U.S. presidents of different political parties, and civic leaders—including proud veterans—determined to chart a new course for our peoples that is about the future, not the past. I recommend Ted's book as both an authoritative history and a colorful account of an ambassador's life in a country of strategic importance to the United States."

—Cindy McCain, chair of the Board of Trustees of
the McCain Institute for International Leadership at
Arizona State University

"This remarkable book is a tribute to the power of reconciliation between former enemies—the United States and Vietnam. It also reveals the power and promise of diplomacy and the extraordinary American ambassador, Ted Osius, who led the way in building a new peace with the Vietnamese people and government."

—Nicholas Burns, former ambassador (ret.), Harvard
University professor, and former U.S. under secretary of state

"From his direct engagement in the establishment of the U.S. embassy to his 2014–2017 ambassadorship in Hà Nội, Ted Osius has demonstrated outstanding commitment and perseverance in the complex and difficult journey toward his stated goal of Vietnam–U.S. reconciliation. I applaud Ambassador Osius's remarkable contribution to this worthy cause. His memoir provides us a needed American perspective from a top U.S. diplomat. Let us hope that in the near future there will also be Vietnamese perspectives offered on the topic of Vietnam–U.S. reconciliation."

—Tôn Nữ Thị Ninh, former ambassador of Vietnam
to the European Union

"Ted's evocative book, *Nothing Is Impossible,* instantly took me down a path of very fond memories. His story is an extremely personal one for me as well; one that brings back countless recollections of people, places, events, and hard decisions, some of which evoked forgotten moments when history was made. His lively firsthand account of the timing, the key players, and the complex circumstances leading to the reconciliation and development of diplomatic relations between the United States and Vietnam will keep readers glued to the book's pages. Anyone interested in an expertly detailed account of U.S.–Vietnam relations will discover that *Nothing Is Impossible* is a gold mine of historical and interesting anecdotal information."

—Pete Peterson, former U.S. ambassador to Vietnam

"Ted Osius and I started our ambassadorship in each other country's capital, Hanoi and Washington, DC, almost at the same time in late 2014. We committed ourselves to working together and we witnessed remarkable achievements: President Obama visiting Vietnam and Party General Secretary Trọng's first-ever historic visit to the United States, among others. Ted has been much appreciated by leaders of both countries for his dedication and wise counseling. And, featured as the title of his new book, *Nothing Is Impossible* has been, not only Ted's famous remarks, but more uniquely, an attribute of the U.S.–Vietnam relationship."

—Phạm Quang Vinh, former ambassador of Vietnam to the United States

"Ted Osius has been the tip of the U.S. diplomatic spear in some of the most critical areas around the world. In his nearly thirty years in the U.S. Foreign Service, Ted has successfully navigated the ever-changing chessboard of U.S.–Asian relations in a political landscape populated with both fierce U.S. allies and determined opponents. All at a time that has seen the ever-growing influence of China on the world stage. Ted has shown he is a diplomat's diplomat and his story—as riveting and touching as it is detailed—is ultimately one of courage, devotion, and dedication."

—Alan Lowenthal, U.S. representative for California's 47th district

"Ted Osius has written a wonderful book about his, and America's, relationship with Vietnam. He shows vividly how through diplomacy—not just government to government, but people to people and culture to culture—former wartime enemies surmounted differences once thought unbridgeable, and makes the case for pursuing goals still thought impossible, like the advancement of human rights in Vietnam. His story is fascinating, fun to read, and a primer for how America can regain its standing and influence in Vietnam and beyond."

—Tom Malinowski, U.S. representative for New Jersey's 7th district

"Ambassador Ted Osius has written an illuminating, engaging, and often moving story of the quarter century he has dedicated to helping the United States and Vietnam overcome their painful past. It is a narrative of political, economic, environmental, and educational policies, of cultures and traditions, of losses and memories, of the lingering devastation of war, and the commitment to work for reconciliation and peace."

—Drew Gilpin Faust, Arthur Kingsley Porter University Professor and president emerita, Harvard University

"This is a book you cannot put down. Set in the corridors of power, Ted Osius's insider account offers fascinating insights about Vietnamese politics and geopolitical relations. Highly recommended to anyone who is interested in contemporary Vietnam."

—Đỗ Nguyễn Mai Khôi, Vietnamese artist and activist

"This is an outstanding account of a rare transformational moment in history, when two peoples formerly divided by bitter ideological differences and scarred by warfare, were able to find their ways towards a reconciliation of the spirit, long after the swords were put away. As US ambassador to Vietnam, Ted Osius was far more than a detached observer and reporter of these events, in the classical manner of diplomats. Without ever losing perspective as an exponent of US policy, he invested heart and soul in furtherance of this process, and, as an unintended consequence of his respect for the values and cultures of the people of Vietnam, and by virtue of the examples he set in the details of his personal life, became in his own right a symbol of the best we have to offer as a nation."

—Leon Fuerth, Founder and Director of the Project on Forward Engagement, former National Security Adviser to Vice President Al Gore

"Ted Osius expertly weaves the personal and the political into an engaging and insightful story of how Vietnam and the United States have come so far so fast since diplomatic relations were established twenty-five years ago. 'Dealing honestly with the past . . . was key to carving out a different future,' he writes, and the most challenging part of that past is Agent Orange. Today the United States is giving material assistance to victims of Agent Orange and cleaning up the dioxin residue left behind at former American bases in Vietnam. But reconciliation is not yet complete and these and other measures which address the legacies of war will require continuing American attention and commitment."

—Charles Bailey, former Ford Foundation representative in Vietnam and coauthor, *From Enemies to Partners: Vietnam, the U.S., and Agent Orange*

"I had the pleasure of spending time with Ted in 2016 while I was filming in Vietnam. He instantly impressed me as a diplomat who not only held a strong commitment to U.S. diplomacy, but more importantly as someone who cared deeply about the people of Vietnam with whom he interacted daily. He later demonstrated great personal integrity and courage by standing up against an unjust and misguided policy that would have abandoned people who had sacrificed greatly for our country. More Americans should follow his example of genuine communication, deeper understanding of others, and courageous living!"

—Samuel L. Jackson, actor

"Ted Osius has shared such an important story about how America and Vietnam made the remarkable transition from enemies to friends, and what it means, truly, to come to terms with epic tragedy and loss."

—Lynn Novick, co-director/producer, *The Vietnam War*

"How do countries move from war to peace to friendship to cooperation to partnership? The dynamic is exceedingly, and unfortunately, rare. But Ted Osius had the good fortune to be engaged in America's reconciliation with Vietnam from its earliest days. In the finest tradition of diplomatic memoirs, he effortlessly synthesizes grand strategy and humanitarian affairs, tense negotiations and touching bicycle rides, to definitively document the course—and the enormous potential—of one of America's most vital partnerships in Asia."

—Parag Khanna, author of *The Future Is Asian*

"Warriors and prisoners turned diplomats, revolutionaries and political activists turned statesmen, soldiers and draft dodgers turned national leaders: such are the extraordinary people whose unimaginable determination and resilience helped to overcome the impossible aftermath of war—and succeeded at a magnificent act of reconciliation. As brilliantly told by former ambassador Ted Osius, two former deadly enemies become bound into a reflection of one another through a desire for peace. *Nothing Is Impossible* deserves to be read for generations."

—Nguyễn Quí Đức, former National Public Radio
journalist and author of *Where the Ashes Are:
The Odyssey of a Vietnamese Family*

"While millions of pages have been written about the terrible war between the United States and Vietnam, the two countries' fraught and complicated efforts to rebuild diplomatic and economic relations afterward has been understudied and misunderstood. Ted Osius's *Nothing Is Impossible* beautifully fills this important gap. Told from the perspective of a diplomat on the front lines of the negotiations, the story Osius shares is both deeply personal and revelatory. Readers will learn new facts about the incremental steps toward reconciliation while being introduced to a cast of compelling characters who shaped the process."

—Edmund Malesky, professor of political economy and director of the
Duke Center for International Development

"*Nothing Is Impossible* reminds me of *Vietnam Now* by former *Los Angeles Times* bureau chief, the late David Lamb. Like David, Ted is a great storyteller connecting the people he's met along the way to the pivotal moments in Vietnam's modern history. From lifting the U.S. trade embargo by President Clinton in 1994 to Vietnam's crackdown on civil society leaders during President Obama's visit in 2016, one can sense Ambassador Osius's frustration as well as his jubilation in his dealing with Washington, DC, or Hanoi where he once called home. Someday he will return with his family to call it home again. For he is an American at birth, but a Vietnamese at heart."

—Trịnh Hội, lawyer and television host

"Despite a tortured history, America's relationship with Vietnam is now evolving into a strategic partnership as Southeast Asia becomes a testing ground for China's rise and the epicenter of U.S.–China rivalry in the world. This illuminating book by Ted Osius tells the dramatic story—through the people who lived it—of how the two countries transitioned from implacable enemies to cooperative partners on the regional stage. As a central player in this transition, Osius has written the rare volume that is both important diplomatic history and an engrossing and enjoyable read."

—Jonathan Stromseth, Lee Kuan Yew Chair in Southeast
Asian Studies, Brookings Institution, and former member
of the secretary of state's policy planning staff

Nothing Is Impossible

Nothing Is Impossible

• • • • • • • • • • • • • • • • •

America's Reconciliation with Vietnam

TED OSIUS
Foreword by John Kerry

Rutgers University Press

New Brunswick, Camden, and Newark, New Jersey, and London

Library of Congress Cataloging-in-Publication Data

Names: Osius, Ted, author. | Kerry, John, 1943– writer of foreword.
Title: Nothing is impossible : America's reconciliation with Vietnam / Ted Osius ;
    foreword by John Kerry.
Description: New Brunswick : Rutgers University Press, [2022] | Includes bibliographical
    references and index.
Identifiers: LCCN 2021006631 | ISBN 9781978825161 (hardcover) |
    ISBN 9781978825178 (epub) | ISBN 9781978825185 (mobi) | ISBN 9781978825192 (pdf)
Subjects: LCSH: United States—Foreign relations—Vietnam. | Vietnam—
    Foreign relations—United States. | Osius, Ted. | Ambassadors—United State—
    Biography. | Ambassadors—Vietnam—Biography. | United States—
    Foreign Relations—1989–
Classification: LCC E183.8.V5 O85 2022 | DDC 327.730597—dc23
LC record available at https://lccn.loc.gov/2021006631

A British Cataloging-in-Publication record for this book is available from the British Library.

www.rutgersuniversitypress.org

Manufactured in the United States of America

To Clayton, my life's partner,
and
TABO and Lucy, who give their papa the greatest joy

Nothing is impossible in United States–Vietnam relations.

PETE PETERSON, former prisoner of war and the first U.S. ambassador to postwar Vietnam

Contents

List of Photographs

Foreword

It's almost clichéd now to suggest that America has no permanent enemies. After the horrors of World War II, through the Marshall Plan, the United States helped rebuild Germany as a pivotal player in a peaceful Europe. The United States helped transform Japan into a boisterous democracy, a contributor to stability and prosperity in Asia. These were simply some of the best investments even a war-weary United States could ever imagine making: instead of turning inward, we turned adversaries into close allies, and that has defined seventy-plus years of progress.

In retrospect, there was both an ease and almost an inevitability to those decisions. After all, in both cases, the United States was the victor on the battlefield, and we were entering a new global struggle between ideologies that would shape the second half of the twentieth century. Helping rebuild capitalist democracy was part of our post–World War II mission. The rare question for the United States is, what happens afterward when we don't win the war?

Enter Vietnam: seven letters that have meant everything from misunderstanding to division and from civil war to proxy war, and which a generation of unlikely allies—in the United States and in Vietnam—chose to redefine not as a war or as a bitter memory but as a partnership between two proud nations. How improbable, and how rewarding.

In *Nothing Is Impossible: America's Reconciliation with Vietnam*, my friend Ted Osius, former U.S. ambassador to Vietnam, tells the extraordinary story of how two enemies became friends. Relationships are at the core of this story, because for reconciliation and for diplomacy relationships matter. As ambassador, Ted showed that demonstrating respect and building trust could strengthen the U.S.-Vietnam partnership. Working together on important challenges—climate change, global health, and peacekeeping—built trust. These diplomatic lessons should inspire us as we redefine and rebuild our relationships with the rest of the world.

This is also a story of diplomacy lived every day, in ways big and small. Not all diplomacy is grand strategy. Ted had fun doing his job. He loved Vietnam, and it showed. Each time I visited, I saw how thoroughly he enjoyed the opportunity to represent America abroad. Riding his bicycle or traveling with his young children, Ted touched the hearts of many Vietnamese. Because he embraced Vietnam's people, history, culture, and language, Ted won over not only Vietnam's leaders but also its citizens. He made full use of a moment in history when it was possible to create meaningful friendships for the United States.

Flash back to a very different but not too distant time in our two countries' history, and such diplomacy seems a world away. The early days—after the war and before we normalized diplomatic relations with Vietnam—were difficult. Ted describes the imperfect but determined people on both sides who took risks to bring Vietnam and America together. Writing about my friendship with John McCain, he recounts what drew us to the same conclusion: we needed to make peace with Vietnam. We needed to end the war about the war because it was in America's interests to do so. On an overnight flight to Kuwait in late February 1991, John and I began to talk about our very different experiences in Vietnam, and even about our disagreements in the 1970s. That conversation literally lasted for decades. We both saw the need to have a relationship with a country as important as Vietnam.

We served together on a Senate select committee to dig into a seminal and haunting question: Were there American soldiers still alive in Vietnam? A historic effort was launched to bring people home—and to bring answers and closure to their families. Never in the history of warfare have a former foe and its opponent engaged in such exhaustive accounting of the missing.

Healing wasn't easy. Reconciliation requires hard work, courage, compromise. and—most important—recognition of the humanity of brothers, sisters, friends, and loved ones on both sides. Vietnam and the United States have pursued this process every day for the past twenty-five years. Together, Vietnamese and Americans found and returned the remains of soldiers who perished, blew up unexploded ordnance, and cleaned up Agent Orange. Step-by-step, Americans and Vietnamese deepened the pool of trust that allowed us to become, if not allies, at least close economic and security partners.

Today, Vietnam participates in more military engagements with the United States than it does with any other country. Vietnam has twice welcomed a U.S aircraft carrier to its shores, and the largest ship in its fleet came from the United States. Vietnam and the United States collaborate on challenges in the South China Sea, the Mekong River, and North Korea. Our diplomats work together in multilateral fora, including the United Nations, the World Health Organization, the Asia-Pacific Economic Cooperation forum, and the Association of Southeast Asian Nations. These actions demonstrate trust, and they advance the process of reconciliation.

To build trust, we must keep earning it, and that means doing what we say we will do.

The task of reconciliation is not complete. As Ted notes, even after Washington and Hanoi were reconciled, divisions persisted. The war was simultaneously a fight for independence, a contest of ideologies, and a civil war. Reconciliation needed to take place not only between victors and vanquished, but also between north and south, and between Americans of Vietnamese origin and citizens of Vietnam. Reconciliation between the Vietnamese diaspora and the motherland involves deeply emotional matters, including honoring the dead and acknowledging past horrors. It depends on ties between people: the back-and-forth activities of businesspeople, veterans, students, tourists, and family members. It requires more time.

Reconciliation requires continued nurturing. The United States and Vietnam must continue to engage on challenges that matter not only for dealing honestly with the past, but also for the future—including clean energy, climate change, economic transformation, human rights, and education.

For twenty-five years, the United States has shown respect for and built trust with Vietnam by being honest about the past, even as we've both been determined to overcome it. We both chose the path of reconciliation, and as a result, we are walking toward a better future—together. What better story could any of us write than this account by Ambassador Ted Osius to explain the difference that determined diplomacy can make in the twenty-first century?

John Kerry

Preface

• •

Biên Hòa Cemetery

The cemetery wasn't much to look at. Broken slabs of concrete covered many of the graves. Some were tilted, threatening to fall onto the caskets beneath. The scraggly trees looked gray and were covered with a thin layer of dust from a nearby industrial zone. Unkempt grass, coated with the same dust, was bunched around the tombstones that remained upright. The dry season made the air still and hot.

A guard was seated on a broken cane chair at the entrance, smoking cigarettes and feigning indifference as our motorcade snaked inside. He rose to follow us. After our visit, the local police would require him to fill out a report. When I lit incense at a hulking, moss-covered concrete monument at the cemetery's highest point, I saw the guard hovering in the background. Attracted by the stir, onlookers had drifted in and were skulking by the gray trees.

Could this grubby, abandoned cemetery northeast of Hồ Chí Minh City really be a pivot point for reconciliation? Vietnam's Communist Party wanted it forgotten. Its graves contained soldiers who had fought for Saigon, and the government in Hanoi had let Biên Hòa Cemetery go to seed. Some feared that the cemetery could be a rallying point for those who opposed Vietnam's Communist Party.

The Vietnamese American community, whose members agreed on little else, was united on the importance of restoring Biên Hòa, of cleaning up its graves and honoring the souls buried there who had fought for South Vietnam. Community leaders, many based in Southern California, insisted that the cemetery be remembered and its dead treated with respect.

I had waited until I was halfway through my tenure as ambassador to visit the cemetery. A few years before, a South Vietnamese veteran piloted a small plane over Biên Hòa and dropped leaflets calling on the Vietnamese people to overthrow the Communist regime in Hanoi. I had needed to establish some credibility in Hanoi before I could make even a quiet visit to the cemetery. The government needed assurance that the American ambassador had no intention of destabilizing the fragile peace between north and south.

Months after I visited the cemetery, my husband, Clayton, and I were hosting an official dinner, and our honored guest was Drew Gilpin Faust, president of Harvard University. A distinguished historian of America's Civil War and its aftermath, Faust knew a lot about reconciliation.

"Biên Hòa Cemetery has symbolic importance," I said to her. "Properly burying the dead, in their homeland, matters to the Vietnamese, whatever part of the country they come from. But the government won't allow the Vietnamese American community to maintain it. What should I do?"

"After the U.S. Civil War," Faust replied, "it took a long time before Southern soldiers could be buried at Gettysburg. In cemeteries, the victors and the vanquished honor the dead and their sacrifice. But the victors choose who can be honored, and they may not show equal respect to those who fought on the losing side.

"Ambassador, let me offer a suggestion," she continued. "Instead of talking about 'The Dead,' with a capital T and capital D, try speaking instead about honoring people who died."

Faust was speaking from her seat in the grand dining room of the colonial mansion that served as the U.S. ambassador's residence. Pink and white flowers adorned the dining table, and each gold-rimmed plate was embossed with the Great Seal of the United States. Masterpieces from American photographers and Vietnamese artists adorned the walls. We were the sixth American family to occupy the stately home. In front of the building was an enormous American flag, while statues of Presidents George Washington and Abraham Lincoln watched over the back. It was fun to show it off.

Faust was seated next to Vietnam's deputy foreign minister, Lê Hoài Trung. I said to him, "A small gesture from the victors would mean a lot."

He shook his head. "This matter of Biên Hòa Cemetery is very difficult. People who oppose us have turned it into a political issue." Deputy Minister

PHOTO 1 Colonel Tuấn T. Tôn; Consul General Mary Tarnowka; Ambassador Ted Osius; and Nguyễn Đạc Thành, president of the Vietnamese American Foundation, Biên Hòa Cemetery, Bình Dương province, October 2017 (Credit: Personal photos of Tuấn T. Tôn).

Trung remembered the pilot and his leaflets, as well as many attempts to raise the flag of South Vietnam in Biên Hòa.

Another guest, a former Việt Cộng guerrilla, Lê Minh Khuê, interjected, "According to Vietnamese tradition, death washes away all differences."

"Those with whom I have spoken only want to honor people who died," I told Deputy Minister Trung. "No capital letters. When the rainy season comes, they don't want the caskets to float away. They don't want tree roots to burst through the graves. No flags or symbols or politics," I promised. "Just two requests: let them dig ditches and cut tree roots."

He thought for a moment, then smiled: "Ditches and tree roots. Let me see what I can do."

Months after my ambassadorship ended, a friend wrote to me, knowing I still cared about Biên Hòa. He told me that ditches had been dug in the cemetery and tree roots had been cut. The rainy season had come, causing the trees to turn from gray to green. Death had washed away the differences. Reconciliation had progressed a meaningful step further.

When the Vietnam War ended with Saigon's fall on April 30, 1975, U.S. President Gerald Ford wanted Congress and the American people to shift their focus away from the chaos we had left behind. Henry Kissinger, Ford's secretary of state, rebuffed Vietnam's efforts to establish communication. Exhausted by the war and its damage to our own society, Americans didn't want to hear about Indochina. Veterans, activists, and Vietnamese refugees tried to bring attention to those left behind. As Vietnamese Americans in California, Texas, and Louisiana began to prosper and acquire some political clout, they insisted that their elected representatives pay attention to human rights and religious freedom in Vietnam, as well as to the treatment of buried soldiers who had fought for Saigon.

For twenty years, reconciliation between the governments in Washington and Hanoi progressed slowly. Only after President Bill Clinton established full diplomatic ties in 1995 did it appear possible that the United States and Vietnam could begin anew. Reconciliation involves deeply emotional matters, including honoring the dead with proper burials and acknowledging the pain and horrors of the war.

It depends on ties between people: the back-and-forth activities of businesspeople, student exchanges, tourists, and family visits. These ties continue to grow, because brave people from all sides decided to face the past squarely, build trust with former adversaries, and create a better future. They learned how to dig ditches and cut tree roots, to create the conditions for reconciliation one step at a time.

Nothing Is Impossible: America's Reconciliation with Vietnam is about that process, rooted in the tangible stories of some prominent individuals as well as ordinary citizens. Their stories show that friendship between old enemies is possible. A former prisoner of war, Pete Peterson, could serve as America's first postwar ambassador to Vietnam. Another former prisoner of war, Senator John McCain, and his ideological opponent, Senator John Kerry, could become champions of reconciliation. President Clinton, who dodged the draft, could help heal deep wounds.

As Washington and Hanoi were formally establishing ties, I requested an assignment as one of the first U.S. diplomats in a united Vietnam. It felt like a great stroke of luck to witness firsthand the early days of government-to-government reconciliation.

Making friends in Hanoi, and later in Saigon, turned out to be remarkably easy. The Vietnamese people chose not to harbor grudges but rather to open their arms, even to representatives of a government that had waged a terrible war in their country. I had studied the Vietnamese language before my assignment began, and each time I met someone new during those heady early days, we built a bit more of the trust needed to create a partnership.

I came to know the heroes who reconciled former adversaries: not only McCain and Kerry, but also former Vietnamese Foreign Minister Nguyễn Cơ Thạch and Vietnam's first ambassador to the United States, Lê Văn Bàng. I served on the staff of a true American hero, Ambassador Pete Peterson, who spent nearly seven years as a prisoner of war in the Hỏa Lò Prison (nicknamed the Hanoi Hilton) and then returned to that city as President Clinton's personal representative.

As a young political officer and later as ambassador, I collaborated with behind-the-scenes heroes of reconciliation, including Tommy Vallely, a Harvard professor; Virginia Foote, a trade expert; Tim Rieser, a Senate staffer; the Ford Foundation's Charles Bailey; Bùi Thế Giang, a member of Vietnam's Communist Party; diplomats Nguyễn Vũ Tú and Nguyễn Xuân Phong; and "superconnector" Thảo Nguyên Griffiths.

Pursuing diplomacy with Vietnam for twenty-three years—under four presidents and seven secretaries of state—I became, in 2014, the first U.S. ambassador who spoke fluent Vietnamese, and the second openly gay career ambassador in U.S. history. When President Barack Obama visited Hanoi in 2016, he asked about my family. I offered to introduce him to my spouse, who is Black, and our children, who are of Mexican descent. Smiling, he referred to us as a "walking Benetton ad."

Becoming the U.S. ambassador to Vietnam was a dream come true. I love Vietnam. I love its people, history, language, and culture. During my first tour as a relatively junior diplomat in the 1990s under President Clinton, we laid a foundation for a new relationship, and as ambassador under President Obama, I had the privilege of building upon that foundation. My history with the country helped me enjoy unstinting support from leaders in Washington and Hanoi, who shared the goal of making our new partnership work. The United States pushed the process of reconciliation through joint action with the Vietnamese on multiple fronts.

President Obama and Secretary of State Kerry provided a vision for transforming U.S.-Vietnam relations that I believed in passionately. While I served as ambassador, I was honored to host many U.S. visitors to Vietnam, including Supreme Court Justice Ruth Bader Ginsburg, President Clinton, the actors Samuel L. Jackson and Brie Larson, Nobel Prize winners, cabinet officials, members of Congress, and activists of all kinds.

Traveling to Vietnam with President Clinton in 2000, working as a diplomat in Asia during the administration of President George W. Bush, and hosting President Obama in Vietnam in 2016, I witnessed the power of a U.S. president's showing respect and how that builds trust and creates partnership

PHOTO 2 The author, Secretary of State John Kerry, and President Barack Obama, Hanoi, May 2016 (Credit: AFP/Jim Watson).

with former adversaries. In India, President Bush's commitment to a new partnership altered the trajectory of history. In Indonesia, I witnessed a transformation of relations under President Obama's leadership. As ambassador in Hanoi, I had the privilege of arranging the first visit to the Oval Office by Vietnam's Communist Party chief and of persuading President Obama to visit Hanoi and Hồ Chí Minh City. Presidents Clinton, Bush, and Obama understood the value of real partnerships for the United States.

Early in my tour as ambassador, Vietnam's press dubbed me "the People's Ambassador." I spoke Vietnamese and rode a bicycle everywhere, and that helped me make friends with citizens from all walks of life. On a bike and up close, I saw how Vietnamese turned their country from a ravaged war zone into a strong, prosperous, and independent friend of the United States. *PBS News Hour* broadcast a profile of me titled "Meet Bicycle Diplomat Ted Osius, America's Modern Ambassador to Vietnam."[1]

On bicycles and in our travels, my embassy team and I learned important lessons about reconciliation. The war had left massive scars. Our only chance to shape a different future was by being honest about our history. And there are many versions of that history. As Ken Burns and Lynn Novick said in their documentary *The Vietnam War*, "There is no single truth in war."[2]

We learned that the United States casts a long shadow. Showing respect meant figuring out what was truly important to our Vietnamese partners and taking that seriously. We learned the lesson of ditches and tree roots. To build trust required efforts large and small. U.S. military and civilian leaders understood that ties between Vietnam's armed forces and the U.S. military would help advance America's security goals in the Asia-Pacific. My job, and that of my team, was to figure out how to build enough trust to allow those ties to develop. We had to remember that many of Vietnam's current leaders had come up through the ranks while fighting against the United States. Applying the ditches and tree roots concept—that is, one step at a time builds trust—was the only way to go. It required patience and determination.

Step by step, by finding the remains of soldiers who perished, destroying unexploded bombs, cleaning up Agent Orange, and assisting Vietnamese with severe disabilities in provinces that were heavily sprayed with the defoliant, Americans and Vietnamese built a foundation of trust that allowed them to become close security partners. The stories in this book show that when the United States commits itself to strong relationships, we create opportunities for a more prosperous and safer America. America's relationship with Vietnam has arisen from the ashes of war and become something unique. Our countries' remarkable transformation from enemies to friends shows that, truly, nothing is impossible.

A Note on the Text

Wherever possible, I have used the Vietnamese spelling of names and places. In Vietnamese, the family name comes first, followed by the middle name and then the operative name. For example, Nguyễn Cơ Thạch, Vietnam's foreign minister from 1980 to 1991, may be referred to as Foreign Minister Thạch, or simply Thạch, but not Nguyễn. Hồ Chí Minh, widely referred to as President Hồ, is an exception. I have also made exceptions in writing "Vietnam" and "Hanoi," because they are commonly written in English as a single word rather than Việt Nam and Hà Nội.

Nothing Is Impossible

An Improbable
Friendship

● ● ● ● ● ● ● ● ● ● ● ● ●

In late February 1991, on a Boeing 757 headed for Kuwait, a conversation took place that would accelerate the reconciliation between the United States and Vietnam. The flight was the first leg of a Congressional delegation's journey to the Persian Gulf to survey the results of Operation Desert Storm, which had begun in January and had just ended.

Seated facing one another on this overnight flight were Massachusetts Senator John Kerry and Arizona Senator John McCain. The two men had served together in the Senate for four years, Kerry as a Democrat and McCain as a Republican, and they regularly found themselves on opposite sides of important issues. In part, that may have been an extension of their different experiences as soldiers during the Vietnam War and in particular their reactions to the war when they returned from it.

Lieutenant Commander John McCain was the son and grandson of admirals. He graduated from the U.S. Naval Academy in 1958, trained as a fighter pilot, and flew a Naval A-4 aircraft that dropped bombs on targets in North Vietnam. On October 26, 1967, the thirty-one-year-old McCain was shot down over Hanoi's Trúc Bạch Lake after he had tried to destroy a power plant.

Ejected from the plane as it spiraled downward, McCain had two broken arms and a broken leg even before he hit the water, hard. Men swam out to him, but saving his life was not foremost in their thoughts. McCain and his fellow pilots had destroyed their city's infrastructure and killed many of its citizens. The Vietnamese soldiers swimming toward him wanted him dead.

The men who pulled McCain from the water held him responsible for the deaths of their loved ones, and they stuck a bayonet in his groin. He was dragged to shore with one leg bent at a 90-degree angle and the bone protruding from the skin. McCain's captors threw him into a cell in Hỏa Lò Prison; its name translates as "fiery furnace." Built by the French at the end of the nineteenth century, the prison housed generations of Vietnamese nationalists long before any American prisoners of war (POWs) were held there. Weeks passed before McCain received any medical attention. Two of his broken limbs were set without anesthetic. The third, and the wound in his groin, were left to heal on their own—or not. Fellow prisoners, who had also endured torture at the hands of the Vietnamese, kept McCain alive.

Over the coming months, McCain shrunk down to a hundred pounds, and when he was brought before the warden in June 1968, he was barely able to stand. The Vietnamese had by then learned that McCain's father was the commander of America's entire Pacific Fleet.

"You may go free," the warden said.

McCain sought the advice of his friend and fellow prisoner Bob Craner, who argued that seriously injured prisoners could be considered exempt from the U.S. military's Code of Conduct, according to which POWs should go home in the order of their capture. But McCain chose to adhere to the code and refused to accept the offer. He would not go home out of turn.

The warden told him, "Now, McCain, it will be very bad for you," and ordered guards to beat him. They broke his ribs, rebroke his arm, knocked out his teeth, and threw him into solitary confinement, where he stayed for two of the next four years.

The decision to remain in prison, in solidarity with other POWs, defined McCain. Previously a playboy and a rebel, McCain experienced prison as a kind of enlightenment. He had inherited a legacy from his father and grandfather, who had passed on to him a deep loyalty to the United States and especially to the U.S. Navy. Service, sacrifice, and honor became the foundations of his character. Many years later, in his memoir *Faith of My Fathers*, McCain reflected on "the honor we earn and the love we give if at a moment in our youth we sacrifice with others for something greater than our self-interest."[1]

In December 1972, President Richard Nixon ordered B-52 attacks on Hanoi, which became known as the Christmas bombings. McCain and the other American POWs cheered when they heard U.S. planes overhead. A month later, the Paris peace talks between the governments of the North and South Vietnam and the United States ended with an agreement that included the release of POWs. They were released in order of the dates they had been shot down, and McCain was among those who departed from Vietnam on March 15, 1973. President Nixon was a hero to McCain, and they first met when the president welcomed McCain and other POWs to the White House in May 1973.

As a former POW, McCain could choose his next military assignment. He became the commanding officer at Cecil Field, in Jacksonville, Florida.

Like McCain, John Kerry was also a member of a military family: his father had served as a pilot during World War II. Kerry graduated from Yale University in 1966 and enlisted in the U.S. Navy. He arrived in Vietnam in November 1968 as a lieutenant and was soon captaining Swift Boats on the intricate web of rivers that make up the Mekong Delta.

On the night of February 28, 1969, Kerry and his crew were patrolling the Bảy Háp River on a mission to destroy enemy boats, structures, and bunkers when they ran into an ambush. Kerry directed the boats he commanded "to turn to the beach and charge the Viet Cong positions," and then he "expertly directed" his boat's fire and coordinated the deployment of the South Vietnamese troops, according to Admiral Elmo Zumwalt, the commander of U.S. naval forces in Vietnam, who later awarded him the Silver Star.

Kerry pursued the people who had staged the ambush, leaping ashore to pursue, and ultimately kill, a fleeing Việt Cộng who was carrying a B-40 grenade launcher. The mission was judged successful for having destroyed numerous targets and confiscated substantial combat supplies, while sustaining no American casualties.

Less than a month later, Kerry earned a Bronze Star by rescuing Jim Rassmann, a Green Beret, from a different tributary of the Bảy Háp River. Kerry crawled out onto the deck of his damaged Swift Boat and, though injured and under fire, pulled Rassmann out of the water. Kerry also earned three Purple Hearts. He was sent home on March 26, 1969, as a decorated war hero who had been wounded three times.

Returning full of questions, Kerry wondered what the United States was actually accomplishing in Vietnam. He had discovered that most Vietnamese he saw along the rivers were apolitical. They didn't support the Việt Cộng or the Saigon government. They just wanted to be left alone to go about their lives. He questioned whether the domino theory of countries falling to communism one after another made sense. In his 2018 autobiography, *Every Day Is Extra*, he wrote that "the blind repetition of missions . . . was symbolic of our whole failing commitment to a war that I was now convinced was wrong."[2]

While Kerry admired the bravery and sacrifice of the men with whom he served, he could not justify their deaths—nor did he believe that the U.S. government could do so. Kerry connected with the antiwar movement and gradually began to speak in favor of an accelerated end to the war. In 1970, he received an honorable discharge from the Navy and began working with the Vietnam Veterans Against the War (VVAW), a national veterans' organization that by then was active throughout the United States. Kerry argued that the VVAW should take its arguments to Washington, DC, where in April 1971 he participated in a five-day antiwar protest.

During the protest, someone from Senator William Fulbright's staff heard Kerry speak and hustled him into a Senate hearing room. The young veteran said, "Each day to facilitate the process by which the United States washes her hands of Vietnam someone has to give up his life so the United States doesn't have to admit something that the entire world already knows, so that we can't say that we have made a mistake. Someone has to die so that President Nixon won't be, and these are his words, 'the first President to lose a war.' We are asking Americans to think about that, because how do you ask a man to be the last man to die in Vietnam? How do you ask a man to be the last man to die for a mistake?"[3]

Kerry's testimony drew so much attention that he was asked to give speeches around the country for the VVAW. In 1972, he ran for Congress. In that election President Richard Nixon defeated Senator George McGovern, and Kerry also lost. After the Paris Peace Accords were signed in January 1973, Kerry attended law school.

Graham Martin began serving as ambassador to South Vietnam in September 1973. Accredited to the Republic of Vietnam, that part of the country below the 17th parallel, Martin was chosen for the job of ambassador by Secretary of State Henry Kissinger, who correctly believed that Martin would refuse to depart from Saigon until the bitter end. By March 1975, the North Vietnamese were advancing quickly and overtaking the south.

In April 1975, Saigon was a city under siege, and although Martin had not yet ordered a general evacuation, the Marines began assisting thousands of Vietnamese employees of the U.S. government to leave from Saigon's Tân Sơn Nhất Airport in the twelve days before South Vietnam surrendered. Some of these Vietnamese had worked for the U.S. government over the past decade and a half, and they knew that the invading North Vietnamese would treat them brutally as enemies.

Most of the Vietnamese employees were evacuated with their immediate families, flying out on U.S. military transport aircraft and chartered jetliners. Vietnamese personnel working for the Defense Department (nearly all of whom worked for the Central Intelligence Agency) got out on the airlift, as did a number of those employed by the State Department, the U.S. Agency for International Development, and the U.S. Information Agency.[4] The U.S. ambassador determined the timing of the evacuations from the country.

Serving as ambassador is like captaining a ship. Only the U.S. president has a higher protocol rank than an ambassador in the country where he or she is accredited. The ambassador's letter of instruction generally gives him or her full responsibility for all executive branch officials in the country. Most of those officials adhere strictly to the chain of command and find it difficult to challenge the ambassador's decisions. Martin's decisions to hold off on evacuations in the spring of 1975 had life-or-death consequences.

At this time, General Fred Weyand, the last U.S. commander in Vietnam, recommended to President Gerald Ford an additional $700 million in U.S. assistance to mobilize fresh South Vietnamese units to hold back the Communists. Kissinger made a last-minute appeal to the Senate Appropriations Committee on April 15, arguing that the funds would enable the Saigon regime to negotiate with Hanoi on terms "more consistent with self-determination."[5] Congress would have none of it and denied the request.

On the same day, Lance Corporal Darwin L. Judge arrived in Saigon to supplement the twenty-four Marine Security Guards who were divided between the embassy compound and Tân Sơn Nhất Airport. The stretched and exhausted detachment's first mission was to secure classified material. Its second was to protect American citizens, and six Marines were assigned to protect the ambassador.

Growing up in Marshalltown, Iowa, Judge had played Little League Baseball; delivered newspapers on his bicycle; and, as an Eagle Scout, shoveled snow for the elderly. During hay-making season, he often helped farmers load hay bales onto a hayrack. During his senior year of high school, Judge joined the Marines.

On April 21, Judge was providing security at a defense attaché facility at Tân Sơn Nhất Airport. Doug Potratz, another Marine, recalled that as thousands were trying to flee the city, he was frantically trying to evacuate his wife and his daughter, Becky. Potratz wrote that Judge "rushed us to the plane . . . put my 4 year old daughter on his back, 'piggy back ride' style, picked up my wife's suit cases, and walked them up to the plane."[6]

On April 22, Corporal Charles McMahon Jr. arrived in Saigon. His sister wrote, "At that time the fall of Saigon to the North seemed imminent, so nobody at home thought he would have to go there."[7] In his hometown of Woburn, Massachusetts, McMahon was a strong competitive swimmer and diver. He "had a great way with the kids," his sister explained, and he taught swimming at the Woburn Boys' Club. Joining the Marines at the age of nineteen, McMahon served first with the military police and then joined the elite Marine Security Guards, graduating from the training program in March 1975 with orders to go to Saigon. McMahon, too, was assigned to Tân Sơn Nhất Airport.

On April 25, a forty-man force attached to the Seventh Fleet augmented the beleaguered Marines. At 3:45 A.M. on April 29, the North Vietnamese army attacked the airport, and their heavy shelling forced an immediate halt to the evacuation. The first rocket landed on the main road, killing Judge and McMahon. In the chaos that ensued, their remains were left behind. At the U.S. embassy, the order for a helicopter evacuation was finally given.

Some have speculated that the killing of Martin's adopted nephew, Marine First Lieutenant Glenn Dill Mann, near Chu Lai in November 1965 contributed to Martin's refusal to listen to those who said in early April that it was time to prepare for an evacuation. Martin made the staff wait until the North Vietnamese had already entered Saigon before they could cut down a large tamarind tree on the embassy grounds to make room for a possible helicopter landing. He ranted in an internal message (a cable, in State Department lingo) that his bureaucratic foes were criticizing him in the press.

Martin's opposition to giving the general evacuation order until too late resulted in many people who worked for U.S. civilian agencies being left behind. The helicopter airlift was initiated at the last possible moment and was too disorganized to rescue many of the locally employed staff who had been told to wait in safe houses for transport to the airport.

Martin contended, against the strong protest of senior U.S. staff at the embassy, that a mass evacuation would have caused panic in South Vietnam's army and the Marine units defending Saigon and end hopes for a negotiated cease-fire. Martin was still committed to Kissinger's tripartite scheme—according to which power would be shared between North Vietnam, the Việt Cộng, and the Saigon government—when Tân Sơn Nhất Airport was closed by the North Vietnamese bombers and the shelling that killed Judge and McMahon.

In retrospect, the North Vietnamese (and probably the Soviets) were likely colluding in a disinformation campaign to dupe the United States while running out the clock on South Vietnamese military resistance. U.S. intelligence at the time showed the north's rapid gains on the ground, and it confounds reason that Martin believed they would stop at the gates of Saigon and accept a power sharing arrangement. Yet by delaying evacuation until the airport in Saigon had been destroyed, Martin failed the Vietnamese who had supported the United States and were left behind.

Judge and McMahon were the last Marines to die in Vietnam. Their commander, Master Gunnery Sergeant John J. Valdez, from San Antonio, Texas, commanded the Marine Security Guards and dispatched Judge and McMahon to Tân Sơn Nhất Airport. For twenty-four hours without a break, Valdez loaded helicopters from the embassy compound. Just before 5:00 A.M. on April 30, Valdez and Ken Moorefield, a foreign service officer and former infantry captain, put Martin, dazed and suffering from pneumonia, aboard one of the last helicopters to take off from the embassy roof. Moorefield later reported that, as he rode in another helicopter headed for the U.S. fleet, "I realized my war, our war, was finally over."[8]

When the ambassador departed, the coded message "Tiger is out" was issued, causing confusion among some of the helicopter pilots—who thought the message meant that the evacuation was complete. Still on the embassy roof with the last of his Marines, Valdez noticed that the flow of choppers had decreased: "No birds in sight. But I never thought for one minute that the choppers would leave us behind."[9] A helicopter returned and lifted the Marines off just before 8:00 A.M. Valdez was the last Marine to climb aboard. Three hours later, North Vietnamese troops crashed through the gates of Saigon's presidential palace.

In 1966, Ann Mills Griffiths had an experience that would become all too common among American families. Her brother, Commander James Mills, was listed as missing in action (MIA) when the Navy F4B on which he served as radar intercept officer disappeared on a low-flying mission at night over North Vietnam. Ann and her family discovered how painful it was to be denied closure.

Starting in 1970, the National League of Families of American Prisoners and Missing in Southeast Asia focused on the families of servicemen whose questions remained unanswered. With its black-and-white POW/MIA flag, the League provided a symbol used by some politicians to help foster a deep sense of grievance about the first war America had lost. Active in the League since its founding, Ann Mills Griffiths relentlessly sought answers for the families of the missing and, over time, her support was sought and opposition feared by American leaders of both parties.

The stories and images coming out of Vietnam appalled Americans. When the POWs were released in 1973, they brought with them horrific stories of the torture they had endured, among them McCain's. Two years later, Americans witnessed both the humiliation of the helicopter airlift of U.S. citizens and some Vietnamese and the tragedy of the South Vietnamese who were left behind. The north's takeover of Saigon was followed by images of reeducation camps, as well as the miseries of the boat people and other refugees fleeing from the Communists. From 1975 to 1979, reports trickled out about the slaughter in Cambodia, reviving American memories of the Indochina conflict.

Above all, Americans held onto the belief that additional POWs were being held in secret camps in Vietnam's jungles, a view supported by the *Rambo* films and by politicians including Ronald Reagan. Emotional debate centered on the fate of these imagined POWs and those considered missing in action from the conflict.

In 1982, Griffiths traveled to Laos and Vietnam, beginning a dialogue that led to the fullest possible accounting effort—and to the normalization of relations between the United States and those countries. Starting in 1987, John Vessey, former chairman of the Joint Chiefs of Staff and a retired general, and Richard Armitage, assistant secretary of defense, made several trips to Southeast Asia. Consulting closely with Griffiths and the League, the 1987 delegation led by Vessey succeeded in convincing the Vietnamese to permit U.S. teams to operate in the country, seeking information about American service members still unaccounted for from the war.

America's crippling economic embargo on Vietnam after the Communist takeover, along with collectivized agriculture and two wars—in Cambodia and on the Chinese border—had led to economic ruin and famine in Vietnam. The possibility of ending the embargo incentivized the Vietnamese to cooperate on the POW/MIA effort.

By the time I met her, Griffiths was a prominent figure in Washington, with years of experience lobbying U.S. presidents and military leaders. A chain smoker, she spoke in a gravelly voice about providing answers to families who had lost a loved one. As leader of a grassroots movement, Ann pursued answers relentlessly, determined to achieve the fullest possible accounting about Americans missing from not only the Vietnam War but also from World War II, the Cold War, the Korean War, and conflicts in the Middle East and

North Africa. A familiar figure in the halls of Congress and the White House, Ann was also accorded respect at the highest levels in Hanoi.

Ann believed that the U.S. government had to keep its promise to those who had made the ultimate sacrifice in service to their nation. Soldiers might have been lost, but she was determined that they would never be forgotten. The U.S. military's creed, she knew, was never to leave a fallen comrade behind. Military families knew that, too, and over time the creed that defined her mission became enshrined in the ethos of the U.S. government.

Ann and the League helped guarantee that when it came to Vietnam, commercial and strategic considerations took a back seat. No issue mattered more to the United States than the fullest possible accounting of those lost during the war.

From 1977 to 1981, McCain was posted to the Navy Office of Legislative Affairs in Washington, DC. Speaking of his new assignment, McCain said that it was a "real entry into the world of politics and the beginning of my second career as a public servant."[10] Two Republican senators—John Tower of Texas and William Cohen of Maine—took an interest in the nation's most famous former POW and war hero. McCain also became friends with Senator Gary Hart of Colorado, a Democrat who had managed McGovern's presidential campaign when he challenged Nixon. In 1980, when McCain married his second wife, Cindy, the daughter of an Arizona beer magnate, Cohen and Hart served as groomsmen.

In 1982, backed by his father-in-law's fortune and political contacts, McCain was elected to the U.S. House of Representatives, defeating his Democratic opponent by 35 percentage points. He became one of Reagan's conservative warriors and four years later ran for Barry Goldwater's Senate seat, which he won by 20 percentage points.

Kerry may have lost his first election, but he wasn't finished with politics. After graduating from law school in 1976, Kerry went to work in the district attorney's office of Middlesex County, Massachusetts, and in 1982, the same year that McCain won his race for Congress, Kerry was elected lieutenant governor of Massachusetts, second in command after Governor Michael Dukakis. In 1984, Kerry ran for the Senate seat vacated by Paul Tsongas. John McCain visited Massachusetts to rally veterans for Kerry's opponent, Republican Ray Shamie, but Kerry won in spite of the Reagan tide that swept other Republicans into office in Massachusetts that year.

During the Reagan administration, while many political leaders wanted to ignore Vietnam, debates about the war continued. Republicans such as

McCain argued that America had failed to prosecute the war with sufficient determination. Democrats such as Kerry argued that the United States should never have entered the war in the first place. In 1985, Kerry and McCain appeared together on CBS's *Face the Nation* to present these different views. POWs despised Kerry's antiwar protests, as McCain recalled in their tense on-air encounter. Kerry said that the war had accomplished little with enormous costs to both sides.

The two senators' different experiences in Vietnam seemed to lead them to hold contrasting worldviews that played out in other issues. A hawkish Republican, McCain was quick to call for military action when the United States faced a challenge. An antiwar Democrat, Kerry knew the costs of war personally and never gave up on diplomacy. However, what they had in common moved them forward with regard to Vietnam. Both men were patriots to the core. They believed in service to their country and in honor. They knew American families that desperately wanted answers about what had happened to their loved ones in Vietnam. Thousands of servicemen remained unaccounted for, and their families needed closure.

The two senators brought that common commitment with them on the flight to Kuwait in 1991 and, despite their differences, they agreed that binding the wounds of the Vietnam War was essential for the families of U.S. servicemen. Closure was also essential for America to allow the country to move forward. The United States was still torn over the meaning of the Vietnam War, and McCain and Kerry agreed that the Vietnam Syndrome had lasted long enough.

As senators and veterans, they thought that together they could help bring about closure, and that the United States might even benefit from having a relationship with Vietnam. That night in 1991, they agreed to put party disagreements aside to achieve the fullest possible accounting of those whom America had lost in the hills, rivers, and forests of Vietnam. Too many unanswered questions haunted America, and as veterans who knew the cost of war, McCain and Kerry could do something that would allow America to move forward.

McCain was then at the end of his first term in the U.S. Senate, and Kerry was at the beginning of his second. Their decision to work together took place sixteen years after the fall of Saigon. Upon their return from Kuwait, the two senators set up a select committee that dug into the question of whether any Americans were still alive in Vietnam. McCain made clear that full diplomatic relations with Vietnam would not be possible unless the United States could be certain that no Americans remained in the country and that all Vietnamese political prisoners had been released from reeducation camps.

As Kerry and McCain worked together on the Senate Select Committee on POW/MIA Affairs, they continued the discussion that had begun that night on the plane—one that lasted for decades—and they formed an improbable friendship. At first, their staff members and political advisors warned them against the undertaking. The task of proving a negative was too complex. It was likely to cost them votes and place their promising careers at risk. Veterans and the families of veterans would suspect a cover-up by the Vietnamese and perhaps one by the U.S. government.

Still, Kerry and McCain began an intense process of collaboration. The so-called Gang of Five supporting them—Ginny Foote, Mark Salter, Nancy Stetson, Tommy Vallely, and Frances Zwenig—swung into action to tackle this seemingly impossible challenge. Few Americans at that time traveled to Vietnam, but Foote did so multiple times, often taking delegations of U.S. veterans with her and staying at Vietnam's government guest house. She worked closely with General Tom Needham, who directed the POW/MIA work in Vietnam.

Foote had taken her first trip to Vietnam in May 1989, in support of her boss, William Sullivan, then the leader of the International Center, a non-governmental organization. Sullivan had served as deputy chief of mission at the U.S. embassy in Saigon; ambassador to Laos; and ambassador to the Philippines from 1973 to 1977, when hundreds of thousands of Vietnamese were escaping through that country. In the mid-1960s, as a member of the team negotiating with the North Vietnamese in Geneva, Sullivan had met Nguyễn Cơ Thạch, and they had learned to trust each other.

Thạch, who had become Vietnam's deputy prime minister and foreign minister, reached out to his old friend, seeking a way to contact senior U.S. government officials. Sullivan asked his former colleagues at the State Department, including Assistant Secretary John Negroponte, if he could meet with Thạch and see what his friend had in mind. As Vietnam was still bogged down in Cambodia, Negroponte first said no.

After some progress in the Paris peace talks over Cambodia,[11] Negroponte decided to take a risk and let Sullivan go to Vietnam as a private citizen. If things went wrong, the State Department would distance itself from Sullivan. During those 1989 meetings in Hanoi, Thạch and Sullivan were happy to see each other and caught up on family news, including the death of Thạch's daughter—who had also been a Vietnamese diplomat. Although Foote did not realize it at the time, with that trip she had embarked on a lifelong adventure with Vietnam.

The two senators, the Gang of Five, and their administration allies gradually persuaded Vietnamese leaders that cooperation on the POW/MIA effort was in the Communist nation's interest and would eventually lead to an easing of the economic embargo. Kerry, McCain, and other members of the select committee needed to prove that no evidence suggested that Americans had been held back in Vietnamese prisons. They had to ensure a bipartisan conclusion, agreed to by all of the committee members. McCain's and Kerry's efforts, and those of their collaborators, led to the most exhaustive accounting of soldiers lost in a war that the world has ever seen.

After he agreed to work with Kerry, McCain became the object of many veterans' wrath. He was called "Songbird" and "Manchurian candidate," first for his commitment to fully account for American POWs and MIAs and later for supporting normalizing diplomatic relations with Vietnam. He endured heckling and protests for his work on the select committee. Veterans questioned the honor of a man who for more than five years had endured torture and deprivation at the hands of his captors. Similarly, Kerry had long faced the wrath of veterans who resented his antiwar stance.

Ann and the League, and later the select committee, insisted on absolute transparency from Vietnamese officials, a challenge in a political system enshrouded in secrecy. Americans searching for remains had to be able to go wherever leads took them, even on short notice, and the Vietnamese and Americans engaged in that historic effort gradually learned to trust one another.

After the Soviet Union dissolved in December 1991, Vietnam sent emissaries to Washington seeking peace, and President George H. W. Bush established a timeline for normalization. In January 1992 he directed the Department of Defense to create the Joint Task Force–Full Accounting, which soon opened an office in Hanoi.

In 1992, after McCain and Kerry had been working in the select committee for a little more than a year, domestic politics intervened. Arkansas Governor Bill Clinton defeated President Bush and won the presidency. Like Kerry, Clinton had led antiwar protests. Unlike McCain and Kerry, he had avoided military service. Senate Majority Leader Robert Dole, a Kansas Republican who had served in World War II, stridently opposed lifting the economic embargo on—or establishing full diplomatic relations with—Vietnam.

McCain and his fellow Republicans had no incentive to make the new president's job easier. For McCain, however, honor and duty mattered more than party, especially when it came to relations with Vietnam.

2

A Time to Heal and a Time to Build

● ● ● ● ● ● ● ● ● ● ● ● ● ●

Bill Clinton, the former governor of Arkansas, became president in 1993, with Al Gore, a former U.S. senator from Tennessee, as vice president. Clinton selected Warren Christopher as his first secretary of state and, along with Assistant Secretary Winston Lord, they devoted the United States' initial diplomatic efforts in Asia to advancing human rights in China. The focus with regard to Vietnam continued to be on achieving the fullest possible accounting of prisoners of war (POWs) and those missing in action (MIAs) from the war.

Anthony Lake—who had served as a junior diplomat in Vietnam, first as a consular officer in Saigon and Hué, and later as assistant to Ambassador Henry Cabot Lodge—became President Clinton's national security advisor. In 1969, Lake had gone to Paris with Henry Kissinger, President Richard Nixon's national security advisor, on his first secret meeting with North Vietnamese negotiators. Given Lake's experience and the political sensitivities of the POW/MIA issue, the Clinton administration decided that the White House, instead of the State Department, would make the key decisions about America's relationship with Vietnam, in consultation with Congress and with Ann Mills Griffiths and the National League of Families of American Prisoners and Missing in Southeast Asia.

Senator John Kerry chaired the Select Committee on POW/MIA Affairs—with Republican Senator Bob Smith, also a Vietnam veteran, as vice chair. Senator John McCain had declined the position as vice chair, though he was a member of the committee. Other Vietnam veterans on the committee included senators Bob Kerrey, Chuck Robb, Tom Daschle, and Hank Brown. They all had to contend with the cantankerous North Carolina Senator Jesse Helms, the Republican who chaired the Foreign Relations Committee, and the wild conspiracies believed in by Smith. The committee pursued an exhaustive inquiry, involving more than two hundred hours of public hearings that included the testimony of active and former U.S. government officials, a former Vietnamese army colonel, and family members of missing servicemen. The committee required the Defense Department to declassify more than a million pages of documents, and committee investigators examined archives in Russia, North Korea, and Southeast Asia for any evidence that Americans were still being held in captivity. Kerry and other senators visited Vietnam more than twenty times, seeking information from the Vietnamese government and military. In January 1993, the committee concluded that there was no compelling evidence that any American POWs were still alive in Vietnam.

Finding those still missing was America's overriding goal in Vietnam from 1975 to 1995 and beyond. During that period, Vietnam faced America's economic embargo and struggled with two wars, famine, and a devastated economy. The United States made it clear that an end to Vietnam's economic and diplomatic isolation could be achieved only if the Vietnamese fully cooperated with the Americans on the POW/MIA issue.

Soon after the war ended, there were quiet attempts to lift the economic embargo and establish diplomatic relations with Vietnam. In March 1977, President Jimmy Carter sent a delegation to Hanoi, led by Leonard Woodcock, president of the United Auto Workers, to investigate the POW/MIA question. In May 1978, Cyrus Vance, Carter's secretary of state, instructed Assistant Secretary Richard Holbrooke to negotiate the terms of normalization with Deputy Foreign Minister Phan Hiền in Paris, followed by two rounds of talks in New York with senior official (later Foreign Minister) Nguyễn Cơ Thạch.

Holbrooke described six requirements for normalization: (1) increased Vietnamese cooperation with the United States on possible POWs and those considered MIA from the conflict; (2) the end to Vietnam putting refugees out to sea in iron ships; (3) a guarantee that Vietnam would not invade Cambodia (the United States knew Hanoi was preparing to do so); (4) the end of Vietnam's cozying up to the Soviet Union; (5) the Vietnamese would stop raising the Agent Orange issue; and (6) the Vietnamese would no longer push for reparations.

A secret letter from President Richard Nixon to North Vietnam's prime minister, Phạm Văn Đồng, a side agreement to the 1973 Paris Accords, could be interpreted as an American promise to provide nearly $5 billion in war reparations.[1] This letter prompted first Hiền, and later Thạch, to push repeatedly for reconstruction assistance, based on a moral obligation to provide aid. Holbrooke told both officials the U.S. Congress would not accept reparations. Still, the Vietnamese said that they would not raise the issue of Agent Orange and agreed to the other requirements. The Vietnamese were also willing to help with the POW/MIA issue.

Mike Eiland, a member of Holbrooke's negotiating team, said that at the second and final meeting in New York, Thạch told Holbrooke that Vietnam agreed to normalization without preconditions and suggested they work out a memorandum of understanding on the spot. Holbrooke said that he would report the Vietnamese position to President Carter.

National Security Advisor Zbigniew Brzezinski persuaded President Carter that relations with China were too important to risk by normalizing diplomatic relations with Vietnam. China, which had supported Vietnam during the war with the United States, felt betrayed when Vietnam pushed back on territorial disputes and opposed the Chinese-backed Khmer Rouge in Cambodia's civil war. After Deputy Assistant Secretary of State Bob Oakley went to New York in November 1978 to tell the Vietnamese that the deal was off, Thạch flew directly to Moscow and signed a treaty of friendship and cooperation with the Soviet Union and, a month later, Vietnam invaded Cambodia to defend its borders against Cambodian incursions—thus ending the horrors of the Khmer Rouge, which had ruled Cambodia since 1975. This action prompted Vietnam to continue its expulsion of refugees from Cambodia, most of whom were ethnic Chinese. Clearly this had been planned well in advance, and we will never know if the Vietnamese would have followed through with the Soviet treaty and invasion of Cambodia if the United States had continued the normalization process.

A month after the invasion, Chinese Premier Deng Xiaoping visited the United States and warned President Carter that China would teach Vietnam a swift lesson, which lengthened into a twelve-year border war. Ten thousand Vietnamese and ten thousand Chinese soldiers perished in 1979, and thousands more died during the next eleven years of fighting. Vietnam's presence in Cambodia revived the deep historical animosity that many Cambodians felt toward the Vietnamese. In addition, Hanoi also further aligned Vietnam with the Soviets against the West by permitting the Russian military to use its Cam Ranh Bay, one of the most strategically important bays in all of Asia.

Following the unsuccessful Carter-Holbrooke attempt to lift the economic embargo and establish diplomatic relations with Vietnam, the United States did not revive high-level diplomatic efforts during the eight years of Ronald Reagan's presidency. The administration of President George H. W. Bush engaged in Cambodian peace talks with the five permanent members of the U.N. Security Council: China, France, the United Kingdom, the Soviet Union, and the United States. In 1989, the State Department had sanctioned unofficial talks between William Sullivan, the former ambassador mentioned in chapter 1, and Thạch, which led to a visit by Thạch to Washington in 1990. There he received a U.S. proposal for a road map to the normalization of relations.

The road map laid out specific conditions, including full Vietnamese cooperation in investigating reports that POWs had been seen alive after the end of the war. Although Thạch stated that no living POWs remained in the country, he agreed to the U.S. conditions as humanitarian. As China considered Thạch to be too friendly to the United States, Chinese officials told their Vietnamese counterparts that firing him was a precondition for Vietnam's maintaining diplomatic relations with China. The admirable and talented diplomat resigned in March 1991, remaining under house arrest for nearly five years. In October 1991, the five permanent members of the U.N. Security Council agreed to a comprehensive political settlement of the Cambodian conflict, a key step toward meeting the U.S. conditions for establishing full diplomatic relations with Vietnam.

President Clinton proceeded cautiously. Some form of embargo had been in place since 1945, when the United States first attempted to bolster France's colonial authority by sanctioning the Việt Minh, the organization that led the struggle for Vietnamese independence from French rule. Ending that half-century of sanctions had to be handled carefully, especially by a president who had famously avoided military service in Vietnam.

Fortunately, Kerry and McCain provided President Clinton with the political cover needed to lift the economic embargo. The senators' thorough and dogged work in the select committee led to a Senate resolution in January 1994 urging the president to lift the trade embargo. McCain promised to do whatever was necessary to back the president's actions. On January 26, when Smith sought to block the president from lifting the embargo, Kerry,

McCain, and others joined forces to defeat Smith's motion by a vote of 58 to 42. Kerry and McCain then sponsored a bipartisan resolution that urged the president to lift sanctions, which passed 62 to 38.

"The vote will give the President the kind of political cover he needs to lift the embargo, and I expect that relatively soon," McCain said. "I think it's a seminal event in U.S.-Vietnamese relations."[2] The president lifted sanctions on February 3.

In May 1994, the United States and Vietnam formally established consular relations and then opened liaison offices in Hanoi and Washington, DC. Scot Marciel, the first diplomat assigned to the liaison office in Hanoi, worked out of the Joint Task Force–Full Accounting (JTF-FA) compound while searching for a building to serve as the U.S. embassy. Only after full diplomatic relations were established between the two countries could the United States send a chargé d'affaires (also known as an acting ambassador) or a confirmed and credentialed ambassador to Hanoi.

That next step was still fraught with political risk. Three hundred U.S. companies had opened offices in Vietnam after the embargo was lifted. Still, Lake would not speak with U.S. companies about doing business in Vietnam, stating that more progress was needed on the POW-MIA issue before full diplomatic relations could begin. It was not until 1995 that Lake was persuaded by his deputy, Samuel "Sandy" Berger, and Senior Director for Asia Sandy Kristof, together with support from the Veterans of Foreign Wars, that enough had occurred on the POW-MIA issue to obtain Congressional support for normal diplomatic relations with Vietnam.

Even so, U.S. businesses would have to wait years before economic relations were truly normal. These companies wanted the kind of support that the U.S. government typically provided overseas, including having the Overseas Private Investment Corporation, Export-Import Bank, and Trade and Development Agency operate in Vietnam. And ultimately, businesses needed a bilateral trade agreement to bring tariffs down to normal levels. Diplomatic relations alone did not provide a sufficient basis for robust trade relations.

Debate over the Vietnam War continued after the 1994 midterm elections that resulted in new majority leaders in Congress: Newt Gingrich in the House of Representatives and Bob Dole in the Senate. With Republicans controlling both houses of Congress, President Clinton needed at least some Republican support if he hoped to establish full diplomatic relations with Vietnam. Specifically, he needed support from McCain, the senator with the most credibility on Vietnam.

Berger, who became the national security advisor in President Clinton's second term, also worried about the threat to the establishment of full diplomatic relations from the Vietnamese diaspora. He made annual pilgrimages to Southern California, where he was pelted with eggs and tomatoes by Vietnamese Americans who opposed establishing ties to Hanoi. He also heard from U.S. veterans who believed that their service would be dishonored by establishing diplomatic relations with Communist Vietnam.

In the mid-1990s, many Vietnamese Americans considered that too little progress had been made on human rights. "Business interests have been put in front of human rights," said Do Diệm, an opponent of normalization living in Orange County, California.[3]

Some were ready to move on. Frank Jao, a property developer who owned significant real estate in Little Saigon, a neighborhood in Westminster, California, said, "Speaking in the context of being an American businessman— nothing to do with Vietnamese American, because I am no longer a Vietnamese—[full diplomatic relations are] good for the United States."[4]

In early 1995, former Defense Secretary Robert McNamara publicly expressed his shame over the war's conduct. McNamara said what most Americans already knew: U.S. leaders had let down members of the armed forces when they sent them into battle and had failed the American people by their prosecution of the war. Twenty years after the fall of Saigon, the debates remained personal and painful, and a politician's war record (or antiwar record) still evoked praise or scorn. (Five years later, when Vice President Gore ran for president, he mentioned his military service in Vietnam during all three debates to draw a contrast with Governor George W. Bush.)

In mid-May 1995, a presidential delegation headed by Deputy Secretary of Veterans Affairs Hershel Gober visited Vietnam and found the government remarkably forthcoming with information about the American servicemen lost during the war. The delegation reported that "more than 800 separate POW/MIA documents have been turned over to U.S. officials by the SRV [Socialist Republic of Vietnam] Government since the inception of JTF-FA." The success of Gober's mission allowed President Clinton to argue that genuine collaboration with the Vietnamese was the best way to achieve the fullest possible accounting of the Americans lost in the war.

By July 1995, the president had determined that America's overriding goal in Vietnam—the fullest possible accounting for Americans missing from the war—could best be achieved by establishing diplomatic relations. Flanked by almost every Vietnam veteran serving in Congress, as well as Bobby Muller, chairman of the Vietnam Veterans of America, in a wheelchair, President Clinton announced his decision on July 11.

Drawing on Abraham Lincoln's words, the president said: "This moment offers us the opportunity to bind up our own wounds. They have resisted time for too long. We can now move to common ground." He closed by quoting scripture: "Let this moment . . . be a time to heal and a time to build."[5]

Ann boycotted the event, despite having worked so hard and contributed so much to establishing diplomatic relations. "I couldn't in good conscience attend," she wrote, "since provisions on the 'Roadmap to Normalization of Relations' with Vietnam had not been met, despite the President's and Tony Lake's pledge to me in front of all the VSOs [Voluntary Service Organizations] and staff to adhere to it." She continued, "I didn't want to see respected, prominent figures giving their version of how we got to that important moment which I knew to be untrue, then be asked by media, also present, and have to tell the truth or say no comment. . . . I'm still very honored to have been a part of those post-war, challenging efforts, secret dinners and meetings in NYC and long hours in Hanoi with the most incredible, capable and intelligent, as well as visionary, diplomat I've ever met, Nguyen Co Thach."[6]

According to Ann, progress on the road map had been insufficient, though the U.S. government believed that Vietnam had done enough to move forward. It was a bittersweet moment for many.

Warring op-eds summarized the controversy greeting the president's announcement. Jan Scruggs, a decorated Army veteran and founder of the Vietnam Veterans Memorial Fund, wrote: "The time is now" for full diplomatic relations. "What better way to resolve the issue of missing U.S. servicemen than to have tens of thousands of American tourists roaming around Vietnam and U.S companies doing business there?"[7]

The Veterans of Foreign Wars passed a resolution at its annual convention in the summer of 1995 to support full diplomatic relations as a way to strengthen work on the MIA challenge.

David Varney, the American Legion's New York State Commander, made a different case. "It's too soon to give in," he wrote, arguing that Hanoi had been sluggish in responding to U.S. requests for information about MIAs. He described the overall history of this accounting as "one of inaction, manipulation and, increasingly, a willingness on the part of the U.S. government to portray Vietnamese cooperation as more than it is."[8]

The White House released supportive statements from military heavy-weights such as former Secretary of State General Alexander Haig; former Defense Secretary Harold Brown; former Chief of Naval Operations Admiral Elmo R. Zumwalt Jr.; former Commander in Chief of the U.S. Pacific Command Admiral Charles Larson; and two former chairmen of the Joint Chiefs of Staff, General David Jones and Admiral William Crowe. Sixty-one percent of the American public agreed that it was time for full diplomatic ties.[9]

Veterans in Congress also spoke up, including Senator Frank Murkowski, the Republican who chaired the Committee on Veterans' Affairs; and Democrats such as Senators Kerry, Kerrey, and Bennett Johnston, and Congressman Pete Peterson. Most important, McCain declared that "tangible progress" had been made toward the fullest possible accounting. "We have looked back in anger at Vietnam for too long," he added. "I cannot allow whatever resentments I incurred during my time in Vietnam to hold me from doing what is so clearly my duty."[10]

McCain also pointed out the strategic advantages of a positive relationship with Vietnam. Noting that Vietnam would join the Association of Southeast Asian Nations, McCain wrote that "an economically viable Vietnam, acting in concert with its neighbors, will help the region resist dominance by any one power."[11]

In July 1995, days after diplomatic relations were established, I met a Vietnamese official for the first time. There was nothing bittersweet about the experience. I was jubilant. After joining the State Department in 1989, I had served my first tours in the Philippines and at the Vatican. In 1994, during a two-year stint as an advisor to U.S. Ambassador to the United Nations Madeleine Albright, I had requested that my next assignment be to Vietnam. I was convinced that no diplomatic posting could be more meaningful than one where I could help build the foundation of a new relationship with a former adversary. Gradually, I would come to understand how difficult reconciliation was for so many people who had suffered from the war.

When I met Lê Văn Bàng during a conference at the Washington Hilton, he had just become his country's chargé d'affaires to the United States. I was struck by his warmth, especially as protestors followed him to every public event in which he participated. Later, Bàng became the Socialist Republic of Vietnam's first ambassador to the United States. A perpetual optimist, Bàng gave me wise advice when I first met him, and he did so again many years later, when I became U.S. ambassador to Vietnam. He never failed to see possibilities in U.S.-Vietnam relations, and he played a key role in the countries' reconciliation.

For many who had supported or opposed diplomatic relations, Bàng was the human face of Vietnam. He first visited Washington in 1991 for a three-month fellowship set up by Ginny Foote, president of the U.S.-Vietnam Trade Council, which had been founded by Sullivan and Foote. Since the two Americans' trip to Vietnam to meet with Thạch in 1989, Foote had returned to Vietnam a number of times, and she had organized visits by Vietnamese diplomats to Washington, DC, where they met members of Congress, State Department officials, and representatives of NGOs and the business community. During his 1991 visit, Bàng met Kerry, McCain, Peterson, Lane Evans (another Vietnam veteran in Congress), and other key U.S. players. Bàng's personal relationships were critical during the political battle over establishing full diplomatic relations. Optimistic and disarmingly honest, Bàng over time gained the trust of the administration officials and members of Congress engaged in the debate.

Senators Dole, Smith, and Helms strongly opposed diplomatic ties with Vietnam. Still, Bàng managed to charm Helms, who was from the tobacco-producing state of North Carolina, saying that one day Vietnam would banish cigarettes, but until then he would urge all Vietnamese to smoke two cigarettes at a time. Helms laughed, and though he never changed his position, he was willing to engage with Bàng.

In August, as Secretary of State Christopher traveled to Hanoi to cut the ribbon on a new U.S. embassy, I began learning Vietnamese. It is a hard language. While the grammar is straightforward, pronunciation is exceedingly difficult. Most words have a single syllable, pronounced staccato fashion, with two-syllable compounds that are difficult to identify as words unless you already know their meaning. In the north, the language has six tones, while in the south it has five, and there are regional dialects all over the country that are almost mutually unintelligible. Vowels come in more than one form, so you must listen very carefully for subtle differences. Distinguishing between the tones, the strange vowels, and the slight variations between words that sound almost exactly alike can be a real challenge.

I struggled for months to have the language make sense, and then I experienced a breakthrough when I visited Vietnam for the first time in the spring of 1996 for a two-week immersion tour. Another language student and I would park ourselves in a club in Hồ Chí Minh City, where bar girls would chat with us, happy to be paid for doing nothing more than talking. Being able to ask a question and understand the answer from a hotel clerk or cyclo (pedicab) driver felt like a miracle.

After I passed my Vietnamese exams and arrived in Hanoi in September 1996, I reported to Bàng's counterpart, the U.S. chargé d'affaires, Desaix Anderson. Desaix had led the U.S. mission in Hanoi since late August 1995, and he would continue leading it until the first ambassador arrived in May 1997. Desaix had spent most of his thirty-five-year diplomatic career in East Asia, including seven tours in or focused on Indochina. He was a brilliant political analyst with a deep understanding of Vietnamese history and culture that allowed him to read his Asian counterparts.

Our embassy team loved working for Desaix. Born in Mississippi, he was a thoughtful, kind, and decisive gentleman. He was also an accomplished artist, whose paintings of Vietnam have been exhibited in New York, Washington, and Paris.[12]

Those of us on Desaix's embassy staff particularly valued his calmness under pressure and his devotion to the truth. Desaix spoke simply and directly, deploying his gracious Southern ways of speech to good effect, and the Vietnamese respected him greatly. He was Secretary Christopher's choice to serve as the first U.S. ambassador in Hanoi, though it is not clear whether the Senate would have confirmed him.

I was one of two fairly junior political officers in the embassy. The other was Bryan Dalton, whose understanding of the Vietnamese language and the country's internal politics far surpassed my own. He became a close friend as well as a colleague. Bryan and I cheerfully divided our workload, often while we were hunched over a charcoal stove in a local eatery, slurping noodle dishes that cost about fifty cents each. If one of us was busy shepherding a visiting delegation, the other would do the office work that was due to go to the State Department. We were thrilled to be pioneers.

Desaix let Bryan and me know that building a new relationship with Vietnam required two parallel efforts. As Vietnam's economic and diplomatic isolation ended, the country needed to integrate itself successfully into the region and to become part of the global economy. The United States needed our embassy to support the POW/MIA efforts of the JTF-FA. Desaix also prioritized health and education as nonpolitical areas of collaboration that would receive Congressional support.

In each of these efforts, we worked closely with Nguyễn Xuân Phong, director both of the Americas office at the Foreign Ministry and of Vietnam's Office for Seeking Missing Persons, which had begun working with Americans in 1988 to create the fullest possible accounting. Phong, a smart and engaged diplomat with a cool and proper demeanor, was dedicated to building U.S.-Vietnam relations, while continuing to represent Vietnamese interests.

He certainly did not give us everything we wanted, but he was not like the brick wall we and others had encountered with the government in the early days. He was willing to take risks within the Vietnamese system, and without that we could not have made as much progress on the fullest possible accounting or on anything else we tried. The JTF-FA made steady progress, year after year, in finding and repatriating the remains of American MIAs. Despite following hundreds of leads, its dedicated team never found any evidence that POWs remained in Vietnam.

Our longer-term goal was to create a security partnership with America's former enemy, and to do that, it was essential to address the past honestly. We also needed to take a step-by-step approach so that two militaries, once adversaries that had very different traditions, could learn to understand one another.

The first tentative steps took the form of military-to-military visits, a process the U.S. military pursued to understand and collaborate with the armed forces of any nation. American military leaders had worked with allies and partners for two centuries, but the People's Army of Vietnam had been long isolated from everyone but the Soviets. I served as the Hanoi embassy's first political-military officer in 1996–1997, and I apprenticed under the first defense attaché, Colonel Ed O'Dowd, who had established the office in 1995. He taught me that reciprocal visits by military leaders were essential to build the trust and understanding needed for the armed services of different nations to work together toward common security goals.

Lake had visited Hanoi in July 1996, a few weeks before I arrived. True to his promise to Ann and the League, Lake focused his visit on the effort to achieve the fullest possible accounting. The centerpiece of his trip was a visit to a remote helicopter crash site in Quảng Trị province, where six U.S. soldiers had been lost in 1968.

Lake's meeting with President Lê Đức Anh, whose responsibilities included leadership of the military, broke new ground. President Anh had convinced the military to support the POW-MIA recovery effort, and Lake's visit made it possible to initiate a military-to-military relationship and open the consulate in Hồ Chí Minh City. With Party Leader Đỗ Mười and Prime Minister Võ Văn Kiệt, Lake reached an agreement on resettlement opportunities for Vietnamese refugees.

In the autumn, Deputy Assistant Secretary of Defense Kurt Campbell followed Lake and designed a step-by-step approach that would lead to contacts between the U.S. military and the Vietnamese military that went beyond the POW/MIA accounting effort.[13] Vietnam's military leaders wanted Campbell to explain what steps could be taken to build a bilateral security partnership and to engage in multilateral arrangements such as those of the Association of Southeast Asian Nations. Campbell assured officials in Vietnam's Communist Party, the foreign ministry, the defense ministry, and other central government offices that the United States wanted to have a better—and broader—relationship with Vietnam.

In 1997, O'Dowd and I helped organize a reciprocal visit by Vietnamese senior colonels to Washington, DC, and Honolulu. Commander-in-Chief of the Pacific Admiral Joseph Prueher visited Vietnam the same year, followed by a series of visits from U.S. officials—including one from U.S. colonels representing all the services to Hanoi, Hồ Chí Minh City, Đà Nẵng, and Huế and a delegation from the National Defense University. Vietnam established a counterpart defense attaché's office in Washington in March 1997, and this led to Vice Minister of Defense Lieutenant General Trần Hanh's visits to Washington and Honolulu.

These meetings provided the U.S. military with a better understanding of Vietnam's military capabilities and limitations. The United States viewed the accounting of POWs and MIAs as the first essential step for building confidence in the countries' relationship, and for the Vietnamese, the first step was the United States' showing a sincere interest in Vietnamese concerns—such as the tons of land mines and unexploded ordnance still littering Vietnam's soil and the remnants of Agent Orange still poisoning its citizens. Addressing the painful past helped the Vietnam Ministry of Defense deflect criticisms from the old guard within the Communist Party who rejected a closer relationship with the United States. A bilateral security relationship needed to rest on a foundation of trust and collaboration in addressing the legacies of the American War, as the Vietnamese called it.

Full diplomatic relations between the two countries also brought tangible benefits to American citizens traveling in Vietnam, and to one in particular. Many Americans may not know that if they are overseas and have a problem, someone at the American embassy will answer the phone at any time when they call, day or night. If there is a bombing, someone will come looking for Americans known to be in the area, including in all hospitals, and will call each traveler's family with news. If there is a coup, embassy personnel will try to round up citizens and get them to a safe place. If Americans are hurt and in need of help, people at the embassy will assist them.

At 6:10 P.M. on October 26, 1996, I was the embassy duty officer when the phone rang. Embassy Marines were patching through an administrator calling from a provincial hospital in remote Yên Bái province, northwest of Hanoi.

Although the telephone line was bad and the administrator spoke in a local Vietnamese dialect, I could make out that an American had been in an automobile accident. I knew he was in serious trouble, because health care in the provinces at that time was terrible.

Then an Australian came on the line and told me his friend, thirty-six-year-old Timothy Vickers, had been hit by a truck while riding a motorcycle. Vickers had suffered massive internal injuries and was bleeding to death. With multiple pelvic fractures, as well as a ruptured spleen and kidney, he was fighting for his life.

Vickers had quit his job to take a dream trip around the world. Vietnamese doctors wanted to operate on the injured American, but to prevent them, the Australian had thrown his body across that of his friend. "The scalpels are rusty," he told me. "I'm a veterinarian, and I wouldn't want one of my animals to be treated in this hospital."

I was new to the embassy and to Vietnam, and I didn't know what to do, so I called my friend Kristen Bauer, a consular officer. Kristen advised me to call the embassy doctor. An Israeli with a strong sense of duty, Rafi Kot quickly got on the line with the hospital in Yên Bái. He then told me he needed enough blood to stabilize Vickers's condition and a helicopter to retrieve him from Yên Bái.

Hanoi's blood bank was not safe, so Kristen and I called members of the embassy community who had Timothy's blood type, O positive. All thirteen of them came forward to donate, waiting their turns until 2:00 A.M. in Kot's clinic, none of them complaining.

Unfortunately, we didn't have access to a helicopter, but two embassy drivers took Kot and a makeshift ambulance on the rough roads at night to Yên Bái. Meanwhile, I tracked down Vickers's parents in Peoria, Illinois, and told them all I knew. Distraught, his mother said to me: "Please, please save him. I've already lost one son. I can't lose another."

I told her, "We're doing everything we can, ma'am." At that point I wasn't sure her son would make it.

Kot drove back to the city with Vickers, at 6:00 A.M. reaching the airport, where we had arranged for an evacuation flight. There were no cell phones in those days, so every call to the people near Vickers had really been a series of calls via landlines. The blood we had collected from our embassy community was not enough, and we had reached out to a number of other Americans in our consular network. They came to the clinic to donate blood, and we delivered several liters of O positive blood to Kot when he reached the airport.

Kot loaded Vickers onto the evacuation plane, which was equipped with an intensive care unit, and flew with him to Singapore, using every unit of blood we had collected. At Mount Elizabeth Medical Center in Singapore, the doctors said that our efforts, and especially the blood, had saved Vickers's life.

A few days later, Desaix received a telegram from senior State Department leaders: "Your staff's successful management of the Vickers case, despite considerable obstacles, strongly reinforces in a most tangible way the immeasurable value of our presence in Vietnam." Assisting Americans abroad is the first task of any U.S. embassy.

After Vickers had recovered enough to board another plane, he flew home to Illinois, where he was met on the tarmac by his mother and sister. Given the extent of his injuries, doctors did not expect him to walk again, but he was determined and endured very tough rehabilitation. A year later, he came back to Hanoi. He walked through the embassy and thanked everyone there for saving his life.

In nearly thirty years as a diplomat, I handled many emergencies, including ones that occurred during a coup attempt in Manila in 1989, a terrible bombing in Mumbai in 2008, and an earthquake in Padang in 2009. In each situation, I joined other embassy staff members in assisting Americans in these countries, but I still feel especially proud that my colleagues and I were able to help save Vickers.

Safe travel between the United States and Vietnam—by tourists like Vickers, Americans of Vietnamese origin, businesspeople, or students—reinforced the human ties between the two nations. Safe travel for Americans involved providing assistance when they were hurt or in trouble, and saving Vickers was another step along the path to reconciliation.

A Vietnamese proverb, "Đi một ngày đàng, học một sàng khôn," says that when you go on a journey, you come back with wisdom. As a political officer in the Hanoi embassy in early 1997, I knew that I needed more wisdom—or at least a better understanding of the country where I served. Having discovered a few years earlier that I liked long-distance cycling, I persuaded eight biking friends from the United States, Vietnam, and Australia to ride 1,200 miles with me from north to south through Vietnam. This was certainly a way to get to know the country, and it seemed like it would be fun.

It was, but it was also a tough ride. We pedaled against headwinds every one of our fourteen days on the road. The heavily trafficked Highway One passed over mountains and through deserts, and the road was rough and under repair everywhere. Still, that highway is Vietnam's lifeline, its edges crowded with people growing and selling crops, educating their young, feasting and celebrating, and sometimes dying. Everyone in our group felt profoundly connected to the country while riding along that lifeline.

Our trip was punctuated by a series of bright images of Vietnam's varied landscape. And our challenging days of biking were broken up by a glorious afternoon on China Beach, a stroll through imperial Huế, having ice cream in the ancient Japanese port city of Hội An, dancing wildly to the Spice Girls' "If You Wanna Be My Lover" in Nha Trang, and scrambling onto the roof of the old U.S. embassy in Saigon—the roof from which helicopters had ferried thousands of people to safety. Most vivid for all of us, however, were the images of the Vietnamese people, especially young children.

When we rode into small towns, clad in Lycra on our fancy modern bikes, the kids didn't just wave and shout greetings but bounced to the edge of the road and greeted us with excitement about our passing. Most of us were Westerners, and we were like the circus coming to town. One rider, six-foot-four-inch Sam Shelton, distributed colored wind-up frogs, berets, and Polaroid photos to astonished and delighted children. Another rider, Dan Fern, wrote that although aggressive drivers caused us frustration, "then a young child would run up to the side of the road with a big smile and greeting, and my frustrations would disappear."[14]

Older kids, smiling and friendly, pedaled furiously to keep up with us for a few miles, eager to practice their English. "What is your name? Where are you from? Where do you go? Are you tired?"

Near the demilitarized zone that once divided north from south, I stopped on a bridge for a granola bar and a photo. A woman in her forties pointed out bomb craters, which were gradually filling in with water or brush after twenty-five years. We spoke in Vietnamese. She said that the Americans had destroyed the bridge where we stood many times. The Americans, she continued, killed people she knew.

As a U.S. citizen and diplomat, I felt that I had to tell her my nationality. She looked at me thoughtfully and said that America and Vietnam are friends now. Touching my arm, she said in the intimate language used for family members—language that conveys so much in Vietnamese—"Today, you and I are younger brother and older sister."

I told that story seventeen years later, when I testified before the Senate Foreign Relations Committee in my confirmation hearings. To me, it says a great deal about the Vietnamese spirit of forgiveness and reconciliation.

In 1997, our group of bikers responded enthusiastically to Vietnam's beauty, its subtle cuisine, and the warmth of its people. Nina Fuerth was on her first overseas trip and didn't know a word of Vietnamese, but she managed to connect with people everywhere. Her father—Leon Fuerth, my friend and mentor who was then national security advisor to Vice President Gore—called us regularly along the route to make sure his youngest daughter was safe.

The only woman cyclist on the trip, Nina was nervous about climbing the Hải Vân Pass, but when we finally got there, she was the first biker to reach the top. Nina pointed out that traveling north to south, we witnessed all the stages of growing rice, which constitutes the agricultural cycle and the central element of Vietnamese culture. First, farmers plant seeds in the wet paddy field, then they transplant the seedlings, harvest and thresh the rice, and finally dry the rice by the side of the road.

Stephe McMahon believed that the trip was about forgiveness and reconciliation. After we had laid waste to the country, Vietnam welcomed us back with open arms. For me, I learned about strengths and limitations during the long hours of pedaling, and the possibilities that arise when meeting an extraordinary challenge.

On the last day of biking, I was bloody and bruised from a spill I had taken as I dodged maniacal trucks, buses, and motorbike drivers for the final 116 searingly hot miles. Still, I remember feeling incredibly alive, from our 5:00 A.M. fogbound start to a downhill rush through thick jungle, past sugarcane and rubber plantations, and through busy marketplaces to the ferry ride across the Saigon River into the heart of Hồ Chí Minh City.

Exhausted and exhilarated—as well as caked with sweat, sunscreen, diesel fuel, and bike grease—all nine riders plunged fully clothed into a swimming pool, giddy with triumph and relief that we'd made it, alive and more or less unscathed. We had seen deadly accidents along our route, but luckily our mishaps were minor enough that we'd already forgotten them.

It was a great adventure. And true to the proverb, each of us had returned from our journey with some wisdom, or at least greater knowledge of a country we'd grown to love.

President Clinton chose to nominate as the first ambassador to a unified Vietnam Pete Peterson, a Vietnam veteran who was then a three-term congressman from Florida. Other contenders had included Jim Kimsey, a war hero

PHOTO 3 Nine bikers and friend Lê on Mỹ Khê Beach, Đà Nẵng, March 1997. From left to right: The author, Sam, Nina, Stephe, Tom, Daniel, Minh, Lê, Owen, and Ed (Credit: Sam Shelton).

and cofounder of AOL; Gober; and Under Secretary of State Peter Tarnoff. Clinton listened to his friend Bill Richardson, who had served in the House of Representatives with Peterson and strongly recommended him.

Clinton wanted an ambassador whose confirmation was assured. Peterson knew Vietnam from the perspective of a POW. He had been imprisoned for six and a half years, and he had spent some of that time in the infamous Hỏa Lò Prison—along with six hundred other American POWs, including McCain. Peterson should have emerged embittered and angry at those who had tortured him and deprived him of food and freedom. Miraculously, he walked out with hope, and as a member of Congress he became one of the architects of reconciliation.

Peterson had seen the worst of war, and President Clinton knew it would be hard to label someone who had endured such horror at the hands of his captors as soft on communism. Peterson wanted to return to Vietnam and build peace. In addition, as a former Congressman, he could do what a career diplomat could not: get on the phone in the middle of the night in Hanoi and call Senator Smith while he was on a fishing trip in New Hampshire to insist that he get out of the way so Peterson's team could do its job of peace building.

Peterson's confirmation hearings reignited the battles in American politics over normalization of relations with and full recognition of Vietnam, with some legislators and commentators believing that this was not the best way to achieve the national goal of having the fullest possible accounting for the POWs and MIAs whose families wanted news—any news—that would give them the closure they needed. Senator Smith was determined to delay full normalization. He was joined by Representatives Bob Dornan, Chris Smith, Dana Rohrabacher, and Ben Gilman and Senators Dole and Helms. They believed that the Vietnamese were dragging their feet on full accounting and thought that establishing full diplomatic relations was a premature reward.

On the other side were Vietnam veterans such as Senators Kerry, McCain, Kerrey, and Richard Durbin; Representatives Evans and Jack Reed; and former Representative Jay Rhodes. This argument continued to play out during the confirmation hearings for Peterson.

His confirmation was first delayed because of the ineligibility clause, an obscure rule that says a member of Congress cannot take a job that was created during his tenure. Peterson had to wait until a new Congress took office in January 1997. Then President Clinton had to certify that Vietnam was "cooperating in full faith" with efforts to answer questions about missing Americans, including those lost in Laos.[15] Senator Smith put a hold on Peterson's nomination for several months.

Peterson lobbied senators directly, asking for his nomination to be put to a vote. No one questioned his credentials or qualifications for the job, and the delay in voting was a matter of Congressional politics and the passions that Vietnam still elicited. Madeleine Albright became engaged to a greater degree in Peterson's nomination than is usual for a secretary of state and made numerous calls to senators. Finally, in April, the Senate voted unanimously to confirm him. Peterson's arrival in Hanoi in May heralded a new time for healing and building.

3

The Story of Pete
Peterson

• • • • • • • • • • • • • •

May is the hottest month in Vietnam, but the sun was especially relentless on May 9, 1997, when an excited crowd waited on the tarmac at Nội Bài Airport for the arrival of the first U.S. ambassador assigned to Hanoi. The last U.S. ambassador to Vietnam, Graham Martin, had departed from Saigon on a helicopter twenty-two years earlier. I was happy to join American and Vietnamese war veterans, expats, and kids, some waving American flags, at the airport that hot afternoon.

Ambassador Pete Peterson strode purposefully down the stairs from the plane to loud cheers from those of us assembled on the tarmac. Members of the press surrounded Pete and began thrusting microphones over the heads of those assembled. They snapped photos when a gray-haired veteran, Mai Văn Ôn—one of the men who in 1967 had fished John McCain out of Hanoi's Trúc Bạch Lake—stepped in to wrap Pete in a warm embrace.

Pete told the crowd that the exchange of ambassadors between the United States and Vietnam marked the "full normalization of our relations. . . . This is the beginning of a new era of constructive relations." A man of his word, he repeated the promise of his confirmation hearings to focus first on obtaining the fullest possible accounting of the more than two thousand Americans still listed as missing from the Vietnam War.

Pete also expressed his hope that a bilateral trade agreement could be concluded during his tenure. "Simply put," he said, "U.S. policy is to help Vietnam to become a prosperous country, at peace with its neighbors and integrated into this dynamic region."[1]

Shortly after the airport ceremony, Pete headed to the embassy and gathered those of us on his team around an oblong black table. He recounted a story from his days as a young Air Force lieutenant: "My commanding officer told us, 'You'll get it right 98 percent of the time. As for the other 2 percent, I'll eat it!'" His message to us was to get out and do our jobs and take risks to build a new relationship with Vietnam. He would have our backs. Pete's words epitomized his leadership style and have stayed with me over the years.

Days after arriving, Pete was called to the Presidential Palace, an imposing French colonial–style mansion with a sweeping set of steps carpeted in red. All ambassadors are asked soon after they first arrive to visit the country's head of state and present credentials from their home country. Pete said after the ceremony that the trip to meet President Lê Đức Anh had felt strange. "I rode to the palace in a white limousine," he told me. "In front and behind were white motorcycles flying white flags. The last time I was in a Vietnamese vehicle I was shackled to the floor."

Throughout his time as ambassador, Pete's infectious optimism contributed to the loyalty and affection our team felt for him. We were all committed to Pete's mission of bringing together two nations that had been enemies. "I had six and a half years to build up my animosities. Then I left my hate at the gate," Pete said. He had known more than his share of suffering in his sixty years.

In 1966, as he was flying his sixty-seventh mission over northern Vietnam as an Air Force pilot, Pete's plane was brought down by a surface-to-air missile between Hanoi and Hai Phong. After the crash, with a broken knee, shoulder, and ribs, Pete knew he couldn't escape those who were searching for him. He ordered his copilot, Bernard Talley, to leave him behind and escape (Talley was captured a day later).

Pete's family did not even know he was alive for first three years he was in Hỏa Lò Prison.[2] When I asked Pete about his time in prison, he didn't say much. I knew that he never ate pumpkin soup because pumpkin was the only food the prisoners were given to eat for six months at a time.

Finally, in March 1973, with the Paris Peace Accords signed, Pete and other soldiers—including John McCain—were released as part of the prisoner exchange. After returning to his home state of Florida, Pete worked as a businessman and educator. In 1981, Pete's teenage son Douglas, who was just six years old when his father was freed, died in a tragic car crash. Elected to Congress in 1990, Pete represented Florida's Second Congressional District for three terms. In 1995, the year before Pete was nominated by President Bill Clinton to become ambassador, he lost his wife, Carlotta, to her brave battle with cancer. Pete had faced many difficulties, and perhaps that explains why he was impatient with whiners. He was also a man who only told the truth, and he didn't tolerate dishonesty in others.

During their first meeting, Communist Party's eighty-year-old General Secretary Đỗ Mười asked Pete where he had been tortured. At first, Pete didn't answer. That prompted Đỗ Mười to roll up his sleeves and show his scars. Pete then rolled up his sleeves, also revealing scars. Both men had been tortured in the same prison—Đỗ Mười by the French and Pete by the Vietnamese.

We began preparing right away for a visit by Secretary of State Madeleine Albright—her first trip to Vietnam—just six weeks after Pete's arrival. This trip was important in its own right but also because we knew it could be paving the way for a visit by President Clinton. Secretary Albright had personally sworn Pete in as ambassador, recognizing his integrity, ability to overcome tragedy, and steady focus on the future. Pete knew that I had served as Madeleine's staff aide and political officer when she was ambassador to the United Nations, and he asked me to take responsibility for planning her visit. I admired Madeleine greatly, and I enjoyed this challenge. Once we had the actual dates for her visit, there were only ten days to organize the trip, and I threw myself into every detail.

Madeleine was enchanted by Vietnam, and she enjoyed traveling around the country with Pete. On all of her trips, she tried to carve out a little time for shopping. She knew that Hanoi had a vibrant local art scene, and after official meetings, she and Pete visited a gallery where she admired a painting. Madeleine was not carrying any local currency, but Pete stepped up and said, "I'm the man with the *đồng* [Vietnamese currency]." This provoked a lot of laughter.

It was fun being with Madeleine again and seeing that she was the same smart, gracious, funny, and charismatic person she had been when she served as U.N. ambassador. She took time in the middle of a wildly hectic schedule to see me and renew our ties. After a few days in Hanoi, she and her entourage traveled to Hồ Chí Minh City, where we would be opening the U.S. Consulate General. On June 28, 1997, Madeleine symbolically troweled in a brick at the foundation of the new consulate, in the shadow of the

PHOTO 4 Madeleine Albright, the author, and Pete Peterson, Hồ Chí Minh City, June 1997 (Credit: Author's personal collection).

embassy from which Americans had fled on April 30, 1975. Pete stood beside her.

After the event, Madeleine spontaneously walked out through the gate, to the consternation of her security detail, and plunged into a crowd of Vietnamese onlookers. She sparked a flurry of happy excitement and handshakes that perfectly captured the sense that we were moving forward. For me, this was a moment when my work for an old boss was meeting my work with a new one, two diplomats whom I admired tremendously. Madeleine's visit enabled us to open the consulate, and I could begin my assignment as the first U.S. political officer in Hồ Chí Minh City in twenty-two years—since the city lost its former name, Saigon.

Madeleine's visit wasn't all celebration, though. She met Đỗ Mười in Independence Palace, once the home of South Vietnam's presidents. As note taker at that meeting, I appreciated Madeleine's direct and forthright manner as she pressed the old war leader on his country's miserable human rights record. Đỗ Mười wasn't accustomed to being challenged in this way, but he knew he had to engage with her if Vietnam hoped to have a relationship with the United States.

Madeleine also pressed Prime Minister Võ Văn Kiệt and Foreign Minister Nguyễn Mạnh Cầm to ease emigration curbs so that the United States could waive what were known as the Jackson-Vanik restrictions, imposed by legislation that since 1974 had precluded the participation of nonmarket economies in any U.S. government program that provided credit and investment guarantees if the country restricted emigration. Aimed at the Soviet Union, the restrictions prevented U.S. companies in Vietnam (a nonmarket economy that restricted emigration until 1997) from having access to government trade support. Madeleine urged these leaders to have the Vietnamese government release political prisoners, and she spoke specifically about Đoàn Viết Hoạt and Nguyễn Đan Quế. Two years later, both were offered release. Hoạt and his family agreed to leave Vietnam and went into exile in the United States.

However, Quế refused to leave Vietnam. Vice Minister of Public Security Nguyễn Văn Hưởng was furious and told an interlocutor, "That was the deal." Friends urged Quế's brother, Nguyễn Quốc Quân, to persuade his sibling to leave Vietnam. "If his conscience dictates that he remain in Vietnam, who am I to talk him out of it?" Quân replied.[3]

The U.S. government owned a small compound a few blocks from the old Saigon embassy. Before its renovation into an office space, it had two small apartments. Briefly during the summer of 1997, those apartments served as a hiding place for Danish Crown Prince Frederik; his then-girlfriend, Maria Montell; and two burly Danish bodyguards. It had been my idea to hide them there, as the paparazzi who followed Frederik everywhere wouldn't look for him on a U.S. diplomatic compound. A few years before, I had hosted Frederik in Washington, and we had remained friends. When he called to ask for help arranging a getaway to Vietnam, I was happy to take part.

Frederik had just finished leading a large Danish trade delegation to Thailand, where King Bhumibol had feted him with banquets, honor guards, and a grand parade. The Thais have great respect for monarchy, and the Thai royal family had long ties with the thousand-year-old Danish royal family. In Vietnam, Frederik, who was then twenty-nine years old, seemed relieved to be free of all the pomp, circumstance, and pressures of his position as well as the omnipresent press that followed him when he traveled.

Frederik told me the journalists accompanying him to Thailand expected him to return directly to Copenhagen. As the crown prince's plane taxied down the Bangkok runway, one journalist realized that the prince was not on board and tried to persuade the pilot to stop the plane. The pilot refused.

Some journalists later wrote admiringly of Frederik's clever escape. Unable to pinpoint Frederik's location, the tabloids made up stories, juxtaposing photos of the prince in Thailand with those of Maria in Denmark and file photos of famous Vietnamese scenes.

A recognizable pop star, Maria was spotted by a Dane on her flight from Bangkok to Hồ Chí Minh City, and the plan was almost ruined. Attractive and irreverent, Maria at that time was cutting best-selling albums in Europe and the United States. She and Frederik loved Vietnam, and together we had marvelous dinners with fine champagne and good Danish beer, and we danced in the best Hồ Chí Minh City discos. The prince's bodyguards always sat at a discreet distance, but they were immensely tall and blond and not exactly invisible. Frederik said he hoped to return to Vietnam with his father, who had grown up in Hanoi during the French colonial era and gone to school in Saigon.

With the help of the Danish ambassador, we traveled to Hạ Long Bay, a six-hour journey from Hanoi. We sailed on an old wooden junk with red canvas sails, drank marvelous wine, skinny-dipped in the moonlight, climbed the limestone outcroppings, ate fresh crabs and shrimp, swatted cockroaches, and got sunburned. Relaxed and happy, we swam in pristine waters.

Back at work, the U.S. consulate team opened a temporary office with six Americans and a small number of local staff members. We had one landline and a fax machine for the entire office. The landline was a rotary phone connected to a wall jack via a long cord. That single phone had been difficult to obtain and was very precious, and we passed it from desk to desk based on who needed it most urgently. Every day, it seemed, someone tripped over the cord, causing the phone to crash to the ground. We all gasped, horrified that we had been cut off from the world. The phone took its battering and never stopped functioning.

An early task was a request from the Gerald R. Ford Presidential Library and Museum for the staircase atop the U.S. embassy that people had climbed toward a helicopter that would lift them to safety on the last night of the U.S. evacuation from Saigon. The staircase had been made famous by a photograph taken by the Dutch photojournalist Hubert van Es, but it turned out that van Es's photograph had actually been taken not at the embassy but at the home of the Central Intelligence Agency station chief and on April 29, a day before the last flight out.[4] When we told this to the people at the library, they instructed us to send the staircase from the embassy roof anyway.

PHOTO 5 The U.S. embassy in Saigon just prior to demolition, 1997. Pen mark points to where friend Jeannette Piña stood (Credit: Jeannette Piña).

The State Department had been dithering about what to do with the old Saigon embassy. Should we keep it as a museum? Try to renovate it? Pete instructed us to hire a company to demolish it. He said it was the symbol of a wartime headquarters, and America was now at peace with Vietnam. In addition to the bad memories it held, the building was dilapidated and full of asbestos. My apartment overlooked the embassy grounds, and I was able to watch as manual laborers knocked it down, brick by brick, day by day. A laborer died after falling into an elevator shaft during the demolition, adding to the sense that the embassy was haunted.

Our small team held multiple symbolic openings of the new Hồ Chí Minh City consulate. A succession of veterans and members of Congress visited the consulate, and each time we held U.S. flag raisings because this was the first time a U.S. flag had flown in what was once Saigon since the war. Pete had told each visitor that returning to Vietnam and seeing a country at peace was a cathartic experience.

Like Lieutenant John Kerry, Illinois Congressman Lane Evans, another Democrat, had opposed the war as a Vietnam veteran after he returned to the United States. A close friend of Pete's, Evans had championed full diplomatic relations and reconciliation, and he pushed the U.S. government to acknowledge that Agent Orange was harmful to both American personnel and Vietnamese civilians. In August 1997, Evans led a delegation of congressmen to Vietnam who all flew coach and arrived well briefed. Unlike other Congressional delegations, this group was not focused on sightseeing. Its members did not share the Clinton administration's reticence about discussing the effects of dioxin (a persistent, highly toxic residue left behind from Agent Orange) with the Vietnamese. They advocated for programs to clean up land mines and unexploded ordnance in Vietnam and urged Vietnam's leaders to pursue economic reform.

On August 13, I joined this delegation and flew in an old Russian M17 helicopter to a site in the north. The Joint Task Force–Full Accounting was working to achieve the fullest possible accounting of Americans missing from the Vietnam War. Its mission members sifted through the wreckage of a plane that had crashed into a hillside in 1964 while trying to bomb a nearby factory. The young soldiers carrying out the excavation task were jubilant about the previous day's find: an arm bone, likely from a twenty-four-year-old pilot from North Carolina who had died years before they were born. His remains would return to America in a small, flag-draped coffin.

At a dinner that night at a Cuban-built hotel in Huế, a Vietnamese general who had fought for fifty years against the Japanese, French, Americans, Cambodians, and Chinese spoke passionately of his desire for peace. The next day, two of the congressmen, Vietnam vets, argued bitterly as we stood in Huế's citadel, where hundreds of U.S. Marines and two thousand civilians had lost their lives during the 1968 Tết offensive. Both marines, they clashed over the significance of American and Vietnamese atrocities during the war and had to cool their tempers a day later with a dip in the sweet waters off China Beach (renamed Mỹ Khê).

In Đà Nẵng, one Congressional staffer who had flown bombing runs out of that city hugged a grizzled pair of uniformed Vietnamese veterans. Their embrace physically embodied the reconciliation we sought. An older Vietnamese general told us that the only other time he had met Americans was on the battlefield. "Now," he continued, "my comrades and I dream only of peace and hope that cooperation with America will bring prosperity to Vietnam."

Evans, who served in the U.S. Congress for another ten years, did ultimately succeed in forcing an honest discussion about dioxin's pernicious effects on Americans, and much later the U.S. government assumed some responsibility for the harm it caused to Vietnamese citizens. Evans visited Vietnam many times. On his last visit, Parkinson's disease had deprived him of the ability to speak. He left the trip early in poor health, retired from public life in 2006, and passed away in a nursing home in 2014.

In addition to supporting efforts to determine what had happened to American soldiers lost during the war, Pete quickly stepped up our exchanges with the Vietnamese related to science, technology, health, agriculture, and aviation. During Desaix Anderson's time as U.S. chargé d'affaires, agreements had been reached to resolve Vietnam's wartime debt to the United States, protect U.S copyrights, and expand educational exchanges. First Desaix and then Pete established foundations for business to flourish, knowing that productive long-term ties between nations depend on private-sector relationships. Pete also directed American negotiators to work with Vietnamese counterparts on a wide-ranging trade agreement between the two nations.

I held the labor portfolio, and a U.S.-Vietnam bilateral trade agreement was the test for whether we could negotiate any trade agreements during Clinton's second presidential term. A trade agreement would have to include strong labor rights provisions if we hoped to secure the support needed from Congressional Democrats.

The Vietnam General Confederation of Labor (VGCL) was the Communist Party's only organization responsible for representing workers in Vietnam and overseeing all labor unions. The VGCL was a part of the Vietnam Fatherland Front, an umbrella for mass Party organizations that included women, veterans, and youth. Although the VGCL was good at organizing weddings and funerals for its members, it did not engage in collective bargaining or the other core functions of modern labor unions in the United States and Europe. Instead, it collected significant membership dues and doled out a portion of those funds to the families of workers who were injured or who had lost their lives. With few exceptions, the VGCL was isolated from the world's labor unions.

In the summer of 1997, as I moved from the embassy in Hanoi to the consulate in Hồ Chí Minh City, a controversy surfaced in the United States when the widely syndicated cartoonist Garry Trudeau lampooned the footwear giant Nike—and especially its celebrity booster, Michael Jordan—for producing expensive shoes in Vietnam while paying poor wages to workers who toiled in sweatshop conditions.[5] Nike responded defensively at first and provided little information. Then company leaders realized that there was some truth to the accusations and they had more than just a public relations problem. Nike faced a fundamental challenge due to its lax oversight of contract factories, many of them run by Taiwanese and Korean contractors.

In one incident, a Taiwanese line manager had "lined up 125 assembly-line workers and slapped them with the sole of a sneaker."[6] In another, a dozen female Vietnamese workers fainted after being forced to run around the perimeter of three warehouses in the blazing hot sun as a disciplinary action. A Korean foreman "made workers lick the factory floor for misdemeanors, and employees at yet another factory were led in chants of 'Loyalty to the boss!'"[7] Nike belatedly realized that it had a responsibility to improve workers' conditions, and the company sharply stepped up its oversight of contract factories.

In December 1997, Deputy Chief of Mission Dennis Harter and I conducted a fact-finding tour of several shoe factories in the south that supplied Nike. My improving Vietnamese language skills came in handy. While my boss interviewed line managers and labor relations directors, I spoke directly with factory workers. I asked about wages and working conditions, customs problems, union activities, and relations with local officials. I walked through assembly lines, cafeterias, and parking lots, talking with workers about their lives.

By this time, Phil Knight, Nike's CEO, knew that the company needed to take decisive action, and as the purchaser of most of the factories' output, it was in position to make a difference. Nike hired a nongovernmental organization (NGO) to investigate labor rights challenges in Vietnam and placed a Nike representative in every factory to monitor workers' conditions.[8] Nike also became more transparent, and from 1999 through 2002 it let thousands of American college students, NGO representatives, government officials, media representatives, and athletes (including Carl Lewis) visit the factories to see for themselves what working conditions were like.

Dennis and I found that even though conditions and management attitudes varied from factory to factory, Nike had pushed and prodded its contractors to upgrade working conditions. Fearful of losing Nike's business, the contractors had complied. Powerful ventilation systems had been installed in places where workers had earlier breathed dangerous fumes. Pregnant women had been moved to areas where no gluing took place. Lighting and reconfigured work spaces now existed where previously workers had struggled for light and space.

Referring to the Taiwanese factory, a spacious, clean, well-lit, and well-maintained facility, Joel Enderle, Nike's regional labor practices director, said: "The problem there is not with the hardware, it's with the software—in the managers' heads. It's not easy, but we're trying to convince them to change the way they manage the factory." Many of the Taiwanese managers had received military training and needed to change their authoritarian methods to adapt to the more relaxed environment of Vietnam.

Dennis and I were struck that employee turnover rates at all factories had sunk to less than 1 percent per year in some cases, indicating improved worker satisfaction. This resulted not only from improved conditions but also from wage increases that had made jobs producing Nike shoes some of the most lucrative factory work in Vietnam. Demand for these factory jobs was tremendous. Each job opening produced scores of applicants because the Vietnamese would take on even boring, repetitive tasks if doing so could boost them out of poverty and provide better lives for their children.

At one of the rural factories, I encountered a relaxed young employee in soccer clothes, trotting toward a playing field. Surprised that a foreigner was addressing him in Vietnamese, he stopped to chat. "I play for Team Nike," he told me happily. Nike's public relations advisors couldn't have scripted it better.

Enderle told me, "It's possible to create humane working conditions in all our factories." He and the Nike team set out to prove it. Nike had raised the bar, and all shoe manufacturers in Vietnam felt that they had to follow suit and improve working conditions. This was a significant progressive step, but it was not the end of the story of labor rights in Vietnam.

Our small consulate staff held its first reception in December 1997 to honor a group of Vietnamese American singers who had returned to their homeland for the first time since the war had ended twenty-two years earlier. We thought it was important to focus these singers' *Về Nguồn* ("Homecoming") concert on youth awareness of HIV/AIDS prevention. Since 1990, when Vietnam's first HIV case was detected in Hồ Chí Minh City, the virus had spread rapidly among injecting drug users and, to a lesser extent, sex workers and their clients.

Our team wanted to show the Vietnamese that U.S. diplomats cared about more than just business. The result was encouraging, with the entire community devoted to combating HIV/AIDS attending: officials from the local department of Labor, Invalids, and Social Affairs, which was responsible for managing the country's growing epidemic; directors of Hồ Chí Minh City's Louis Pasteur Institute; representatives from the Youth Union and Women's Union, Communist Party organizations that were effective at mobilizing grassroots activity in the health field; and local organizations working with young people to prevent HIV infections.

A month later, Kerry visited Hồ Chí Minh City on one of his many trips to follow up on the work for POWs and MIAs. Kerry's agenda included human rights as well as cooperation between the United States and Vietnam in education, science, technology, and addressing environmental challenges. He was also interested in health, including HIV/AIDS prevention.

Kerry wasn't with us for the *Về Nguồn* concert, but during his visit, I persuaded him to drop by the popular Condom Café at the Youth Cultural Center. A colleague told me I was crazy taking a U.S. senator to a place that featured condom balloons and T-shirts, but Kerry—never the stodgy Brahmin some see him as—loved the Condom Café and enjoyed its humor while appreciating its serious purpose. Even though intravenous drug users were most at risk for HIV/AIDS, the café aimed its prevention activities at young people in a city where more than half the population was under twenty-five years old. Kerry laughed when the waiter brought a condom with the check.

I like to think my friendship with Kerry began with that visit to the Condom Café, but we really bonded on a bicycle trip a few days later. The trip began when we took a ferry to Vũng Tàu with Pete and joined the final leg of the 1,250-mile World T.E.A.M. Sports's Vietnam Challenge, in which eighty cyclists—many of them war veterans, some of whom were disabled—rode the 1,250 miles from Hanoi to Hồ Chí Minh City. The cyclists visited hospitals and orphanages along the route, making this journey part of a long process of reconciliation between former adversaries.

Eight veterans without the use of their legs rode hand-powered cycles, an unthinkable feat of determination on hundred-mile days. Participants ranged in age from eleven to seventy-eight years, including a father riding with his blind son (two other cyclists were also blind). They rode over the towering Hải Vân Pass and the Hiền Lương Bridge spanning the 17th parallel that had separated north from south during the war.

Kerry, Pete, and I rode the seventy-eight miles to Hồ Chí Minh City with three-time Tour de France winner Greg LeMonde and Diana Nyad, who later became the first person to swim from Cuba to Florida without using a shark cage. Years later, when Kerry described the bike ride, he liked to give the impression that I had ridden circles around him. But Kerry is an avid biker, on top of being intensely competitive. I recall his tall, lean profile being well ahead of me on the long, hot ride to Hồ Chí Minh City. Pete was close behind Kerry, his friend and fellow veteran.

We crossed the finish line on the day that began a year-long celebration of Saigon's three hundredth anniversary. There were lion dances, fireworks, and celebrations to mark the first day of the Year of the Tiger. The Vietnamese cheered the fact that paraplegics, amputees, and blind people would attempt such a feat and folded them into a grand ceremony, complete with acrobats, a dragon dance, and a high-wire act.

Kerry and Pete had to depart before the ride's closing ceremony, which meant the group got me as the token U.S. government representative. I told them the senator and ambassador considered their journey not only a personal triumph for each participant, but something even more meaningful.

By returning to Vietnam and riding the length of the country, accompanied by journalists from *Sports Illustrated* and the local and international press (who generally focused on LeMonde), the veteran riders contributed to the long process of healing taking place in Vietnam and the United States. The riders helped reconcile our peoples, build a new relationship, and establish trust. The disabled bikers showed Vietnam's many disabled citizens what can be done.

I addressed the Vietnamese citizens and acknowledged the importance in the Vietnamese tradition of the first guest of the lunar new year (Tết). I expressed my hope that the arrival of the cyclists and their determination to further reconciliation marked an auspicious beginning to the Year of the Tiger. I recited the same Vietnamese proverb that had guided my earlier bike trip, "Đi một ngày đàng, học một sàng khôn"—when you go on a journey, you come back with wisdom.

In early 1998, I had the opportunity to meet Phạm Xuân Ẩn, a remarkable man who had lived through much of Vietnam's recent history. Ẩn told heart-stopping tales in the relaxed atmosphere of his garden—with its birds, plants, and fish—and his faithful dog, King, at his side. According to Ẩn's biographer, Larry Berman, the birds symbolized freedom, while the fish served as a reminder that one should often remain silent. The dog symbolized loyalty to friends and country.[9]

Ẩn considered himself a nationalist and a patriot, and during the war, he had worked as a double agent. He conveyed to Hanoi everything he learned as a reporter for *Time*, the Associated Press, and Reuters. In the north, Ẩn was not a reporter but a general. After an American reporter was captured in Cambodia, the reporter's wife appealed to Ẩn, who risked blowing his cover by using his clandestine connections to secure the reporter's release.

After the fall of Saigon, Ẩn sent his wife and children to California. Only when he received a hero commendation from General Võ Nguyên Giáp in December 1976 was it clear to his former colleagues that Ẩn had been a double agent. Still, his former journalist colleagues raised funds so that Ẩn could send his son, Phạm Xuân Hoàng Ẩn, to study journalism in North Carolina in 1990. The younger Ẩn later served as a diplomat, working with me in Hồ Chí Minh City in 1997.

Phạm Xuân Ẩn served as the inspiration for the main character in *The Sympathizer*, Nguyễn Thanh Việt's 2016 Pulitzer Prize–winning only partly fictional account of Saigon's fall, the plight of Vietnamese American refugees, and the horrors of reeducation camps. No one has chronicled the feelings of people in the Vietnamese diaspora more effectively than Việt, who has noted that Vietnamese American literature forces its readers to acknowledge that a narrow definition of war featuring only soldiers is inaccurate.[10]

Việt's character is an assassin, fighter, and counterrevolutionary. Ẩn (a gentle and engaging man, brilliant raconteur, and devoted husband and father) would likely have laughed at the portrayal. He was an enigma except in one respect: like many Vietnamese, he was motivated by a fierce desire to rid his country of a foreign presence—even if the invader was the United States, a country he loved and admired.

For Ẩn, the war was a battle for his country's independence. It was also a civil war, but primarily it was a battle to drive out a foreign invader.

Days after Pete arrived in Hanoi, at a cocktail party at the Israeli ambassador's residence, he met Vi Lê, the Saigon-born commercial counselor at the Australian embassy. It was love, or at least a strong mutual attraction, at first sight. A few months later, the Australian ambassador, Sue Boyd, hosted a dinner where the couple announced their engagement.

Their wedding on May 23, 1998, had journalists referring to it as the social event of the year in Hanoi. Like the day when Pete arrived a year earlier, it took place on a very hot afternoon. In the capital's Grand Cathedral, candles wilted, with some listing to the left and others to the right. Pete's oldest son, Michael, stood by his father as his best man.[11] The ushers, including Dennis Harter and Science Officer Michael Eiland, sweated through their tuxedos. The groom was drenched, too, and he said his shoes squished when he walked. Only the bride, Vi, didn't show a bead of perspiration. She just glowed.

The Reverend Nguyễn Văn Thái, who presided over the ceremony, never mentioned the arm-twisting that authorities had subjected him to when he sought permission to marry two foreigners in Vietnam. For many, the wedding of a former American prisoner of war to a Vietnamese-born Australian was the ultimate gesture of reconciliation. Sadly, no Vietnamese officials attended the wedding or the reception at the U.S. ambassador's residence.

One minor official attended a separate reception at the Horison Hotel for embassy staff. This showed that the work of reconciliation and even normalization had not been completed simply by the ambassador's arrival. It also reflected Vietnamese uncertainty about how to deal with a situation—a U.S. ambassador's wedding in Hanoi—for which there was no precedent.

Soon after Pete's wedding, I left Vietnam to serve on the staff of Vice President Al Gore, whom I advised on Asia policy and international trade and finance. At the White House, I closely followed negotiations over the Bilateral Trade Agreement (BTA) between the United States and Vietnam. Desaix had begun the negotiations while he was chargé d'affaires, and they would last until the agreement was signed in July 2000.

Soon after normalization of diplomatic relations, the U.S. Agency for International Development (USAID) contracted with Ginny Foote, the president of the U.S.-Vietnam Trade Council, and Dan Price, an attorney, to provide technical assistance to Vietnam during BTA negotiations, as for the most part the country's economy had been closed to the rest of the world, and there were gaps in Vietnamese knowledge of market economics.

I recall charging into the chargé d'affaires' office once to complain when I was frustrated about Ginny's requests of the embassy. "I don't work for Ginny Foote," I announced. "I work for the United States government." Desaix replied gently in his Mississippi drawl, "Ted, we all work for Ginny Foote."

Desaix admired Ginny, valued her contributions, and knew that official efforts would succeed only if they were supported by the business community—and especially nongovernmental facilitators like Ginny who were trusted by both sides. Pete trusted her at least as much as Desaix did.

July 1999 was a historic turning point for Vietnam and for U.S.-Vietnam relations. Not knowing whether the talks would succeed or fail, Deputy U.S. Trade Representative Richard Fisher went to Hong Kong and awaited news from the chief negotiator, Joe Damond.

"Vietnam's Politburo met for much of the day on July 20, presumably to get a feel of where things were and to make decisions on the Vietnamese side," Ginny wrote a few days after the BTA agreement in principle was inked.[12] There weren't a large number of differences still to be resolved, and both sides wanted to wrap up negotiations before President Clinton's trip to the Asia-Pacific Economic Cooperation summit meeting in mid-September in Auckland, New Zealand, where he would meet Vietnamese Prime Minister Phan Văn Khải.

Feeling that the two sides were close, Fisher came to Hanoi. On the evening of July 22, Minister of Trade Trương Đình Tuyển met Fisher at the government guest house. When the meeting broke and as participants were about to head across the hall for a dinner hosted by Tuyển, Ginny noticed that Pete's face was white. Ginny quietly asked him if he was okay. In fact, he was furious that the discussion with Tuyển had not resolved any of the remaining issues. She suggested that Pete call his car to take him home. Pete and Fisher skipped the dinner to call U.S. Trade Representative Charlene Barshevsky to break the bad news. Ginny remained behind at the dinner and warned Vietnam's chief negotiator, Nguyễn Đình Lương, that negotiations had "hit rock bottom." She joined Lương and Price for an overnight session to produce language that could bridge the gap.

Ginny described the next days of negotiations, which included Deputy Prime Minister Nguyễn Tấn Dũng, as "intense." On July 24, negotiations still didn't seem promising, and a senior U.S. official arrived at the Trade Ministry only to find the front door chained and bolted from the inside, "hardly a good omen."[13] A gala celebratory event was scheduled for that evening, but it turned out to be more like an election night party with an uncertain outcome.

Ginny said that Fisher and Pete "arrived at the gala at 1:30 A.M., the two sides having finally reached—at least—an Agreement in Principle." A reporter added, "The ambassador is always the most upbeat, optimistic guy in the room, and even he was beginning to look a little fatigued."[14]

The next afternoon, Fisher held a joint press conference with Tuyển. Not all of the issues had been resolved, but at least the framework of the agreement under negotiation showed Vietnam's willingness to open up its highly protected economy to the outside world. The negotiations dragged on, in part because Vietnam wanted to allow state-owned enterprises several years to prepare for the rough-and-tumble of the global economy.

The negotiators were dealing with Vietnam's internal politics, which they had glimpsed in March 1998—when Minister of Planning and Investment Trần Xuân Giá was about to arrive in Washington to sign an agreement welcoming the Overseas Private Investment Corporation (OPIC) to Vietnam. Vietnam's first ambassador to the United States, Lê Văn Bàng, suddenly received word that the Politburo, Vietnam's highest-level decision-making body, was reconsidering its support for the agreement.

When a U.S. official told Bàng that postponing the signing would set back bilateral relations, the ambassador replied, "We have our politics, too. You may think because we're a Communist country that we can just decide things. Our country's leadership is just as complicated as yours." Even so, he knew that the OPIC agreement was important, and he worked successfully to get it completed during the minister's visit.

Bob Schiffer told me a story about Pete that has stayed with me as a lesson in effective diplomacy. At a low point in the BTA negotiations, the U.S. team became discouraged. According to Bob, American officials blamed the Vietnamese for delays and groused that "if they knew what was good for them," Hanoi's leaders would move forward with the deal.

Pete gathered the team and told them a story. "During my imprisonment," he said, "when I was taken in for one of my many interrogations (we called them 'quizzes'), there was an older Vietnamese officer wearing a well-tailored uniform sitting next to my regular interrogator at the interrogation table. The presence of this older 'guest' was unusual. The 'quiz' took place after I had been locked up for over four years. By that time, I was fed up with everything and fiercely resisted whatever the Vietnamese threw at me.

"The interrogator began by asking me a number of questions related to my treatment in camp. 'How are your accommodations?' he asked. I replied that they were awful. 'And the food we provide you, how is that?' Even worse, I replied. Not fit for human consumption.

"'How are the guards treating you?' Horrible treatment, I said. There were a few more questions of that nature, and I answered negatively to each one. All during the 'quiz,' the older man sat passively at the side, did not say anything, and didn't react to any of my negative responses.

"Just as the interrogator was finishing, the older man abruptly stood up, looked me straight in the eye, and in perfect English said, 'You must remember where you are!' It was a perfect squelch that has had a profound impact on me to this day."

Bob wanted to be sure that he had interpreted the story correctly, and he followed Pete into his office, asking, "What did you want us to draw from that story?" Pete replied simply, "We must 'remember where we are' and work hard to achieve our goals while respecting Vietnam's cultural and political differences."

Soon after the July negotiations in Hanoi resulted in an agreement in principle, Damond and Lương, his counterpart, met in Washington to hammer out differences over six outstanding items, still with the goal of signing the BTA at the Asia-Pacific Economic Cooperation summit in September. Unfortunately, Vietnam's leaders had not reached consensus on the changes to be made in the country's economy, and Washington wouldn't budge. Talks in Auckland failed, and bitterness ensued.

Vietnam wanted to be a member of the World Trade Organization (WTO), but the BTA was a U.S. prerequisite to that. By implementing its commitments (on market access, investment, trade in goods and services, intellectual property rights, and transparency), Vietnam could show that it could and would meet WTO trade standards. The agreement would grant Vietnam trade and market access to foreign investors; provide for the protection of intellectual property; and, most significant, enshrine a commitment to treat all investors equally.

It took many months before the United States and Vietnam resolved the few remaining issues. The agreement was finally signed on July 13, 2000, fulfilling President Clinton's goal of a comprehensive BTA with Vietnam that would lead to more open markets and to Vietnam's integration into the global community. By then, Vũ Khoan had replaced Tuyển as Minister of Trade and Deputy Prime Minister, and he was able to close the negotiations with Barshevsky just before a ceremony in the White House's Rose Garden with President Clinton.[15]

To attend the signing ceremony, President Clinton interrupted his meetings at Camp David with Israeli Prime Minister Ehud Barak and Palestinian Authority Chairman Yasser Arafat. Returning to Camp David right after the ceremony, the president told Barak and Arafat that the U.S. agreement with the Vietnamese was proof that former enemies could be friends.

The agreement had to be approved by Congress, and by then the presidential election campaign was under way. Congress delayed action until the new president, George W. Bush, introduced the agreement to Congress in 2001. In describing the agreement, the *Wall Street Journal* wrote: "After four years of hemming and hawing, the Vietnamese government finally signed a trade pact with Washington."[16] The *Journal* added that "America's largest labor federation, the AFL-CIO, opposes the deal—ostensibly on the grounds that Vietnam exploits its workers and bars union formation. But then that's exactly why the trade agreement is needed: The deregulation of the Vietnamese economy will lead to new enterprises and capital formation in Vietnam, which in turn will lead to the creation of a merchant class. And middle classes inevitably demand political change."[17]

With diplomatic relations established and the BTA signed on his watch, in November 2000, Bill Clinton made the first U.S. presidential visit to a united Vietnam. A victory lap of sorts just a few weeks before he left office, the trip occurred at a time of solid progress on the POW/MIA issue and four months after the two countries had signed (though not yet ratified) the BTA. Just prior to the trip, Congressional leaders including McCain lobbed a warning shot across the president's bow, insisting that he devote considerable attention to Vietnam's poor human rights record.

I was still working at the White House as Vice President Gore's Asia advisor and, as someone who knew Vietnam, I was asked to assist with preparations for President Clinton's visit, including a briefing to the president from Vietnam experts. Stanley Karnow, the greatest chronicler of the war, joined the briefing, as did Harvard University's Tommy Vallely; Fred Brown of Johns Hopkins University; Ginny; and Mike Jendrzejczyk, the Human Rights Watch's director for Asia in Washington.

President Clinton outlined his goals for the trip: focus on achieving the fullest possible accounting of those lost in the war; consolidate the process of diplomatic normalization; help the American people see Vietnam as a country, not just a war; and help the Vietnamese see that America supported their economic development.

President Clinton's trip followed the contested presidential election of November 2000 by a little more than a week. Each evening during the trip, we staffers raced to our hotel rooms to watch newscasters discuss hanging chads and butterfly ballots in Florida. If Vice President Gore were to prevail, I would likely become his senior Asia advisor. If Governor George W. Bush won, I did not expect warm treatment from the new administration.

President Clinton followed the events in Florida carefully. When Katherine Harris, Florida's secretary of state, certified results that showed Bush ahead of Gore by more than seven hundred votes, President Clinton was apoplectic. Believing that the election had been stolen, he wanted to make a statement. His traveling staff prevailed on him to remain publicly silent.

Still, the turmoil at home did not detract from the excitement of the enormous crowds that welcomed the U.S. president. An iconic photo of that visit shows two young Vietnamese reaching from an adjoining window to touch President Clinton's hand. In advance of the trip, the president had insisted that he wanted to deliver a nationwide address that would air live on television, something that had never before happened in Vietnam. During a visit to China in 1998, President Clinton had delivered a live speech to the people, and he insisted on equal treatment by the Vietnamese. The leaders in Hanoi reluctantly agreed, knowing that the trip would not take place otherwise.

In his speech, President Clinton noted that one of his predecessors, Thomas Jefferson, had tried to obtain rice seed from Vietnam two hundred years earlier. Then he added, "In 1945, at the moment of your country's birth, the words of Thomas Jefferson were chosen to be echoed in your own Declaration of Independence."

President Clinton thanked those who had focused on achieving the fullest possible accounting, making full diplomatic relations possible: Senators Kerry, McCain, Bob Kerrey, and Chuck Robb; Pete; and Veterans Affairs Deputy Secretary Hershel Gober. They came to Vietnam, the president said, "determined to honor those who fought without refighting the battles; to remember our history, but not to perpetuate it; to give young people like you in both our countries the chance to live in your tomorrows, not in our yesterdays."[18]

The president spoke of Vietnam's progress from isolation to the political and economic reforms called *đổi mới*, enabling the country to begin reaping the benefits of globalization. "Globalization is not something we can hold off or turn off," he said. "We can work to maximize its benefits and minimize its risks, but we cannot ignore it."[19] The bilateral trade agreement with the United States, he predicted correctly, would lead to Vietnam's entry into the WTO and to the country's integration into the global economy.

In his speech, the president announced USAID support for implementing the recently signed BTA, and he drew attention to Kerry's initiative, a debt-for-education swap that created the Vietnam Education Foundation. He also spoke about human rights, religious freedom, political dissent, and freedom of the press. Authorities in Hanoi took advantage of the slight delay needed for the Vietnamese translation to tone down his criticism of human rights, but the president was still able to convey his message.

Separately, the president's visit facilitated an expansion of the Fulbright scholars' exchange program and the Fulbright Economics Teaching Program in Hồ Chí Minh City; new efforts to locate and clean up land mines and unexploded ordnance; new agreements on combating narcotics and boosting collaboration in science and technology; HIV/AIDS prevention efforts by the U.S. Centers for Disease Control and Prevention; environmental and agricultural assistance programs; the sale of Boeing aircraft to Vietnam Airlines; expansion of the Leahy War Victims Fund and Displaced Children and Orphans Fund; and, a favorite of Pete's, motorcycle helmets for kids.

President Clinton had outlined the key elements of a diplomatic agenda he hoped the United States and Vietnam would pursue. Negotiations continued behind the scenes to bring about the release of Vietnamese prisoners of conscience and to broaden the country's official recognition of religious groups. Despite this area of continuing tension, the visit's large tranche of "deliverables," in White House parlance, helped lay the foundation for even more significant collaborative activities in the future.

Showing great respect to his hosts, President Clinton visited Hanoi's thousand-year-old Temple of Literature and its equally ancient citadel. The Secret Service worried about the difficulty of controlling the crowds if the president entered the temple from the front. After the Vietnamese agreed to close the street, President Clinton, always the extrovert, stopped to shake scores of Vietnamese hands.

In a toast at the state banquet, the president spoke about Vietnamese history, culture, art, film, and poetry. To illustrate the thaw in relations, he quoted from the *Tale of Kieu*, the country's greatest literary work: "Just as the lotus wilts, the mums bloom forth; time softens grief, and the winter turns to spring."

Clinton also met with each member of the triumvirate ruling Vietnam: the president, prime minister, and general secretary of the Communist Party. The first two meetings were warm and friendly, but the meeting with General Secretary Lê Khả Phiêu quickly descended into acrimony when Phiêu departed from his script about nations with different political systems cooperating and tried to co-opt President Clinton by associating him with the antiwar movement. Phiêu said he had seen Chelsea Clinton's "sweet face" on television, and she reminded him of the daughter of an antiwar activist who had immolated himself in front of the Pentagon. He then noted President Clinton's own antiwar past.

The president gave a masterful reply, acknowledging that in the past he had opposed the war, but stating that he also knew that many brave American warriors like Pete had served in Vietnam in the sincere support of ideals of democracy and freedom. Phiêu could only respond with a non sequitur: "well, we never invaded California."[20] To limit the damage, at the press conference after the meeting, Giáp and Khải spoke effusively about how much Vietnam's leaders appreciated President Clinton's visit.

At the Ninth Party Congress in April 2001, Phiêu—the last of a string of military leaders to lead the Communist Party—was pushed aside and replaced by General Assembly President Nông Đức Mạnh. The disastrous meeting with Clinton may have contributed to Phiêu's ouster.

President Clinton was accompanied on the trip by the first lady, Hillary Rodham Clinton, who had just been elected to the U.S. Senate from New York; their daughter, Chelsea; and the first lady's mother, Dorothy Rodham. The president and first lady toured an art exhibit organized by Catholic Relief Services that featured drawings and paintings by young boys and girls who had been injured by unexploded ordnance in Quảng Trị province. Four of the boy artists were present, and President and Mrs. Clinton visited at length with two brothers, who shared their stories.

Noting that the United States had just provided $3 million in demining equipment to Vietnam, President Clinton announced the donation of a surplus field hospital to Quảng Trị. He said that the United States would work on cleaning up unexploded ordnance until the last mines were removed.

Even twenty-five years after U.S. troops left Vietnam, the war was still a scar across America's psyche. What a U.S president said was important—but what he did not say was equally important. Reporters were looking for any sign of an apology from President Clinton, and his opponents still viewed him as a draft dodger and would pounce on any suggestion of an apology to the former enemy in Hanoi. Veterans wanted to know if the United States was putting business interests ahead of POW-MIA concerns, while human rights groups wanted the president to press Vietnam on the issues of religious freedom and prisoners of conscience. President Clinton and his team weaved their way through these pitfalls with a skill that came from eight years on the job.

It would also have been dangerous politically for President Clinton to lean too far forward on Agent Orange or to discuss reparations. In his capacity as president of the Red Cross, President Clinton met with Dr. Nguyễn Trọng Nhân, president of Vietnam's Red Cross, to discuss Agent Orange. Pete had recommended that the president make a public commitment to cleaning up dioxin in Vietnam, but the National Security Council said it was too late for the administration to make a promise that would need to be implemented by President Clinton's successor. Instead, the Red Cross made a grant of $1.5 million to Vietnam's Red Cross for training and prosthetic devices, and Pete signed a new science and technology agreement on the president's behalf. The agreement included a provision for a joint U.S.-Vietnam study of the effects of dioxin on human health, and that began progress on the last and most difficult of the war's legacy challenges.

The worst flooding in a generation had just hit the Mekong Delta, and the United States had an opportunity to show how its government's scientific expertise could support Vietnam in a time of need. As Vice President Gore's representative on the trip, I met with the director of Vietnam's Disaster Management Center and officials responsible for flood control and relief efforts. I provided them with maps and data, and USAID donated one million dollars for flood mapping and the strengthening of warning and forecasting capabilities.

President Clinton had included a reference to this in his speech: "We want to bolster our efforts on disaster relief and prevention, including our efforts to help those suffering from the floods in the Mekong Delta. Yesterday, we presented to your government satellite imagery from our Global Disaster Information Network—images that show in great detail the latest flood levels on the Delta that can help Vietnam to rebuild."[21] The president participated in a disaster relief event with the Red Cross, the United States provided flood relief supplies, and a USAID senior official joined me in visiting flooded areas of the delta by boat.

One event in Hanoi was particularly meaningful to those of us who cared about Pete. Schiffer, who had helped stage-manage the president's visit and who was a close advisor to the ambassador, worked closely with Heather Davis in the White House to arrange for Pete to receive the Presidential Citizens Medal, one of the highest possible honors a civilian can receive. Pete was completely stunned when first John Kerry, then Hillary Clinton, and finally the president spoke about Pete's service to the United States. It was a surprise to everyone else, too. Pete's and Vi's diplomatic friends, as well as other government officials and business representatives, were there, not knowing that they would witness this emotional moment.

The president read the medal citation: "As ambassador, three-term member of Congress, and highly decorated Air Force pilot, Pete Peterson has devoted his life to protecting and strengthening democracy. While in our Armed Forces, he survived 6 ½ years as a prisoner of war in Vietnam and returned there in 1997 as America's first postwar ambassador to begin the process of reconciliation. With diplomatic skill and sensitivity, he has worked to heal the wounds of the past while actively pursuing a full accounting of all missing Americans. Through his selfless and inspiring service, Pete Peterson has demonstrated an unwavering devotion to duty, honor, and country."[22]

Pete replied humbly: "I bombed Vietnam during the war. Then I had the opportunity to come back and do good things. Few people have that opportunity."

President Clinton was unhappy that he had to depart for a state dinner and cultural performance and didn't have time to shake hands with those who had waited to meet him, including embassy staff members and Pete's friends. "I'm a thug," he told his wife, because he felt deprived of an opportunity to show his appreciation to the embassy team.

Vietnam's leaders were surprised by the huge throngs of people who lined the streets to see America's president. Vietnam had never before received a delegation the size of President Clinton's, which had more than 1,500 people and the longest motorcade ever to pass through Hanoi's streets.

President Clinton was also traveling to Hồ Chí Minh City, and before Air Force One took off, he and his family attended a ceremony at the airport where uniformed Americans provided full honors to the remains of U.S. servicemen lost in the war and watched as the small coffins were loaded onto military aircraft. On the flight, Schiffer listened with wonder as Chelsea Clinton (then a student at Stanford University) asked her father about the meaning of the airport repatriation ceremony. She had prepared well for the trip, even reading a dense biography of Hồ Chí Minh.

President Clinton spoke with great feeling about the importance of bringing closure to families by locating and returning the remains of their loved ones. The trip's most moving moment, he said, was at an excavation site, where the two sons of a fallen Air Force pilot, Lawrence Evert, watched Americans and Vietnamese working together to find their father's remains. Lieutenant Colonel Rennie Cory, mission director of the Joint Task Force–Full Accounting, oversaw that excavation and the subsequent POW-MIA repatriation ceremony, in which flag-draped remains were sent home to America.

The president told his daughter that the airport ceremony held great meaning for him personally. It was important, he added, to help the Vietnamese recover their dead. The country had lost as many as three million people in the war, and according to Vietnamese tradition, until remains are properly interred, the souls of the dead wander the earth. Vietnamese families deserved to find closure as well.

In Hồ Chí Minh City, the turnout for President Clinton was even greater than in the capital. As I rode in the motorcade, I was stunned by the size of the crowds. Young people could be seen everywhere, and they surged toward the president during the few times he broke out of the Secret Service's bubble around him.

President Clinton made up for any lost handshakes at the embassy by spending extra time with consulate staff on the rope line. He reached out to touch the hands of young and old, with half his body leaning into the crowd. I noted that Senator-elect Hillary Clinton held back. She didn't appear to relish the touch of the crowd the way her husband did.

A year after the trip, on April 7, 2001, Lieutenant Colonel Cory, the leader of the remains recovery mission, and six other American and nine Vietnamese mission members were killed when their Russian-made M17 helicopter, lost in fog, crashed into a mountainside in Quảng Bình province. I knew those helicopters. I had traveled in a M17 with Evans and his delegation. And when my mother and stepfather visited Vietnam for my first Christmas in the country, I had taken them to the beautiful Hạ Long Bay in another M17 helicopter, flown by the Northern Service Flight Company. My stepfather, who was then eighty years old, had been a fighter pilot in World War II. He worried about the safety of the helicopter, and as it turned out, he had reason for concern.

Fortunately, our trip in an M17 had been uneventful. As we flew over Hạ Long Bay's stunning limestone karst landscape—made famous in the 1992 film *Indochine*, with Catherine Deneuve—I thought it was possibly the most beautiful place on earth. Helicopter crashes were far from my mind.

President Clinton remembered Cory from the excavation site near Hanoi and the airport repatriation ceremony. He was no longer president when Cory died, but Clinton went to great lengths to track down the officer's wife and offer his condolences. Relationships mattered to him. Cory's wife was deeply moved.

David and Goliath

● ● ● ● ● ● ● ● ● ● ● ● ●

During Bill Clinton's presidency, significant strides were made toward reconciliation between the United States and Vietnam. Those of us involved in
this process recognized the importance of seeing reconciliation through the
lens of history, both recent and longer ago. We knew that American ignorance of Vietnamese history, culture, and politics had helped draw the United
States into war in a country it never came to comprehend.

Desaix Anderson, the scrupulously honest former chargé d'affaires who
served seven diplomatic tours in or focused on Indochina, directed the Prince-
ton Global Summer Seminar from 2007 to 2009. Its mission was "to use the
historical events of the American role in Vietnam to illustrate the importance of studying history."[1]

In *United States–Vietnam Reconciliation: Through Wars to a Strategic Partnership*, Desaix asked, "How had American leaders so misjudged the nature
of the struggle in Vietnam, the strength of nationalist sentiment, the determination of North Vietnam's leaders, and Hanoi's attitude toward China and
the Soviet Union? Had none of the American leaders been aware of Vietnam's
history?"[2]

Today, it is common to question the underlying belief in the domino
theory—the idea that once one Southeast Asian country fell to communism,
its neighbors would tumble behind it—in the administrations of Presidents
Dwight Eisenhower, John F. Kennedy, and Lyndon Johnson. Reasonable
scholars differ over that theory's relevance to Vietnam. However, it is

astonishing that presidential advisors who held that view seemed not to consider the context of the long history of Vietnam's battle for independence against China. The beginnings of this can be seen as far back as the tenth century.

938: Bạch Đằng

For eleven centuries, China has been the single most important determinant of Vietnam's foreign policy. In 938, after more than 750 years of Chinese occupation, General (later Emperor) Ngô Quyền led his military forces to defeat the Chinese in the first battle of Bạch Đằng. Ngô Quyền knew that Liu Hongcao, the Chinese commander, planned to sail his Southern Han fleet up the Bạch Đằng River to reach the Red River plain, the heart of northern Vietnam. Anticipating this move, Ngô Quyền and his troops sharpened stakes, tipped them with iron, and buried them into the mud so they would be beneath the water level at high tide.

When the Chinese ships pursued Ngô Quyền's troops, who traveled in boats with shallow drafts, the tide fell and Ngô Quyền counterattacked, driving the heavy Chinese warships back downstream, where they were impaled on the stakes. More than half of the Chinese troops were drowned, including Liu.

In 981, Emperor Lê Đại Hành had to repel a Song dynasty fleet in the second battle of Bạch Đằng, and he too used stakes planted in the water.

A diorama in Vietnam's Museum of National History shows the first battle of Bạch Đằng, illustrating how weak local forces defeated a Chinese armada supported by the full weight of an established empire. Visiting Hanoi in September 2016, my friend and mentor, Leon Fuerth, former national security advisor to Vice President Al Gore, was fascinated by the exhibit. He noted, "When the Chinese fleet moved in to attack, they did so at high tide. When the tide went down and the water receded, the stakes pierced their hulls, sinking every vessel. The strategy of allowing the strong to use its own power for self-impalement is not a single event, but a pattern."[3]

The five centuries after Ngô Quyền's victory at Bạch Đằng are referred to as Vietnam's independent period, when the country was ruled by the Ngô, Đinh, Lê, Lý, Trần, and Hồ dynasties. (Those six names, plus Trịnh and Nguyễn from later centuries, are the most commonly used surnames in Vietnam today.) Even so, during this time, the Vietnamese were forced to push back against encroachment from the north. In 1288, General (later Emperor)

PHOTO 6 Stakes in the Bạch Đằng River, October 2017 (Credit: Debra Book-Barrows).

Trần Hưng Đạo used the "self-impalement" strategy for a third time, in that instance to repel Kublai Khan's Mongol armies. Like Ngô Quyền and Emperor Lê Đại Hành before him, General Đạo used iron-tipped stakes to achieve victory in the third and final battle of the Bạch Đằng River. More than four hundred Mongol vessels were lost or captured, ending Kublai Khan's attempt to invade Vietnam and also effectively ending the Mongols' campaign to conquer Southeast Asia.

When I visited Bạch Đằng River, near Hai Phong, I stood beneath towering statues of three Vietnamese leaders who had successfully guarded the country against northern aggression: Generals (and later emperors) Ngô Quyền, Lê Đại Hành, and Trần Hưng Đạo. There, I read a poem in Vietnamese:

> The Emperor of the South reigns over mountains and rivers of the South,
> as it stands written forever in the Book of Heaven.
> How is it then that you strangers dare to invade our land?
> Your army shall be shamed and beaten.

This poem, written in the eleventh century, is sometimes referred to as Vietnam's first Declaration of Independence. According to mythology, it was

PHOTO 7 Three kings, Lê Đại Hành, Ngô Quyền, and Trần Hưng Đạo, at the Bạch Đằng River, October 2017 (Credit: Debra Book-Barrows).

read by God's envoys in support of Vietnamese troops who fought against invaders from the north.

In later centuries, other countries—France and the United States—would come and go, but China was always there. Every town in Vietnam has streets named after the national heroes who fought the Chinese, including Ngô Quyền, Lê Đại Hành, Trần Hưng Đạo, Lê Lợi, the Trưng sisters, Bà Triệu, Lý Thái Tổ, and Lê Thánh Tông. China has represented an existential threat to Vietnam from its birth as a nation to the present.

Obsessed by worries about Chinese and Soviet influence in Asia, Americans who led the war effort applied the domino theory to Vietnam and considered North Vietnamese leaders to be controlled by Moscow or Peking. This theory ignored the history of Vietnam's quest for independence and the mythology and culture that surrounded it. Even if fraternal links existed between the Soviet, Chinese, and Vietnamese Communist Parties, Vietnam would never blindly follow the Soviet Union, much less China. Vietnam absorbed Confucian values and Chinese customs, and many Chinese terms made it into the Vietnamese language, but Vietnam would not let itself be assimilated. The common thread running through Vietnam's history and legends is resistance to foreign powers, whether they be Chinese, Soviet, French, or American.

1945: Tân Trào

European colonialism in Vietnam began quietly in the sixteenth century, when Portuguese traders settled in Faifo, now the town of Hội An, fifteen miles south of Đà Nẵng. In the seventeenth century, the first French traders arrived in Vietnam as a civil war raged between the Trịnh in the north and the Nguyễn in the south. Even after commerce between Europe and Vietnam waned, Catholic missionaries remained and gained influence. In the early nineteenth century, Emperor Minh Mạng sought to curb the missionaries' influence, which provided a pretext for French attacks that later led to the overthrow of Minh Mạng's grandson, Emperor Tự Đức, Vietnam's last independent ruler. He capitulated in 1861 to the French, who established a protectorate over southern Vietnam. By 1863, the French were in charge in Hanoi and Saigon. In 1887, France established the Indochinese Union, consisting of Cochinchina in the south, Annam in the center, Tonkin in the north (the three parts of what is now Vietnam), and Cambodia. Laos was added six years later.

If the French believed that they could overcome Vietnamese nationalism and forcibly assimilate the citizens of their colony, they were wrong. Vietnamese resistance to French rule grew during the late nineteenth and early twentieth centuries, led by nationalists such as Phan Bội Châu and Phan Châu Trinh. The most effective leader in mobilizing Vietnamese nationalism was Hồ Chí Minh. In 1940, the Japanese swept into Southeast Asia and imprisoned leaders of the French administration in Vietnam. A year later, Hồ slipped into the country after three decades of wandering, ready to seize his moment.

After World War II ended in 1945, as the Allied war with Japan was winding down in the Pacific, officers in the Office of Strategic Services (OSS)—the predecessor of the Central Intelligence Agency, which was founded in 1947—began training an elite force of two hundred Việt Minh guerrillas. The OSS knew something about two of its members, Hồ and his most famous general, Võ Nguyên Giáp. Henry Prunier of Worcester, Massachusetts, and six other Americans had parachuted into Tân Trào village on a clandestine mission. Prunier taught the diminutive General Giáp how to throw a grenade.

The OSS's Deer Team wanted the Việt Minh to use modern American weapons and fighting techniques to harass the Japanese, who were occupying Indochina. The Việt Minh had supported the Allies in World War II, saving downed pilots. When I visited Tân Trào in March 2017, a guide showed us a massive banyan tree in a clearing at the heart of the Việt Minh's jungle base. She said one of Deer Team's agents had parachuted into the tree and gotten tangled in its branches. Armed men emerged from the jungle, and he fired his revolver, thinking they might be some kind of pro-Japanese militia. They retreated, and at daybreak the OSS agent, still stuck in his harness, woke from a fitful sleep to see a bamboo mat below on which someone had written two words in English: "Welcome friend."

Relieved, he called out to the Việt Minh, and they cut him down from the tree. Once in camp, he found out that the words that had lured him down had been written by the one person in the guerrilla band who knew some English: their leader and the future president of Vietnam, Hồ.

Hồ, Giáp, and the Việt Minh welcomed the Americans. Paul Hoagland, an OSS medic, treated Hồ for malaria and may have saved his life. After grenade lessons, Prunier instructed "Mr. Văn" (Giáp) in the use of American rifles, machine guns, bazookas, and other arms. Prunier earned a bronze star for these exploits and returned to Vietnam in 1995 to meet Giáp, who demonstrated the grenade-lobbing technique Prunier had taught him.[4]

Hồ introduced himself to the OSS officers as C. M. Hoo, and when he learned that Prunier was from Massachusetts, he told stories of his time as a pastry chef at the Parker House hotel in Boston. Hồ asked for a copy of the U.S. Declaration of Independence, which the OSS arranged to be air-dropped into the camp.

My visit to Tân Trào was with a small team that included Brett Blackshaw, the U.S. embassy's talented political counselor and someone with a personal connection to the village. His British grandfather, Peter Morris Williams, had been one of the Allied pilots who had brought food, medicine, and other supplies to the encampment. It is even possible that, along with food and medicine, Williams and his Royal Air Force special duties squadron may have been the ones who dropped the U.S. Declaration of Independence—the document that declared the American colonies' independence from Britain. During our visit, Brett left a photo of his grandfather at the base of a monument to Allied soldiers, just below the hut where "C. M. Hoo" had recovered from malaria.

In August 1945, after the United States dropped atomic bombs on Hiroshima and Nagasaki, the OSS helped protect Hồ as he traveled to Hanoi to announce Vietnam's independence. In Hanoi's Ba Đình Square, he paraphrased the U.S. Declaration of Independence in declaring, "All men are born equal: the Creator has given us inviolable rights, life, liberty, and happiness!"[5]

I repeated these words in Vietnamese to the press in Tân Trào, near the spot where Allied planes had dropped the Declaration of Independence for Hồ to study. Hồ had told the United States something important with his use of Thomas Jefferson's words to announce Vietnam's independence from France on September 2, 1945, but by then America was too alarmed by encroaching communism in Europe to listen.

The OSS argued against President Harry Truman's decision to support France in its war against the Vietnamese nationalists. Invoking the "Spirit of 1945"—referring to when the United States had been the prime supporter of Vietnam's independence—Hồ sent a telegram to President Truman on February 28, 1946: "FRENCH POPULATION AND TROOPS ARE MAKING ACTIVE PREPARATIONS FOR A COUP DE MAIN IN HANOI AND FOR MILITARY AGGRESSION STOP I THEREFORE MOST EARNESTLY APPEAL TO YOU PERSONALLY AND TO THE AMERICAN PEOPLE TO INTERFERE URGENTLY IN SUPPORT OF OUR INDEPENDENCE AND HELP MAKING [sic] THE NEGOTIATIONS MORE IN KEEPING WITH THE PRINCIPLES OF THE ATLANTIC AND SAN FRANCISCO CHARTERS RESPECTFULLY HOCHIMINH."[6]

Hồ's message to President Truman did not reach the president and went unanswered. Vietnamese leaders told me that Hồ wrote seven times, but he never received a response.

In 1946, the United States was already obsessed by communism. That obsession had only increased by 1950, when Senator Joseph McCarthy announced that he had a list of supposed Communists working in the State Department. Theodore H. White describes in his masterful *In Search of History* what happened to the United States during the decade after World War II, as the Cold War became Americans' focus and McCarthyism had a significant influence on our political culture. White showed how decimating the team of Foreign Service Asia experts—people who would have known about the history of enmity between Vietnam and China—left the State Department unprepared for the coming conflict in Southeast Asia and contributed directly to the debacle of our engagement in the Vietnam War. White wrote:

> The ultimate impact of McCarthy on American diplomacy, and thus on the world, came many years later, in Vietnam. . . . The purging ended with a State

Department full of junior diplomats, who knew their future career was pawn to political passion at home, who knew that prediction of a Communist victory would be equated with hope for a Communist victory, and who learned to temper their dispatches of observation in the field with what their political superiors wished to hear. No field-grade American diplomat, in the long period between 1964 and 1975, had the courage flatly to predict the potential for disaster in Vietnam. Many recognized that potential, but none dared say it aloud or in print until it was too late. They reported what their political masters wanted to hear.[7]

1954: Điện Biên Phủ

Since their independence declaration in 1945, the Việt Minh had been fighting against the French. From 1950 to 1954, the United States provided substantial military assistance to the French,[8] but the battle that would ultimately decide the fate of French Indochina occurred near the end of that period. By March 1954, General Giáp had forced the French to retreat to their base in Điện Biên Phủ. With help from the Chinese, Giáp installed artillery in tunnels and caves in the mountains overlooking the base and began pounding the French with mortar rounds. After fifty-four bloody and dispiriting days, the French position was hopeless. Under a barrage of artillery fire and surrounded by the enemy's trenches, the number of French troops had dwindled from nearly 16,000 to 13,000, with more than a third severely wounded.

By the afternoon of May 7, it was clear that the French could not hold their jungle fortress until nightfall. Still, in his office 220 miles away in Hanoi, Theater Commander General Réné Cogny didn't want Colonel Christian de la Croix de Castries to surrender. Their exchange was recorded by radiotelephone.

> Cogny: "Mon vieux, of course, you have to finish the whole thing now. But what you have done until now surely is magnificent. Don't spoil it by hoisting the white flag. You are going to be submerged [by the enemy], but no surrender, no white flag."
>
> De Castries: "All right, mon général. I only wanted to preserve the wounded."
>
> "Yes, I know. Well, do as [*sic*] best you can, leaving it to your [static: subordinate units?] to act for themselves. What you have done is too magnificent to do such a thing. You understand, mon vieux."

There was a silence. Then de Castries said his final words:

"Bien, mon général."

"Well, goodbye, mon vieux," said Cogny. "I'll see you soon."

A few minutes later, de Castries's radio operator methodically smashed his set with the butt of his Colt .45, and thus the last word to come out of the main fortress, as it was being overrun, came at 5:50 P.M. . . . : "We're blowing up everything around here. Au revoir."[9]

When the French forces were overtaken at Điện Biên Phủ in May 1954, it marked an end of French military influence in Asia and showed that Asians, who had been subjugated for centuries, could beat the whites at their own game. In September 2016, I went to Điện Biên Phủ with Võ Hồng Nam—the son of Giáp, the general who had defeated the French there. We visited de Castries's bunker with Leon, my friend and mentor. We tried to imagine what it would have been like to survive there, underground, for fifty-five days, living on cigarettes and whatever meager supplies dropped from the air that were a direct hit (most of the supplies fell into enemy hands).

Giáp was a former teacher, and he had studied Vietnam's victories at Bạch Đằng. At Điện Biên Phủ, he had designed and executed one of the greatest victories in Vietnam's long martial history. It was a sort of self-impalement not in a river but in a remote valley, where French military leaders could not have imagined that thousands of Việt Minh could carry heavy guns over rough terrain and dig tunnels around the French positions.

Giáp later used the same principles that had worked for Vietnam in its many wars with China and its long war with France in the effort to drive the United States out of Vietnam. He understood that America's vast power had to be used for self-impalement. Giáp told the historian Stanley Karnow in 1990 that his principal concern had been victory. When Karnow asked how long Giáp would have resisted the U.S. onslaught, he replied, "Twenty years, maybe 100 years—as long as it took to win, regardless of cost."[10] And the human toll was horrendous. In addition to 58,000 Americans, as many as three million North and South Vietnamese soldiers and civilians perished.

As we climbed to Giáp's jungle command center, Nam told us that his father never left his troops and always remained with them, even in the mud and the trenches. He drew a contrast to Cogny and to General Henri Navarre, who commanded all of the French forces in Vietnam, both of whom stayed 1,200 miles away in their air-conditioned offices in Saigon while their men fought at Điện Biên Phủ.

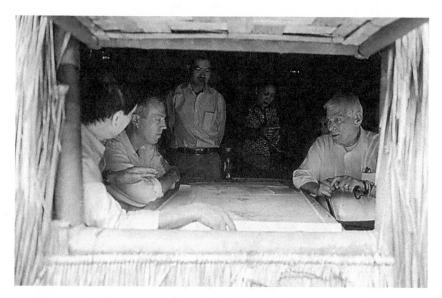

PHOTO 8 Võ Hồng Nam, the author, Leon Fuerth (all seated), Điện Biên Phủ, September 2016 (Credit: U.S. Department of State/Pope Thrower).

This seems to be a lesson worth considering. Leaders who ask their followers to take great risks do better if they are willing to share their followers' hardships, such as mud and mosquitoes in the jungle.

Of course, the French faced bigger disadvantages than distant commanders. Giáp's Vietnamese troops may have been inexperienced, but they were deeply motivated by the idea of independence. Forty thousand Vietnamese carried heavy artillery a thousand miles over rough terrain from China to Điện Biên Phủ. They died in larger numbers than the French. Still, as Hồ told Vietnam's colonizers in 1946: "You can kill 10 of my men for every one I kill of yours, yet even at those odds, you will lose and I will win."[11]

The French appealed to the United States to save them at Điện Biên Phủ. France had occupied Vietnam since the 1860s and did not want to lose its imperial jewel. Secretary of State John Foster Dulles and Vice President Richard Nixon urged President Eisenhower to intervene. Some urged a nuclear strike. The president said no.[12]

Nam unfolded a large map on a table in Giáp's jungle command center. He had carefully researched and drawn the map so it showed the movements of troops, where trenches had been dug, and the placement of artillery. "On this table," he said, "my father signed this map to certify its accuracy."

Sure enough, Giáp's signature was in the corner, along with a date: April 19, 2004. Nam gave a copy to Leon and another to me. I framed the map and bequeathed it to my successor, Ambassador Daniel Kritenbrink, as a reminder of Vietnamese determination and unwillingness to bow to an outside power, no matter how strong or wealthy.

Leon pondered the lessons of Bạch Đằng and Điện Biên Phủ. "They are David versus Goliath stories," he said. "And it's not just a specific event, but a meme." In some explanations of the David versus Goliath story, the giant is blind. At Bạch Đằng and Điện Biên Phủ, the Chinese and French giants certainly operated blindly.

Leon sat on a bench and listed some other David versus Goliath stories in history:

- Jewish rebels against Roman legions
- American colonies against British rule
- Indians against British rule
- Irish against British rule
- Algerian rebels against France
- Afghan tribes against the Soviets
- Somali tribes against the United States
- Taliban against the United States
- Islamic State of Iraq and Syria against the United States

In Vietnamese history, the theme is repeated:

- Vietnamese against China
- Vietnamese against France
- North Vietnamese against the United States

Leon understood that in Vietnam's history, the David and Goliath story repeats itself again and again. "The weak stalemating and sometimes even defeating the mighty," Leon commented. "The mighty permanently altered as a consequence." In writing about the United States and Vietnam, he added, "We won our battles militarily, but lost the war politically, which has become our pattern ever since. In the process, our country has paid an immense price, measured in terms of lost treasure and lives, and of the slow weakening of our polity."[13]

1963: Diệm in Saigon

In *United States–Vietnam Reconciliation*, Desaix examined a second question that President Kennedy's senior advisors must have considered: "How did we come to expect that a corrupt regime in Saigon could earn the respect and support of the population? Was it understood that the widespread sympathy in South Vietnam toward the Vietminh (Vietcong) did not represent support for communism as an economic or political system, but rather for the unfinished struggle for national independence?"[14]

Not only did President Kennedy's advisors fail to consider Vietnam's long history of enmity with China, but they also badly misunderstood the current regime in Saigon. Until Henry Cabot Lodge was appointed America's ambassador to South Vietnam in 1963, U.S. diplomats and leaders saw President Ngô Đình Diệm as an effective, if ruthless, leader of South Vietnam who was more or less aligned with U.S. interests. That view changed dramatically and quickly, and Diệm was then viewed as a leader who had become tiresome, unresponsive to American advice, and a perceived liability in winning the war. When President Kennedy and Ambassador Lodge gave tacit permission to assassinate Diệm—in the jargon of the time, he was "terminated with extreme prejudice," the Central Intelligence Agency's euphemism for a political assassination—it sent a message to the Vietnamese in the north and south about the limits of American loyalty and American staying power.

American complicity in Diệm's overthrow had a significance that far transcended Vietnam, as Karnow wrote in *Vietnam: A History*: "It meant, in theory at least, that the United States reserved the right to manipulate a dependent government that failed to conform to its standards."[15]

When Lyndon Johnson became president and inherited the war, he concluded that "Losing the Great Society was a terrible thought, but not so terrible as the thought of being responsible for America's losing a war to the Communists."[16] However, an independent, non-communist Vietnam could not be achieved by the series of corrupt and antidemocratic leaders whom the U.S. government propped up. The body count mounted, year after year, as President Richard Nixon took over the war, handing it over to President Gerald Ford—who saw it end in defeat.

When I joined the U.S. embassy in Vietnam in 1996, Robert McNamara, who had served as defense secretary under Presidents Kennedy and Johnson, had just published *In Retrospect: The Tragedy and Lessons of Vietnam*, and he was on what many critics referred to as his mea culpa tour. During a June 1997 visit to Hanoi, he took part in a six-day "Missed Opportunities?" conference organized by Brown University. As one participant noted, "McNamara probed, pushed and prodded in an effort to get our Vietnamese hosts to agree that both sides had some responsibility for misperceptions and lost opportunities" in the pursuit of a negotiated settlement instead of war.[17] He did not succeed.

The Vietnamese adhered to a preapproved script, a narrative in which the Americans were wrong in their judgment about Vietnam but the Vietnamese were correct in their assessment of the United States. Public Affairs Counselor Bill Bach noted that Vietnamese conference participants agreed about one missed opportunity: President Truman's failure to reply to Hồ's letters asking for U.S. support against the French. (I recall sneaking Christiane Amanpour, a correspondent for CNN, onto the back of my motorbike and through the rainy city to a reception during the conference. CNN had been promised an opportunity to film the proceedings, but the Vietnamese government canceled the arrangement at the last minute.)

In a meeting with his former nemesis, General Giáp, McNamara acknowledged that the United States "gave short shrift to Vietnam's strong nationalist tradition and aspirations" and that Americans "were held in thrall by the Domino Theory and our conviction that Vietnam was a potential steppingstone for China's thrust into Southeast Asia."[18] Before he departed, McNamara chatted with journalists at the bar in the Metropole Hotel. Bob Schiffer, Pete Peterson's friend and economic advisor, asked McNamara what he thought about Vietnam after a few days of visiting. "I know a lot about China," McNamara replied dismissively. "I know nothing about Vietnam."

The Pentagon Papers show that McNamara knew as early as 1967 that the war was unwinnable, but he didn't say this publicly. When confronted with this fact later, McNamara at first said that he had kept quiet out of respect for the president he served, Lyndon Johnson. But even after he had obtained a sinecure at the World Bank and Nixon was in the White House, McNamara stayed quiet, attended Georgetown dinner parties, and enjoyed his summers on Martha's Vineyard while Americans and Vietnamese continued to fight and die. His interviews in the 2003 film *Fog of War*[19] suggest that McNamara went to his grave tormented by the choices he had made.

1979–the Present: China and the South China Sea

Vietnam's foreign policy is primarily determined the same way now as it was in 938, when Emperor Ngô Quyền won the first battle of Bạch Đằng and ended more than 750 years of Chinese occupation. The same compulsions drive Vietnam today as they did in 1427, when Emperor Lê Lợi defeated a Chinese army and China first accepted Vietnam's independence.

Hannah Beech, the Southeast Asia bureau chief for the *New York Times*, wrote, "While the American War, as the Vietnamese call the conflict, lingers in American memories as a bloody and ideologically charged confrontation, Vietnamese animosity toward China runs much deeper."[20] The Communist fraternity between Beijing and Hanoi has at times eased tensions, but it has never erased the lessons of history for Vietnam. Scarcely 8 percent of Vietnamese view China as their nation's friend.

In mid-February 1979—four years after the last Americans withdrew from Saigon—200,000 Chinese troops from the People's Liberation Army entered Vietnam, and in an initial spasm of violence, tens of thousands of soldiers on both sides lost their lives in less than a month. In annual skirmishes for the next dozen years, thousands more lost their lives. The administration of President Jimmy Carter, having given up on efforts to establish diplomatic relations with Vietnam, ignored the Vietnam-China war, and the administration of President Ronald Reagan continued that approach.

In 1974, China had seized the Paracel Islands from South Vietnam. In recent years, Chinese and Vietnamese troops have fought over ownership of the South Johnson Reef in the Spratly Islands, where Vietnam occupies more islands and reefs than any other country does.

China has engaged in three phases of claims in the South China Sea, all aligned with the country's foreign policy narratives. Nguyễn Thị Lan Anh, an associate professor at the Diplomatic Academy of Vietnam and an expert in international law, described those phases: (1) Deng Xiaoping's "hide your strength, bide your time" approach of creeping claims; (2) bullying behavior since 2008, when China began to strive for a bipolar global order; and (3) the present, when China seeks to change the rules of maritime demarcation.[21]

Though Vietnam and China are the only countries with claims on the Paracel Islands, six governments (of Brunei, China, Malaysia, Philippines, Taiwan, and Vietnam) have competing claims on the Spratly Islands. Vietnam in particular has watched warily for the past decade as China, through extensive reclamation, has transformed the bits of rock and reef it controls into sprawling artificial islands that now double as military bases.

During the past decade, China's overt aggression and bullying in the South China Sea have led Vietnam to seek other friends in the region and develop its strongest security partnership with the United States, a former adversary.

Vietnam used self-impalement principles to defeat first China and the Mongols, then France, then the United States, and finally China again. In the 1960s and 1970s, the United States made a huge error by ignoring Vietnam's history of resistance to foreign dominance. Vietnam's history and nationalist aspirations provided the context for everything that diplomats and U.S. government officials tried to do in the mid-1990s to bring the two countries together. That history also served as the background for what I later tried to do as ambassador, attempting to create a long-lasting partnership between two former adversaries.

5

The Legacies of War

● ● ● ● ● ● ● ● ● ● ● ● ●

Thảo Nguyễn Griffiths was born in the northern province of Hà Giang three years after Saigon's fall. She began attending boarding school in Hanoi at the age of fourteen, and her trips home to see her family weren't easy because she had to ride twelve to sixteen hours each way in the back of an open newspaper truck. At least the trucks were reliable, and riding among the newspapers and bags of mail didn't cost much. The spot where the newspapers were loaded was near the dike that prevents the Red River from inundating Hanoi, and Thảo would climb in there with the newspapers and bags of mail before they headed out to Hà Giang.

Although riding in the back of the trucks was cheap, it was not comfortable. The newspapers smelled terrible, like fermented bamboo, and the road to Hà Giang is full of many elephant-size potholes, which caused the trucks and their smelly cargo to lurch from side to side. In winter, the open trucks were freezing cold, with the rain and wind sweeping in. For the first twenty-one years of her life, Thảo never saw an electric heater.

The 1980s were years of famine and the deepest poverty in Vietnam, but by the time Thảo went to boarding school in 1992, the economy had slowly begun to improve. At school, she lived alone on a small stipend in the big city of Hanoi. Her parents were not able to send her any money, so starting in her first year at boarding school, Thảo worked to support herself. "I never felt self-pity," she told me. "I shared poverty and suffering with the rest of Vietnam.

The years after the war were tough. Those who were privileged didn't have the experience of the real Vietnamese people."

From 1995 to 1999, Thảo studied at the Diplomatic Academy of Vietnam, and to make money, she sometimes taught Vietnamese to foreigners. That is how she met her husband, Patrick Griffths, an Australian who fell in love first with Vietnam and then with Thảo. After Thảo graduated, she was expected to stay in Hanoi, but after marrying a man who is not a Vietnamese citizen, she was not allowed to work for the Foreign Ministry.

Thảo also missed her parents, and she and Patrick returned to Hà Giang. Her mother and father were Confucian in their values, with scholars at the top of the pecking order, and they believed that education provided the ticket to a good life. They also believed in giving to the community, and they worked on a development project to improve the lives of ethnic minority peoples. When Thảo was twenty-one years old, she saw her father pay great respect to a Vietnamese man who had studied overseas on a Fulbright scholarship. She knew that such a scholarship was the key to something important.

Even before full diplomatic relations between the United States and Vietnam were established, the Fulbright exchange program began to build a web of educational ties between the Vietnamese and American people through its exchange of scholars. Thảo applied and was awarded a scholarship. Patrick said that a Fulbright scholarship was a passport to a new life, and she must accept it.

Thảo was a Fulbright scholar from 2004 to 2006, and that time marked the beginning of her love affair with America. She received support from Vermont Senator Patrick Leahy; his longtime foreign policy advisor, Tim Rieser; and Bobby Muller, president of the Vietnam Veterans of America Foundation (VVAF), a hallowed veterans' organization. Muller had risked censure from other veterans when he championed reconciliation with Vietnam. In 1995, Muller, in his wheelchair as a result of an injury he sustained in combat in Vietnam, joined President Bill Clinton for the historic establishment of full diplomatic relations.

Thảo took to Washington, DC where she was exposed to a lifestyle that included bicycling, museum visits, and many new ideas. She developed an appreciation for art, and as she told me, "The country girl from Hà Giang—still in the nineteenth century—jumped into the twenty-first century. Those years in the USA transformed me into a new person. My parents gave birth to me, but my Fulbright friends gave me a second chance in life."

Thảo recognized that she had been given a rare opportunity, and she felt a need to give back. She was part of a new generation of Vietnamese who were exposed to U.S. values. Back in Vietnam, from 2006 to 2016, she managed the Vietnamese programs of Muller's VVAF. Thảo told our mutual friend Irene Ohler, who was gathering stories of remarkable Vietnamese women, "This was the first time that a Veterans' Organization had, first, a Vietnamese national, and, second, not a veteran. And born after the war, and a woman!"[1]

"We've gone so far," Thảo said about her work at the VVAF, "from almost next to nothing between the U.S. and Vietnam on Agent Orange to probably more than $80 million in collaboration between Vietnam and the U.S., and it has been a success. There has been a lot of progress, and being part of that is a moment of joy."[2]

Thảo's work at the VVAF focused on war legacy issues such as cleaning up Agent Orange, removing land mines, and addressing the mental health challenges of people who had experienced terrible things. Thảo was Vietnam's first Rotary Peace Fellow in 2011 and the youngest fellow in the first batch of Eisenhower Fellows from Vietnam in 2013. She was named an outstanding international alumna of the Royal Melbourne Institute of Technology in 2016. Having grown up after the war, she focused her career on strengthening U.S.-Vietnam ties, and her story reflects that of the postwar reconciliation. Her story and mine intersected in 2015, and ours became a meaningful friendship.

George W. Bush, a Republican, was inaugurated president on January 20, 2001. Normally, when a new president assumes office, political ambassadors (in contrast to career diplomats) must tender their resignations. However, President Bush and Secretary of State Colin Powell knew that the United States and Vietnam were still negotiating the Bilateral Trade Agreement (BTA) that would benefit both countries. Recognizing that continuity was essential to these negotiations in Vietnam, President Bush asked Pete Peterson, President Clinton's ambassador and a lifelong Democrat, to stay on through the agreement's ratification.

Pete had devoted much of his tenure to negotiating the BTA, which he saw as the final act of diplomatic normalization. On March 9, 2001, Pete gave a speech to the Asia Society, during which he said that "Congressional approval of the [trade] agreement and ratification by Vietnam are the final acts in this fifteen-year-long bipartisan process [of diplomatic relations]."[3] Vietnam's attempts to join the world economy began in the mid-1980s, when Trường Chinh and then Nguyễn Văn Linh headed the country's Communist Party. The United States facilitated that economic integration, and its decision to pursue the BTA prepared Vietnam to join the World Trade Organization, catapulted Vietnam into the world economy, and helped lift it out of poverty.

In his speech, Pete described the importance of the BTA and explained that it would "point Vietnam toward compliance with the requirements it must meet to join the World Trade Organization." He concluded with a telling anecdote: "A reporter interviewed in November an old Vietnamese war veteran who was among the crowd waiting to see the American president. He asked the old man why he was so eager to see an American president after his experience fighting against the Americans. The man replied with a proverb: 'A thousand friends are not enough. One enemy is too many.' A lot of people there and here would agree."[4]

Vietnam joined the World Trade Organization six years later, in 2007. In the preceding years, Vietnam had changed key laws and launched a process to meet its international trade commitments that continues today.

In July 2001, Pete told *Vietnam News*, "The U.S. has long offered to engage in serious, joint scientific research with Vietnam to reach a well-founded understanding of the environmental and health effects of dioxin, an element in Agent Orange that has been claimed to cause health problems."[5] By this time, Pete was serving his last months as ambassador. He was succeeded by Raymond Burghardt in February 2002.

In retrospect, it seems obvious that the United States would eventually take some responsibility for war legacies, including its use of Agent Orange, an herbicide and defoliant chemical used to clear brush and forest where enemy forces hid. Dioxin, a highly toxic byproduct of the manufacture of Agent Orange, has been demonstrated to have long-term harmful physical effects on people exposed to it and is linked to birth defects. But during the first years of diplomatic relations, most U.S. officials (including me) were instructed to avoid discussing the topic with Vietnamese officials or in public. The U.S. government did not want to face culpability for birth defects, children's diseases, and other medical problems that might be related to use of the defoliant.

Silence with regard to Vietnamese victims of dioxin stood in contrast to the U.S. government's payment of billions of dollars each year in disability to U.S. veterans who later developed one of seventeen diseases associated with dioxin exposure. The government admitted guilt when it came to U.S. veterans exposed to dioxin but denied any responsibility for harming Vietnamese citizens.

The Vietnamese side also bore responsibility for the very slow pace of discussions on Agent Orange. Science Officer Mike Eiland told me he could not avoid Agent Orange discussions, but they were never fruitful. He credited Pete with "help[ing] establish a basis for honest dialogue that eventually paid off."

Senator Leahy, Thảo's patron, helped end the silence. "My goal, to put it simply," he said in a speech in June 2015 at the Center for Strategic and International Studies in Washington, "was to turn Agent Orange from a source of antagonism and resentment into another example of the U.S. and Vietnamese governments working together to address one of the most difficult and emotional legacies of the war."[6]

As ranking member of the Senate Appropriations Committee, Leahy played a major role in securing funding to deal with Agent Orange in Vietnam and to clean up unexploded ordnance (UXO) in Vietnam, Laos, and Cambodia, legacies of war that still plague those countries. Leahy also provided political leadership in the international campaign against land mines and cluster munitions.

For thirty years, Rieser never flagged in trying to do what was right to resolve the legacies of the past. He said that "changing the way we talked to each other" was key to overcoming mistrust between the two former adversaries. Rieser continued: "We turned issues of anger and resentment into joint problem solving [to clean up UXO and dioxin]. That transformed the relationship. Together we overcame initial reluctance, resistance, and antagonism. It was a function of personal engagement."[7]

Charles Bailey was another hero of the Agent Orange saga. First he headed an initiative on Agent Orange while directing the Hanoi office of the Ford Foundation from 1998 to 2007, then led a program at the Foundation's New York headquarters from 2007 to 2011, and continued the work at the Aspen Institute from 2011 to 2014. Bailey's mission was to have the United States honestly address the legacy of dioxin contamination. He began by researching the facts about lingering effects of Agent Orange.

From 1996 to 1999, the Canadian government funded a study by Hatfield Consultants that involved Vietnamese Health Ministry officials and focused on the status of dioxin in soils in the Aluoi valley. This remote area in Thừa Thiên-Huế province, near the border with Laos, had been repeatedly sprayed during the war. The study discovered that dioxin was still at dangerous levels at one former U.S. base, but not in the surrounding countryside.

In 2002, under Bailey's direction, the Ford Foundation funded a study by the same Vietnamese-Canadian team to assess the dioxin status at all former American military bases in southern Vietnam. The U.S. government did not support this effort, but the Ford Foundation—a private philanthropic organization—did not rely on the government for funding, nor did it require approval of its activities. Completed in 2006, the study established that dioxin was a present danger at a small number of former bases, in particular the air bases at Phù Cát, Đà Nẵng, and Biên Hòa. The United Nations took responsibility for the smallest of the three, Phù Cát, where 7,000 cubic meters of soil were found to be contaminated with dioxin. The soil was moved to a passive landfill, a large lined pit in a remote part of the base where the soil was secured and monitored to guard against any leakage.

Today's commercial airport at Đà Nẵng and the military air base at Biên Hòa were much bigger challenges. Đà Nẵng had 95,000 cubic meters of dioxin-contaminated soils and lake sediments, and Biên Hòa had more than five times as much soil (495,300 cubic meters) requiring remediation. In Đà Nẵng, about two dozen local residents regularly ate fish from the dioxin-laced lake at the northeast corner of the airport. An even greater number of people who lived in the area surrounding the Biên Hòa air base were potentially exposed to the dioxin-contaminated lakes nearby that were used to raise fish and ducks.

Bailey worked closely with each U.S. ambassador to develop a vocabulary that American and Vietnamese officials could use to discuss the issue. In 2009, his Đà Nẵng study led him to propose that the U.S. government focus its health and disability assistance on the Vietnamese with severe disabilities in the most heavily sprayed provinces. For eleven years he used his Ford Foundation budgets to move the Agent Orange issue forward, providing $7.4 million to assist Vietnamese with disabilities, $2.7 million for dioxin surveys and remediation, and $7.1 million to update the American people about this legacy of the war.

When my boss, Vice President Al Gore, lost the presidency to George W. Bush, I took a short sabbatical. I had received a Council on Foreign Relations–Hitachi Fellowship in Tokyo, and I spent six months researching and writing a book about the U.S.-Japan security alliance. Undecided about whether to rejoin the diplomatic corps, I was surprised by an offer to serve as environment, science, technology, and health officer for Southeast Asia and the Pacific. I began the job days after the tragedy of 9/11. It was an unusual assignment for a political officer, but it suited me. As a science officer, I never had to defend President Bush's decision to invade Iraq, and I learned crucial lessons that would help tremendously when I returned to Vietnam many years later.

In March 2002, I participated in the first U.S.-Vietnam Science and Technology Commission meeting, which was held in Hanoi. Our delegation was instructed to discuss areas of scientific collaboration between the countries but not the effects of dioxin. Even so, American and Vietnamese scientists met and presented their research on dioxin and its effects on the margins of that meeting, in a conference at Hanoi's Daewoo Hotel.

The third U.S. ambassador to Vietnam, Michael Marine, assumed his duties in September 2004. "I wanted to know why we hadn't made more progress on the Agent Orange issue," Marine said. "The basic attitude I found in my discussions with American officials from various departments was that this was an issue they really didn't want to deal with, they didn't want to touch, because it was too hard. . . . I decided I wasn't going to accept the status quo and that we would try to do better on the issue."[8]

A key turning point in the dioxin debate came in November 2006 when President Bush visited Vietnam to participate in the Asia-Pacific Economic Cooperation summit. Prior to the visit, Ambassador Marine obtained a State Department grant of $400,000 and additional funds from the Environmental Protection Agency to help cover the cost of dioxin remediation at Đà Nẵng. At a press conference in Hanoi, Bailey announced Ford Foundation grants of $2.2 million to add to the funding for Đà Nẵng and for three American nongovernmental organizations to pilot assistance for disabled children in Đà Nẵng and neighboring provinces. In March 2007, Senator Leahy and Tim Rieser arranged for a Congressional appropriation of $3 million, the first in a stream of annual appropriations that continues to this day to address Agent Orange in Vietnam.

President Clinton announced the first efforts by the United States to map and clean up land mines and UXO, but action really began during the Bush administration and extended into the administration of President Barack Obama. During the past twenty-five years, the United States spent more than $230 million on cleaning up UXO. The amount reached $12 million per year when I was ambassador.

The challenge concerned explosive weapons left behind by U.S. military forces (many of which had been buried underground) that could explode and kill or maim Vietnamese citizens. The United States had dropped 7.5 million tons of bombs on Indochina, mostly on Vietnam—a country about the size of New Mexico. By comparison, the United States dropped 2.25 million tons of bombs on all of Europe, Asia, and Africa during World War II. Early estimates suggested that hundreds of years would be needed to clean up all the

UXO in Vietnam. But a consortium of nongovernmental organizations (NGOs), working with Vietnamese officials, set a more realistic goal: instead of trying to eliminate every shred of metal, they would rid Vietnam, village by village and province by province, of UXO that could be harmful.

If land was to be used for agriculture, the NGOs and military would remove from UXO to the depth of a plow. If buildings were to be constructed, they would clean up UXO to the depth of the foundations. Occasionally cluster bombs would rise to the surface. These are small bomblets designed to kill people and destroy vehicles, but they look like toys and can fit in a child's hand. Therefore, over the past quarter-century, a massive effort has been made to educate more than 500,000 of central Vietnam's residents to identify different kinds of UXO, and what to do when they see it.

During my time as science officer in President Bush's first term, I learned that one way to build trust and advance the process of reconciliation was to engage the Vietnamese in matters of importance to them—those related to environmental challenges, health, or science and technology. The longest-lasting work I carried out was related to the fate of the Mekong River (the world's eighth largest), which begins in the Himalayan snows and flows three thousand miles before it spills into the South China Sea. My responsibilities included the Mekong countries of Southeast Asia, from the river's mouth in Vietnam upriver to Cambodia, Laos, Thailand, and Myanmar.

The Mekong Delta, known as Vietnam's rice bowl, produces half of the country's rice and 80 percent of its fruit and vegetables. Of the more than sixty-six million inhabitants of the Mekong basin, 80 percent depend on water-related resources such as rice and fish for their livelihoods. During the Vietnam War, the river was a front line between capitalist and communist forces. Naval officers such as Lieutenant John Kerry had experienced the Mekong by traversing it in Swift Boats, which drew only five feet of water and were able to glide into the river's narrow, shallow tributaries in the delta. In Phnom Penh, Cambodia's capital, the sluggish Mekong River meets Tonlé Sap Lake, which in spring is so swollen from the annual monsoon that it backs up and runs in reverse.

On a 2003 trip I made upstream, along the Laotian-Cambodian border, I saw some of the critically endangered freshwater Mekong dolphins. In Myanmar, on the Irrawaddy River, freshwater dolphins[9] help Burmese fishermen by herding fish into their nets and picking off those that slip through the mesh. Fishermen value the dolphins, and the symbiotic relationship is an important cultural tradition in many Burmese villages. In Cambodia and

Laos, the Irrawaddy dolphin's Mekong cousin is similarly beloved, credited with saving fishermen from drowning and from marauding crocodiles.

I visited a pod of thirteen to fifteen of the three-foot gray cetaceans a few miles south of the Mekong's majestic Khone Falls. As mammals that need to come up to the water's surface for air, the dolphins provide a guaranteed source of tourist income for villagers. Laotians, Cambodians, and Burmese do not capture dolphins for food or sport, but in the 1970s, the Khmer Rouge shot thousands of the dolphins in Tonlé Sap Lake in an attempt to crush local beliefs and also to extract oil from the dolphins for war machinery. During Vietnam's occupation of Cambodia, Vietnamese soldiers reportedly set up machine guns and shot at the dolphins for sport. The former Burmese strong-man Ne Win "bathed in dolphin's blood, believing it kept him youthful," according to an obituary.[10]

The dolphins' habitat is near Siphandone, a Lao term that can be trans-lated as "four thousand islands." Located in southern Laos, the region is one of the mighty Mekong's geological and scenic wonders. A major fault line there causes a drastic, sixty-foot drop in the river. Cutting across the stream, the fault line forces the river to spread out into a nine-mile-wide maze of chan-nels, rapids, and majestic waterfalls. The channels contain countless islands, some large enough to support towns and others so small that only a few shrubs and itinerant birds live there. Some of the smaller islands are entirely sub-merged for six months each year during the rainy season.

The 150-feet-tall Khone Falls are a serious obstacle to shipping on this stretch of the Mekong. During colonial times, the French operated a nine-mile narrow-gauge railway to haul cargo from below the falls to a wharf in Siphandone above. The French hoped the railroad would help transform the Mekong into a commercial thoroughfare. No railroads exist in Laos today. Although the falls prevented the dolphins' migration further north into Laos, they might be the dividing line that prevented a broader ecological disaster on the Mekong. Thus far even China's most ambitious channel-widening plans, supported by Laos, Burma, and Thailand, do not include blasting away the Khone Falls.

Upstream, in Luang Prabang, the Mekong's light-chocolate water runs fast, and shallow-draft boats must navigate carefully between sharp rocks. At dusk, the river turns pink, orange, and green, and kids swim and shriek along its banks. From the river, the red-and-gold peaked temple roofs of Laos's ancient imperial capital are barely visible in the gathering dark. Early in the morn-ing, while the cocks crow and mist still hangs over the river, long lines of monks walk barefoot along the still streets, carrying brass bowls suspended from their necks by saffron-colored cloth. Doors open, and the women of the town emerge with steaming baskets of sticky rice. As the monks file by, each woman places a bit of rice in every bowl. Not a word is said.

Anyone who has experienced the Mekong's beauty and magic must worry that efforts to improve river navigation with dynamite threaten the reefs and rapids between China's border and the city of Luang Prabang, as well as the Siphandone. China, Myanmar, Laos, and Thailand have agreed to destroy rocks in the river that make the passage of commercial boats challenging.

In 2003, the freshwater Mekong dolphins—as well as those in the Yangtze River in China, Mahakam River in Indonesia, Songkhla Lake in Thailand, and Chilka Lake in India—were perilously close to extinction, and today their situation has worsened. The pod I visited has reportedly shrunk to only three dolphins, which are among the last of a species that has lived in Southeast Asian rivers since the last Ice Age. Without changes in fishing practices, habitat protection, and an increase in community awareness and education, these dolphins and those in two other remaining pods, at Stung Treng and Kratie, will be gone in a few years. Other threats to the dolphins include being entangled in gill nets; electric and explosive fishing techniques; cyanide fishing; and, in the Irrawaddy, mercury poisoning.

The 600-pound Mekong giant catfish,[11] the world's largest freshwater fish and one of the river's great treasures, once lived in the stretch between Thailand and Laos, but it is also nearly extinct.[12] In addition to its size, it has another attribute that may contribute to its doom: it spawns late in life, and fewer and fewer of the catfish survive to that stage.

In 2013, China began its Belt and Road Initiative, which includes massive infrastructure investments stretching from East Asia to Europe. A part of that initiative had China blasting rapids and rocks to make the Mekong River navigable for cargo vessels and making the river safer for travelers and merchants in countries where development needs are great and poverty is high— countries that welcome the Chinese investments. In the process, dynamite and dams have destroyed spawning and breeding grounds and almost wiped out the catfish and the dolphins.

More than one thousand species of fish live in the Mekong Basin. According to the Stimson Center's Southeast Asia director, Brian Eyler, a world expert on the Mekong and the author of *Last Days of the Mighty Mekong*, the river's annual catch is "thirteen times more than the catch that comes out of all of North America's rivers and lakes combined."[13] It is among the top three rivers in the world (after the Amazon and Zaire) in terms of fish biodiversity. By comparison, the Amazon basin, which is nine times larger, supports three thousand species. Sixty percent of the Mekong's rich fish harvest (worth

$1.7 billion annually) consists of migratory species. These so-called white fish—including the giant catfish—depend on the annual flood pulse for spawning and access to necessary nutrients. If the Mekong's fisheries hope to continue producing, its fish need sufficient water flows, the sediment- and nutrient-rich silt the river provides, and free migration routes, and these things are all affected by dams, dikes, and irrigation mechanisms built on and along the Mekong and its tributaries.

The region's governments have been trying for decades to improve the living standards of some of Asia's poorest people. More than a third of those living along the Mekong subsist on about a dollar per day. Cambodia's sixteen million people get up to 70 percent of their protein from fish that live in the Mekong River system, especially the Tonlé Sap Lake. One-tenth of Cambodia's population is engaged in fishing full-time, and more than half of the population fish at least part-time. Yet China plans to build a nine-mile-wide dam at Sambor in Cambodia that would wipe out the fish catch and block the flow of rich alluvial soil to Vietnam's delta.

Sediment flow in the Mekong has been reduced significantly since China's first dam, the Manwan, opened on the river's upper reaches in China in 1995. Even though China contributes only 16 percent of the total flow of water in the Mekong, it accounts for half of the estimated 150–170 million tons per year of sediment load. Since 1995, the sediment reaching the Mekong Delta—needed for fish but also to fertilize crops—has diminished by two-thirds. Instead of growing as in the past, the delta is shrinking. At the same time, rapid sediment buildup threatens to fill in the Manwan reservoir and incapacitate the dam, yet the environmental damage is already done. China has completed eleven dams on the upstream portion of the Mekong in its territory, and some of them are among the largest dams in the world.

For Vietnam, the farthest downstream of the six countries straddling the Mekong, dams threaten the nation's prosperity and the livelihoods of twenty-two million citizens living in delta provinces. As the dams produce electricity, and land-locked Laos exports mostly electricity and timber, Laos alone has built more than sixty dams, hoping to become the battery of Southeast Asia. There are two hundred new dams on the drawing boards. While not all will be constructed, each one would lower the amount of water reaching Vietnam's Mekong Delta, reduce the amount of rich silt for Vietnam's crops, and inflict permanent damage on the river basin's biodiversity.[14]

As a science officer, I was also responsible for tracking diplomatic developments involving public health in Southeast Asia and the Pacific. In April 2003,

Thaksin Shinawatra, the prime minister of Thailand, convened a meeting on ten days' notice of the Association of Southeast Asian Nations (ASEAN) to address the recent outbreaks of Severe Acute Respiratory Syndrome (SARS). In an unprecedented move, China's leaders were invited to participate.

The summit produced decisions on key disease-prevention measures, including information sharing, regular reports on the status of SARS outbreaks, and collaboration on epidemiology and laboratory work. Chinese and Southeast Asian leaders wanted to show the world that they were united, confident, and exercising leadership in tackling the disease and slowing its spread. The ASEAN summit marked the first emergency leaders' meeting since Vietnam's 1979 invasion of Cambodia. China's participation, and reports that Vietnam and Singapore had made major strides in controlling SARS's spread, brought about a recovery in Asian stock markets.

SARS cut East Asian economic growth as much as 2 percent that year, costing the region $11–18 billion, including $800 million worth of damage to the airline industry.[15] Tourism-dependent economies, such as those of Hong Kong, Singapore, Malaysia, Thailand, and Cambodia, suffered most. SARS cut growth in those five economies by 0.5–2.0 percent. Growth in Vietnam, where tourism accounted for only 4 percent of the nation's gross domestic product, dropped less.

Fear of SARS probably caused greater economic loss than the disease did, and Asian leaders wanted to spread accurate information about the disease as quickly as possible to quell rumors and stop the panic that, in three months, had caused serious damage to economies. As COVID-19 would almost two decades later, SARS scared the people who spent money in East Asia: investors, tourists, and the traveling public. For that reason, SARS demanded international collaboration and a quick, decisive response.

China's Wen Jiabao, making his first official trip abroad as premier, came to Bangkok with a strong team, including Hong Kong's chief executive, Tung Chee-hwa. The Chinese delegation described the measures taken in China and Hong Kong to cope with SARS and pledged $1 million to a Chinese-ASEAN fund for bilateral programs. Thailand contributed $250,000 and Cambodia $100,000. China also offered to host a high-level international symposium on SARS control and treatment.

ASEAN members divided up some of the tasks. Indonesia took the lead in disseminating information through the ASEAN SARS Containment Information Network. Member countries also pledged to use the ASEAN secretariat to notify their neighbors about SARS-infected people traveling between ASEAN countries. ASEAN took responsibility for informing the public and asked the World Health Organization (WHO) to help spread accurate information and forestall panic. Malaysia took charge of laboratory work to evaluate tests that could be used to determine if an individual had contracted SARS. Thailand took the lead on coordinating epidemiological tracking of SARS.

China's attendance at the summit implicitly acknowledged the country's responsibility for spreading SARS. Only a week earlier, Chinese leaders had agreed that serious shortcomings had occurred in their handling of the epidemic. President Hu Jintao admitted that there had been a cover-up, and at an extraordinary press conference on April 20, a deputy health minister, Gao Qiang, announced a ninefold increase in the number of probable SARS cases in the nation's capital.

The next day, Xinhua News Agency announced the firing of China's health minister, Zhang Wenkang, and Beijing's mayor, Meng Xuenong. They were the highest-profile officials expelled from the Communist Party for negligence (as opposed to corruption) since the Party had forced General Secretary Zhao Ziyang out during the 1989 Tiananmen Square protests. The firings placed all Chinese health officials on notice that further cover-ups would not be tolerated. (Seventeen years later, in February 2020, China fired several senior officials in Hubei province for their mishandling of COVID-19.)

In the first months of 2003, Beijing had handled SARS in the secretive way it would later use in dealing with COVID: beginning with denial, the government moved to reluctant acknowledgment, followed by a mobilization of resources. With COVID, the process happened more quickly than it had with SARS.[16]

During the 2003 SARS outbreak, the U.S. Centers for Disease Control and Prevention (CDC) collaborated closely with Vietnam's Health Ministry. The CDC's work in Vietnam had begun during Pete's time as ambassador, when Mike Linnan was the U.S. embassy's first health attaché. Linnan had previously spent five years with the CDC in Vietnam, and he had helped start the Hanoi School of Public Health. CDC scientists were the ones who identified the virus that causes SARS within a month of Beijing's announcement of the mysterious new illness.

In October 2003, when President Bush visited SARS-free Bangkok, leaders of the Asia-Pacific Economic Cooperation forum launched a health security initiative, an additional diplomatic mechanism for dealing with the region's health crises. Three lessons from dealing with SARS proved to be particularly relevant in the case of COVID-19: the public health infrastructure needed strengthening; governments had to practice openness, transparency, and accountability in dealing with health challenges; and the microbial world remained a significant health threat.

In 2007, in response to SARS, the WHO overhauled the international system of infectious disease control. At the time, 194 member countries agreed to comply with international health regulations that require them to report any potential global health threat instantly to the WHO. Years later, when leaders in East Asia were faced with COVID, they knew they had to respond as quickly and effectively as the tools of public health would allow.

A month after the ASEAN summit in Bangkok, where I was based, a number of friends bound to Vietnam by personal and professional ties traveled to a small wedding on Bintan Island, a short ferry ride from Singapore. Bob Schiffer, the master of ceremonies, stood between the bride, Shiu Mei Lin, and the groom, Chris Helzer, on a small wooden platform over a pool where a half-dozen shimmering candles floated.

Behind them, waves crashed against the rocky South China Sea coast, and palms swayed in the light breeze. The water in the pool reflected an image of Shiu Mei's pink and ivory Vera Wang dress. Chris wore a vest but no jacket. The evening was pleasant, but we were only a few degrees from the equator— which meant that it was hot, and we welcomed whatever breezes drifted in from the Malacca Strait. Sarong-clad waiters circulated among the guests, distributing champagne.

Many of the same guests had sweltered through Ambassador and Mrs. Pete Peterson's wedding in Hanoi's great cathedral, exactly five years earlier. But this May was during the peak of the SARS epidemic, and as part of the ceremony, Bob delivered goodwill messages from Pete and Vi, who had been prevented by SARS from traveling to the wedding. Two other friends of the groom were not able to attend because their U.S. company was strictly enforcing a travel ban. Other guests found ways to elude restrictions that had disrupted travel and commerce throughout Asia.

For weeks before the wedding, Chris had sent upbeat bulletins to the guests, such as this wire report: "Singapore continues to receive visitors for business and leisure, from around the world. It is business as usual." He cited the *Straits Times*: "Singapore's battle against the virus has won a vote of confidence from foreign investors." Indeed, Singapore's strict measures to control SARS exceeded guidelines set by the WHO and the CDC. On my Thai Airways flight, crew members dispensed face masks to the passengers, and at Singapore's Changi Airport, a thermal imaging machine informed public health officials if travelers' temperatures were low enough for them to proceed. Officials took passengers' temperatures coming and going on the ferry from Singapore to Bintan, using procedures now familiar to anyone living through COVID-19.

During the spring of 2003, SARS crowded out virtually all other news in East Asia's media, including America's war in Iraq. The U.S. State Department and the CDC issued frequent warnings to travelers, suggesting that they avoid East Asia until SARS could be brought under control. For a time, East Asia and SARS seemed synonymous. The symbol of SARS—a white face mask covering the mouth and nose, with Asian eyes peeking out above—could be seen everywhere.

Some Southeast Asians favored homegrown wisdom over medical science, as doctors seemed helpless in the face of SARS. In Cambodia, a story spread that a miracle baby had been born, able to speak only moments after he emerged from the womb. "Eat mung beans," he told his parents, "before the clock strikes midnight, or you will die of SARS." Quickly the neighbors spread the baby's warning, and thousands flocked to the streets where vendors sold mung beans. Prices rose by the hour as the demand for mung beans outstripped supply. Their mung beans devoured, at midnight the citizens of Phnom Penh remained SARS-free. His mission accomplished, the miracle baby died.

SARS spread from southern China to twenty-nine countries in eight months[17] and caused eight thousand deaths. SARS frightened people because infected individuals were highly contagious. Globalization—especially the ability to travel by air at great speeds—vastly increases the potential for spreading infectious disease widely. Seventeen years later, COVID reached 215 countries and territories in only four months.

Vietnam learned important lessons from SARS, Middle East Respiratory Syndrome (MERS) and H1N1 (swine flu) that helped the country effectively contain COVID-19 in 2020. A coronavirus originating in southern China caused SARS, a coronavirus from the Middle East caused MERS, and a coronavirus from Wuhan caused COVID-19. Identifying the origin of a virus can help scientists figure out how it evolved and found its way into people. SARS arose in southern China because people there raise pigs and ducks, and many farmers live close enough to their livestock for the disease to jump from animals to humans. The flu epidemic of 1918–1920, which killed 20–40 million people around the world, probably originated this way in China. The Asian flu of 1957 and the Hong Kong flu of 1968 most likely passed in similar fashion from animals to humans.

Some scientists believe that most influenza epidemics originate in bird populations, but others focus on the threat caused by Chinese proclivities for consuming wildlife. The coronavirus that causes SARS is nearly identical to one found in civet cats, raccoon dogs, and badgers—and all of those animals are eaten in southern China. If the virus can still infect its animal host, it may be impossible to eliminate even by breaking the chain of infection among humans. This is especially true if the host is a wild animal that cannot be rounded up or isolated.

On July 5, 2003, the WHO's director general, Gro Harlem Brundtland, said: "SARS is a warning. . . . Next time, we may not be so lucky. We have an opportunity now, and we see the need clearly, to rebuild our public health protections. They will be needed for the next global outbreak, if it is SARS or another new infection."[18] SARS was contained worldwide because quarantines and isolation had broken the human chain of transmission. But Brundtland warned that SARS was not gone. A single case can start a new outbreak. Like other coronaviruses, it could reappear as soon as the winter flu season began. In September 2003, a medical researcher contracted SARS in a Singapore lab while studying the West Nile virus. Mistakes can occur, and SARS has not disappeared forever.

As COVID-19 has demonstrated, a virus can infect tens of millions and plunge the world into an economic depression. A virulent pandemic can wreak havoc long before a vaccine is ready. New dangerous microbial strains can mutate and infect humans at great speeds in an increasingly interconnected world.

SARS came and went relatively quickly. As a diplomat and as a man who lost many friends to AIDS, I devoted significant effort to combating the HIV/AIDS epidemic. In 2004, President Bush designated Vietnam as a focus country—the only one in Asia—for the President's Emergency Plan for AIDS Relief (PEPFAR), making it eligible for targeted technical assistance with wiping out the AIDS epidemic. Focusing on the threat of HIV to prosperity, democracy, and regional stability, the Bush administration acknowledged that AIDS was not only a public health issue but also a challenge with profound economic and security implications.

In East Asia, the HIV/AIDS epidemic initially hit Thailand, whose first AIDS case was discovered in 1984. By the late 1980s, one-third of Thailand's injecting drug users had been infected by HIV. A thriving sex industry and widespread intravenous drug use facilitated the disease's rapid spread to the general population. By 1990, the number of new HIV infections in Thailand had reached 150,000 annually. If trends had continued, 15 percent of Thais would have been infected. Instead, Thailand fought the epidemic and succeeded in cutting new infections by a factor of six.

One man did more than any other to reverse this situation. Senator Mechai Viravaidya, Thailand's most recognized advocate of family planning and safe sex, was affectionately known as the condom king. In Thailand, the popular term for a condom became "mechai." A man like Mechai, who came from a respected, high-society family linked to Thai royalty, might have objected to this sobriquet. Instead, he relished it. The condom was Mechai's banner in a tireless crusade against HIV/AIDS. He made this simple device the symbol of a social revolution, one that began with family planning and moved quickly into the realm of AIDS prevention.

Mechai employed humor—very effective in Thai culture—to popularize the condom. First, he staged condom-blowing contests, awarding the winners T-shirts adorned with condom-shrouded anthropomorphic penises. Captain Condom cruised the go-go bars in Patpong, Bangkok's red-light district, urging customers to practice safe sex. Mechai crowned the queens in Miss Condom beauty contests. His Cabbages and Condoms Restaurant sold colorful condom bouquets and condom mugs, pens, and bathmats. Instead of an after-dinner mint, the check came with a condom for each patron. Condoms were placed under the pillow at Mechai's Cabbages and Condoms beach resort. Cabbages and Condoms convenience stores sold condoms all over Thailand.

At an international AIDS conference in Montreal in 1989, Mechai's keynote speech sounded the alarm about AIDS in Thailand. He called on the government to lead a massive public education campaign. For two years, while the government dithered, Mechai and his condom crusade remained a focal point for anti-AIDS activism. Then in 1991, Prime Minister Anand Panyarachun made AIDS prevention a national priority, chairing a National AIDS Committee and putting Mechai in charge of waging the public education campaign he had called for in Montreal. The media, government, and non-governmental organizations promoted universal condom use in commercial sex. The policy in brothels was clear: no condom, no service—and no refund. This campaign reduced visits to prostitutes by half, raised condom usage above 90 percent, cut sexually transmitted diseases dramatically, and achieved significant reductions in HIV transmission. All segments of society were involved, from government officials, teachers, and monks to prostitutes and drug addicts.

With one million people infected by HIV/AIDS, Thailand was one of the world's hardest-hit countries. But matters could have been far worse.

Courageous political leadership altered the public debate and changed behavior. In South Africa, by contrast, President Thabo Mbeki raised doubts for years about whether HIV causes AIDS. He claimed that evidence from the internet proved his peculiar thesis that HIV did not cause AIDS. Millions of unnecessary deaths followed.

In Vietnam, as in Thailand, HIV/AIDS mostly affected marginal populations: drug users, prostitutes, men who have sex with men, and transient populations. The Bush administration, recognizing that the disease would move into the general population, took action to help head off what might have become a devastating epidemic in Vietnam.

Fortunately, Vietnam also had a courageous champion in the fight against HIV/AIDS. Though not as flamboyant as Senator Mechai, Deputy Prime Minister Vũ Đức Đam seized the political third rail of drugs and sex and for more than a decade pushed for a rational public health response to HIV. Vietnam is a socially conservative country, and HIV remains associated in the public mind with drug users, homosexuals, and prostitutes—in short, with sin. Đam realized that discrimination had to be addressed because it was a major obstacle to combating HIV. He pushed back against those who focused on sin and instead emphasized condom use and clean needles, sex education, and strengthened public interventions.

In Vietnam, injecting drug users made up the bulk of the affected population. Strong links exist between the drug user and sex worker epidemics, since addicts also visit prostitutes or sell their bodies to fund their drug habits. In urban areas where drug use and prostitution fed off one another, such as Hanoi and Hồ Chí Minh City, HIV rates rose fast. With this disease, as much as a decade can pass between infection and illness—a decade during which most people show no symptoms of the disease and can unknowingly infect many partners. In contrast to images of intravenous drug use in the West, injecting drug users in Vietnam and elsewhere in Asia generally hold down jobs, have partners and even families at home, and tend to function if not in the mainstream, at least not just on society's outer edges.

President Bush's PEPFAR program was informed by the experience of Brazil. Since 1997, Brazil had proved that a commitment to treat every citizen with HIV/AIDS who needed it was a good economic bet. The treatment efforts worked and strengthened prevention campaigns. Data from Brazil showed that the cost of hospital and ambulatory care services for AIDS patients ($2.2 billion in a six-year period) exceeded the cost of antiretroviral therapy ($1.8 billion), and that did not include the benefits of keeping parents with their children, teachers in schools, and farmers working their lands. Although still costly, antiretroviral therapies made economic sense. When antiretroviral drugs are given in combination (three drugs together), the rate at which the virus reproduces itself is reduced, and the body's immune system can partially regenerate—thereby restoring health and improving the quality of life.

After three years as science officer for Southeast Asia and the Pacific, I moved back to Washington, DC, to serve as deputy director of Korean affairs at the State Department. There, in a monthly business meeting for LGBT+ diplomats that was devoted to strategizing for equal rights during the Bush administration, I met Clayton Bond, a fellow diplomat serving in the department. We married in 2006 in Vancouver, Canada, as same-sex marriage was not yet legal in most of the United States. We were posted together to New Delhi, where Clayton worked on public diplomacy and embassy management, while I was responsible for political affairs—including the U.S.-India civil-nuclear initiative that transformed relations between the world's oldest democracy and its largest.

My experiences in the Bush years—as science officer and working on Korean affairs and then in India—taught me that apolitical initiatives, such as collaborations on challenges related to the environment, health, and education, were particularly effective in advancing reconciliation after a break in relations.[19] In the case of Vietnam, those apolitical endeavors needed to be supplemented by joint work to build economic ties and address the legacies of war.

Reconciliation advanced during the Bush presidency, especially because the United States took seriously the need to boost trade with Vietnam and clean up dioxin and unexploded ordnance left over from the war. President Bush's decision to include Vietnam in PEPFAR deepened public health collaboration between the two countries and demonstrated to Vietnam's leaders and people that the United States wanted a broad partnership. Military-to-military ties proceeded more slowly, but as the legacies of war were addressed, a more complete, mutually beneficial relationship became increasingly possible.

6

Think Unthinkable Thoughts

● ● ● ● ● ● ● ● ● ● ● ●

By 2008, more than a thousand Vietnamese scholars had earned either master's or doctoral degrees in the United States, and one of them, Nguyễn Vũ Tú, was already a rising star in Vietnam's diplomatic corps. At that time Tú served as deputy director of the Foreign Ministry's satellite office in Hồ Chí Minh City. He had served multiple tours in that city, where he and his wife raised their two children.

I first met Tú there in 1996, when he was a young diplomat whose tasks included interacting with incoming U.S. officials and visitors. Like Thảo Nguyễn Griffiths, Tú had learned about the United States as a Fulbright scholar. He and Phạm Bình Minh—who succeeded his father, the legendary Foreign Minister Nguyễn Cơ Thạch, in that position—were among the first diplomats to earn a U.S. master's degree in international relations when they studied together at the Fletcher School of Law and Diplomacy at Tufts University from 1992 to 1994.

Tú's parents were Communist Party royalty, and I once saw a photo of him as a toddler sitting on Hồ Chí Minh's knee. Also like Thảo, Tú returned from his Fulbright experience with a determination to give back to Vietnam. Tú and I had monthly lunches with his boss, Deputy Director Lương Văn Lý, always at a different restaurant. At first, Lý was not friendly to the United

States. Educated in Switzerland, he was somewhat disdainful of Americans, initially tolerating our lunch meetings only because he trusted Tú. Gradually, Lý began to trust me as well. By the end of a year, he had decided that Americans did not have horns on our heads, and he was willing to visit the United States himself, on a six-week exchange tour that I arranged for him. He had become another friend for the United States.

Crucially, Tú believed in the Harvard-Fulbright Center's mission in Hồ Chí Minh City. He moonlighted there, working closely with Tommy Vallely, founder of the center and director of the Harvard Vietnam Program. Vallely was a Marine veteran and had been John Kerry's comrade since the war. He had supported Kerry in Massachusetts politics and remained his lifelong friend. Along with Kerry, Vallely wanted the State Department–administered economics teaching center to bear the name of Senator J. William Fulbright. Later renamed the Fulbright Economics Teaching Program (FETP), it was dedicated to educating Vietnam's decision makers in the fundamentals of modern economics.

The Fulbright brand resonated in Vietnam, where it had a relatively long history. Fulbright had been chair of the Senate Foreign Relations Committee longer than anyone else, and he had transformed himself from a close ally of President Lyndon Johnson to one of his toughest critics in terms of the goals and execution of the war in Vietnam. The FETP drew its inspiration on education from Fulbright's belief that "we must dare to think about 'unthinkable' things. We must learn to explore all the options and possibilities that confront us in a complex and rapidly changing world."[1]

Tú realized that educating provincial officials in modern economics could be a game changer, and he threw himself into making the program work. He took on the difficult and unglamorous task of translating complex economic terms into Vietnamese, knowing that provincial officials, who rarely spoke any English, could drive economic reform at the local level. I remember Tú as being in overdrive, balancing his FETP and diplomatic duties and regularly traveling to Hanoi to help Communist Party leaders figure out what the United States was planning.

From 1994 to 2018, the FETP transformed the way Vietnamese officials thought about and managed their country's economy. Year by year, the program gained credibility by producing graduates who returned to their provinces or Hanoi and systematically changed systems of governance in ways that helped the market economy, as well as foreign investors, flourish. Officials who used what they had learned at the FETP to attract foreign direct investment (FDI) to their provinces were promoted, and others took note. As more foreign investment came into the country, it created pockets of success—in Đà Nẵng and around Hồ Chí Minh City—that grew and grew.[2]

Kerry continued to support the FETP, but he also established the Vietnam Education Foundation, an independent executive branch agency that sent scholars such as Thảo, Tú, and Phạm Bình Minh to the United States for study. Kerry knew that this exchange would have a significant impact on U.S.-Vietnam relations and enable friendships between American and Vietnamese citizens.

Even after I left Vietnam, Tú and I remained in touch as our careers progressed. In 2004 and 2005, when he was in Washington, DC, serving as political counselor in Vietnam's Embassy, and I was at the State Department covering Korean affairs, Tú and I were able to get together for a bowl of *phở* (Vietnamese noodle soup) on a regular basis.

In 2006, Vietnam began to take off as a destination for FDI when the government revised its laws related to land ownership, and *Euromoney* (an influential guide for investors) held its annual general meeting in Hanoi. Investors decided that Vietnam was the new China, and FDI—especially in banking and real estate—rose rapidly. The 2008–2009 financial crisis did not affect Vietnam too much. Capital was looking for return, and Vietnam appeared attractive.

President Barack Obama's first year in office was largely devoted to recovering from the financial crisis and building a domestic constituency for health care reform. In July 2009, I began serving as deputy chief of mission at the U.S. embassy in Jakarta, Indonesia. As a boy, President Obama had lived with his mother and stepfather in Indonesia, and the Indonesians relished the connection. Early in his presidency, a visit to Indonesia was announced, and Clayton and I prepared for it. Twice the trip was canceled—first because of a critical vote on health care and second when the president needed to remain in the United States to manage the Deepwater Horizon oil spill.

In November 2010, when President Obama at last arrived in Jakarta, excited crowds greeted him at every stop. To overcome past differences, he formally launched a comprehensive partnership between the United States and Indonesia that included collaboration in key areas of mutual interest: education, trade, environment, security, and international diplomacy and security. In July 2011, the president returned to Indonesia for the East Asia Summit in Bali, accompanied by Secretary of State Hillary Clinton. My job as deputy to Ambassador Scot Marciel (who, years before, had been the first diplomat to serve in the U.S. liaison office in Hanoi) was to oversee the preparations for that visit, as I had for the earlier one.

In Bali, the president and secretary engaged in diplomacy that led to Clinton's landmark trip to Myanmar in the autumn and to the administration's rebalance to Asia. In October, Clinton outlined the new approach to Asia in *Foreign Policy*, writing that "the United States stands at a pivot point."[3] In November, President Obama said, "Asia will largely define whether the century ahead will be marked by conflict or cooperation, needless suffering or human progress."[4]

As secretary, Clinton visited Vietnam twice—the first time in 2010, when she participated in the Association of Southeast Asian Nations regional forum in Hanoi and declared that the United States had a vital strategic interest in preserving freedom of navigation in the South China Sea. By the beginning of President Obama's second term, it was clear that Vietnam was crucial to the administration's pivot toward Asia. In July 2013, Vietnamese President Trương Tấn Sang met with President Obama in the Oval Office, where jointly they announced a U.S.-Vietnamese comprehensive partnership that would provide an overarching framework for advancing the countries' relationship. Dave Shear, then the U.S. ambassador to Vietnam and a skillful diplomat with deep experience in Asia, had worked with President Sang and other leaders to launch this new partnership.

At a celebratory luncheon at the State Department honoring President Sang, the new Secretary of State, John Kerry, departed from his prepared remarks and said, "I noticed that in 1966, [President Sang] joined the Communist Party of Vietnam; in 1966, I joined the United States Navy. In 1969, he became a guerrilla leader in a district south of Saigon . . . ; in 1969, I was in the Mekong Delta at war. Subsequently in 1984, he took on major responsibilities in Vietnam, ultimately becoming the mayor of Ho Chi Minh City . . . ; in 1984, I was elected to the United States Senate and took on not so major responsibilities, but—(laughter)—I tried to upgrade that at one point."[5]

I was thrilled to be a witness to this history. Clayton and I had ended our Indonesia tour and had recently returned to Washington. I was delighted to be at this event and to see so many old friends—Vietnamese and American—gathered to celebrate how far our two countries had traveled together.

While in Jakarta, Clayton and I had tried to adopt a baby girl, but we had three strikes against us: we weren't Muslim, Indonesian, or straight. After that disappointment, we decided to start our family in the United States. While the adoption process took some time, our patience was rewarded in

December when our son TABO (our nickname for Theodore Alan Bond-Osius) was born in El Paso, Texas.

By then I was teaching at the National War College and under consideration for an ambassadorship. When the Bureau of East Asian and Pacific Affairs put my name forward for a posting to Fiji, I sought the advice of a wise friend and experienced diplomat, Glynn Davies. Glynn had served as executive director of the National Security Council at the White House when I worked for Vice President Al Gore, and by 2013, he had completed the first of his two tours as an ambassador. "While I'm grateful that I might have the chance to go to Fiji," I said, "Vietnam has always been my dream." Laughing, Glynn replied, "you speak Vietnamese, and you have the credentials. Go for it."

Diplomats more experienced than I wanted Vietnam, and I questioned whether I had a chance. Hours before the deadline, I asked two friends, Dan Baer and Uzra Zeya, if the Bureau of Democracy, Human Rights, and Labor would put my name forward for nomination. Dan and Uzra said that they would be happy to do so.

Twelve senior diplomats vied for the position of ambassador to Vietnam, but I was the only one who had served there and spoke Vietnamese. I wondered if Secretary Kerry remembered how much I loved Vietnam, or if he recalled our bicycle ride with Pete Peterson and our visit to the Condom Café. I do not know whether Kerry weighed in directly, or how the State Department's decision-making process played out, but when the director general of the Foreign Service called and told me my name was going to the White House as the State Department's candidate, I was surprised and overjoyed. A few months later, I learned that President Obama would request that the government in Hanoi grant *agrément* (diplomatic acceptance) of my nomination as the sixth U.S. ambassador to Vietnam.

In April 2014, now the sleep-deprived father of a colicky four-month-old, I showed up at the ambassadorial seminar, known affectionately as "charm school." In our seminar, three of the nominees were political appointees—fund-raisers for or friends of President Obama—and five were career diplomats. One classmate, Marcia Bernicat, who had already done one tour as an ambassador, served as our class mentor.

Ambassador Nancy McEldowney, director of the Foreign Service Institute, asked me, "Do you want to be known as the gay ambassador, or would you rather be considered the best ambassador?" I had worked for Pete Peterson and would always consider him America's best ambassador to Vietnam.

I also thought that being simply "the gay ambassador" might be limiting. I wanted to be the most effective ambassador I could be. Being an authentic, effective leader would require me to be proudly who I was. It did not have to be an either-or choice.

When I joined the State Department in 1989, it was unthinkable to imagine an openly gay foreign service officer rising to the position of ambassador. During the administration of President George H. W. Bush, gay officers who were identified as such by the Bureau of Diplomatic Security were typically stripped of their security clearances and forced to resign.

In 1992, a few of us banded together. While carefully protecting our membership list for fear of retaliation, we formed a group called Gays and Lesbians in Foreign Affairs Agencies (GLIFAA). Quietly, we began to advocate for nondiscriminatory treatment, simply hoping to keep our jobs. We achieved our goal during President Clinton's first term in office. More important, I met my future spouse through GLIFAA.

Attitudes in the United States had changed significantly by the time President Obama nominated me to be ambassador to Vietnam. I asked Ambassador Bernicat whether I, a white man, might be considered a "diversity candidate." "Yes," she replied, "you certainly are." What had once been a debilitating liability could now be a neutral factor or even an asset.

I wasn't at all sure that my sexual orientation would be viewed with equanimity by the leadership in Vietnam, nor did I know how Vietnamese society—where the concept of traditional family is revered—might react to an openly gay ambassador. As I awaited Hanoi's response to the president's request, I contacted my friend Tú, who by this time was back in Vietnam after serving as ambassador to the Philippines from 2010 to 2013. Ever the careful, discreet diplomat, Tú did not give away any secrets. He also did not indicate that there would be a problem receiving agrément.

I took nothing for granted. I had discovered during my first tour in Vietnam how socially conservative its leaders could be. In 1996, the Communist Party had launched a campaign to rid Vietnam of so-called social evils such as prostitution and homosexuality. I didn't know how much had changed, but my worries proved unfounded. After seven weeks, Hanoi granted agrément, and President Obama sent my name to the Senate for confirmation on May 14, 2014. Next, I had to wonder if sexual orientation would play a role in my confirmation.

A U.S. president had only once before nominated an "out" career diplomat, when President George W. Bush named Michael Guest as ambassador to Romania, and the State Department did not give him much support.

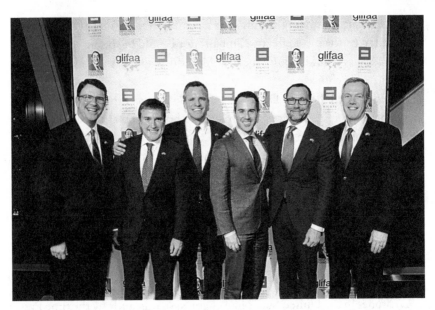

PHOTO 9 Six openly gay ambassadors, John Berry, Wally Brewster, Rufus Gifford, Dan Baer, James Costos, and the author, Washington, DC, March 2015 (Credit: Blake Bergen).

Secretary of State Colin Powell didn't want Guest's partner, Alex Nevarez, to play a visible role at Guest's swearing-in ceremony. Later, Secretary of State Condoleezza Rice refused to recognize Nevarez as part of Guest's family when it came to benefits such as medical evacuation, an integral part of the package for every foreign service officer.

However, in May 2012 President Obama had come around to supporting marriage equality. Since his reelection, the president had appointed five openly gay political ambassadors: Dan Baer, John Berry, Wally Brewster, James Costos, and Rufus Gifford. I felt confident that he would be supportive even if there was controversy.

Surprisingly, at no point in the confirmation process was my sexual orientation an issue. I spoke Vietnamese, was a Southeast Asia specialist, and had the policy and management experience to do the job. In the end, Glynn was right: I had the credentials.

In June 2014, as I began calling on key senators before my confirmation hearings, China had threatened Vietnam's sovereignty by moving an oil rig into its coastal waters. When I met with members of the Senate Foreign Relations Committee, including Chairman Robert Corker and Ranking Member Benjamin Cardin, they asked about South China Sea tensions. I also met with Senator Sheldon Whitehouse, whose father had served as deputy chief of mission to Ambassador Ellsworth Bunker in 1972–1973 and who had fond memories of bicycling from one end of Saigon to another.

The most critical meeting was on June 16 with Senator John McCain. I knew that if McCain supported my appointment as ambassador to Vietnam during my confirmation hearings the next day, the other senators would as well. If he opposed my nomination, my chances weren't good.

During that meeting, I gained much more than the senator's vote. McCain gave me a glimpse into who he was. He took me by the arm and walked me over to a framed State Department telegram dated September 13, 1968. Sent by Ambassador-at-Large Averell Harriman, who was in Paris heading the U.S. delegation at the 1968 peace talks, it read, "Lê Đức Thọ . . . mentioned that DRV [North Vietnam] had intended to release Admiral McCain's son as one of the three pilots freed recently, but he had refused."

When McCain pointed to that telegram, he revealed a truth about the pivotal moment in his life, a decision that made him the man he became. I had met McCain first during his 1997 visit to Vietnam, and again when he and Senator Joe Lieberman visited India in December 2008, but I knew him then as a senator and not as a man.

McCain had earned the right to decide who should, and who should not, be the United States' ambassador to Vietnam.

Though obtaining the senator's vote was my sole objective, that outcome had already been secured—and not by me. McCain told me that Pete Peterson, his fellow prisoner in Hỏa Lò Prison, had called to vouch for me. After their shared suffering as POWs, McCain and Peterson later shared a commitment to U.S.-Vietnam reconciliation. "If Pete supports you as ambassador, then I will vote to confirm," McCain said.

McCain then told me that in 1985 a small monument had been erected at Trúc Bạch Lake in Hanoi, next to the place where he had been pulled from the water. "The monument is pretty dirty," he said. "Could you ask that it be cleaned up?" I joked that as long as he was supporting my confirmation, I would clean it myself with a toothbrush if that's what it needed.

McCain laughed along with me, but if I had listened more carefully, I might have realized how serious this request was. That monument marked the spot where he was pulled ashore with three limbs broken following his crash into the lake. It stands at a critical point in McCain's story.

A year earlier, Phạm Quang Nghị, Secretary of the Party Committee in Hanoi, met with McCain in his Capitol Hill office and gave him a photograph of the monument. The senator noted that first, a bird was pooping on it, and second, his title was inaccurate: he was listed as a U.S. Air Force squadron leader, and he was a U.S. Navy lieutenant commander. Even worse, the senator's name was misspelled. The only monument to McCain had the facts wrong, and McCain wanted people to know the truth.[6]

During my confirmation hearing on June 17, I spoke in broad terms about where I hoped to take the relationship between the United States and Vietnam. I described my cycling trip in 1997, when a Vietnamese woman had approached me on a bridge between north and south. "Today, you and I are younger brother and older sister," she had said. The "brother and sister" reference, which revealed a spirit of forgiveness and reconciliation, made me choke up, even seventeen years later, and my mother had warned me against repeating it. I had to practice it a few times so I could say it clearly, with dry eyes.

I acknowledged that the United States and Vietnam had major differences regarding human rights. "If confirmed, I will face those differences squarely and directly with the leaders in Hanoi," I pledged. "I will say that when Vietnam's government respects human rights it will grow stronger, not weaker, and our partnership's potential will grow as well. I will press the government to protect universal human rights, including by releasing prisoners of conscience and by making systemic changes, so that Vietnam can fully integrate with the world community. Because even as in families, among brothers and sisters, differences can be worked out, and history can be overcome."[7]

McCain asked the toughest questions I received during the hearing. He had assured me in advance that I had his support, but he still made me sweat through the session. McCain knew how serious an ambassador's responsibilities were, and he expected me to work hard for the honor. After the afternoon hearing, the Foreign Relations Committee voted unanimously to send my nomination to the full Senate.

Shear had served as ambassador in Hanoi since 2011, but he was leaving the post in early August. I lobbied hard for a full Senate vote on my nomination, saying that the United States needed an ambassador in Hanoi during a time of great stress in the South China Sea, final negotiations about the Trans-Pacific Partnership trade agreement (TPP), and human rights disagreements with Vietnam. Some nominees had waited two years for a vote, and I didn't want that to happen in my case. While I waited, I began to meet as many experts as possible, not only to help prepare for the challenges of the job, but also to have friends in the United States to contact when problems arise—as they always do.

Before confirmation, the ambassadorial candidate can call only on executive branch officials and members of the Senate because going further would suggest presumption that the Senate will confirm the nominee. After confirmation, the ambassador can call on members of the House of Representatives, businesspeople, and influential or knowledgeable private citizens.

I refreshed my knowledge of the Vietnamese language, which had grown rusty over eighteen years of sporadic use. I met with executive branch officials to learn about the challenges ahead, starting with State Department officials—including those in the important fields of human rights, religious freedom, and the rule of law. I wanted to build trust with Tom Malinowski, the new assistant secretary for democracy, human rights, and labor. Although Dan and Uzra, who worked under Tom, had supported my candidacy, my most difficult and delicate work as ambassador would be with him.

I called on the presidents of the Export-Import Bank, Overseas Private Investment Corporation, and Trade and Development Agency, as well as officials in the Treasury, Commerce, and Agriculture Departments, to learn how I could best help U.S. businesses in Vietnam. I met with U.S. Trade Representative Mike Froman's senior negotiators, who were hard at work on the TPP and wanted to include Vietnam.

During my assignment as science officer for Southeast Asia and the Pacific, I had learned that apolitical collaboration offered rich possibilities for building trust and advancing America's overall diplomatic goals. I learned from the Environmental Protection Agency's administrator and from officials at the Department of Health and Human Services what joint activities we could pursue with Vietnam in the areas of health and the environment. At the Centers for Disease Control and Prevention in Atlanta, I learned about its work on HIV/AIDS and other infectious diseases in Vietnam. And I studied our foreign assistance programs, most of which were administered by the U.S. Agency for International Development, knowing that members of Congress would pay particular attention to how the embassy spent precious assistance dollars.

At U.S. Special Operations Command headquarters, I learned about U.S. military capabilities for helping an embassy in a time of crisis. The ongoing crisis in the South China Sea gave these lessons a sense of urgency. I spent considerable time with members of the intelligence community and colleagues at the Department of Defense, knowing that a strong military-to-military relationship with Vietnam could yield strategic dividends for the United States.

President Obama wanted to establish a Peace Corps mission in Vietnam, and I met with leaders of that organization. I had helped establish a Peace Corps presence in Indonesia—where experts had said that doing so would be impossible—and I believed that we could repeat the trick of overcoming a host government's suspicions about the Peace Corps.

My letter of instruction from President Obama, delivered after my confirmation, would say that any executive branch official must report to his or her agency through the ambassador. "As Chief of Mission," the President wrote, "you have full responsibility for the direction, coordination, and supervision of all U.S. executive branch employees in the Socialist Republic of Vietnam . . . except those under command of a U.S. area military commander."[8]

I would be responsible for overseeing all eighteen agency representatives in Vietnam, and I met with members of an alphabet soup of law enforcement agencies, including the Drug Enforcement Administration and Immigration and Customs Enforcement. I needed to understand their priorities and know what they were doing, including their representatives who were engaged in classified operations.

On September 24, Senator David Vitter placed a hold on my nomination, slowing down my final confirmation. He stated in a letter that he had concerns about the safety of shrimp and catfish imports from Vietnam. He said that Vietnam had engaged in dumping and other unfair trade practices that placed shrimp and catfish from Louisiana, the state he represented, at a disadvantage.

Vitter's hold risked putting me at the end of the line for confirmation, and I was determined to do something about it. I reached out to McCain through his staff, hoping he would help me get a vote. I felt certain that he would not want the ambassador's seat in Hanoi to remain empty for too long.

A friend in my ambassadorial seminar who was headed for Europe told me how unimpressed he was with the State Department's efforts to persuade senators to vote on nominees. "My strategy," he said, "is like that of a laboratory rat: if you press enough buttons, eventually a pellet will drop out." He had gotten the pellet to drop, and he headed to his post in July. With that in mind, I began pressing as many buttons as I could.

I asked for advice from my longtime friend and mentor, Leon Fuerth, about unfreezing my nomination. "You need to learn everything there is to know about shrimp and catfish and Louisiana," he told me. "Then go and see Senator Vitter."

I learned that Louisiana was the sixth biggest exporting state in the United States, that 300,000 Louisiana citizens were employed in export industries, and the state had doubled its exports to Vietnam in the past three years. Most exports were agricultural products: cotton, soybeans, poultry, and consumer goods. Poultry was a $2 billion industry in the state. Also, much of America's agricultural exports went overseas through the port of New Orleans.

Louisiana's shrimp and catfish producers had been hit hard, first by Hurricane Katrina, then by the Deepwater Horizon oil spill in the Gulf of Mexico, and then by a disease that affected Gulf shrimp. A proud industry had been brought to its knees, and Vitter believed that subsidies to Vietnam's shrimp and catfish farmers made for unfair competition. I could see his side and understood that he cared about his constituents. Brushing him off with a formulaic response would not work.

The rules of trade, enshrined in the World Trade Organization, permitted countries to levy tariffs on imports that were highly subsidized. Even though Vietnam's shrimp and catfish exports were already subject to high tariffs, they were still gobbling up a huge share of the market and driving Louisiana's seafood prices so low that the state's farmers and fishermen faced bankruptcy. Vitter and others also said that Vietnamese shrimp and catfish were unsafe to eat and posed a health threat to U.S. consumers.

Julia Frifield, assistant secretary of state for Congressional affairs, wrote Vitter on October 20 that the Obama administration had strengthened its catfish and shrimp safety inspection regime. She argued that if I were confirmed and sent to Vietnam, I would be in a position to advocate for U.S. trade and food safety interests. That led to a meeting for me with Vitter on November 12. Friendly and affable, the senator described his constituents' painful plight. I assured him that I would ensure the full implementation of U.S. law. I offered to visit Louisiana, if he thought that would be useful, and he urged me to do so.

My friend and colleague Jillian Bonnardeaux, an officer on the Vietnam desk at the State Department, supported me as I learned everything there was to know about Louisiana trade and catfish. Five days after I met with Vitter, on November 17, 2014, the Senate voted unanimously to confirm me as ambassador. After our success together, Jillian presented me with a cloth catfish with long whiskers. It is still a favorite toy for my children.

The next day I met with a former college classmate, Pennsylvania Senator Pat Toomey, a member of the Finance Committee. Toomey was confident that his committee would pass Trade Promotion Authority (TPA), allowing President Obama to conclude negotiations about the TPP. During our one-on-one meeting, Toomey, a Republican, named the two Democratic committee members he believed would buck their party's Congressional leadership to support TPA. He also predicted that if the administration succeeded in negotiating a high-standard TPP, with labor, environmental, and digital economy provisions, the Senate would ratify it. In a demonstration of how quickly the politics of trade shifted, Toomey distanced himself from TPP during his 2016 campaign, when he was in a tight race for reelection.

Within hours of being confirmed by the Senate, I met with members of the business community. With that first public meeting after confirmation, I wanted to signal that my door would always be open to businesspeople, and I would go the extra mile to support U.S. businesses in Vietnam. I recognized that private-sector ties were needed to make long-term partnerships between the United States and any other nation possible, and success for U.S. businesses meant jobs for Americans—a top priority for any president.

My hardest tasks as ambassador would involve defending human rights, including the freedom to worship, freedom of speech, and freedom to associate. I had promised the Senate Foreign Relations Committee that I would address human rights challenges squarely, and so I showed members of the business community that I carried in my shirt pocket a small, laminated cheat sheet that listed prisoners of conscience and key human rights requests for the Vietnamese government. Mark Lambert, the U.S. embassy's political counselor, had come up with the idea of the card to make sure that there were no mistakes about what mattered to the United States.

I also joined Tom Malinowski when he met with activists committed to changing Vietnam's human rights situation. Later on the same day, Nguyễn Quốc Quân, brother of the famous Nguyễn Đan Quế (known as the "dean of dissidents"), introduced me to his friends in the Vietnamese American community. I would meet with Quân regularly in the coming years and benefited from his measured, wise counsel. I also met with Rabbi David Saperstein, the incoming U.S. ambassador at large for international religious freedom. He and Tom were intently focused on Vietnam and visited numerous times while I served there.

I wanted the advice of my former boss, Pete Peterson, but he was living in Melbourne, Australia, so it came via email. In Washington I met with his successors as ambassador, Raymond Burghardt, Michael Marine, and Michael Michalak, and each provided valuable insights into the challenges he had faced and the people in Vietnam with whom I needed to forge relationships. Over lunch with our spouses, Shear gave me practical suggestions and wise strategic guidance. I also met with key members of the House of Representatives and sought out elder statesmen with a personal knowledge of Vietnam, including former Deputy Secretaries of State Rich Armitage and John Negroponte.

As soon as I could, I met with Ann Mills Griffiths, who by then had been president of the National League of Families of American Prisoners and Missing in Southeast Asia for more than four decades. Since the 1970s, Ann had effectively advocated for the fullest possible accounting of those whom the United States had lost in the Vietnam War.

I had to be especially careful about the people I chose to meet in the Vietnamese American community, as some activists were so passionately committed to reversing the results of the war that the government in Hanoi would mistrust me if I were seen as being too close to them. The Việt Tân network had members committed to overthrowing the Communist regime and had used violence against its opponents in the Vietnamese American community. I quietly met with a Việt Tân representative, but I allowed no photographs. Even though most of its influence in the community had waned, the organization could still stir up trouble.

Others in the community I embraced without difficulty. I met with Vietnamese American human rights activists, businesspeople, educators, and leaders of nongovernmental organizations. Some were committed to reconciliation between the diaspora in the United States and the people of Vietnam, and some were not. Increasingly successful, prosperous, and politically influential, the diaspora community was critical for the long-term success of ties between the two countries. It was also the key to reconciliation.

Largely divided along age lines, similar to the divisions within the Cuban American community, the Vietnamese diaspora directed activities that shaped the most important aspects of the bilateral relationship, the links between people: ties of family, education, business, and tourism.

My priorities as ambassador could be achieved only if leaders in Hanoi and in Washington shared them. It was important to establish publicly— before I arrived at my new post—what my objectives were. As a mission statement, I echoed the words of Secretary Kerry, who in December 2013 said, "A strong, prosperous, and independent Vietnam that respects the rule of law and human rights will be a critical partner for the United States on many regional and global challenges that we face together."[9] Shear repeated that statement again and again, and I included it in my early remarks in the United States and after my arrival in Vietnam so that Vietnamese leaders would recognize the continuity in U.S. policy and our diplomatic approach.

I had an opportunity to use social media to present myself to the Vietnamese leadership and people even before I arrived in Hanoi. A recent tradition at the State Department was for new ambassadors to produce a short video introducing themselves and their families to the people of the country where they would serve and to send it out via television and social media. At the Foreign Service Institute, we watched videos made by our predecessors and other ambassadors, and we considered what would work best in our specific situations. In my video, I wanted to establish the right tone and to show what my family looked like. The key, I decided, was to speak only in Vietnamese, to show respect for Vietnam's culture and to indicate that I had a real love for the country's language and people.

I practiced for two weeks to perfect my pronunciation of a difficult language and to make the delivery as friendly and natural as possible. I wanted to introduce the idea that I liked biking, because most Vietnamese, especially in rural areas, still traveled at the speed of a bicycle. We filmed the video at the edge of the Potomac River on a sunny day. Clayton brought our infant son to the river's edge, so that our modern family—two dads and a child— could be seen in the closing shot.

For the sound track, I persuaded guitarist An Trần, the friend of a friend, to play a popular song, "Bèo Dạt Mây Trôi" ("Water ferns drift, clouds float") on the guitar. An had grown up in Hanoi, but as a music student at Yale University, he symbolized the educational links between our two countries.

We also needed a photograph that the local press would publish when we first arrived. We were a black-and-white gay couple whose son, TABO, had Mexican American roots. We planned to arrive in Hanoi with my eighty-five-year-old mother, so at least we would offer something Vietnamese could relate to: a three-generation family.

Before my swearing-in ceremony, I met with Secretary Kerry in his ornate, ceremonial State Department office. "Ted, you're going to *my* country. I will visit you often," he said. Kerry had appointed me to my dream job. He had my back, and I was eager to host him as often as possible.

John Kerry and Teresa Heinz Kerry supported Clayton and me, not just as staff members but as a family. In 2005, when I visited their home in Pittsburgh while Kerry was in Washington, Teresa was still smarting from her husband's narrow loss to George W. Bush in the race for the presidency. During the campaign, she had told the LGBT+ community, "If you have any problems, you just knock on the door of the White House and ask for Mama T."

As we cut into roast pork loin and looked out over the Pennsylvania hills, I told Teresa how much her commitment to equality meant to us. She was unable to attend my confirmation ceremony, but her husband made certain that all members of my extended family felt welcome, greeting my friends and relatives, and ushering my spouse, mother, and son onstage. I regretted that

PHOTO 10 John Kerry, the author, Clayton Bond, Nancy Zimmerman, and TABO at the author's swearing-in, Washington, DC, December 2014 (Credit: U.S. Department of State).

Guest, the only "out" career ambassador to precede me, had not received the same gracious treatment from Secretary Powell.

Secretary Kerry often had to delegate the task of swearing in a new ambassador to other officials. I considered it a great honor when he officiated personally over my December 10 ceremony. It had been a long journey to get to that moment, and many people who had helped were there. Vietnam's new ambassador to the United States, Phạm Quang Vinh, attended the ceremony, and I hoped that he would report to Hanoi his first thoughts about my goals and aspirations. We promised to check in with each other whenever he visited Hanoi or I visited Washington. Over time, we became friends, and we stayed closely synchronized during my entire tenure as ambassador. Congressman Alan Lowenthal, cochair of the Congressional Caucus on Vietnam and a representative of California's Orange County, joined Ambassador Vinh as a special guest.

"I want to welcome Ted's family starting with his husband, Clayton, and their 11-month-old son who is decked out in the best seersucker suit I ever saw at that age," Secretary Kerry began. "There he is. . . . You can record the day that TABO stole the show."[10]

He continued, "I first met Ted in January of 1998, when I traveled to Vietnam to take part in a disabled veterans bike ride. They had come down all the way from Hanoi; I joined it in Vung Tau, and we biked up to Ho Chi Minh City with a bunch of veterans who had been wounded in the war. And the heat and the humidity were pretty intense, as you can imagine, but the worst part of it was every time I'd look up Ted was just kind of biking along— (laughter)—easy Saturday afternoon, whatever, leading the trail with ease, sort of a Sunday stroll for him. And I found out later that it was a Sunday stroll for him because he'd ridden the full distance of 1,200 miles between Hanoi and Ho Chi Minh City, not just the final leg."

Kerry had not forgotten.

After I swore to "support and defend the Constitution of the United States against all enemies, foreign and domestic," I outlined my top policy priorities. Knowing that Vietnam's leaders would pay close attention to what I said, I repeated Kerry's mantra that the United States supported a strong, prosperous, and independent Vietnam. I said that we had "a unique opportunity to deepen our comprehensive partnership in ways that will make it last. A successful Trans-Pacific Partnership trade agreement will create jobs and growth in both countries. On rule of law and human rights, we will continue to show the government and people of Vietnam that the United States is on the side of openness, transparency, and respect for the individual."

I spoke of the founding legend of Vietnam, when two winged creatures—a dragon from the sea and a fairy from the mountains—gave birth to the people of Vietnam. In this legend, the dragon lays one hundred eggs, and a boy hatches from each egg (yes, it's sexist, but that is the myth). Fifty of the boys went with their mother, the fairy, to the mountains, and fifty went to the sea with their father, the dragon. The eldest boy became Vietnam's first king. Presumably, the hundred boys found girls in the country's mountainous interior or along the coast, because they gave birth to the Vietnamese people.

Speaking in Vietnamese, I told Vinh that through partnership, the United States stood ready to support the people of Vietnam, the children of the dragon from the sea and the fairy from the mountains, as they soar higher and farther. The next day, as I had hoped, Vietnamese media reported not only the substance of my remarks, but a full recounting of the story of the dragon and the fairy.

Before closing, I thanked members of GLIFAA, the LGBT+ affinity group that had supported my nomination:

> Twenty-two years ago, when we founded GLIFAA to end discrimination against LGBT personnel, we had to keep our member list secret or risk losing our jobs. Ten years ago, when I met Clayton at a GLIFAA meeting, we didn't

expect that we could marry, that we could raise children, or that we could represent our country at the highest levels. We made progress because of people like our cousins Julian Bond and Pam Horowitz, who took risks. We made progress because of Madeleine Albright and Hillary Clinton, Secretary John Kerry, and Teresa Heinz Kerry. When it was very unpopular to do so, Teresa stood with us and said, "You can count on Mama T." . . . You are our heroes. And as President Obama said, each time we make a step toward inclusion— whether in Seneca Falls or Selma or Stonewall—we help fulfill the promise of a more perfect union.

My heart was filled with gratitude as I looked out on my mentors, family members, and dear friends who had come to my sweaing-in ceremony in large numbers. I said it was a "dream come true" to serve as America's ambassador to Vietnam, and it was.

7

Diplomacy from a Bicycle Seat

● ● ● ● ● ● ● ● ● ● ● ● ● ●

As we were landing at Hanoi's Nội Bài Airport on December 15, 2014, I remembered that Ambassador Nancy McEldowney had told us we had only one chance to make a first impression. Accompanied by my mother, we showed up as a three-generational family, a concept very familiar to every Vietnamese citizen. I hoped the Vietnamese would see our multihued, two-dad family as both modern and traditional.

We were greeted by members of the press, and I spoke to them entirely in Vietnamese, while Clayton held our son in his arms and my mother looked on. I repeated the story of the dragon from the sea, the fairy from the mountains, and the origins of the Vietnamese people. Through partnership, I said, the United States stood ready to support the people of Vietnam as they soared farther and higher. That was part of the headlines in all of the next day's media stories, accompanied by our family photo.

Vietnam had changed dramatically in the twenty years since I'd served there during the administration of President Bill Clinton. Its buildings were taller, there were Louis Vuitton and Hermès shops in the cities, and bicycles had been replaced by cars and motorbikes. Everyone had a mobile phone, and the internet had changed the way people communicated. Social media, especially Facebook, was a big deal.

PHOTO 11 Clayton Bond, TABO, Nancy Osius Zimmerman, and the author arriving at Nội Bài airport, Hanoi, December 2014 (Credit: U.S. Department of State).

On December 16, eighteen hours after arriving, I was invited to present my letter of credence—popularly known as credentials—from President Barack Obama. The government in Hanoi had been four months without a credentialed U.S. ambassador, and the president's office moved swiftly to schedule what was usually a quarterly ceremony. A four-motorcycle escort roared up to the residence, and I was driven in the embassy's black Cadillac to the president's palace. Coached by the embassy team on what to expect, I mounted a long stairway on a red carpet between two lines of uniformed men. In what seemed like an elaborate minuet of side and forward steps, I presented President Obama's letter to President Trương Tấn Sang.

After the ceremony, we moved to another room with aides from the U.S. embassy and the Vietnamese government for a private talk. Mark Lambert, our political counselor, later said that President Sang "twinkled" several times—a sign of pleased agreement—as we talked for another hour. Mark thought that the president was impressed by my ability to speak (though not perfectly) in Vietnamese, which showed a sincere commitment to understanding the country's language, people, and traditions.

Vietnamese media reported on President Sang's statement, in which he said he hoped that "the two sides will continue removing obstacles in bilateral cooperation as well as in negotiations on the Trans-Pacific Partnership (TPP) Agreement."[1] Reports also focused on the resolution that had recently been passed by the U.S. House of Representatives opposing Chinese claims in the South China Sea and supporting a peaceful resolution of maritime territorial disputes in accordance with international law.

I reiterated to the president that I was eager to conclude TPP negotiations and that I looked forward to the twentieth anniversary of full diplomatic relations in 2015, as a chance for the United States and Vietnam to strengthen our partnership. He and I spoke about the South China Sea and my hopes to deepen our countries' collaboration on education, health, and the environment.

During my return to the residence in the same Cadillac, the American flag now flew on the right front fender, an honor reserved for a credentialed ambassador. It was a thrill. I felt sorry for ambassadors in less safe countries, who could not fly the Stars and Stripes because it exposed them as targets. The embassy security officer told me, "It's the only Cadillac in Hanoi. Everyone will know who is in it, whether you fly the flag or not, so you might as well fly it."

It is tradition in an ambassadorial vehicle for the highest-ranking official to be seated in the right rear seat behind the flag. When the door opens at the curb and the press takes photographs, the first pictures taken should be of that official, not of an aide.

This tradition carries with it a story that is probably apocryphal. According to State Department lore, when Madeleine Albright, then ambassador to the United Nations, visited Berlin, she rode in a limo with Richard Holbrooke, who was then ambassador to Germany. He had relegated her to the less important seat. Later, when she was secretary of state and President Clinton nominated Holbrooke to be U.N. ambassador, Albright reportedly held up the appointment for a few weeks to remind Holbrooke who was the boss.[2]

Remembering this story, I always put my guest in the right rear seat when we traveled in the limo. Only Secretary of the Navy Ray Mabus, who had been an ambassador himself, insisted on the left-hand seat. "As ambassador," he said, "you outrank every U.S. official except the president." Ray was right, yet I continued to offer the honored seat to my guests. You never know who might be the next secretary of state with a long memory.

The same day I presented my credentials to President Sang, I also met with Pacific Fleet Commander Admiral Harry Harris, who shortly after became commander of all U.S. armed forces in the Pacific—a position once held by Senator John McCain's father. President Obama had written in his letter of instruction: "You and the area military commander must keep each other currently and fully informed and cooperate on all matters of mutual interest."[3] I considered Admiral Harris a friend from that moment on. That day we began a dialogue that lasted for years, with significant results for U.S.-Vietnam relations. He sought my opinion on matters regarding Vietnam, and I appreciated his ideas and experience. By the end of our three-year collaboration, we had transformed the U.S.-Vietnamese security relationship, and Vietnam had more military-to-military interaction with the United States than with any other country.

The next day, I met with my new team at the embassy. I called upon the words Ambassador Pete Peterson had used with his team seventeen years earlier and said, "You'll get it right 98 percent of the time. I will trust you to do your jobs, and I will have your backs." Two-thirds of our six hundred Hanoi employees were Vietnamese, so I spoke to them in their own language, and they responded enthusiastically. A few members of the local staff were people I had hired during my first assignment to Hanoi in 1996, and they in particular regarded me as their ambassador.

An embassy tends to be organized around the work of different agencies and sections. Instead of having senior staff members operate in silos, I wanted to ensure that our work was centered on the five themes I had spoken about when I was sworn in as ambassador: (1) deepening the commercial relationship between the United States and Vietnam, while pressing Hanoi for further economic reforms; (2) increasing Vietnam's respect for the rule of law and human rights; (3) strengthening security ties between the two countries; (4) enhancing educational exchanges; and (5) carving out areas for productive collaboration on health and the environment. This meant that the efforts of all our diplomats, our public activities, and internal working groups had to remain focused on those themes, regardless of agency affiliation.

When I served at the United Nations, the U.S. political counselor there, Cameron Hume (by the time he retired, a four-time chief of mission who served forty-two years in the State Department), engaged in a practice that none of his predecessors had dared to undertake. He placed a junior action officer—sometimes a low-level diplomat—directly behind the U.S. permanent representative to the Security Council. When Ambassador Albright turned around to ask what she should say about Cyprus or the Western Sahara, for example, she was faced with me. Whenever I would be sitting in the hot seat, I knew I had to have mastered the subject before each council meeting. If a cabinet-level officer like Albright was going to use my words, they had to be accurate because they instantly became U.S. policy. Cameron was there as backup and for matters that required more experienced judgment. But each action officer knew that he or she had to be thoroughly prepared.

That experience informed how I relied on my action officers at the embassy. Deputy Chief of Mission Claire Pierangelo and I made certain that action officers "owned" their portfolios. We let them know that they could still seek guidance from their direct supervisors or from Claire or me, but we trusted that they would do so bringing ideas and their own deep knowledge of the problem at hand. Working with Cameron on three separate assignments had taught me that when a diplomat designs and then implements a strategy—and sees it through to completion—he or she is changed in the process and will never settle for less in the future.

We had arrived in Hanoi just ten days before Christmas, and we didn't have much time to rest in our new home before we decided to let the Vietnamese people see an American family enjoying our own traditions. My oldest sister, Meg, had joined us, and she pitched in on December 23, when we invited children from a local orphanage to the residence—where they could see the Christmas tree, eat Christmas cookies, and receive small gifts. A local choir, whose members were all blind, led us in singing Christmas carols.

The press loved it. Photos of our gathering made the front pages of many newspapers, and the public affairs team quickly put me in front of television and internet-based media for exclusive interviews in which I described our embassy's plans for 2015, especially our joint celebration of the twentieth anniversary of full diplomatic relations. I repeated (in Vietnamese) Secretary John Kerry's mantra that the United States supported a strong, prosperous, and independent Vietnam that respects the rule of law and human rights. We wondered if the press would include the second half of that phrase, and every reporter did.

The Vietnamese have a hierarchy of partnerships in their diplomatic system. Vietnam had a comprehensive partnership with America. But with China—a fraternal Communist nation—Vietnam had a strategic comprehensive partnership, which outranked its relationship with America. I told *Tuoi Tre* (a newspaper) that "I think the content of the partnership is more important than what term you use. I'm perfectly happy with '*đối tác toàn diện*' [comprehensive partnership]."[4] Naturally, the press focused on the U.S.-China competition for influence in Vietnam and in the region. Though I, too, was interested in that competition, I thought a zero-sum approach did not fully capture the complex factors each Asian nation had to consider in its relations with the United States or China. No matter what label our

PHOTO 12 Clayton Bond, first Christmas in the ambassador's residence, Hanoi, December 2014 (Credit: U.S. Department of State).

partnership with Vietnam bore, I wanted it to be substantive and wanted our joint activities to build trust.

My introductory video had shown that I liked biking, and that, combined with speaking mostly in Vietnamese in roundtable meetings and on-the-record interviews, led the local press to call me "the people's ambassador." Not many contemporary Vietnamese leaders would let themselves be filmed while riding a bicycle, but I was determined to project an image of accessibility and friendliness.

On my first visit to the south, a month after arriving in Vietnam, I rode through the streets of Hồ Chí Minh City with some local students, and the press loved it. We quickly expanded our social media following as a way of communicating ideas to the Vietnamese people through photographs, short videos, quizzes, and words.

"Create a plan for the first one hundred days of your tenure as ambassador," Bill Burns had advised us at the ambassadors' "charm school." "You'll be amazed at how quickly your tour will go by." A career officer, Bill had served as ambassador to Jordan and Russia; undersecretary of state for political affairs; and deputy secretary of state, a job normally reserved for political appointees. He was a legend in the foreign service.

When Bill told us this, it reminded me of something Cameron had told me. "If you want to do something important and meaningful," he said, "you need to get it moving at the beginning of your time as ambassador, because most significant initiatives take at least two or three years to complete." When Cameron was ambassador to South Africa, he chose three big goals and pursued them energetically. As ambassador to Indonesia, he created the comprehensive partnership launched by President Obama in the world's largest Muslim-majority nation, and then he worked to fill in that framework with joint endeavors—areas of mutually beneficial activity that would build trust.

My predecessor in Vietnam, Ambassador Dave Shear, had established the framework of a comprehensive partnership that Presidents Obama and Sang had announced in 2013. If it was to last, this new partnership needed substance. Before I left Washington, I had created a strategic plan for my new mission, a hundred-day plan organized around the five themes of economic engagement, human rights, security ties, educational exchange, and health and the environment.

When I arrived in Hanoi, my plan in hand, I discovered that Vietnamese leaders had their own strategies and plans for where we needed to focus our energies. I began learning what their plans and priorities were from my counterpart, Vice Minister of Foreign Affairs Hà Kim Ngọc. Ngọc, a talented diplomat who later became Vietnam's ambassador to the United States, began to discuss with me how much a visit by the general secretary of the Communist Party to Washington, DC, could transform our countries' relationship. I heard this from other leaders as well, but I did not initially recognize the proposal's significance. Some observers thought that General Secretary Nguyễn Phú Trọng would soon retire, eclipsed by the charismatic prime minister, Nguyễn Tấn Dũng. I believed these erroneous predictions and thought that the State Department—not the embassy—would sort out a visit by Trọng.

At a conference in January 2015, the twentieth anniversary of U.S.-Vietnam relations, Ngọc proposed that our comprehensive partnership could be transformed from one of bilateral cooperation to one of regional and global collaboration. That's what we would accomplish over the next three years, especially in the areas of peacekeeping, nonproliferation, climate change, global health challenges, and biodiversity. At the same conference, Pete summarized his views on the future: "Nothing is impossible in this relationship." As always, Pete was optimistic while still speaking the truth. I decided to make his statement the leitmotif of my ambassadorship.

We used the ambassador's residence for much of our official business. I preferred holding meetings with guests in the historic, beautiful residence,

PHOTO 13 U.S. ambassadors to Vietnam Michael Michalak, the author, and Pete Peterson, Hanoi, January 2015 (Credit: U.S. Department of State/Lê Đức Thọ).

rather than in the main embassy building, a ramshackle "temporary" structure that the U.S. government had leased in 1995 and expected to occupy for only a few years but that was still serving as the embassy when I returned as ambassador. In 1997, we had found a dead rat on a colleague's desk one morning, its corpse having fallen through a collapsed ceiling during the night. Each U.S. ambassador attempted to move into a more suitable office space. I looked at dozens of possible sites for a new embassy and, just before my term ended, was fortunate to locate an appropriate site where a new embassy could be built.

Clayton and I were honored to host Pete and Vi Peterson as our first official overnight guests in the residence, the colonial-era home where they had spent a year as newlyweds. Half of the house staff had worked first for Desaix Anderson and then for Pete. Vi had brought the other half to the home. All of them remained on the job nineteen years later and helped our family.

This historic residence, built in 1921, is one of only twenty properties on the Secretary of State's Register of Culturally Significant Properties, and it is the most architecturally distinguished ambassadorial home in Hanoi. Designed by M. LaCollonge, principal architect and chief of civil construction

PHOTO 14 U.S. ambassador's residence, Hanoi (Credit: US Department of State).

service in Tonkin, the residence had weathered the ups and downs of the past hundred years of Vietnam's history.

After the French colonial government built the home, Indochina's financial governors lived in it until 1948. I imagined them carrying their baguettes out the front door (which had become the back door) and strolling to the Central Bank in an era when the neighborhood did not include so many fences. Then, until 1954 the residence had been assigned to the highest-ranking Indochina tariff officer. Its façade, genteel and elegantly Parisian, is defined by tall windows, wrought-iron balconies, and a high-style mansard roof punctuated with dormers. It resembles Hanoi's Opera House, designed by the same architect and located only a few blocks away.

When the French left Southeast Asia in 1954, Vietnamese government officials occupied the building. The last Vietnamese resident, Vice Minister Phan Kế Toại, had been the special envoy of Emperor Bảo Đại, the thirteenth and final emperor of the Nguyễn dynasty, the last ruling family of Vietnam. Toại was also the highest-ranking representative from the royal Huế Court under the Japanese occupation in the northern part of the country. Assigned to his post when the Japanese seized power from the French in 1940, Toại served until the Japanese surrendered to the Allies on August 15, 1945, and pulled out of Southeast Asia. Toại later joined the Việt Minh government, having secretly collaborated with resistance forces during the Japanese occupation.

After Toại's death in 1973, the house became the headquarters for the Committee for Foreign Culture Exchange. Afterward, the Ministry of Foreign Affairs Press Office used the building until 1994. One official showed me where his cubicle had been located, in what had become the dining room. Now it was the room where subsequent U.S. ambassadors hosted their guests.

Tết—Vietnam's lunar new year celebration, which is like Christmas, Easter, and Hanukkah all wrapped into one holiday—lasts for days, and little work gets done during this time. Most Vietnamese flee their city offices and head home to the countryside to reconnect with family members, and an important part of Tết is visiting the graves of ancestors and paying respect to them. The North Vietnamese Army chose this holiday for the January 1968 Tết offensive, knowing that South Vietnamese leaders and soldiers would be spread thin and at their least vigilant.

In 1996, my first Vietnamese language teachers, Cô Hiền, Thầy Độ, and Thầy Duy (from the south, north, and center of Vietnam, respectively), taught our small group of students to appreciate the significance of this holiday and especially its food. Members of the Vietnamese diaspora, no matter where they lived, celebrated Tết, even if they couldn't visit the graves of their ancestors.

As the new U.S. ambassador, I asked the Vietnamese staff for recommendations about which Tết traditions were important for me to observe. With the embassy team's encouragement, my family and I celebrated the Day of the Kitchen Gods a few days before Tết in February 2015. On that day, according to legend, the kitchen gods ride to heaven on the backs of carp to give a report on each family's doings in the preceding year—essentially, saying whether the family has been naughty or nice.

Many Vietnamese mark the day by releasing carp into the nearest body of water. In Hanoi, the most popular spot is near the Trấn Quốc pagoda on the edge of West Lake. The idea is to facilitate the gods' report.

Like many Vietnamese legends, this one involves true love and dramatic death. When Trọng Cao and his wife, Thị Nhi, quarreled, he threw her out of the house. Later, in a fit of remorse, he went looking for her, but by then she had married a much kinder husband, Phạm Lang. Understandably, when Trọng Cao knocked on Thị Nhi's door looking for food, she must have had mixed feelings.

When her new husband returned home, Thị Nhi, fearful of being discovered with her ex, hid him under a pile of straw. Her second husband lit the straw on fire, and her first husband, rather than expose her to charges of infidelity, burned to death. Thị Nhi then jumped into the flames, followed by her second husband, and all three perished. The Jade Emperor in heaven, moved by this story, decided to let the ménage à trois remain together for eternity. He changed them into three hearthstones around the cooking fire, and they became the kitchen gods.

With the Trấn Quốc pagoda as a backdrop, I did my best to relate this story in Vietnamese to the gathered press, and then I released a bucketful of fat carp into West Lake as the cameras whirred. With our toddler son strapped to Clayton's chest, our nontraditional family was an unusual sight for the Vietnamese, and the story went viral on television and social media. Reporters and Vietnamese citizens in general liked the United States and made us, its representatives, feel welcome. China was less popular. As I crouched near the edge of the water, one reporter quipped, "If you had been the Chinese ambassador, we would have pushed you into the lake."

I went to the Hanoi marketplace—recalling an experience during my first Tết, when ten Vietnamese students to whom I taught English brought me gifts of peach blossoms and orange kumquat trees—to pick out the branches and trees that would decorate our home. I bought peach blossoms (a northern tradition) and yellow apricot blossoms (a southern tradition), and later I released more carp into Huế's Perfume River (we couldn't leave out central Vietnam!). The Vietnamese media covered all of this, and when I painted meaningful sayings with a calligraphy master, the video of that, too, went viral. We attracted so much positive press that my fellow ambassadors in Vietnam, especially the Europeans, began competing to see who could get the most media attention for celebrating Tết.

The press filmed us preparing *bánh chưng* in the ambassador's residence. Every child in Vietnam knows the story of the most important Tết foods, *bánh chưng* and *bánh dày*, and I repeated the story in Vietnamese on television. Emperor Hùng Vương had eighteen sons. He staged a contest among them to bring him appropriate food, with all his sons knowing that the winner would succeed him as emperor. As the youngest prince, Lang Liêu didn't stand much of a chance. But he had a dream in which a fairy came to him and said, "Think of a food that represents all that parents do for their children."

Lang Liêu's seventeen older brothers scoured the earth for the most exotic dishes. They brought the emperor seafood from the depths of the oceans and rare plants and animals from the highest mountains. Lang Liêu took the simplest foods, sticky rice and mung beans, and made two dishes. He wrapped them in banana leaves in two distinct shapes and, with a bit of pork fat in the center, cooked them overnight. When Lang Liêu presented the simple dishes to the emperor—he was the last of all the sons to give his father food—he explained: "The round cake represents the heavens; the square cake represents the earth. What parents do for their children is as great as heaven and earth. The rice, beans, and pork represent the love and care that parents give to their children. They are staple ingredients that children need to grow up." Impressed, the emperor made Lang Liêu his successor, and thousands of years later, *bánh chưng* and *bánh dày* are still cooked for every Tết celebration.

Tradition dictates that the Tết celebration, which is observed primarily by family members, is followed by visits to friends. Clayton suggested that I seek the advice of not only staff members but also of Thảo Nguyễn Griffiths, whom we'd gotten to know through Tim Rieser, Senator Patrick Leahy's foreign policy advisor. "She knows everyone," Tim had said, and that was no exaggeration. He continued, "And she is my friend—a real friend."

I asked Thảo whom to meet, what to say, and how to behave. Although I remembered my language lessons and the appropriate Tết greetings ("I wish you prosperity, happiness, health, and long life"), I didn't want to make a misstep. For example, the first visitor on the third day of Tết is supposed to bring good luck—if he or she is an auspicious guest. I asked Thảo whether a gay couple should visit a family whose hope was to bear children. I wondered if it would be a burden for a Vietnamese family to have as the first people to step across their threshold in the new year the U.S. ambassador and his spouse. Thảo said that it would not, and she recommended that we visit Đỗ Thanh Hương, a businesswoman and designer, and her husband, Tom Bowen. They lived in a beautiful traditional home in old Hanoi, where they joyfully celebrated Vietnam's cultural and culinary traditions. We made new friends that day.

Thảo also had friends in the military—an institution that was not particularly friendly to Americans. She took me to meet the family of Vietnam's legendary general, Võ Nguyên Giáp. Such a simple gesture was meaningful, it seemed. Word got back to military leaders that I had paid my respects to Giáp, and those leaders became more willing to see me than they had been before.

Lãn Ông Street in Hanoi has a number of stores where customers can buy special herbs, roots, and leaves used in traditional Chinese medicine.

A knowing customer can also go to the back of many stores and buy slices of rhino horn, pulverized pangolin scales, tiger's testicles, bear paws, and elephant tusks—all of them erroneously thought to be aphrodisiacs. Hopes that the availability of Viagra would slow down the illegal wildlife trade unfortunately had not panned out.

The embassy organized a bicycle ride in spring 2015 that drew attention to the country's illegal wildlife trade. Hundreds of students wearing "Buy No Rhino" T-shirts joined me to ride past the traditional medicine shops on Lãn Ông Street to help create a media campaign that extended to several endangered species. Freeland, a nongovernmental organization, partnered with the embassy in this campaign and posted graphic photographs of rhinos whose horns had been hacked off, bears without paws, and cute pangolins. These posters emphasized that pieces of endangered animals had been proven not to elevate anyone's libido.

The pangolin is the most trafficked mammal of all, and it is in serious danger of extinction. Although its meat is sold as a delicacy, its scales—which are sold on the black market—are what makes it so lucrative. Pangolin scales are given as a gift during the lunar new year, to help the recipient feel that he has his mojo back.

Our team also organized "WildFest," a film festival and awareness event at Hanoi's thousand-year-old citadel. An audience of several thousand people watched short films made by young Vietnamese about the dangers of the illegal wildlife trade. We later repeated our bike rides on Lãn Ông Street, to the delight of students and the media.

I quickly found out that Thảo not only knew everyone, she also knew all the best biking routes around Hanoi, and we soon established a regular routine of biking on weekends. A natural athlete, Thảo rode fast. Once we biked with her thirteen-year-old daughter, Aimee, and she was almost as fast as her mom. Usually we began with a ride across Long Biên Bridge—a historic cantilever bridge across the Red River that was closed to cars but not to motorbikes or bicycles—to the eastern outskirts of Hanoi.

Thảo's friends joined us, and sometimes we boarded simple ferries to cross the Red River, our bikes perched precariously on the deck. Like Thảo, her friends enjoyed biking, and they wanted to see Vietnam at a cyclist's pace.

As often as she could, Thảo joined bike rides organized by the embassy or the consulate in Hồ Chí Minh City that were meant to show the Vietnamese people that we were interested in exploring and learning about Vietnam. That first spring in Vietnam, we bicycled through the rice fields and mango groves of Cần Thơ, in the heart of the Mekong Delta, Vietnam's agricultural

PHOTO 15 The author greeting people at the roadside, Quảng Bình province (Credit: US Department of State/Lê Đức Thọ).

core. I once rode on the back of a motor scooter, stopping at Saigon's street food stalls. I did all this for the television cameras but also because it was fun, and a good way to strengthen the team spirit of our diplomatic mission.

When I had lunch with the South Korean ambassador, who had lived in Vietnam for twenty-one years, I asked for the secret of his success. "If you love Vietnam and its people, then let it show," he said. I hoped that by biking and meeting the people throughout the country, I could show how much I loved the country and that the United States was open to a deeper friendship.

When I wrote my hundred-day plan, I'd had a hunch that speaking in Vietnamese and respecting the nation's traditions would be received well. But I underestimated the impact of a U.S. ambassador's actions, at first not realizing that releasing a bucketful of fat carp into Hanoi's West Lake would leave more of an impression on the people of Vietnam than any press statement could. I gradually came to understand that learning about and observing ancient traditions also made an impression on Vietnamese Americans. Every Vietnamese citizen—and every member of the Vietnamese diaspora in America—celebrated Tết, and acknowledging the significance of that shared experience seemed to contribute, in some way, to reconciliation.

I also discovered that I had less time than expected to carry out a hundred-day plan because after only three months in Hanoi, Clayton and I learned that our daughter, Lucy, had been born, and we flew with our son, TABO, to Texas for her adoption. Some things matter more than work.

I fretted that I would not be in Vietnam for the arrival in March 2015 of a Congressional delegation led by Nancy Pelosi, minority leader of the House of Representatives. When she heard why I would not be there to greet her, Pelosi wrote to congratulate us on adopting our daughter, adding, "What a joyous, exciting and wonderful occasion."[5] She was right.

Even with this interruption, I was pleased that we had managed to set the stage for three productive years. I had already seen throughout my diplomatic career that the United States casts a long shadow, and I knew that when Americans show respect, it has a big impact. Showing respect meant figuring out what was truly important to America's partners and taking that seriously. Respect cost America very little and gained us almost everything. With that in mind, I focused on areas of collaboration that I believed would matter to the Vietnamese.

Showing respect builds trust. Real, powerful partnership comes from building trust, and diplomats can help build trust by finding where interests converge and then doing things together. The diplomat's job is to find those shared interests and make them the basis for action. All diplomatic reports, contact work, and outreach should lead to action.

A real partnership in this case also required the Vietnamese to address U.S. concerns. We needed to be honest, direct, and respectful with each other about even our most profound differences, especially those related to human rights such as the freedom of speech and the freedom to worship and to associate. Success in building a long-term partnership would depend also on another important area of engagement—reconciliation—and at first, I didn't believe that required ambassadorial leadership.

Even though the governments in Hanoi and Washington, DC, had established a normal and productive relationship, many of our citizens had yet to achieve reconciliation after the war. Only over time did I come to appreciate that an ambassador could use carefully planned and thoughtful engagements to help promote that process.

8

Châu, Khiết, and the Students of Vietnam

● ● ● ● ● ● ● ● ● ● ● ● ● ●

Early in 2015, Consul General Rena Bitter and I visited Vietnam's ancient imperial capital, Huế, where severe damage had been done to the city's citadel and monument complex during a titanic battle between Americans and North Vietnamese during the 1968 Tết offensive. My predecessor, Dave Shear, had obtained a grant from the Ambassador's Fund for Cultural Preservation, managed by the State Department, to restore three royal altars of the Triệu Tổ Temple from the Nguyễn dynasty. The royal family in Huế had used the altars for ancestor worship.

The grant was small ($29,000), but its symbolism was large. When the project was launched in 2014, Huế's conservative political leaders, decidedly cool to the U.S. government, had turned out in large numbers and paid close attention to progress on the renovation. Phan Thanh Hải, director of the Huế Monuments Conservation Centre, said at the launch: "The altars must be indispensable in the traditional ceremonies of Vietnamese people, especially in the royal ancestor worshipping activities." He spoke about the significance of carved symbols on the altars and about how preserving them also helped keep alive "the masterpieces of the carving and lacquering techniques of the period."[1]

Restoration work was still under way at the site when Rena and I visited it. We had come because the consulate team had recommended that we apply for a large ($700,000) grant, also from the Ambassador's Fund for Cultural Preservation, to restore the Triệu Tổ Temple, one of the five most important temples of the Nguyễn dynasty in Huế. Built in 1804 to worship Nguyễn Kim and his empress, the ancestors of the Nine Nguyễn Lords, it had been declared a UNESCO World Heritage site in 1993. The Triệu Tổ Temple housed the three newly restored royal altars.

We joined Đỗ Kỳ Mẫn, an experienced heritage artisan, as he mixed lacquer and applied it in layers to the temple columns. This complex process involved more than a dozen layers of lacquer and endless drying and sanding between each layer. When applied correctly, the lacquer would last more than a century. I told the media, "Cultural protection is not just about preserving achievements from the past but also to tell our stories to our children." Clayton and our son were with me, and I added, "My family is here together as I want my son to understand what I learned 20 years ago, that Vietnamese heritage sites are the world's treasures."[2]

I didn't need to say that we had chosen to restore a temple that had been damaged during the war. Without apologies, the United States was quietly acknowledging the painful past. Our group burned incense sticks on the royal altars and spoke with workers at the site. Then we joined local chefs in making *bún bò* Huế, the city's signature spicy soup with rice noodles and beef.

Rena and I returned to Huế a year later to unveil the completed renovation of the Triệu Tổ Temple.[3] We had started small by restoring the three altars, and then we restored the building where they were housed, giving us the opportunity to show respect to the Vietnamese people and gradually to build trust between our two nations. Our diplomatic engagement followed the same track. When it began, Huế officials were suspicious of U.S. intentions, but by the time we had the large project rolling, we had clearly made a breakthrough.

The Huế Monuments Conservation Centre described the temple project as "an achievement of the cooperation in the cultural heritage preservation between the U.S. Consulate in Vietnam and Thua Thien Hue Province in the past years. Furthermore, it helps strengthening the friendliness of the two countries in the future."[4]

All of this became possible because a local consulate employee, Nguyễn Hữu Luận, who had grown up in Huế and once worked for the local commission charged with preserving the monuments, helped Alex Titolo, the consulate's public affairs officer, choose the right projects and partners. Alex was able to go beyond the cultural projects and gain approval to pursue many other initiatives in Huế, including student exchanges between U.S. educational institutions and Huế University, English-language teaching, and a small U.S. cultural center in the city.

Later, I led the U.S. delegation to the Asia-Pacific Economic Cooperation forum on a visit to Huế, during which local authorities and Hải of the Conservation Centre hosted us at a grand dinner in the citadel, where the U.S. delegates were the most honored guests. When other diplomats asked why I knew the local officials so well, I pointed out the newly restored Triệu Tổ Temple.

Courtney Marsh's 2015 film, *Chau—Beyond the Lines*,[5] became one of five finalists for an Academy Award in the category of short documentaries. This extraordinary film told the story of Lê Minh Châu, a young man born with severely deformed limbs because of his mother's exposure to dioxin. Refusing to live as a victim, Châu created an independent life as an artist, painting with a brush held in his teeth. Châu is incredibly talented and has a winning personality, making this film a tale of overcoming the greatest odds and finding satisfaction, not tragedy, in life.

Our team screened the film at the embassy in Hanoi and the consulate in Hồ Chí Minh City. Châu attended the latter screening, and the audience welcomed him with a standing ovation. Châu grinned and nodded happily.

Charles Bailey, former director of the Ford Foundation's Vietnam office, organized a screening of the film on Capitol Hill and continued his marathon efforts to persuade legislators that Agent Orange is a humanitarian concern the United States could and should do something about. Bailey urged the U.S. government to help people like Châu who had been harmed by dioxin.

In spring 2015, I quietly visited the dioxin cleanup project at the Đà Nẵng Airport. The project had taken a long time to reach the operational stage. In 2007, Ambassador Michael Marine first visited the site, the second largest dioxin hot spot in Vietnam. In 2011, his successor, Ambassador Mike Michalak, outlined in a letter to Prime Minister Nguyễn Tấn Dũng a two-year project for cleaning up Đà Nẵng. At that time, the project was expected to cost $34 million, and the United States had committed $20 million. In 2012, Ambassador Dave Shear and Senior Lieutenant General Nguyễn Chí Vịnh officially launched the cleanup. In 2014, Senator Patrick Leahy, who had led the effort in Congress to back efforts to undo the damage caused by Agent

Orange in Vietnam, visited the area to ceremonially light an "oven" the size of a football field.

During that 2012 visit, Leahy also visited a family whose members had been affected by Agent Orange. Two boys, Tri and Hau, suffered from severe mobility and intellectual disabilities and had received support from the U.S. nongovernmental organization (NGO) Children of Vietnam since 2010. Leahy's visit was the first by a high-level U.S. official from Washington to see what some Vietnamese families had endured as a result of dioxin contamination. Prior to Leahy, the only senior U.S. official to visit an Agent Orange victim was Ambassador Marine in 2007.

Dioxin threatened additional harm to citizens in Vietnam even forty years after the war ended. Scientists had determined the way to rid soil of dioxins left there by the use of Agent Orange was to "cook" the dioxin-contaminated soil at a temperature of 335 degrees Celsius—more than three times the boiling point of water—and keep the dirt at that temperature for twenty-eight days. The soil was heated in a vast structure that was surrounded by thirty-foot-high concrete retaining walls and a roof.

Progress had been steady, though the costs of the cleanup had increased to more than $100 million. By the time of my 2015 visit, one huge batch of dioxin-free soil had been removed and replaced with a second batch of dirt, and the process would be repeated again.

A year later, I returned to Đà Nẵng with Senior Lieutenant General Nguyễn Chí Vịnh, who had by this time accompanied three ambassadors in scoping out, launching, and at last completing the project. Vịnh always played a key role in matters related to the U.S.-Vietnamese security relationship, and every time he and I met, I could count on him to raise the dioxin cleanup—first in Đà Nẵng and later in Biên Hua.

We were also joined in the celebration of the successful Đà Nẵng cleanup by Deputy Prime Minister Vũ Đức Đam. His presence showed how seriously the Vietnamese government took the joint effort. The press snapped dozens of photos when Vịnh and I plunged our hands into the newly decontaminated soil. The government displayed one of these photos in the War Remnants Museum in Hồ Chí Minh City, a reminder that it was possible to overcome the legacies of war. I knew that together, Vietnamese and Americans had made the soil safe. Otherwise, as the father of two small children, I would not have touched soil that still contained dioxin.

When Shear handed the dioxin baton to me, he warned that an even bigger challenge than that in Đà Nẵng was the dioxin hot spot at the Biên Hua

PHOTO 16 Senior Lieutenant General Nguyễn Chí Vịnh and the author at the dioxin cleanup site in Đà Nẵng, May 2016 (Credit: U.S. Agency for International Development).

air base. There, the health of current residents was still at risk from residual dioxin. I wrote to leaders in the State Department, Defense Department, and the White House: "U.S. leadership on the cleanup of Biên Hòa air base, the largest and most complicated dioxin 'hot spot' . . . draws a line under a delicate history and demonstrates our good faith as a partner. Vietnam's leaders often say U.S. efforts to resolve these issues are essential to building the trust we need for a more forward-looking defense relationship."[6]

In addition to Agent Orange, we needed to address the vast amount of unexploded ordnance (UXO) that the U.S. military had left behind in Vietnam. The United States dropped more than three times as many bombs on Vietnam as it did on all of Europe, Asia, and Africa during World War II.

In summer 2015, I visited the central province of Quảng Trị, near the former demilitarized zone, to see work that was being funded by the United States to remove land mines and UXO that still remained in the countryside. All of Quảng Trị's villages had been destroyed during the war. So many bombs had exploded in the province that parts of its landscape were as cratered as the moon. Yet 10 percent of the bombs dropped on the province didn't explode. In 1989, Vietnam's military estimated that over 80 percent of the province was contaminated with UXO. Eighty-five hundred people had been killed or injured since the war ended, 31 percent of whom were children.

Brave technicians from a small number of NGOs performed the hot, dangerous, and dirty work of demining, swinging their metal detectors from side to side as they crisscrossed the landscape. Every minute or two, a detector emitted a telltale "bzzt," and more often than not, experts found cluster munitions under the ground. Sometimes they found much larger bombs or land mines. The field where I stood was littered with cluster bombs and other varieties of UXO. These technicians also used dog sniffers because they could smell metal buried as deeply as two meters beneath the surface.

If the bombs could not be removed, they had to be destroyed in place. I was given the honor of pressing a detonator button and watching one bomb explode. At least that was one more spot where a farmer wouldn't lose his leg while plowing the earth and a child wouldn't lose hands or eyes after picking up a cluster bomb. Day after day, year after year, these teams mapped the terrain, discovered UXO beneath the ground, and destroyed it, gradually making Quảng Trị province safe.

The nerve center for this extraordinary effort—involving close collaboration between Peace Trees, Project RENEW—Norwegian Peoples' Aid, the Mine Action Group, local officials, and Vietnam's ministry of defense—was a warren of offices called the Legacy of War Coordination Center. The NGOs and Vietnamese officials divided up what needed to be accomplished, and every day they made progress toward getting it done.

The United States first signaled that it would support cleaning up UXO in Quảng Trị in the final weeks of the administration of President Bill Clinton. In Hanoi, the president noted that the United States had just provided $3 million in demining equipment to Vietnam, but he also announced the donation of a surplus field medical hospital to Quảng Trị province. He promised that the United States would work on cleaning up UXO until the last mines were removed. Over the past twenty-five years, the United States spent more than $230 million on removing UXO and related programs.[7]

On the day I visited Quảng Trị, I met forty-five-year-old Ngô Thiện Khiết, a Project RENEW team leader who was responsible for demining. A father and husband, he spent his days doing dangerous work that would save the lives of his fellow citizens. Nine months after I met him, Khiết was killed in an explosion while directing his team in an area where cluster bombs had been found.

I was angry and sad when I wrote my condolences to Khiết's widow. We should never have dropped those bombs in the first place. Project RENEW's

PHOTO 17 Ngô Thiện Khiết recording GPS coordinates of a cluster bomb, Xuân My village, Cam Tuyền Commune, Cam Lo District, Quảng Trị province, July 2015 (Credit: Ngô Xuân Hiến / Project Renew—NPA).

explosive ordnance disposal specialists and clearance technicians were highly trained and professional. Safety was their top priority. Since 2001, they had destroyed more than thirty thousand bombs and other munitions without a single accident, injury, or death—until Khiết's.

Khiết's team was undaunted and so committed to making Quảng Trị and Vietnam in general safe from UXO that team members were back in the field the day after his death. They returned to the site where Khiết was killed and continued the task of neutralizing cluster bombs and making the land safe for the local people and their new crop of rice. As of this writing, no further injuries or accidents have occurred in Quảng Trị.

Making Quảng Trị province impact free, so that farmers, children, and other citizens will not have to fear a sudden, deadly explosion, can be achieved by 2025 if work proceeds at the current pace. These efforts have gradually been replicated in Quảng Bình, the second most heavily bombed province, and in Thừa Thiên-Huế province and other places where UXO remains.

The creed of an American warrior is to leave no one behind, and I knew as ambassador how important it was for the U.S.-Vietnam partnership that I continue the work that others had already begun to find those whom the United States had lost in the war. Since 1997, I had visited many sites where Vietnamese and Americans worked side by side to recover the remains of the lost. After so many years in Vietnam's acidic soil, the clues might consist of no more than a zipper or a fragment of a pilot's face mask. If we were lucky, the searchers would find a tooth, a bone fragment, or even a wedding ring.

While serving as ambassador, I took a helicopter to a remote 7,200-foot-high mountain in Kon Tum province. A Defense POW/MIA Accounting Agency (DPAA) team that included U.S. servicemen and women and Vietnamese soldiers and civilians combed the steep hillside for remnants from a U.S. Air Force plane that had crashed there in 1968. To see the work under way, we climbed a muddy hillside, and we had to hold onto exposed roots to keep from sliding down the 45-degree slope. I asked a young serviceman who was swatting away mosquitoes while he sifted through dirt and mud what he thought of his job.

"I am proud to do this mission," he told me. "I signed up a second time. If I were to die in the line of duty, I would want others to do the same for me. We don't leave our comrades behind."

By 2015, the DPAA had excavated approximately twenty sites per year. As they had promised, the Vietnamese permitted the DPAA to send investigators almost anywhere, at any time, to search Vietnamese land for the remains of those still missing. The only exceptions where the Vietnamese imposed limited restrictions were near disputed international borders.

Due to Ann Mills Griffiths's advocacy, the U.S. Congress in 2015 approved limited funding for the Unidentified Remains Project to help the Vietnamese identify the remains of the estimated 300,000 people still missing on the Vietnamese side. The U.S. Agency for International Development signed a statement of cooperation with the Vietnam Academy of Science and Technology that included a $980,000 grant so the Academy's laboratory could conduct DNA testing and analysis.

U.S. backing of the Unidentified Remains Project is a critical part of the reconciliation effort because it recognized a significant Vietnamese belief—that the souls of people whose remains are not properly buried wander the earth for eternity—and it was an attempt to respect that belief. The Vietnamese referred to lost soldiers as martyrs; only once they are properly entombed can they be called heroes.

When I was in Vietnam in the 1990s, I taught English to ten teenage Vietnamese students every Wednesday evening in a dusty classroom in the Institute of Physics in Hanoi. These kids came from middle-class families whose members valued education. The young women were in their last year of high school, and the young men were studying in their first or second year at a polytechnic college or the University of Construction. I cherished my students and looked forward to those Wednesday evenings. I wondered what had happened since I had last seen them in 1997, and as ambassador I was determined to find them.

I had brought the students English instructional books from the United States, and they had given me the gifts a Vietnamese student traditionally gives a teacher: a lacquer painting and a small kumquat tree during the annual Tết celebration. They took me to eat snails and drink beer near West Lake. They taught me far more about Vietnam than I could ever have taught them about the English language.

I decided to try finding them through social media. I had 100,000 Facebook followers, and within days of posting a photo of my former class, I had located all of them. A member of my staff dubbed the communication effort "Operation Former Students." She reached out to the ones still living in Vietnam, and they wanted to hold a reunion.

Six of the former students who were based in Hanoi or Hồ Chí Minh City came to the ambassador's residence, and they were joined by one student who was visiting from her home in Belgium. A good education had helped all of them. Three were CEOs, two of information technology companies and one of a fashion company; and two were diplomats. Only one worked for a state-owned enterprise, although such enterprises still dominated Vietnam's economy. All used social media extensively (as did more than sixty million other Vietnamese citizens).

My former students had excelled in the fields of physics, engineering, and information technology. One of my goals was to enhance educational exchange

PHOTO 18 Former students and teachers. First row: Điệp, Thủy, Trang, Thu. Second row: Sơn, Trực, Theresa (who picked up teaching tasks when the author moved to Hồ Chí Minh City), the author, Hải, Tiến. Missing: Đức and Hoa. Hanoi, 1997 (Credit: Author's personal collection).

between the United States and Vietnam, and I wanted to determine how much the United States had contributed to education about science, technology, engineering, and mathematics (STEM) in Vietnam. I visited programs run by Arizona State University (ASU), an innovative public university that had worked for more than a decade to build partnerships with universities in Vietnam and had contributed to the country's efforts to reform its higher education system. By 2015, ASU had trained more than seven thousand Vietnamese faculty members and administrators, primarily to improve STEM education.

The charismatic sixteenth president of ASU, Michael Crow, was first determined to transform higher education at the university in Arizona. Then he turned to other countries, particularly Vietnam, where he wanted to "have a dramatic impact on the workforce and economy of that country, as well as materially advance economic and social ties between the United States and Vietnam."[8]

ASU's many programs included the Higher Engineering Education Alliance Program (HEEAP), a partnership with eight of Vietnam's top universities and numerous private companies that received significant funding from Intel and support from the U.S. Agency for International Development. In its first phases, HEEAP trained nearly five thousand academic leaders, particularly in engineering. Another industry-academic consortium, Building University-Industry Learning and Development through Innovation and Technology Alliance (BUILD-IT), involved seventeen Vietnamese universities and thirteen industry partners, including Intel, Microsoft, Amazon, and National Instruments.

Vietnamese students in the ASU programs were sparky and receptive, and they loved to study entrepreneurship. There were never enough spaces in entrepreneurship classes—on- or off-line—to keep up with the voracious demand. David Thorne, one of Secretary of State John Kerry's closest advisors and friends, joined me in launching a nationwide contest called the Ambassador's Entrepreneurship Challenge. This competition encouraged innovation and development of Vietnam's entrepreneurial system, and the rewards included exposure and mentorship for the young entrepreneurs and financial support for their best ideas. It was wildly popular. American efforts to highlight bankable, entrepreneurial ideas resonated among Vietnam's hardworking and creative young people.

ASU also worked with the U.S. government to implement the Young Southeast Asian Leaders' Initiative (YSEALI), a program launched by President Barack Obama to strengthen ties between the United States and promising young leaders from all ten ASEAN member nations. Hosting programs in its School of Public Service and School of Engineering, ASU highlighted entrepreneurship and innovation, the focus of YSEALI.

Phạm Quang Vinh, the Vietnamese ambassador to the United States, told me about an effort led by Prime Minister Nguyễn Tấn Dũng and Minister of Planning and Investment Bùi Quang Vinh to identify critical reforms needed for Vietnam's development. Working with an independent group of academics and World Bank economists, Minister Vinh produced an ambitious blueprint for Vietnam to jump from lower-middle-income to upper-middle-income status.

Vietnam 2035: Toward Prosperity, Creativity, Equity, and Democracy, published by the World Bank, is a revolutionary document that maps a route to economic prosperity balanced with environmental sustainability, equity and social inclusion, and governance reform. This ambitious agenda depends on a deep commitment to promoting learning, entrepreneurship, and innovation.

The authors note: "Sustaining high growth over an extended period will depend on an aggressive agenda to spur learning and innovation. Neither enterprises nor knowledge and research institutions are currently motivated to focus adequately on this agenda. A national innovation system can improve the situation. On the demand side, it will encourage firms to seek out the best available knowledge and strengthen the technical and financial support to facilitate their learning. On the supply side, such a system will help build the skills of the workforce beyond its current proficiency in basic education, while raising the quality and relevance of research and advanced training in universities and government research institutes."[9]

Vietnam's Communist Party leaders rejected some of the *Vietnam 2035* recommendations, such as the establishment of independent workers' unions, increasing government accountability, and the creation of an independent media,[10] because these ideas threatened the Party's dominant position. However, the Party and the government did agree that a serious reform of the higher education system was needed. Recognizing that the system was neither meeting Vietnam's labor force needs nor generating economically and socially beneficial knowledge and innovation, leaders looked to the United States for ideas.

Many leaders admired the U.S. higher education system and recognized that it fostered innovation. The Vietnamese Politburo included two officials who had earned graduate degrees in the United States while on Fulbright scholarships. Minister of Education and Training Phùng Xuân Nhạ told me, "we will work in partnership with any nation and will choose what is best to improve our own system." Nhạ had received his PhD from Georgetown University, which meant that he had personally experienced the benefit of drawing from other nations' educational traditions.

This joint work on education—supported by former Fulbright scholars such as Deputy Prime Minister Phạm Bình Minh, Education Minister Nhạ, Planning and Investment Minister Vinh, and my friend Nguyễn Vũ Tú—was an effective investment in the long-term relationship between the United States and Vietnam. Secretary Kerry, his friend Tommy Vallely, and U.S. academic leaders saw it as a vehicle for furthering reconciliation by advancing diplomatic and even commercial interests.

When I first visited Vietnam in 1996, approximately eight hundred Vietnamese students per year were pursuing an education in the United States. Twenty-one years later, more than thirty thousand Vietnamese students went to the United States annually. Returning to Vietnam, alumni of U.S. institutions outperformed and greatly outearned their local peers. In the early years of the two countries' relationship, Vietnamese who studied in the United States were sometimes viewed with suspicion, but by the time

I became ambassador, that was longer the case. U.S. alumni associations, once very secretive, could expand and flourish in the open.

My former students, in their teens in 1996 and in their late thirties when we were reunited, were connected to the world. One element of their success, and of the success achieved by Fulbright scholars and a growing number of Vietnamese alumni of U.S. high schools and universities, was the ability to speak English. Another was a strong network with fellow former students. The single clearest indicator of career success was how effectively each student used the internet. Some had encountered setbacks in their family lives or careers. Yet they had learned resilience and how to pick themselves up, dust themselves off, and move on. They had learned to overcome failure. As a group, they remained enthusiastic and optimistic about the future.

9

China and the Trans-Pacific Partnership

• • • • • • • • • • • • •

The government of Vietnam had big plans to celebrate the fortieth anniversary of reunification on April 30, 2015. I had a different plan that would mark the fall of Saigon. I traveled to Hồ Chí Minh City, where Consul General Rena Bitter and I participated in a memorial ceremony to honor the last two Marines who had been killed in action in Vietnam, Lance Corporal Darwin L. Judge and Corporal Charles McMahon Jr. (Their story is told in Chapter 1.) Both had arrived in Vietnam in April 1975: Judge on the 15th and McMahon on the 22nd. They were ordered to provide security at Tân Sơn Nhất Airport, and both died in the initial rocket attack on April 29. Their remains were initially left behind but were repatriated about a year later.

The Fall of Saigon Marines Association had organized the ceremony on the spot where the U.S. embassy in Saigon once stood. Today it is the location of the U.S. consulate general in Hồ Chí Minh City. The association's members, who come from all over the United States, are U.S. Marines who were serving in Vietnam during the spring of 1975. Since 2000, these Marines have met often—including in Marshalltown, Iowa, where Judge grew up and in Woburn, Massachusetts, where McMahon was raised.

The Marines almost didn't get to the 2015 ceremony because when they were on their way from the Saigon Star Hotel—which had been the Marine House in 1975—they discovered that Hồ Chí Minh City was locked down for a massive parade, during which Vietnam's prime minister was giving a televised triumphal speech excoriating the United States. Ever resourceful, the Marines found their way past the barricades and arrived in time to perform a solemn ceremony in honor of their fallen comrades.

I was proud to stand by these Americans who had served with Judge and McMahon, Marines who had spent decades honoring their comrades' sacrifice. Looking around and seeing the faces of these older Marines—as well as the first young Marines in forty years who had come to Hồ Chí Minh City to stand guard over the consulate—gave me hope that full reconciliation was near.

In April 1975, the older Marines had been in their teens or early twenties. They were the last Americans to be evacuated from Saigon and other U.S. outposts in southern Vietnam. Twenty-one thousand South Vietnamese officials, local employees of American agencies, and their families were evacuated by airlift in the days prior to Saigon's fall. More were left behind because the helicopter airlift was initiated too late and was too disorganized to rescue all of the locally employed staff members who had been told to wait in safe houses for transport to the airport.

The young men serving as Marine security guards worked every day with those local staffers. When the end came, they had to load Ambassador Graham Martin aboard a helicopter and then wait and wonder if any more helicopters were coming. They had to keep back hundreds of their Vietnamese colleagues waiting in the courtyard who had been promised an evacuation and prevent them from climbing onto the roof of the embassy when the last helicopter arrived. These men had to do difficult things that marked them for life.

They had been eyewitnesses to one of America's worst moments, and now they were turning bitter memories into something useful and positive. Since 2002, the association had awarded annual scholarships at the Boys and Girls Club of Woburn, Massachusetts, in honor of Corporal McMahon, and to students in Marshalltown High School, in Iowa, to honor Lance Corporal Judge. Ken Crouse, secretary of the association, told me: "The trips to Marshalltown were at times very challenging and also very rewarding. Speaking at a high school awards night about a friend who died less than a year following high school graduation is not easy—even less so when his mother was sitting in the audience of 200-plus people."

Ken had visited Southeast Asia almost every year since 2004. On one trip to Quảng Nam province, he visited Đông Giang village, where he met a former Việt Cộng soldier, Bàng Khen, who was about his age. When Khen saw

PHOTO 19 Ken Crouse and Bàng Khen, Đông Giang village, Quảng Nam province, November 2017 (Credit: Courtesy of Ken Crouse).

Ken's Marine Corps tattoo of a bulldog, he expressed respect for the U.S. Marines and then revealed scars on his right shoulder and torso from a fire-fight with the Marines. Moved, Ken wrote:

> After the firefight, Marines were mopping up and found [Khen] on the battlefield. They took care of him and apparently sent him to a field hospital where he recovered from his injuries. . . . He then showed me his military awards, a small shrine and other photos. As we walked back out to the jeep, we held hands the way I've seen guys do in some circumstances indicating bonds of friendship. We went back through his home to a back room where three of the walls contained shelves of rice whiskey—something he's apparently known for in the community. Anyway, he asked if I would share a sip with him, and he pulled down a couple of very antique-looking tea cups from the top shelf, and we each had an ounce of his whiskey. The guide told me later that although she had stopped by to greet him more than a dozen times over the previous couple of years, this was the first time she had been into the room with the whiskey. It left a lasting impression on me and remains one of the highlights of the many trips I've taken.[1]

Ken's visits to Vietnam and the Fall of Saigon Marines Association's ceremony were real reconciliation in action. Not organized or directed by any government, they were the deeds of American veterans who were reconciling with their past and had chosen to extend a hand to those with whom they once fought.

A month after the ceremony, in May 2015, Senator John McCain visited Vietnam as the head of a Congressional delegation that also included Senators Jack Reed, Dan Sullivan, and Joni Ernst. McCain guided his colleagues through the Hanoi prison where he had been held during part of his five and a half years as a prisoner of war (POW). Preserved as a museum, Hỏa Lò's exhibits emphasized the brutality of French colonialism. The Vietnamese Communist victors told the story of Hỏa Lò in a manner that glossed over North Vietnamese excesses and portrayed their treatment of American POWs in a bizarre and unreal way.

After looking at a video of POWs playing volleyball, drinking beer, and hanging ornaments on a Christmas tree, McCain laughed. "Yes, it was a party every day," he said. When we came to an exhibit focused on him and featuring a pristine flight suit, he laughed again. "My actual suit had the arms torn off," he noted.

At a quiet dinner afterward, McCain became reflective and told us a story: "Each prisoner had a small cloth, about eight inches square, that we used to wash our dishes and clean our bodies. I left mine drying near the stall we used to wash ourselves. Without any warning, I was hauled off for ten days of 'attitude adjustment.' When I returned, my cloth had been taken from the clothesline on which it was drying.

"Feeling desperate, I saw another prisoner's cloth and swiped it. Our cells were very small, and we weren't allowed to speak with the other prisoners. So I used to tap out messages to the guy in the cell next to mine using Morse code. He tapped this: 'Someone stole my cloth. If I find out who it is, I'll kill him.'

"For days I said nothing. Then one day when washing, I saw another cloth and hung up the one I had stolen. Later I confessed to my neighbor that I was the culprit. For six weeks, he refused to communicate with me. I felt very much alone."

The prisoner next to McCain was Bob Craner. In his 1999 memoir, *Faith of My Fathers,* McCain wrote, "Bob Craner kept me alive. Without his strength, his wisdom, his humor, and his unselfish consideration, I doubt I would have survived solitary with my mind and my self-respect reasonably intact. I relied almost entirely on him for advice and for his unfailing ability to raise my spirits when I had lost heart. He was a remarkably composed man with the courage to accept any fate with great dignity."[2]

Some prisoners curried favor with the guards by ratting on the other prisoners. Rewarded with beer and occasional time out of their cells, they were hated by the majority of those who were incarcerated. When the POWs were released, many wanted the traitors to be court-martialed, but President Gerald Ford gave them a pardon. McCain said he regretted President Ford's decision to pardon men who had betrayed their fellow Americans.

Their time in Hỏa Lò Prison was no party.

Sullivan in particular wanted to visit the spot next to Trúc Bạch Lake where local citizens had pulled McCain ashore after he bombed their city and a monument had later been built. As we drove there in a van, I asked Sullivan what had prompted him to visit Vietnam. He said: "I had a packed schedule. But when Senator McCain asked me to go, I canceled everything. I couldn't say no to seeing Vietnam with John McCain."

I had promised McCain that the monument would be cleaned if I had to do it myself with a toothbrush. It was now pristine. Its text had been revised: McCain's title, U.S. Naval Air Force Lieutenant Commander, was accurate. His name was spelled correctly. The Vietnamese pejorative prefix "*tên*" before McCain's name had been deleted. Honor and truth were preserved. McCain seldom showed much emotion during this visit, but he appeared genuinely pleased by the repairs on the only monument erected to him.

Prior to my confirmation as ambassador, from May to August 2014, China moved its Haiyang Shiyou 981 oil rig into Vietnam's exclusive economic zone in the sea east of Đà Nẵng. Vietnamese citizens responded by rioting in the south and burning Chinese factories. Two Chinese workers died as a result. Vietnam's Politburo, divided on many issues, was united in the view that China once again posed an existential threat. With the oil rig provocation and other bullying actions in the South China Sea, China pushed Vietnam into the arms of the United States. President Barack Obama, Secretary John Kerry, and McCain were determined to return the embrace.

In 2013, the Philippines had brought a case against China to the Permanent Court of Arbitration under the terms of the U.N. Convention on the Law of the Sea. In December 2014, Vietnam, in a rare move, sided with the Philippines by filing its own views, thereby agreeing that the court had the jurisdiction to sort out territorial disputes in the South China Sea.

This was important to the United States because our ships have engaged in freedom of navigation operations since 1979 to uphold the principles of the U.N. convention, which limits excessive claims by coastal states. Freedom of navigation has been a fundamental principle for the United States since the First Barbary War (1801–1805), in the administration of President Thomas Jefferson. In 2015, just before McCain visited Vietnam, China threatened to declare an air defense identification zone (ADIZ) over the South China Sea, which meant that in the interest of national security, China would locate, identify, and control civilian aircraft over international waters. This was a challenge to two centuries of U.S. military doctrine.

Asked about the South China Sea (called the East Sea in Vietnamese) during my first press interview in Hồ Chí Minh City, I said that the United States wanted to see territorial disputes resolved peacefully and in accordance with international law. "That's a fundamental and vital interest for the United States and for other countries in the region," I said. I reminded the press that the United States opposed intimidation and unilateral action, and I added: "When Vietnam made a choice to file a statement with the arbitral tribunal in The Hague, that was a peaceful action and in accordance with a commitment to international law. The U.S. is very supportive."[3]

During their 2015 visit, McCain and the other members of his delegation engaged in substantive discussions with Vietnam's leaders regarding tensions in the South China Sea. They knew that Southeast Asian nations wanted U.S. support for the U.N. decision to uphold international law while they negotiated a code of conduct with China. China had recently militarized the Johnson Reef, located in the Spratly Islands of the South China Sea, making it one of six new man-made islands with runways and fortifications that China was building there. McCain stressed U.S. opposition to an ADIZ and revealed to his hosts that Congress would soon authorize $425 million for new maritime capacity-building efforts for nations threatened by China.

McCain also told Vietnamese leaders that the United States wanted their country to be one of the first members to join the Trans-Pacific Partnership (TPP) trade agreement. Tension in the South China Sea and the TPP were related. Vietnam viewed the TPP as a strategic agreement that would prevent China from dominating its economy and enable it to secure diplomatic support when the Chinese resorted to bullying tactics.

All of Vietnam's top leaders wanted to meet with McCain, and it was a challenge for the embassy to accommodate as many of them as possible. National Assembly Chairman Nguyễn Sinh Hùng, speaking of Chinese bullying in the East Sea, quoted Hồ Chí Minh to McCain: "Nothing is more precious than independence and freedom." Vietnam had fought wars with China in the past, he continued, and it was ready to fight again. Later the same day, when McCain met Nguyễn Phú Trọng, the Communist Party's general secretary told the visiting delegation: "We must be prepared. We will defend our sovereignty."

Defense Minister Phùng Quang Thanh told McCain and the other members of his delegation that China was building islands for logistical purposes, to provide technical services and to establish military bases. "If the international community should use those islands for services," Thanh said, "it would be tacit acknowledgment of Chinese sovereignty." Thanh warned McCain and Sullivan in an aside that if China made good on its threat to declare an ADIZ, it would be viewed in the region as a direct challenge to the United States.

McCain—the delegation's most senior member and a hero in Vietnam for supporting full diplomatic relations in 1995—unusually gave the floor to more junior senators in each meeting. Reed, Ernst, and Sullivan spoke far more than McCain, who could have easily done all the talking.

Vietnamese leaders noticed this as well. Minister of Public Security Trần Đại Quang said to McCain: "I recall your promise to introduce new friends to Vietnam. Thank you for all you have done to promote our relationship." McCain wasn't simply extending senatorial courtesy by bringing along new friends from the Senate and ceding the floor to them. He wanted those who would remain in the Senate after he was gone to understand Vietnam and to see a strong partnership with Vietnam as an important U.S. priority.

His method worked. Sullivan was particularly enthusiastic about the strategic opportunities of a close relationship with Vietnam. When I called on him later in his Capitol Hill office, I noted that Sullivan's commitment to strengthening the relationship had grown. McCain had chosen his protégé wisely. After McCain's death in 2018, no senator mattered more than Sullivan to the future of U.S.-Vietnam relations.

By the time of McCain's 2015 visit, military exchanges between the United States and Vietnam had become regular and frequent. Vietnamese military officials attended a full range of multinational conferences sponsored by the Defense Department, the Joint Chiefs of Staff, and the Pacific Command to discuss military medicine, search and rescue, and peacekeeping logistics and operations.

A month earlier, at the carefully chosen venue of the McCain Institute, Defense Secretary Ash Carter had noted in a speech that "this week . . . in the waters off Da Nang, a U.S. guided missile destroyer and a littoral combat ship are scheduled to engage with Vietnamese navy vessels—an engagement under the tactical command, on the part of the U.S. Navy, of a

PHOTO 20 Defense Secretary Ash Carter aboard a Vietnamese ship in Hải Phòng, May 2015 (Credit: Department of Defense/Photo by Glenn Fawcett).

Vietnamese-American U.S. Navy captain, whose family fled from the Vietnam War when he was five years old."[4]

Stories of Vietnamese refugees making good in America and of humanitarian visits by the U.S. Navy to Vietnam provided our embassy with golden opportunities for public diplomacy. Each humanitarian engagement involved naval doctors seeing Vietnamese patients, engineers repairing schools, training for lifeguards, and dancing and singing to the music of U.S. Navy bands. Vietnam's press published colorful photos and covered the activities extensively.

Carter also spoke about the TTP, saying that, "You may not expect to hear this from a Secretary of Defense, but in terms of our rebalance in the broadest sense, TPP is as important to me as another aircraft carrier. It would deepen our alliances and partnerships abroad and underscore our lasting commitment to the Asia-Pacific. And it would help us promote a global order that reflects both our interests and our values."[5]

Carter then visited Vietnam a few days after McCain. The embassy's political-military team, led by Vietnamese American Colonel Tuấn T. Tôn ("T3") and including the smart and energetic Adam Davis (and later the equally talented Evan Morrissey), worked hard to develop strategies for defense collaboration that would produce results. The team developed an agreement titled "Joint Vision Statement" that Secretary Carter and Defense Minister Thanh signed during Carter's visit.

This enabled the United States and Vietnam to expand maritime cooperation, launch joint work on humanitarian assistance and disaster relief, and together create a role for Vietnam in U.N. peacekeeping. These actions tracked with Vice Foreign Minister Hà Kim Ngọc's proposal to transform the U.S.-Vietnam relationship from one of bilateral cooperation to regional and global collaboration.

Shortly after Carter's trip to Vietnam, he hosted Thanh in the United States. Later, Thanh's successor as defense minister, General Ngô Xuân Lịch, visited the United States, and Secretary Jim Mattis, President Donald Trump's first secretary of defense, visited Vietnam twice during his two-year tenure. Through these back-and-forth senior defense visits, the two countries were building a narrative of trust and collaboration in the security realm. They were also signaling China to proceed cautiously in the South China Sea.

American and Vietnamese strategic interests overlapped not only in the South China Sea but also with regard to managing the North Korean challenge. During President Obama's administration, the United States saw North Korea as the highest-level threat to national security. Vietnam, as one of a handful of Communist nations, had fraternal Party-to-Party ties with North Korea. But with South Korea as one of its top investors, and with 200,000 South Koreans living in Vietnam, Hanoi saw relations with Pyongyang as more of a burden than an opportunity.

North Korea had no funds to operate overseas embassies, so its diplomats often reverted to illicit activities to remain solvent, and Hanoi was no exception to this behavior. The tiny North Korean staff had an enormous fleet of diplomatic vehicles, which they turned over at a (tax-free) profit on a regular basis. They smuggled narcotics through the diplomatic pouch, and when U.N. sanctions took a bite out of their revenue, the North Koreans sought to get around U.N. Security Council resolutions, including by illegally selling coal to Vietnam.

I met often enough with senior Vietnamese Communist Party officials to know that they were suspicious of North Korean activities. That turned to outright hostility when henchmen of the young Kim Jong Un, North Korea's supreme leader, involved a Vietnamese woman in a complex plot to poison Kim's half-brother in Kuala Lumpur. The Vietnamese were outraged by this. North Korean misbehavior made it much easier to persuade the Vietnamese to implement sanctions rigorously.

Poor cybersecurity was another threat that the United States and Vietnam could work together to address. Vietnam's vulnerability to cyber attacks surfaced when Chinese hackers compromised government agencies twice during my tenure as ambassador. In 2015 a group of hackers known as the China 1937CN Team attacked a thousand Vietnamese websites, and in 2016 the same group took over the civil aviation systems at key international airports in Hanoi and Hồ Chí Minh City. Only their self-restraint prevented them from bringing down aircraft. Cybersecurity experts describe Vietnam's vulnerability to cyber threats as dire and its defense capabilities as severely limited.

After the first attack, Minister of Public Security Quang proclaimed that cyber protection was part of national defense and warned of the consequences of cyber warfare. Experts agreed that the attacks were serious and provided examples of deep vulnerabilities. Like its civil aviation system, Vietnam's financial system was also highly vulnerable to cyber attacks. Other Southeast Asian countries confronted similar systemic challenges, but the Vietnamese were acutely concerned about China's using their vulnerability against them, considering the territorial disputes between the two countries and China's formidable cyber capabilities.

In response, Vietnam's Defense Ministry created Command 86, a 10,000-person-strong military cyber warfare unit that, according to the newspaper *Tuổi Trẻ*, was established to counter "wrong" views on the internet and strengthen cyber espionage capabilities. Freedom House reported that Command 86 and the Vietnamese government's "public opinion shapers" monitored and directed online discussions on everything from foreign policy to land rights.[6]

Vietnam's military and public security apparatus had long viewed international cooperation with suspicion. However, the country's leaders began to seek collaboration with multinational technology firms, particularly ones based in the United States, in recognition of the government's inability to respond effectively to potential Chinese attacks.

Late one evening in mid-June 2015, I was asked to come to Prime Minister Nguyễn Tấn Dũng's office at 8:30 the next morning. He wanted to deliver a tough message. When I arrived there, I realized that he had assembled all of his economic ministers, as well as his trade advisors and negotiators, which told me the toughness was intended more for his own government and the country's Communist Party than it was for me. By inserting himself into trade negotiations so visibly, he was issuing instructions to his team and shaping the internal debate over the TPP.

I had slept for only about two hours because I had been in Hồ Chí Minh City, hosting an early 2015 Independence Day celebration, when I received the summons. When Vietnam's most powerful politician called, it was best for me to answer. As luck would have it, one flight after another was canceled, and I couldn't exactly bed down and wait for a morning flight. I caught a budget airline's 2:30 A.M. flight to Hanoi, slept fitfully, and rushed in to see the prime minister.

We affectionately referred to the prime minister's office as "Oz" because it was designed to awe and intimidate, and Dũng had assumed his usual position at the top of a grand flight of steps carpeted in red, his hands planted on his hips and his chest thrust out. The great and powerful Oz watched as I climbed the stairs, exhausted but ready to do battle.

Speaking in his thick Mekong Delta accent, the prime minister ushered me to a seat next to his. He had stood atop Vietnam's political pyramid for a decade, the first real strongman in the country since General Secretary Lê Duẩn, who remained at the peak of power from 1960 to 1986. Dũng had defeated his archrival, President Trương Tấn Sang, in a battle royal four years earlier. For twenty-five years, Vietnamese leaders had ruled as a triumvirate, balancing coalitions within the Politburo. In contrast, Prime Minister Dũng had ruled alone since defeating Sang in the National Assembly. Or so it seemed at the time.

The prime minister and I had discussed the TPP in every meeting we had held. I had forced a few exchanges about human rights, and Dũng had welcomed discussion about the South China Sea. He even took seriously my concerns about relocating the embassy office building to a more suitable and safe location. Yet he had focused most on the TPP. Although he was reluctant to reveal his true position in the negotiations, I sensed that he wanted Vietnam's participation in the trade agreement to be part of his legacy.

The TPP provided Vietnam with opportunities to develop its economy by growing closer to the United States, Japan, and other TPP partners outside of China's orbit. And it served as an essential external force to bring about the wrenching economic reform Vietnam required so desperately. In a country where state-owned enterprises funded the political careers of key leaders, it could be tactically useful to blame external trading partners, especially the United States, when driving through key reforms. And it would be difficult to privatize those enterprises without external pressure.

Vietnam had the least developed economy of all twelve TPP partners. As a result, Hanoi wanted additional time to meet many of its obligations, and for the most part, Washington was willing to grant it that time.

Ambassador Mike Froman, the U.S. trade representative, wanted Vietnam in the agreement, and not just because of the meager benefits that U.S. business would receive from its relatively small economy. He wanted other countries to see that even a developing country such as Vietnam could meet the high standards of the farthest-reaching trade agreement ever negotiated. If Vietnam could do it, then so could non-TPP members such as Indonesia, Thailand, the Philippines, and India—not to mention South Korea and other large, modern economies. A vast swath of Asia could become part of a new and dynamic trade structure.

With almost all of the prime minister's cabinet watching our exchange, I knew I had to respond carefully. He liked to show that he was a tough guy, and his tone was belligerent. "We have ratified seven ILO [International Labour Organization] conventions," he declared. "It's interference in our internal affairs to tell us we must change our labor laws."

Dũng wanted his ministers to report to the Party leadership that he was a resolute, effective negotiator. It was to America's advantage to help him preserve his tough-guy image, but I also had to show that the United States would not budge on some fundamental points. I stayed firm on the U.S. trade representative's key "asks" of Vietnam: tariff reductions, phase-in periods for certain obligations, and especially workers' rights. The prime minister looked me in the eye as he spoke gruffly and sometimes angrily, at least for show: "We are a developing country. We need more time to meet our obligations. Other TPP partners are far richer and more advanced."

I sensed that Dũng was hungry to have Vietnam be one of the TPP's first members, not outside waiting for an opportunity to join later. Strategically, the TPP was good for Vietnam's leaders and its people, since it would prevent China from having a powerful lock on the country's economic future.

The prime minister had willingly taken risks in the past to build a stronger relationship with the United States, and those gambles had paid off, especially in 2014 when (as mentioned earlier in this chapter) China threatened Vietnam by placing an oil rig off the Vietnamese coast. Politburo members who opposed a close relationship with the United States were in a dwindling minority. Dũng proved that he had been right to develop ties with a distant superpower, to balance the one on Vietnam's border.

When I received my summons in Hồ Chí Minh City, I had to abandon my eight hundred Independence Day guests, and I had moved into a private room with the two people I knew could send a message to the prime minister: his daughter and son-in-law. I urged them to tell Dũng that if Vietnam wanted into the TPP, key conditions had to be met. The United States wanted to make it work. Did Vietnam?

Apparently, it did. After my meeting with Dũng, I possessed a much clearer understanding of Vietnam's "red lines"—those elements of the agreement on which the Vietnamese could move no further—but also a strong sense of what Dũng was willing to risk to make Vietnam's joining the TPP part of his legacy.

I dashed off a personal message to Froman. "The political will is there," I told him. "Vietnam is willing to make the tough changes, including on workers' rights."

I also called Ginny Foote, who had been so helpful to Charge d'Affaires Desaix Anderson and Ambassador Pete Peterson during negotiations over the U.S.-Vietnam Bilateral Trade Agreement in the 1990s. Since then, Ginny had moved to Hanoi to continue her work. She operated according to the "Bill Sullivan Rule," as she called it. Her boss and mentor—Ambassador William Sullivan, who played a critical role in helping the United States and Vietnam come together in the late 1980s and early 1990s—had advised Ginny to provide direct and honest feedback to both sides to encourage successful negotiations. "Never spin," he said, "or you'll lose the credibility an honest broker must have."

Ginny and Economic Counselor Laura Stone gave me invaluable advice and insights as Froman negotiated the TPP. Ginny was trusted by both sides because she was not in government, knew so many people in Vietnam, and followed the "Bill Sullivan Rule." She worked hard not to convey her own opinions, instead maintaining the trust of both negotiating parties throughout the TPP negotiations—as she had during the Bilateral Trade Agreement negotiations many years earlier.

After the meeting with Dũng, Ginny, Laura, and I determined that haggling over tariff lines and phase-ins would lead to a mutually satisfactory conclusion. Even so, we recognized that Vietnam would have difficulties meeting U.S. conditions on freedom of association for its workers. The irony of capitalist America telling communist Vietnam how to treat its workers was not lost on us.

The only way President Obama could sell having Vietnam become a TPP member to the Democratic Party—or at least reduce the level of Democratic opposition—was by showing that he had obtained meaningful concessions on workers' rights. Vietnamese Communist Party conservatives strongly resisted the U.S. requirement that workers must be free to form unions and associate with other unions. I determined that Dũng saw this requirement as a price Vietnam must pay to be included in a trade regime that embraced two of the world's three largest economies. Making this concession and joining the TPP would give Vietnam strategic options as well as access to the globe's largest market.

During my first months as ambassador, I met as many of Vietnam's leaders as I could. I heard a consistent message, first from Vice Foreign Minister Ngọc and then from Party and other government leaders: General Secretary Trọng wanted to visit President Obama in the United States.

I gradually began to see the significance of this unusual request. Trọng was among a handful of hard-liners on the Politburo who were most suspicious of the United States. He had risen to power as an expert on Marxism-Leninism and Hồ Chí Minh thought, and he didn't seem likely to become a fan of close ties with the capitalist world. Some members of the Politburo and many in the Party's second most powerful body, the Central Committee, thought that the United States wanted to bring about a regime change in Vietnam. But changes were already afoot, even within the top layers of Vietnam's leadership.

Vietnam had also concluded—following China's decision to park its oil rig in Vietnam's territorial waters, a clear bullying tactic—that its means of resolving disputes with China weren't working. The usual method was to avoid entanglement with China's rivals while engaging Chinese counterparts at all levels of the government and Party to placate Beijing. But every year since 2009, Chinese harassment of Vietnamese ships had grown worse. Beijing backed its South China Sea claims by flexing its military and paramilitary muscle.

The Chinese believed that the U.S. attempt to form a closer relationship with Vietnam was making trouble in the region. But China's bullying of its Southeast Asian Nations neighbors was pushing them into the arms of the United States. Vietnam's people wanted a closer relationship with America. More than 90 percent considered the United States to be Vietnam's closest friend. Strategically, that explained why General Secretary Trọng wanted to visit President Obama.

The problem I faced was that even though the U.S. president hosted heads of state in the Oval Office, that invitation was rarely extended to party leaders. My first requests for a White House meeting were met with a no. U.S. officials told me that Trọng would be welcome to come to America, but he shouldn't count on a meeting with President Obama. This news would not be received favorably in Vietnam. Trọng would meet with the president or with no one at all.

Minister of Public Security Quang visited the United States in March 2015. I made sure that he had top-level meetings and briefed him before his trip. Quang was particularly pleased to meet with Secretary of Homeland Security Jeh Johnson and leaders of the U.S. intelligence services. His visit was seen by many in Vietnam as the warm-up act for the general secretary's visit. Quang was also polishing his own foreign policy credentials prior to the January 2016 Party Congress (when he would become president). His visit to the United States was a big success.

At that point, I had a revelation. If I didn't strongly make the case for why an Oval Office meeting for the general secretary was important, the visit wouldn't happen. I had to show that Trọng's visit could build on progress made by President Sang, who had launched the U.S.-Vietnam Comprehensive Partnership in 2013. I may have been new on the job, but my role wasn't to wait passively for instructions. Instead, it was to shape my instructions, and I got to work.

Fortunately, I found allies. Among them was Tommy Vallely, Secretary Kerry's friend and advisor—who was quite skeptical at first. But he listened carefully, and then helped me persuade Kerry.

Susan Rice, President Obama's National Security Advisor, opposed the visit, saying that it was not the president's job to meet with a party leader.[7] But Kerry went to see the president for one of their regular lunches and argued successfully for the meeting. "I got beat up for making the case," Kerry told me, referring to one of his regular tangles with Rice. "But I got it done." This allowed me to tell the leaders in Hanoi that President Obama had agreed to host Trọng in principle, even though I didn't yet have a date.

China had certainly noticed that a visit was anticipated. When Beijing learned that Trọng was planning a trip to Washington, he received (and accepted) an invitation to visit China. For four days in early April, Beijing rolled out the red carpet for Trọng and his entourage. My Vietnamese interlocutors told me that the visit was high on protocol but included no substantive results.

Next was Secretary Carter's visit to Vietnam after McCain's May trip. In Singapore, just before arriving in Vietnam, Carter said, "There should be no mistake: the United States will fly, sail, and operate wherever international law allows. . . . With its actions in the South China Sea, China is out of step with both the international rules and norms that underscore the Asia-Pacific's security architecture, and the regional consensus that favors diplomacy and opposes coercion."[8] Therefore, on the most critical strategic issue—the South China Sea—we were on the same side as Vietnam.

At a dinner hosted by Defense Minister Thanh, he and Secretary Carter drank a fair amount of red wine. As musicians strummed on instruments fashioned in the central highlands, and dancers in *áo dài* flashed us smiles, Thanh and Carter talked about their families.

Carter asked Thanh where he had met his wife. "She pulled shrapnel out of my hip," Thanh said. He didn't say that Americans were responsible for that war injury. That's when some fine Scotch was brought to the table. After a few glasses and a lot of laughter, Thanh said, "You know, if we had enjoyed a dinner like this back then, there never would have been a war."

Soon after Carter's visit, both sides agreed on an early July date for Trọng's visit to the United States and quietly began making preparations for it, as the visit had not yet been publicly announced. Vietnam's participation in the TPP would show the rest of Asia that a developing country could meet the high standards of a modern trade deal with the United States. Only Trọng could persuade his country's Communist Party to accede to U.S. demands on free assembly for Vietnamese workers, a key human rights provision that was essential to gain support for the TPP from Democratic lawmakers. Also, Trọng could facilitate the growth of security ties between Vietnam and the United States. And only he could ensure that the two countries' partnership would last.

10

The Communist Party

● ● ● ● ● ● ● ● ● ● ● ● ● ●

Ambassador Dave Shear had left a thoughtful memo that helped get me off to a good start, and he specifically urged me to continue deepening ties with the Vietnamese Communist Party. He wanted me to understand that even though Vietnam's government implements policies for the country, the Party sets the government's overall direction. When senior U.S. visitors came to Vietnam, Dave had made a point of taking them to meet both Party and government officials. My team and I kept up that practice.

I was happy that whenever I met with senior Party leaders, I saw a familiar face there. When I first served in Hanoi in 1996, Bùi Thế Giang frequently visited the Yết Kiêu Street residence of Chargé d'Affaires Desaix Anderson. Some Party members maintained a strict distance from U.S. diplomats, but Giang was relaxed and friendly.

On November 6, 1996, Desaix hosted an unusual gathering for Party and government officials (including Giang). Over morning coffee and donuts, Vietnamese and Americans came together to watch CNN election returns when President Bill Clinton defeated his challenger, Senator Bob Dole. This was the first time that many of the Vietnamese had been exposed to the vagaries of democratic governance. They took careful notes.

Desaix gave a speech I had drafted for him. "According to the Constitution of the United States, the election for president is not determined by the popular vote," he said in clear Vietnamese that bore traces of his Mississippi accent. "Instead, each state casts a certain number of ballots based on its population."

I had charts showing each state's number of Electoral College votes as well as the key Senate and House races being decided that day. I was no Wolf Blitzer, and my hand-drawn charts were on low-tech white boards, but our guests—including Giang—were enthusiastic and full of questions. They wondered if U.S. elections were truly democratic, given the Electoral College system and the outsize role that money plays in our presidential politics.

"Why is the U.S. president not elected by a majority of votes? Isn't your Electoral College a peculiar system?" someone asked.

Seeing it through their eyes made me realize how odd it was.

"Is it true that a minority of U.S. citizens hold most of the country's wealth?" another person asked.

At the time, Vietnam was an egalitarian society, with no super rich people, not much of a middle class, and half of the population living on less than $1 per day. Our guests' questions did not have easy answers, especially because I was trying to respond in Vietnamese. Still, the irony of explaining America's complex democracy to Communist Party officials, who never had to face elections, was not lost on me.

In the 1960s and 1970s, Giang had served in three capacities. After leaving college, he was in the infantry during the first months of his military service. Then, together with many of his friends from university, he was assigned to be an antiaircraft gunner in North Vietnamese coastal provinces. In Hải Phòng harbor, he experienced the deadly 1972 Christmas bombings that prompted Lieutenant Commander John McCain and his fellow prisoners to cheer.

After the Paris Peace Accords were signed in January 1973, putting an end to U.S. air attacks against the north, the North Vietnamese military high command restructured its combat forces. Giang was trained as a deminer, an extremely hazardous job. When the war ended, Giang's father, a provincial public servant, astutely advised him to study English for the sake of his career. Most of Giang's contemporaries decided to learn Russian, which was then the most popular foreign language in North Vietnam. Giang was recruited by the Party's External Relations Commission, and he worked as a researcher and translator while also teaching English to the commission's cadres. Later, he served as ambassador and deputy permanent representative at the United Nations when Vietnam was first elected a nonpermanent member of the Security Council.

When Giang and I renewed our friendship eighteen years later, his new double role surprised me. Not only was he a director general who advised top Party officials on how to work with their American counterparts, but he also served as an interpreter for most meetings between top Party leaders and American visitors—including Presidents Clinton, George W. Bush, and Barack Obama. Usually, being a director general was such a senior position that the person holding it wouldn't also work as interpreter, but Giang's double role was not coincidental. Party leaders trusted him, needed his advice, and wanted him to be there to help during top-level meetings. They knew that interpreting the subtle signals and words involved in high-stakes diplomatic encounters required judgment and experience.

I vividly recalled how smart Giang's questions were during the 1996 election party, and in 2015, I saw how thoroughly he understood contemporary U.S. politics and how insightful he was about Americans. He realized that a good relationship with the United States benefited Vietnam, and he worked for decades, into his retirement, to strengthen that relationship. Like many other veterans, Giang was not afraid to take risks for his country.

Giang's greatest political risk was proposing that Nguyễn Phú Trọng, the general secretary of the Communist Party, pay a visit to the United States. Giang saw this trip as high-risk but also high-reward, and his arguments for the visit ultimately prevailed.

In March 2015, I gave a major policy speech at Vietnam National University describing U.S. priorities. A thousand students chanted "nothing is impossible" at regular intervals, but the speech was more than a public relations event. It presented a plan of action whose details were fleshed out in an article I wrote for the *American Ambassadors Review*.[1] My goal was to strike the right chords with Vietnam's leaders. In late May 2015, General Secretary Trọng spoke about the importance of building trust between our nations by working together on economics, security, education, and training. I heard an echo of the ideas I had put forth and thought that we might be on the right track.

By then, Vice Foreign Minister Hà Kim Ngọc had earned my trust, as we met often to resolve bilateral challenges, and he was a practical, reliable interlocutor. He had urged that Trọng pay a visit to the United States. After my Vietnam National University speech, Ngọc told me that Vietnam's leaders were interested in my ideas. I couldn't know that those ideas, and Ngọc's, would soon receive a big boost from an old friend of Vietnam.

"Are you crazy?" I asked. "He'll never come."

Mark Brandt, a senior team member in the U.S. embassy, had suggested that I invite the former president, Bill Clinton, to visit Vietnam to cap our celebration of the twentieth anniversary of full diplomatic relations in July. I doubted that he would come because his wife had just announced in April that she was running for president, but I thought it couldn't hurt to write him a letter. I was surprised and very pleased when he accepted the invitation.

On July 2, 2015, twenty years after normalizing diplomatic relations and fifteen years after his historic trip to Hanoi and Hồ Chí Minh City, Clinton returned to Vietnam. I had worked in the White House during his administration and traveled with him to Hanoi in 2000. I knew him to be vital, brilliant, and wildly extroverted, and none of that had changed. I met him in an anteroom before our event together and saw that he was thinner, the result of quadruple bypass surgery, surgery for a partially collapsed lung and coronary stents, and his adherence to a vegan diet. Still, his blue eyes shone as brightly as ever. Clinton loved people.

Always curious, Clinton peppered Ted—my twenty-year-old nephew, who was a junior at Middlebury College and visiting us for the summer—with questions about his interests and life on campus. Clinton recalled with great warmth Clayton's cousin and civil rights icon Julian Bond, remembering a long chat they had in San Antonio, Texas, years before.

As we prepared to go on stage, Clinton seized Ambassador Pete Peterson's hand. Pete had joined us and two thousand Vietnamese and American guests for the Independence Day–twentieth anniversary celebration. Near the podium, as Deputy Prime Minister and Foreign Minister Phạm Bình Minh warmed up the crowd, the great orator from Arkansas scrawled left-handed notes in his prepared speech, changing and reshaping it until the moment I introduced him.

Clinton opened with warm, off-the-cuff words about Pete and Vi: "To me, the symbol of why we did the right thing will always be Ambassador Pete Peterson and his wonderful wife. Many of you know, he spent more than six years as a guest of the Vietnamese government during the war. He then went home and did his best to put his family back together, ran for Congress, got elected, became our ambassador—our first ambassador, one of the best appointments I ever made—and then married his wonderful wife and moved to Australia so he could come to Vietnam once a month and visit here."

Clinton's prepared message echoed themes of his Hanoi speech fifteen years earlier. He celebrated full diplomatic relations that he said were "for personal, political and geostrategic reasons one of the most important

PHOTO 21 President Bill Clinton, the author, Clayton Bond, Hanoi, July 2015 (Credit: U.S. Department of State/Lê Đức Thọ).

achievements of my career." He marveled at how far the two countries had come together since his visit in 2000.

Recalling his visit with Hillary and Chelsea to the excavation site of a plane downed in 1967, Clinton described the moment when Vietnamese and Americans sought to bring closure to the family of Air Force Pilot Lawrence Evert.

"By then his children, infants when he died, were grown," Clinton said. "But Daniel and Dave Evert were there, and I saw the tears in their eyes when they saw the Vietnamese people alongside the Americans stomping in the mud, desperately looking for shards of bones or other evidence of life." The key to full diplomatic relations—the fullest possible accounting of those we lost in the war—had become a genuine collaboration between two former adversaries.

Clinton then pivoted his speech to the future, just as he had done fifteen years earlier. He spoke of the growing partnership between the United States and Vietnam in trade, health, and especially education, areas of collaboration he had unlocked. In 2000, Clinton had announced an education program designed by Senator John Kerry. By 2015, it had grown from providing a hundred scholarships a year to making it possible for nearly thirty thousand Vietnamese to study in the U.S. annually.

Before speaking, President Clinton asked what I wanted him to include, and he did not disappoint me. "In January," he noted, "Vice Foreign Minister Ngọc opened a conference exhorting our two countries to move beyond bilateral cooperation to regional and global collaboration, a strategy that the current U.S. government strongly supports." Clinton had immediately grasped the significance of Ngọc's thinking and improvised perfectly. Ngọc, in the audience, caught my eye and grinned.

Clinton recalled his Georgetown University mentor, Senator J. William Fulbright, for whom he had worked two years while in college. Fulbright, Clinton said, "was the strongest opponent of the Vietnam War in the United States Congress, the Chairman of the Foreign Relations Committee, and instead of calling the people who disagreed with him names and having a fight all the time, he held the most educational set of hearings I believe ever held by a congressional committee just to teach people about Southeast Asia, to teach people about the history of Vietnam, to teach people about the dynamics of the conflict, and he believed that if he could only get enough people to listen it would change America's core. He was an astonishing man, and we were friends until he died at eighty-seven when I was president."

Clinton closed with a fifty-year-old quotation from Fulbright: "'We should make our own society an example of human happiness, make ourselves the friend of social revolution, and go beyond simple reciprocity in the effort to reconcile hostile worlds beyond our border.' [Fulbright] was right then, he's right today, and in the end it's what we're really celebrating—a decision to go with an outstretched hand, not a clenched fist.

"That decision is at the heart of every conflict in the world today and the decisions other people make about their own identity and whether they are better or worse, stronger or weaker. Whether they choose an outstretched hand or a clenched fist will decide the whole shape of the twenty-first century."[2]

The audience was enthralled by Clinton's spirit, his warmth, and his sparkling words of hope. His aides, trying as always to keep him on schedule, had to tear him away from the rope line. I had seen him with crowds before, and I wondered if the world has ever known a greater extrovert.

While hosting Clinton, I was also preparing for a big announcement. On July 3, the White House stated publicly that General Secretary Trọng would visit the United States just a few days later. Preparations had been finalized during the previous three weeks. This was the first trip to Washington by the general secretary of Vietnam's Communist Party. Trọng was perhaps the most skeptical of all Vietnam's top leaders about partnering with the United States.

Hoàng Bình Quân, chairman of the Party's External Relations Committee, laid out Hanoi's objectives in a *Washington Post* op-ed. He described the visit by the general secretary at the invitation of the Obama administration as a sign of the United States' respect for Vietnam's choice of political regime.

The United States saw Trọng as key to Vietnam's being included in the Trans-Pacific Partnership (TPP) trade agreement. Deputy Secretary of State Tony Blinken published a blog post in which he wrote that the United States considered the Trọng visit an opportunity to advance the TPP which, "if achieved, will establish high standards on labor, intellectual property, and the environment." The agreement, he added, was "a strategic opportunity for the entire region."[3]

On the morning of July 7, Trọng toured the Jefferson Memorial as the cherry tree–encircled Tidal Basin shimmered in the summer sun. President Thomas Jefferson was revered by the Vietnamese. Hồ Chí Minh had echoed Jefferson's words in his 1945 Declaration of Vietnam's Independence from France: "All people are created equal. The Creator has endowed them with inviolable rights. Among these rights are the right to life, the right to liberty, and the right to the pursuit of happiness."

That afternoon, Trọng witnessed Boeing and Vietnam Airlines sign an agreement for the purchase of eight Dreamliner aircraft that would eventually enable direct flights between Hồ Chí Minh City and the United States. Direct flights meant more tourists, businesspeople, students, and family members traveling back and forth. Those flights would accelerate reconciliation.

The next morning, Dan Kritenbrink, who had joined the White House staff just a week earlier as senior director for Asia, asked what I thought President Obama needed to say to Trọng. "The United States respects different political systems," I told him. "If the president says that, it indicates that we don't intend to overthrow Vietnam's government, but rather to work with it." I added: "Hanoi's greatest fear is that the United States wants regime change in Vietnam and will try to bring down the system of one-Party rule. That's why leaders in Hanoi are concerned about our demands for labor reform in the Trans-Pacific Partnership. If we want a constructive relationship with Hanoi and want key concessions that will bring Vietnam into the TPP, we must be clear that toppling a system of Party-led governance is not in our interest."

Moments before the meeting, President Obama pulled me aside in the anteroom and asked what title to use in referring to Trọng. General secretary,

PHOTO 22 President Barack Obama and Party Secretary Nguyễn Phú Trọng, Oval Office, July 2015 (Credit: Associated Press/Evan Vucci).

I told him. He then strode into the Oval Office and greeted Trọng warmly. Earlier, I had urged my friends in the Party, including Giang, to counsel Trọng to leave his notes behind and just have a conversation with President Obama. "Look him in the eye," I asked them to tell Trọng. Trọng did, and the two leaders connected.

President Obama stated that the United States could respect political systems that differed from our own. He spoke respectfully about how deeply the United States valued human rights, saying, "this is just who we are." He urged Trọng to allow Vietnamese labor unions to associate freely with other such unions in the country and elsewhere, noting that Vietnam's membership in the TPP would not be possible without this step. Obama spoke without notes, as if he had been working on the relationship with Vietnam for his entire career. Considering the thousands of demands on the president's time, I wondered how he knew how to be so effective with a Vietnamese Party leader. President Obama had clearly prepared for this meeting.

Scheduled for forty-five minutes, the Oval Office meeting lasted twice that long and broke historic ground. The president and general secretary issued a joint statement after the meeting that included a commitment to "respect . . . each other's political systems," the most important line in the document for the Vietnamese. The two leaders made other significant commitments, such as continuing party-to-party dialogues, dioxin cleanup, human rights, educational exchange, and finishing TPP negotiations.

At a State Department lunch, Vice President Joe Biden said, "Thank heaven we are here today. To see the sun through parting fog and clouds" (*Trời còn để có hôm nay. Tan sương đầu ngõ vén mây giữa trời*). Biden's use of a quote from *Truyện Kiều* (The Tale of Kieu), Nguyễn Du's epic poem, followed the respectful example President Clinton had set in his Hanoi remarks in 2000. Later, when Dr. Jill Biden visited Hanoi, Vietnam's First Lady Mai Thị Hạnh greeted her at the Temple of Literature with a traditional conical hat woven by local women in Huế. When held up to the light, the hat revealed the words spoken by Vice President Biden at the State Department.

The next day, Trọng spoke at the Center for Strategic and International Studies and stressed that when the United States and Vietnam work together on matters of mutual interest, we build trust. I heard echoes of the ideas that Vice Minister Ngọc and I had advanced in the previous months. Just before the speech, Trọng asked me what I thought of the meeting with President Obama. Remembering that he had been a teacher, I gave it a grade: "A plus." The normally reticent general secretary flashed a rare smile.

In their joint statement, President Obama and General Secretary Trọng agreed that Vietnam would grant an investment license for Fulbright University's establishment in Hồ Chí Minh City, and another breakthrough occurred on July 10 in New York City. After twenty-three years of success with the Fulbright Economics Teaching Program, Congress had agreed to provide seed funds for a new university, again bearing the Fulbright name. Congress insisted that the school be nonprofit and independent (that is, it had to have transparent and autonomous governance) and that it should enjoy American-style academic freedom. At the Waldorf Hotel in New York, with Politburo members and government ministers as witnesses, General Secretary Trọng declared that Fulbright University would have full academic freedom and autonomous governance. This was more than we had expected from the Party's chief ideologue. Previously, universities in Vietnam had been permitted to teach only what the Party approved.

Fulbright University would be licensed as a Vietnamese institution rather than a foreign implant, and the government in Hanoi recognized that granting autonomy and promising academic freedom had significant implications for Party control over what students learned. The Hồ Chí Minh City government not only granted the university an investment license that enabled its incorporation, but also donated fifteen hectares of land worth more than

$20 million, where the campus would be built. Translating that verbal promise into an operating license and written guarantee took three more years of concerted, high-level effort. Yet Trọng's declaration of academic freedom and autonomy marked a huge shift, especially because the commitment occurred at the Party's highest level.

Every U.S. ambassador to Vietnam must meet with Vietnamese Americans living in Orange County, California, where shopping centers fly the yellow flag that once flew over South Vietnam. In Little Saigon, it's easier to find *phở* than tacos.

Two days after General Secretary Trọng completed his stop in New York City, I visited Little Saigon. Flanked by local political leaders and members of Congress from both parties—Dana Rohrabacher, Ed Royce, Loretta Sanchez, and Alan Lowenthal—I spoke in Vietnamese with five hundred community members, hoping to learn their concerns. I began by poking fun at my Hanoi accent, giving the southerners permission to laugh and to ask questions in their mother tongue.

When Ed Royce, chairman of the House Foreign Relations Committee, whispered, "good job, Ambassador," I began to relax. Afterward, young and old people approached to shake hands or take a photo with me. One woman asked if she could drape her yellow flag around my shoulders. I smiled and declined, because a photo of me with that flag would not have played well back in Hanoi.

An older man stepped up, seized my lapels, and in clear Vietnamese said, "I spent eleven years in a reeducation camp." His nose near my face, he dared me to respond. I mumbled words of sympathy and asked if I could do anything for him.

"I spent eleven years in a reeducation camp," he repeated. Confused, I asked again, "How can I help?" A third time, he said, "I spent *eleven years* in a reeducation camp." Suddenly, it was clear. He wanted those eleven years back.

This man may have been forty years old when Saigon fell. He spent half his life fighting for a country that no longer existed, followed by eleven years in a horrific place, where jailers beat into him their truth—that he had fought on behalf of a corrupt, spent regime. They told him that real Vietnamese patriots fought for the north, for independence. He had found his way to a new country, the United States, only to face the pain of watching Washington and Hanoi reconcile and seeing his young relatives visit Hồ Chí Minh City along with the other tourists, investors, and businesspeople flocking there.

I promised him that I would do all I could to ensure that his children, and his children's children, would face a different future. Reconciliation was good for Vietnam and the United States, but I understood that this man had lost so much that reconciliation was not possible for him.

My encounter with the woman in Orange County who asked to drape her flag around my shoulders was not the last time I faced the potent symbolism of flags. When I visited the Vietnamese American community in San Jose, I told my hosts: "I am accredited to a country with a red flag. If I am to be successful in addressing the challenges your community cares about—human rights, religious freedom, reconciliation—I would prefer not to be photographed with the yellow flag of the Republic of Vietnam. It will harm my ability to work with the government in Hanoi and carry out my duties."

This request somehow morphed into an instruction that people coming to hear me speak could not display the yellow flag. I explained: "I respect your right to display the yellow flag, the flag for which some of you fought. I ask that you respect my request not to be photographed with it, as that would reduce my effectiveness as ambassador."

My carefulness about not being photographed with the yellow flag wasn't enough to solve the problem. A few days later, the president of the Vietnamese American Community of the USA wrote an outraged letter to Secretary of State John Kerry and members of Congress, asking that I be replaced as ambassador.

In Vietnam, attempts had been made to display the yellow flag in Biên Hòa Cemetery, the primary burial site for southern soldiers. The men and women buried there had lost their lives fighting for the country symbolized by that yellow flag. The Vietnamese Americans in San Jose wanted me to show respect to their flag.

During my preparations before being confirmed as ambassador, I watched Rory Kennedy's film, *Last Days in Vietnam*.[4] Kennedy had unearthed never-before-seen footage from a veteran's attic that showed U.S. and South Vietnamese soldiers on a boat in the South China Sea, headed away from Vietnam after Saigon had fallen. As the boat entered Philippine waters, crew members lowered the South Vietnamese flag and raised the Stars and Stripes. Those Vietnamese soldiers and civilians must have been struck by a profound sadness when the flag they fought for was pulled down for the last time.

The red flag with a yellow star, flown throughout Vietnam today as a symbol of patriotic nationalism, plays a significant role in reconciliation, but so does the old yellow flag of the Republic of Vietnam. I asked Hanoi officials if it would be possible to show respect to the yellow flag as a heritage symbol.

Most found that idea irritating, if not threatening. They wanted to see the yellow flag retired for good. Only the passage of time would lessen the flag's symbolic importance for the victors as well as the vanquished.

The Vietnamese American Community of the USA was based in Texas, and its determined attempts to have me replaced because of the flag incident in San Jose were so impassioned that I decided to visit Houston, where many of the Vietnamese American community's hard-core opponents of reconciliation lived.

A member of the Houston City Council kindly brought together members of the Vietnamese American community, including elders and young members of the business community. I made the case for continued U.S. engagement with Vietnam and outlined my goals for relations between the two countries. I spoke directly about some of our failures in promoting free expression and the kinds of political freedom enjoyed by citizens in most countries in the world.

I also took questions, some friendly, others pointed and critical. An older woman spoke up: "Ambassador, we hear what you're trying to do. So tell us, what can we do to help?"

Asking that question publicly in Houston took courage. The Vietnamese American community there, as in other places, was deeply divided between those who wished to engage with Vietnam and those who thought engagement with an old enemy was too painful.

"If you want to enable young Vietnamese to have options that you didn't have," I replied, "then invest in education, or help develop the private sector in Vietnam, or support an NGO [nongovernmental organization] that engages in health care. My first choice, however, is education. It's not political, and it will transform the future. The most important effort we can make to build a long-term foundation [for relations] between the American and Vietnamese people is to engage in educational exchange and to support improvement in Vietnam's higher educational system."

I don't know if I won over the skeptics, but everyone clapped politely, and the session ended. The students I had taught in 1996 had shown that nothing was impossible as long as they had a world-class education. And even those who remained bitter about the past and were unsure about reconciliation demonstrated that they were ready and willing to support educating the next generation in Vietnam.

In the months after Trọng's visit to the Oval Office, every member of the Vietnamese government and Party, from the Hanoi leadership to the provincial level, was required to study the Obama-Trọng joint statement. Television commentators read on air every word of the text that our teams had negotiated. Analysts thought that Prime Minister Dũng had succeeded in persuading Trọng, the hard-liner, to accept America's key demand—ending the Communist Party's monopoly on labor unions and organized labor—in exchange for entry into the TPP. Most Politburo watchers thought that Dũng was on the rise and Trọng would fade away after the twelfth Party Congress in January 2016.

I continued to be persuaded of this, and two months after Trọng's visit to Washington, I attended a celebration of Vietnam's seventieth National Day, hosted by Dũng. Ten of the Party's sixteen Politburo members attended, as did virtually all the members of the prime minister's cabinet. In a grand banquet hall, with five hundred guests attending, Dũng made a beeline for me. "We need to wrap up negotiations soon," he insisted. "We need a market access offer on textiles and footwear that matches what the EU [European Union] offered in its free trade agreement with Vietnam."

The prime minister then took me around the room, introducing me to dignitaries and insisting that we toast each one. After pressing an enormous glass of red wine into my hand, he looked me in the eye and dared me: "*trăm phần trăm*" (literally, "100 percent"). This meant I had to down the entire glass. "*Trăm phần trăm*," I agreed, and watched him drink his glass as I drained mine. My only regret was that I could not savor the wine.

Negotiations concluded a month later, on October 5. Though a few details still needed to be made final, it appeared that Vietnam was in the TPP.

Just before the Party Congress, Prime Minister Dũng was deposed, driven out of the Politburo in a series of back-room maneuvers. Quiet, low-key General Secretary Trọng surprised most observers with his moves. Dũng may have been as surprised as anyone. One of the most influential leaders in Vietnam's modern history, he managed to extract promises that his family would be shielded from repercussions. He retreated to the south, and Trọng began to drive out of the Party anyone he saw as too loyal to Dũng. A seismic political shift had taken place, and once again the Party, not the government, was firmly in control in Vietnam. While Dũng was prime minister, the government and National Assembly called the shots, but that period had come to an end. The Party and Politburo were back in charge, as they had been for most of the period since the war.

I realized that Trọng had concluded—independently of Dũng—that America did not intend to undercut the Party's primacy. Trọng's visit to

Washington persuaded him and other hard-liners that joining the TPP was essential for Vietnam to preserve its autonomy and increase its prosperity. In a February 2016 side letter to the TPP, Vietnam formally agreed that it would "meet the requirements and procedures for establishing a labour union, organize a labour union and undertake labour union activities once organized, including to bargain collectively, strike, and conduct labour-related collective activities under the [1998] ILO Declaration [of Fundamental Principles and Rights at Work]."[5]

This carefully worded concession effectively ended the Communist Party's monopoly on labor unions and organized labor. Unions could be independent of the Party and could associate freely with other labor unions in Vietnam and around the world.

Trọng's commitment on workers' rights was the biggest human rights concession Vietnam had ever made. Joining the TPP also represented a huge step in the direction of greater prosperity for Vietnam and greater independence for Asian TPP members' economies from the rapacious, mercantilist policies of China.

In the two years after Trọng's Oval Office meeting, our embassy team succeeded in expanding bilateral collaboration in multiple areas, including security, education, science and technology, health, and the environment. The most important was trade. Vietnam had entered the TPP because Ambassador Mike Froman, the U.S. trade representative, had been able to use President Obama's meeting with Trọng to complete the final details.

Facilitating Trọng's meeting with President Obama was the most consequential accomplishment of my tenure. The president's visit to Vietnam in 2016 was also significant, but it would not have been as substantive or meaningful if Trọng had not first visited the United States. Some commentators have suggested that the visit to Washington boosted Trọng's flagging political fortunes,[6] and others said the visit gave Trọng legitimacy as a leader that he could not have attained in a nation with a parliamentary system. At a minimum, Trọng's trip enabled successful U.S.-Vietnamese summits in 2016 and 2017, because each high-level visit built on previous ones.

11

The Notorious RBG

•   •   •   •   •   •   •   •   •   •   •   •   •

When we learned that Supreme Court Justice Ruth Bader Ginsburg and her daughter, Jane, would be visiting us in August 2015, a friend on our embassy team encouraged me to write and ask if she might officiate at a brief ceremony to renew Clayton's and my marriage vows. She replied that she would be delighted.

Justice Ginsburg's visit came a few weeks after the Supreme Court decision in *Obergefell v. Hodges*, which said that our union would be recognized in all fifty states. At a press conference in our home, Ginsburg held in her hands a worn copy of the U.S. Constitution. Asked about the *Obergefell* decision, she described the history of marriage equality that led up to the Supreme Court's historic decision. "Change began in the states," she said, "starting with Massachusetts. Then the Supreme Court heard a case involving a criminal law penalizing same-sex relations. The Supreme Court decided that was unconstitutional."

She continued, "The next case to come to the Court involved the law of another state in which LGBT people could not be protected by antidiscrimination laws. The Supreme Court declared that, too, was unconstitutional. You cannot take one group of people and put them outside the protection of the law. By the time the Court decided the *Obergefell* case, there were already small steps in the direction of marriage equality, and a good number of states had recognized it. So the Supreme Court was taking not a large step but one further step in the direction that was begun at least ten years earlier."

PHOTO 23 Supreme Court Justice Ruth Bader Ginsburg, the author, and Clayton Bond holding TABO, Hanoi, August 2015 (Credit: Lisa Bess Wishman).

Ginsburg argued that social change began at the state level, and that's what made it broadly acceptable. She was not arguing that Vietnam should follow the United States in making marriage equality the law of the land. For her audience in Hanoi, she concluded, simply, that social change leads to legal change.

We hoped that by having Ginsburg renew our vows, we could show the people of Vietnam that it was possible for LGBT+ people to have families. I held our nineteen-month-old son in my arms during the ceremony, and when his five-month-old sister began to cry, a caretaker held her out of sight of the friends and colleagues who had gathered.

Ten years before, when Clayton and I first took our vows, they mattered mostly just to the two of us. This time, those vows also mattered to two small people who are like our hearts beating outside our bodies.

When I placed a ring on Clayton's finger and reaffirmed my commitment "to have and to hold . . . from this day forward through all our life together," our son decided to lunge from my arms into Clayton's. Those vows have only grown in significance because of how fiercely we love our children, and because we know better now what marriage means.

My friend Thảo Nguyễn Griffiths had invited us to bring Ginsburg and her daughter to the gallery of a talented expressionist painter, Nguyễn Thanh Chương. Thảo held Ginsburg's hand as we toured Chương's studio. The justice took home not only a magnificent painting but, she said, "a friend for life" in Thảo.

Toward the end of a reception after the renewal of our wedding vows, Ginsburg pulled Thảo aside and said, "Thảo, sometimes in life you meet somebody, and the chemistry just works. You are one of those people. I want to tell you that I LOVE YOU!"

According to Thảo, Ginsburg gave her "the most loving and tight hug ever." Thảo added, "Tears just came down my cheeks!"

Ginsburg also met with Vietnam's Supreme Court justices and talked about the changes taking place in Vietnam. She held that same copy of the Constitution that I had seen during the press conference, and she referred to it several times. At no point did Ginsburg urge the Vietnamese justices to follow the United States on marriage equality or other matters. However, she did cite examples of judicial decisions that strengthened the rule of law in Singapore, Romania, Turkey, and the United States.

In every meeting she had, Ginsburg showed respect for Vietnam's decisions that shaped its future. American society is not perfect—and neither is Vietnam's—but this wise justice suggested that our two societies still might learn from each other.

Vietnam's 2013 constitution provides for free speech, free assembly, the right of access to information, and the right of association. It envisions a fair and equal justice system. Article 3 states: "The State shall guarantee and promote the People's right to mastery; recognize, respect, protect, and guarantee human rights and citizens' rights; and pursue the goal of a prosperous people and a strong, democratic, equitable, and civilized country, in which all people enjoy an abundant, free, and happy life and are given conditions for their comprehensive development."[1]

Vietnam's constitution is an aspirational document, and efforts to have the country's laws conform with it have been uneven. Days before Ginsburg arrived, Party General Secretary Nguyễn Phú Trọng told Secretary of State John Kerry that Vietnam "intended to synchronize its laws to the Constitution." Previously, when Senator John McCain's delegation visited, National Assembly Chairman Nguyễn Sinh Hùng and Minister of Public Security Trần Đại Quang had used the same words. Hùng had said that in amending its laws, Vietnam showed that it was trying to create a legal and political foundation for progress. Quang had added, "We are focused on balancing social order with individual rights." He noted that when Vietnam amended its penal code, the country had reduced the number of crimes that could lead to the death penalty.

In the summer of 2015, after participating in a two-week leadership seminar at Harvard University, Nguyễn Thị Kim Ngân, the vice chair of the National Assembly (who later became its chair and one of Vietnam's top three leaders) invited me to dinner. She had visited a Boston courthouse, where she had watched the trial of Dzhokhar Tsarnaev, the Boston Marathon bomber.

"Did you know, Ambassador, that the jury in such trials is made up of ordinary citizens?" she asked. I confirmed that the U.S. Constitution makes that a part of our justice system.

"Did you know that the judge is independent and expected to be impartial?" Yes, I nodded.

"Did you know that in the United States, it is hard to bribe a judge?" Surprised by this line of reasoning, I told her I knew that.

Excited, Ngân turned to her aides: "We can learn from this. In Vietnam, we can do this, too."

I took this to mean that our efforts to encourage judicial and legal reform in Vietnam were at long last getting somewhere. U.S. diplomats had worked for years to build trust with the Vietnamese leaders who drafted the laws. That autumn the National Assembly considered a Law on Belief and Religion that incorporated many ideas provided by U.S. legal and religious experts. In November, the National Assembly enacted a Civil Code that also included suggestions from the United States and the U.N. Development Program.

We were not always successful. The Penal Code, which in 2015 was drafted and shepherded through the assembly by the Ministry of Public Security, included many provisions that conflicted with Vietnam's constitution and its international commitments. Still, the United States continued providing training to Vietnamese police to strengthen adherence to the rule of law. We hoped over time to encourage the adoption of laws that respected individual rights and a commitment by the security services to respect such laws. It was a long-term effort.

In the late eighteenth century, America's first diplomat, Benjamin Franklin, pleaded with the French king to protect our young nation's natural right to freedom from oppression. The U.S. Declaration of Independence asserts that "to secure these rights, Governments are instituted among Men, deriving their just powers from the consent of the governed." Ginsburg likely would have added "and among women."

My mother, who was in her eighties, joined our family twice during our tour of duty. Her visit in late August 2015 coincided with Vietnam's commemoration of Mother's Day, the country's second most important traditional holiday. Celebrated on the fifteenth day of the seventh lunar month, the *Vu Lan* festival is an opportunity to show filial piety, as well as a time when lost souls can seek mercy. During this period, wandering souls are believed to return to their former homes.

My sister Alison and I took our mother and my son to the Pháp Vân pagoda in Hanoi. I thought it was a way to show respect for freedom of religion while also honoring Vietnam's traditions. Torrential rain fell as we climbed out of the embassy van, and I tried to protect my toddler from the deluge. A press photo—father and son under an umbrella in a downpour—appeared in many newspapers, on television, and online.

We joined the monks as they prayed for relief from suffering, especially for mothers and fathers, and urged children to treat their parents with respect. Each monk and nun held a flower—red if their parents were living and white if they were deceased. The monks directed my sister and me to present to our mother a red *áo dài* and then pour tea for her.

This visit to the Pháp Vân pagoda had a durable impact. I learned later that for three years in a row, Prime Minister Nguyễn Tấn Dũng and then his successor, Nguyễn Xuân Phúc, told Vietnamese diplomats assembled for an annual conference to pay attention to the lessons of the American ambassador at the *Vu Lan* festival and releasing carp before Tết. "Show respect for traditions," both prime ministers said, "and you will bring good fortune to Vietnam." This was a powerful reminder that showing respect—a simple investment of a few hours—could provide a real boost to diplomatic efforts.

From my first day at the embassy, I told our nine hundred staff members, "we are all human rights officers." I wanted every member of our team to know that America's human rights requests for Vietnam were written on the card that was always in my shirt pocket. The government of Vietnam certainly knew, because its members saw me regularly draw the card from my pocket in meetings with relevant officials, and I made sure that the television cameras caught me referring to it.

PHOTO 24 Nancy Osius Zimmerman, Alison Osius, and the author at the *Vu Lan* Festival in Pháp Vân pagoda, Hanoi, August 2015 (Credit: Trần Thanh Giang).

Even so, America's approach to human rights in Vietnam had yielded limited success. A harmful pattern had developed. In advance of a visit by a high-level U.S official, the Vietnamese would release one or sometimes two people referred to as prisoners of conscience. These brave individuals would generally arrive at Dulles Airport near Washington, DC, sometimes with their families accompanying them. The United States would then hail the release as progress, and after the visit had been forgotten, the Vietnamese would arrest another activist. It was a disappointing and frustrating cycle.

In October 2014, the Vietnamese released an activist blogger named Nguyễn Văn Hải, who was better known as Điếu Cày. He was exiled to the United States, and when I met him in California, I found him sad and withdrawn. Exile, for an activist and a patriot, can be painful.

Tạ Phong Tần, a former police officer, was arrested in 2011 for writing about human rights and corruption on her blog. Under article 88 of the penal code—governing the dissemination of antistate propaganda—Tần was sentenced to ten years in prison in the same trial when Điếu Cày was convicted.

Tần was released in September 2015, not long after General Secretary Trọng's successful meeting with President Barack Obama in the Oval Office. The Communist Party and government in Hanoi knew that the U.S.

Congress would take a careful look at Vietnam's human rights record when it considered ratifying the Trans-Pacific Partnership (TPP) trade agreement.

The number of arrests of dissident bloggers fell sharply in 2015 and, by November, the number of political prisoners of all kinds had dropped to a historic low. I thought that Vietnam's pending entry into the TPP had moderated its behavior. Indeed, I regularly showed letters from members of Congress to Vietnam's prime minister and other leaders, reminding them that for Vietnam to join the TPP, Congress would have to vote in favor of its inclusion in the trade agreement. Therefore, members of Congress who cared about human rights in Vietnam had a say in the country's future. The linkage between Vietnam's TPP ambitions and its human rights record seemed to be working.

I tried to combine cycling trips with my attempts to celebrate Vietnam's history and culture before communism. Not only was this fun, but it was also effective diplomacy that contributed to the gradual process of reconciliation. On November 16, my trusty biking companion, Thảo, arranged a bicycle tour to the Temple of the Hùng Kings, eighteen kings belonging to the Hồng Bàng dynasty (c. 2879–258 BCE), which had ruled over the northern part of modern Vietnam. Their progenitors were Lạc Long Quân and his consort, Âu Cơ, the dragon and fairy whose union was part of the creation myth of Vietnam.

We biked to the temple of An Dương Vuong, who according to folklore defeated the last of the Hùng kings in 257 BCE and founded the kingdom of Âu Lạc, choosing as his capital the site of Cổ Loa, in the northern floodplain of the Red River Delta. Thảo and I also bicycled to Cổ Loa and explored the ancient capital. King Vuong chose this location after difficulties in a previous location had to be resolved by a golden turtle.

Thảo created other bicycle trips for us throughout the autumn, and she once described another origin myth featuring a significant animal. By the tenth century CE, Vietnam's capital had shifted again, this time to the city of Hoa Lư, in Ninh Bình province. A white horse appeared to Emperor Lý Thái Tổ in a dream, urging him to move the citadel—a complex of historic imperial buildings—from Hoa Lư to Thăng Long, which became the center of Vietnam's capital city, Hanoi. The capital and the citadel have remained there for a thousand years.

I was encouraged that, for a few months, the linkage between the TPP and human rights appeared to be working. Unfortunately, in December 2015, a month before Vietnam's twelfth Party Congress, that apparent success came to an end. An unprecedented number of officials with law enforcement experience were jockeying for senior positions. They overruled those who were more concerned about pleasing the international community and improving prospects for economic integration.

December 16, 2015, was the worst day of my tenure as ambassador, because that's when I heard that Nguyễn Văn Đài, a prominent human rights lawyer and blogger, had been arrested on the charge of disseminating antistate propaganda, the same charge levied against Tần and Điếu Cày before him. Đài was arrested as he was about to give a talk on the Universal Declaration of Human Rights. Đài's "crime" was considered to be a national security offense under article 88 of the penal code and could mean as much as 3–20 years in prison.

I knew Đài and his wife, Vũ Minh Khánh. She told me that she had visited the police station where Đài was being held five times in the six days since his arrest and had requested access to her husband so she could give him food and water. The police refused, saying that with national security cases such as Đài's, no one could have access to the accused until an investigation had been completed.

Khánh asked me to press for Đài's immediate release and requested my help in letting her visit him in prison with food and clothing. She also wanted Đài's lawyers to be able to meet with him. Đài was a religious man, and Khanh knew that he would want to read scripture, so I gave her my childhood Bible and wrote to him on the inside cover in Vietnamese: "*Xin Thiên Chúa là nguồn hy vọng, ban cho anh em được chan chứa niềm vui và bình an nhờ đức tin, để nhờ quyền năng của Thánh Thần, anh em được tràn trề hy vọng (Rô-ma 15:13). Hy vọng cuốn Kinh Thánh này sẽ mang lại cho anh niềm vui nho nhỏ* (May the God of hope fill you with all joy and peace as you trust in him, so that you may overflow with hope by the power of the Holy Spirit [Romans 15:13]. I hope this Bible will bring to you some comfort.)" The authorities refused all of Khánh's requests and never gave him my Bible.

I issued personal and public statements criticizing the government for Đài's arrest. At the same time, I also protested violent assaults—most likely carried out by police—against two labor activists, Hoàng Đức Bình and Đỗ Thị Minh Hạnh, who had visited my home and shown me horrific wounds and bruises inflicted by the police.

"This disturbing trend, at this time, threatens to overshadow Vietnam's progress on human rights in recent years," I wrote on social media and said to the press. "I urge the Vietnamese government to investigate reports of these assaults immediately and to hold accountable any officials responsible."

The government was using a common tactic of having thugs follow, threaten, and sometimes attack activists who were critical of the regime.

When I posted my statements on Facebook, thousands of people responded. I expected the government to shut down my Facebook page, but it remained online.

In January 2016, on the eve of the twelfth Party Congress, I spoke out about what was happening:

> [The] TPP has the potential to dramatically improve Vietnam's economy. It's also a powerful symbol of the success of Vietnam's international integration process. However, I fear that continued reports of harassment and detentions of peaceful human rights advocates could place Vietnam in very real jeopardy of losing TPP, and all that it symbolizes. My sincere wish is that Vietnam's leaders recognize what is at stake. The world is watching Vietnam. The U.S. Congress is watching Vietnam, too. And many of its members have made it clear that they will weigh this country's human rights record when they vote on whether to include Vietnam in TPP. I say this as a friend of Vietnam. Vietnam should not lose its place among TPP member countries because this country's leaders decided it was more important to harass and arrest peaceful human rights advocates.[2]

In the short term, this approach didn't work. At this Party Congress, Dũng was ousted and General Secretary Trọng assumed power, bringing about a seismic power shift from the government back to the Party.

Soon after the Party Congress adjourned, the authorities brought the blogger Nguyễn Hữu Vinh (also known as Anh Ba Sàm) to trial, a year and a half after his arrest for defamation of the state. Anh Ba Sàm's father had been a prominent Party leader, government minister, and ambassador to the Soviet Union, but family ties did not protect the blogger. After another postponement, the trial took place in March, and he was sentenced to five years in prison.

In February, I was joined by the Australian and Canadian ambassadors and the European Union's chargé d'affaires in a meeting with Vietnam's minister of public security. We pushed for Đài's freedom and the release of Anh Ba Sàm and other prisoners of conscience. We asked for a moratorium on the harassment of activists. We argued for legal reform, especially of the penal code. We named names and called for free expression on the internet and free association for members of civil society organizations.

A ministry press release afterward stated that we had enjoyed a lovely conversation, with no mention of any of the subjects we had discussed. Even though this was standard practice after meetings with Vietnamese government officials, the Australian ambassador wrote: "On the one hand amusing in its shamelessness. On the other, insulting in, effectively, throwing it in our faces with an implicit 'this is what we say it was and what can you do about it?'"[3] Canada's ambassador also commented about the government's press release, "There appears to be a parallel world out there somewhere."[4]

I shared their frustration while still believing that it might be effective to join hands with like-minded ambassadors when seeking to influence Vietnam's leaders. The European Union was negotiating its own free trade agreement, and the United States, Australia, and other countries were negotiating the TPP, which gave us a kind of leverage that, at least in principle, could help us pressure Vietnam to make progress on human rights.

I compared notes with other ambassadors in monthly meetings, and our staffs met weekly and reported back to us. I also reached out to ambassadors from countries in East and South Asia, Africa, and Latin America. Together, we pressured Vietnam to free political prisoners such as Đặng Xuân Diệu, who was released and exiled to France in January 2017. The work was slow and frustrating, but no one ever argued that we should give up.

Đài was held without bail for more than two years, and no one was ever brought to justice for the police assaults on the labor activists Bình and Hạnh. Anh Ba Sàm remained in jail.

The crackdown on dissent by Vietnamese authorities after the twelfth Party Congress in early 2016 had dampened the hopes of many people for political change. This tightened grip mirrored a similar clampdown by China's Communist Party.

The press had begun referring to Đỗ Nguyễn Mai Khôi as Vietnam's Lady Gaga. A talented singer and songwriter and a strong supporter of LGBT+ rights, Mai Khôi seemed to enjoy provoking the authorities. Commenting on her star power, ABC News said, "She's been called the Lady Gaga of Vietnam, but Mai Khôi arguably has less in common with Gaga than the Russian activist group, Pussy Riot."[5]

Born in 1983, Mai Khôi has been playing music since she was twelve years old. In 2010, her song "Vietnam" won the country's top song-writing award, and she became a celebrated pop star. She used her fame to push for creative freedom and, gradually, for political freedom. As she grew as an artist, Mai Khôi's lyrics became more provocative. "We just want to be free," she sang. "Want the right to be human, living free from tyranny. We want to stop our fear of authoritarianism."[6] When she stopped submitting her lyrics to the censors, her performances were effectively banned, and she was blacklisted.

I invited Mai Khôi to join us for a few U.S. embassy events. She sang at my birthday party, and I met her Australian husband, Ben, and began to think of her as a younger sister. I worried that she would be tossed into jail.

In early 2016, Mai Khôi nominated herself as an independent candidate for Vietnam's National Assembly. The Vietnam Fatherland Front, a Party organ that oversees civil society, disqualified her from participating in the election. That spring, she joined the street protests over an environmental disaster in coastal Hà Tĩnh province that had been caused by a Taiwanese company. The police violence she witnessed in that demonstration affected Mai Khôi deeply and led her to write a song about it, "Cuffed in Freedom."

After naming her band Mai Khôi and the Dissidents, the singer realized that she had crossed a line with the authorities, and she changed the band's name to Mai Khôi Chém Gió (a sardonic name that translates as boasting or exaggerating) when her next album, *Dissent*, was released. "We decided to change because their [members of the band's] families didn't want them performing under that name. In Vietnam, dissidents are talked about on the news like they're enemies of the state," she told Al Jazeera.[7]

Mai Khôi arranged to be in the United States when the album was released. She waited a few weeks before returning to Vietnam. As she expected, the police arrested her upon her arrival in Hanoi, and she was detained for eight hours.

Dissent is autobiographical and it contains social commentary. It charts the artist's moment of political awakening and personal transition from outlandish celebrity to dedicated songwriter and social activist. Compositions such as "Please Sir," "Reeducation Camp," and "Cuffed in Freedom" are explicitly political.

"You won't do anyone any good rotting in a jail cell," I told her.

We took photos together and posted them on social media. I hoped that her having a few photos with the American ambassador, as well as a few with other ambassadors, would make the authorities think twice before arresting her. Still, I warned her, "If you are arrested, don't imagine that I can get you freed." I didn't want Mai Khôi to think that international support would inoculate her if she continued crossing the Party's and government's red lines.

Most of Vietnam, especially in its large cities, has seen significant advancement of freedom to worship. Unfortunately, in some of the country's provinces, especially remote and rural ones, religious practices are still curtailed. In mountainous Lào Cai province, on the Chinese border—where I traveled with Assistant Secretary Tom Malinowski and David Saperstein, the U.S.

ambassador for international religious freedom—we visited a Catholic church, where priests showed us a new and handsome annex.

I admired the ten stained-glass windows depicting the stations of the cross. "Yes, we're happy about these windows," a local priest said, somewhat sheepishly. "But when we applied for permission to show the fourteen stations of the cross, local officials told us we could only install ten."

How stupid. Local officials, in some attempt to show the church who was in charge, had merely demonstrated their thuggishness and ignorance.

During my confirmation hearings, Senator Marco Rubio, a member of the Senate Foreign Relations Committee, had expressed concern about religious freedom in Vietnam. During our exchange, I had promised to seek the freedom of Nguyễn Công Chính, a pastor who had been arrested in 2011 in the central highlands province of Gia Lai. Chính had been sentenced to eleven years in prison for undermining national unity.

I raised Chính's case during my first meeting with Prime Minister Dũng and continued to do so after that. I discussed his imprisonment with other Politburo members, and I asked Ambassador Mike Froman, the U.S. trade representative, to highlight Chính's case during TPP negotiations.

I also tried bicycle diplomacy. I rode with students from Tây Nguyên University (in the central highlands) through coffee and cocoa plantations, and along the central coast through fishing villages. My team and I discussed Chính's case with leaders in Gia Lai province, telling them how important it was to Rubio and other members of the U.S. Congress. Prime Minister Phúc's May 2017 visit to Washington is what finally led to some movement. Five days before the prime minister was to meet with President Donald Trump, the Vietnamese government allowed a member of our consulate staff to visit Chính in prison, and the pastor requested asylum.

Before departing for the United States on July 28, 2017, the pastor's wife, who had also endured a terrible six years, told our team that she did not believe her husband would have survived to see his children grow up if he had not been released early. Chính and others like him should not have been arrested in the first place. His work was pastoral, not political, but it seemed the authorities objected because he ministered to ethnic minority Christians. (Others in the ethnic minority communities were animists.)

When I biked through the central highlands or traveled in the mountainous north, I often asked questions of the people I met along the road or path. I discovered that many members of ethnic minority communities had to spend the first years of school being instructed not in the ethnic minority Ba Na, H'mong, or Thái languages spoken in their communities, but rather in

Vietnamese, which was part of a government effort to mainstream minority peoples. That meant these early years of instruction were a waste for the children. The practice of teaching children in a language that was not their native tongue—coupled with widespread malnutrition—condemned them to an unbreakable cycle of poverty. Discrimination was real and evident, despite perfunctory efforts by Hanoi to alleviate it and boost economic activity in the highlands.

During the war, Americans referred to ethnic minority groups as "Montagnards," and most of them were Christian. U.S. Special Forces studied the tribal differences among the Montagnards in an attempt to work with them effectively. The South Vietnamese government didn't treat the Montagnards much better than the government in Hanoi does today. The presence of U.S. Special Forces helped attenuate some of the more overt discriminatory practices, but the prejudice against these groups by the vast majority of Vietnamese were strong then, and they still are.

In late 1997, when I first visited the central highland province of Kon Tum, it was two years after President Bill Clinton had established full diplomatic relations with Vietnam, and government minders took our group of diplomats to a large Roman Catholic cathedral known as the Wooden Church. Although the cathedral had been built in 1918, a French-speaking priest told us that Catholics had worshipped at the site for 150 years. Church placards were written in Ba Na, and the priest said that he conducted services using a Ba Na bible. He proudly pointed out a stained-glass window designed by a Ba Na artist.

Behind the cathedral was an even larger seminary, whose grand and ornate buildings were nearly empty. Three priests in their late seventies showed us around and bemoaned the lack of younger seminarians. The place seemed deserted except for the three of them.

I asked one of my travel companions, who had earlier served as a diplomat in Havana, Cuba, why the Vietnamese had brought us to this place. "They are showing it to us because they didn't burn it down," she said. "In other revolutions, the victors burned to the ground the monuments left behind by those who lost. In Cuba, Castro would have left nothing to remind people of the past."

As ambassador, I returned to the Wooden Church and seminary in September 2015, nearly twenty years after my first visit. Remarkably, it had been transformed and was bursting with priests of all ages. Seminarians passed between Kon Tum and their school in Nha Trang, a few hours away. One hundred fifty Ba Na ethnic minority children studied at the school. Many wore crosses around their necks, and they sang hymns.

Openness and religious freedom had begun to penetrate even the central highlands, where Christian Montagnards had joined the war's losing side. U.S. veterans and legislators, as well as Vietnamese Americans, cared about their fate. Each seminarian and each Ba Na student who studied Christianity contributed to the advancement of religious freedom and to reconciliation between the United States and Vietnam.

Members of Congress often wrote to me about the case of Thích Quảng Độ, leader of the Unified Buddhist Church of Vietnam (UBCV). The main Buddhist organization in south and central Vietnam prior to 1975, the UBCV has long faced persecution. In 1981, the government dissolved the UBCV and replaced it with the state-sponsored Vietnam Buddhist Church, but the UBCV refused to recognize the authority of the new organization.

Độ was in his nineties when he was released from prison in 1998 and confined to his monastery in Hồ Chí Minh City. I called on him at the monastery and asked about his religious teachings. The monk surprised me by instead speaking about his determination to replace Vietnam's Communist government with a democracy.

Later, I requested and received permission to meet Độ outside of his monastery. The city government said that Độ was welcome to leave the monastery at any time, but he did not have permission to preach. His sermons, officials maintained, were political exhortations, not religious teachings. Độ refused my invitation to meet outside of his monastery. He did not want to be seen walking freely with the U.S. ambassador, as that would have indicated a relaxation of the terms imposed upon him by Vietnamese authorities.

In 2016, Vietnam's National Assembly ratified the Law on Belief and Religion, easing some of the most onerous requirements placed on religious organizations to register with the government and report their activities. This change resulted from hundreds of hours of engagement with U.S. experts, who worked side by side with Vietnamese officials to draft and redraft the law.

The law was not perfect. The United States had been founded on the principle of religious freedom, and Americans preferred that no government registration be required for religious organizations. Still, our collaboration with Vietnamese officials on rewriting the law showed what could be accomplished when the United States built trust and took a practical approach to a challenge.

A number of religious leaders told me that they hoped to open primary schools and clinics to serve the poor in Vietnam. Nguyễn Thiện Nhân, the president of the Vietnam Fatherland Front, welcomed the idea of the Party allowing such steps and said that the Catholic Church and Buddhists had already created kindergartens. Primary schools were the logical next step. He also welcomed private clinics sponsored by religious organizations, as long as they had trained and certified doctors and nurses.

In 1996, when I first arrived in Vietnam, the internet was in its early days. As the *Wall Street Journal* reported in that year, "for a government accustomed to controlling what its citizens read, hear and watch, and suspicious about foreigners prying into Vietnam, the information age is a nightmare."[8] At that time, the government maintained tight control over Vietnam's approximately thirty thousand internet users. Vietnam Data Communications, the only internet access provider, used firewalls to block access to many sites.

When I returned as ambassador, I was astonished that the Vietnamese wrote pretty much whatever they wanted online. With more than seventy million internet users in Vietnam, and nearly sixty million Vietnamese on Facebook, it was far easier to communicate than in the past. Facebook was temporarily blocked in 2009, but so many users circumvented the ban that the government lifted it in 2011. Dialogue on the internet remained surprisingly free.

Vietnam's citizens enjoyed far broader civil liberties than in the 1990s, and this was more a result of Vietnam's rapid globalization and near-universal access to free discussion on Facebook and other internet forums than it was of any conscious action by the state. In January 2015, Prime Minister Dũng told officials that social media is "a necessity and cannot be banned," and he acknowledged that "you are all on social media, checking Facebook on your phones for information."[9] The prime minister encouraged the official use of Facebook for disseminating information and seeking public feedback.

The United States could support this trend. The Vietnamese government set up what it called the Government Information Portal (*Cổng Thông tin Chính phủ*), which quickly acquired 250,000 followers. It disseminated information on issues that mattered to Vietnamese citizens, such as food safety; the availability of water, electricity, and fuel; health insurance; traffic; education and training; and wages.

My Facebook page gradually acquired more than 100,000 followers, and I was able to use it to reach over the heads of Vietnam's leaders to its citizens. I engaged with them in their own language, and when I posted something, I received immediate feedback. Most of my followers were ages 18–34, and this access helped me learn what was of interest to young Vietnamese. Facebook users in Vietnam spend twice as much time online each day as they do watching television.[10]

Political activists and dissidents used platforms such as Facebook to discuss and share materials about human rights and democracy. That explains why the Party cracked down on bloggers like Anh Ba Sàm. I was so troubled by what was happening to those who spoke out that I went to the belly of the beast, the Hồ Chí Minh National Academy of Politics, where Party cadres go for ideological indoctrination. I told its leaders that Vietnam will achieve its greatest potential only when civil society can enjoy greater freedom to peacefully organize, freely exchange views on the internet and social media, and participate in policy making.[11]

Mai Khôi, in an expression of her devotion to freedom, wrote, "In the past, there was nowhere the Vietnamese people could go to express ourselves freely. Government control extended to every aspect of our social life. The advent of social media changed that. It provided a space where we could speak our minds, access uncensored information and organize peaceful protests."[12] She went on to criticize Facebook for "allowing its platform to be abused to divide and isolate people."

Vietnam had a healthy share of feisty journalists, even though most print and television media outlets were owned by the state. The Ministry of Information and Communications met regularly with news editors and issued instructions about which topics could be covered and which could not. In January 2015, at the Party's tenth plenum, leaders laid out a plan to increase state control over the media through 2025. General Secretary Trọng said that the Party and government would make investments in state-owned media, especially in their online and multimedia platforms, while explicitly banning private media.

Clayton and I hoped that having Ginsburg renew our marriage vows would influence Vietnam's evolving attitudes toward gay people. Just before our arrival in 2014, the National Assembly had approved changes to the law on family—changes that decriminalized same-sex marriage. *My Gay Best Friend* was one of the most popular shows on Vietnamese television, an indication that a delicate balancing act was playing out in a conservative society.

The Women's Union, a powerful mass organization with as many as forty million members, had argued that legalizing same-sex marriage threatened traditional Vietnamese values, and it successfully prevented the National

Assembly from taking such a bold step. But Facebook had more users than the Women's Union had members, and the younger generation was ready for change.

We met with leaders of Vietnam's LGBT+ community in Vietnam and, just as important, with some of their parents. Việt Pride celebrations had taken place in forty of Vietnam's sixty-three provinces and Parents and Friends of Lesbians and Gays had established chapters in Vietnam's large cities. We attended a few events aimed at promoting equality, where we learned that Vietnamese parents who were willing to speak up for their LGBT+ children were viewed with respect and sympathy by the general public.

As Ginsburg understood, Americans were not the ones to settle the debate about what kind of society the Vietnamese people wanted. The best way for us to promote inclusion was not by imposing our own values or trying to set an American agenda, but by following the lead of Vietnam's nascent civil society. Leaders of civil society organizations told us that their top two priorities were making it possible for transgender people to change their gender identities legally and supporting equality in the workplace.

The first goal was accomplished in 2015, when the National Assembly passed a new civil code that legalized gender transformation surgery and specified procedures to use in changing gender on ID cards. The legislation was supported by the Ministry of Justice, and it had been shepherded through by the U.S. Agency for International Development and the U.N. Development Program.

The second goal depended on having the private sector step up, and action on that began with foreign companies such as Citibank, Disney, Marriott, and the U.S. law firm Baker McKenzie. The consulting firm KPMG launched a LGBT+ employees' affinity group, not in response to pressure from below but because company managers wanted to recruit world-class talent, and employment discrimination made that harder.

Clayton and I had no precedent to guide us, so we did what seemed right: we showed up at events, granted interviews, and marched in annual Việt Pride parades. Twice, Hanoi's Pride parade took the form of a bicycle ride, and I had fun biking with other ambassadors, rainbow flags on our bikes. In our home, we displayed American artwork whose theme was drawn from President Obama's second inaugural address, in which he spoke about progress "through Seneca Falls, and Selma, and Stonewall."[13] We called the exhibit "Toward a More Perfect Union."

Not all of these activities went smoothly. We timed a visit to Hồ Chí Minh City to coincide with a Việt Pride march, but when city authorities heard that

PHOTO 25 Nienke Trooster, the Dutch ambassador to Vietnam; the author; and TABO biking in a Pride Parade, Hanoi, August 2015 (Credit: U.S. Department of State).

we were participating, they canceled the parade. The LGBT+ community there had worked hard to avoid being viewed as a political group, but getting the required permits from a skittish bureaucracy was difficult enough even when the U.S. ambassador wasn't participating. The city's leaders feared that having me there could lead to a larger-than-expected crowd that could turn into an unexpected protest against the Communist Party.

I met the People's Committee Chairman, Vietnam's equivalent of a mayor, and told him we'd already marched twice in Hanoi. "Is Hồ Chí Minh City less modern and open than Hanoi?" I asked. Quietly, the permit for the parade was granted.

Clayton and I debated how often to have our kids appear with us in public. We wanted to protect them. But we also knew that appearances by our curly-haired, cheerful, and photogenic kids seemed to mean a lot to Vietnam's LGBT+ youth. Most of those young people had never seen a happy family with two dads. We looked for opportunities when we could control how long the kids were exposed to crowds and the media, and when we could take them home quickly if we sensed that they were overwhelmed.

At a restaurant in Đà Nẵng, a young man approached our table. He said that he had seen us on television, and he realized that it might be possible for him, too, to have a career and family. Often, when we traveled outside of Hanoi, hotel staff members came over to us and said how inspired they were that we were visible. We received messages each week in person and on social media—mostly encouraging, occasionally discouraging—from the young people of Vietnam who were curious about a family with two dads.

Clayton is a cousin of the civil rights leader Julian Bond, and the quest for justice and equality is in his DNA. We both admired cousin Julian and his wife, Pam. Julian was the first leader of the civil rights movement to embrace marriage equality, and he recognized that equality for LGBT+ persons was the next phase of the civil rights movement. We accompanied Julian and Pam to a dinner of the Human Rights Campaign (the most influential LGBT+ advocacy group in the United States) at which Julian was guest of honor. I said how much I admired Julian's remarks, and Pam confessed that she had written the speech. "We collaborate on everything," she said. "I do the writing, and Julian gives my words meaning."

We saw Julian and Pam often during our son's first year, as we worked together to plan a family reunion. They regularly volunteered to babysit, understanding how liberating it feels to have a date night while raising an infant.

On August 15, 2015, I wrote to Pam, to provide love and support as she looked after her ailing husband. With no idea how serious Julian's illness was, I told Pam that Clayton and I considered their marriage, and their decades-long collaboration in the quest for civil rights, to be the embodiment of love and purpose. Love and purpose, I thought, were what made life its most meaningful. "We did have that, and I will be forever grateful even though it hurts like hell right now," Pam wrote back. "Julian died about an hour ago."

At Julian's funeral, Pam spoke bravely. The last speaker was Chad Griffin, president of the Human Rights Campaign. "Very few throughout human history have embodied the ideals of honor, dignity, courage, and friendship like Julian Bond," Chad said. "Quite simply, this nation and this world are far better because of his life and commitment to equality for all people. Future generations will look back on his life and legacy and see a warrior for good who helped conquer hate in the name of love."[14]

Clayton and I wanted love and purpose together in our union and our family, as Julian and Pam had had.

I was asked to speak about U.S.-Vietnam relations at a high school for gifted students in the former imperial capital of Huế, a school that counted among its graduates Hồ Chí Minh and General Võ Nguyên Giáp. During the question-and-answer session, a young woman asked what advice I could give to an aspiring actress whose dreams for her future differed from those of her parents. Remembering that students at the school faced many expectations from family members and teachers, I still told her what I thought was right: she must plot her own path.

A teenager stood up, looked squarely at me, and asked if I had encountered any difficulties in my life or career because I am gay. If he had the courage to ask this question in front of eight hundred of his peers, exposing himself to questions, he deserved a truthful answer.

"Yes," I told him, "I have encountered difficulties. When I first joined the Foreign Service, we could lose our jobs for being out. Because there is strength in numbers, we created a group, and we persuaded the State Department to stop discrimination based on sexual orientation. As American society grew more accepting, we insisted that our families be treated with the same respect as traditional families.

"In the group we created, I met the man I later married. While serving together in India, we went to a high-level reception. There, an elegant sari-clad woman asked Clayton about his wife. He pointed toward me, saying I was his spouse. Her eyes widened, and then she replied, 'You live your life.'

"In another conservative society, the world's biggest Muslim-majority nation, the Indonesian president hosted a state dinner for President and Mrs. Obama. Directed toward a table at the front, Clayton and I looked for cards that would tell us where to sit. One read, 'Ted Osius, Deputy Chief of Mission.' Next to it: 'Clayton Bond, spouse of the Deputy Chief of Mission.'

"Since we arrived in Vietnam, our family has received the warmest possible welcome. If I can draw a lesson from these experiences, it is that it is better to be who you are. I don't think happiness is possible any other way. Be who you are."

There was a moment of quiet. The young man who had asked the question smiled broadly. Then the applause began, and it lasted a while.

12

A New Journey

● ● ● ● ● ● ● ● ● ● ● ● ● ●

In early 2016, the U.S. embassy in Hanoi held a contest for a new slogan. We had wrung every drop of goodwill from the previous year's twentieth anniversary celebrations, and we needed something fresh and inspiring. We wanted to say that the relationship between the United States and Vietnam had reached a turning point and could focus on the future while respecting the past.

Four hundred of the embassy's Vietnamese Facebook followers contributed ideas, and our local staff members chose "U.S.-Vietnam: New Journey" (in Vietnamese, *Hành Trình Mới*). A local artist designed a logo showing a cyclist in front of the Vietnamese flag and a star-shaped American flag.

We planned a bike trip to highlight key themes of the relationship: educating the next generation, tackling health and environmental challenges, celebrating entrepreneurship and innovation, and respecting Vietnam's history while being honest about our difficult past.

When the big day came, the heavens opened, sending rain, sleet, and even snow down upon us. I love to bike, but I'm a fair-weather biker. I hate cycling in the rain, and I wasn't happy when our "new journey" to Huế began on the coldest day Hanoi had seen in forty years! The first snow ever recorded in Nghệ An province soaked us as we rode there.

I had encouraged twenty Vietnamese and American friends and colleagues to ride on our 525-mile journey, including a dear friend who flew to Vietnam from Washington, DC, twelve time zones away. Our team had trained for

PHOTO 26 The *Hành Trình Mới* logo (Credit: U.S. Department of State).

months and carefully set up more than twenty events in eight provinces: a
school opening; visits to businesses, temples, and mausoleums; and riding over
a historic bridge spanning the 17th parallel. But the weather gods were clearly
against us. It rained five of the seven days we biked. I could see from the first
day that the ride wasn't going to be easy, and it might not even be fun.

We began with a little damage control. We shortened our biking time on
the first and third days to protect our team's health and reduce the risk of
accidents when visibility was poor. No one complained, even when they were
cold and soaked. Our bus crew poured out mugs of hot chocolate and coffee.
We wrapped ourselves in garbage bags and ponchos. When rural hotels lacked
heat, an enterprising team member went out and purchased electric heaters,
which we later donated to an orphanage in Hà Tĩnh province.

In all eight provinces, we were welcomed so warmly that we forgot about
the cold. In Cúc Phương National Park, we learned about preserving the
world's most trafficked endangered species—the pangolin—and about
the efforts to protect critically threatened langur monkeys. In Thanh Hóa,
we visited a company committed to green growth that had invested millions
of dollars in bamboo plantations and a sugar cane factory. I planted a bamboo plant, a symbol of strength and persistence. Bamboo, which can grow in
any kind of weather, is important in Vietnam and is often used as a fence

around villages. Bamboo is also symbolic of community and solidarity because it grows in clumps rather than alone.

In Quảng Bình, we saw the glorious Phong Nha caves, part of the world's largest underground network. Our stop there was meant to highlight eco-tourism and the role it plays in promoting environmental awareness and pro-tection. This quick stop whetted our appetites for a future visit to Sơn Đoòng, the world's largest cave.

In Nghệ An, we visited a hospital where brave doctors save the lives of people infected with HIV/AIDS and do everything they can to prevent the epidemic's spread. After we met the staff and AIDS patients and their fami-lies, about twenty HIV-infected patients demonstrated their robust health by joining us on a bike ride through the provincial capital city of Vinh. We also opened a U.S.-funded secondary school in Quảng Trị and spoke with university students in Đồng Hới.

We were attempting to show that Americans and Vietnamese care about the same things: good health for our families, clean air and water for our kids to breathe and drink, and educational and economic opportunities that make the future better than the past. We also wanted to learn about Vietnam's history and be honest about our shared past, even its most painful aspects. The Hanoi City Gate, an ancient and iconic symbol of the thousand-year-old capital, served as our starting point. The Ngọ Môn Gate of Huế's imperial citadel marked the finish line.

In between, we visited the Lam Kinh Temple in Thanh Hóa province, a national historic monument in honor of Emperor Lê Lợi that includes his tomb. Lê Lợi is still regarded as a hero in Vietnam for helping create a golden age in Vietnam's history, its second period of independence from China. His dynasty lasted from the mid-fifteenth century to the late eigh-teenth. During Lê Lợi's reign, the Champa Kingdom in the south was virtu-ally wiped out. The kingdom's population followed the Hindu religion and was heavily influenced by India. The Champa Kingdom predated the Chi-nese- and Buddhist-dominated culture that swept Vietnam from the north. During Lê Lợi's reign and the feudal period that followed, Vietnam's admin-istrative system was reformed and traditional Vietnamese culture, law, and literature flourished.

The Hiền Lương Bridge spans the 17th parallel, which during the war served as the dividing line between North and South Vietnam. When we reached that spot, I spoke to provincial officials and the press about the power of reconciliation and looking forward. I was pleased that the media used a photo of our team of riders cycling across the bridge, presenting a powerful

PHOTO 27 Bikers crossing the Hiền Lương Bridge, Quảng Trị province, January 2016 (Credit: U.S. Department of State/Lê Đức Thọ).

image of the new journey. I was also encouraged that millions followed our trip on Facebook.

In Nghệ An province, we visited the childhood home of Hồ Chí Minh, a simple hut with a dirt floor that is a monument to his humble origins. Then we visited the Hà Tĩnh orphanage, where some of the sixty children have birth defects, possibly a result of Agent Orange. Staff at the orphanage was matter of fact about the kids confined to their beds, their limbs distorted, but I felt sorrow and shame. The aftereffects of war were visible in the tiny bodies of these children. We donated a hundred motorbike helmets to the orphanage as part of our effort to promote childhood safety and well-being, as well as the electric heaters that had kept us warm the previous night. An eight-year-old boy named Phú held my hand for the entire orphanage visit, through long speeches and a Frisbee game.

I couldn't help remember biking with friends from Hanoi to Hồ Chí Minh City nineteen years earlier. We didn't have a bus following us, we stayed in simple guesthouses, and no dignitaries welcomed us upon arrival. That ride took place in March, when the weather was warm. Some things were the same, though: kids jumped up and down and shouted hello; green rice fields and slow water buffaloes slid by; and we ate delicious *phở* and received friendly greetings at each stop.

In 2016, Thảo Nguyễn Griffiths joined our ride. She said, "*Vạn sự khởi đầu nan*," a common proverb that means "everything begins with difficulty." We

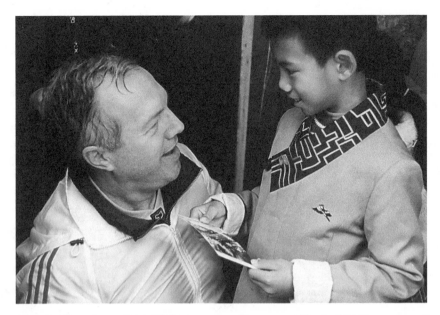

PHOTO 28 The author and Phú, Hà Tĩnh province, January 2016 (Credit: U.S. Department of State/Lê Đức Thọ).

faced difficulty, but we did so as a team. Vietnamese or American, old or young, strong or less strong—it didn't matter as we rode on bikes, on the bus, or in a van. Everyone pitched in, and everyone lent a hand to teammates. We respected each other and the friends we made along the route. That made the ride easier—and more fun—even in the rain.

My friend Ambassador Cameron Hume had taught me that an ambassador would need as much as two years to make substantive preparations for the visit of a U.S. president. (The logistical elements of a visit, such as events and speeches, could be planned relatively quickly.) It was crucial, he argued, to develop strategies far in advance to bring concrete accomplishments over the finish line during a presidential visit. Secretary of State John Kerry had told me that President Barack Obama wanted to visit Vietnam in 2016. After General Secretary Nguyễn Phú Trọng's visit to the Oval Office, we had less than a year before the president was expected to arrive. We had to hurry.

In June 2015, my team and I began the preparatory thinking during a productive workshop. By then everyone knew that I liked to focus on joint endeavors, as opposed to the deliverables (to use the White House's favorite term), because "joint" indicates that efforts by both parties are needed. When Trọng was in Washington, he spoke at the Center for Strategic and

International Studies and emphasized that trust was built when the United States and Vietnam engaged in practical activities together. The success of Trọng's visit gave our partners in Vietnam's government much more room to collaborate with us.

At a second workshop in October 2015, with a new senior team in place, we settled on twelve concrete joint endeavors we could pursue with the Vietnamese. My new deputy, Susan Sutton, helped guide the action officers for each effort, and we challenged them to develop strategies that would complete their actions in time for the president's visit.[1]

By the beginning of 2016, we had developed strategies for the twelve joint endeavors, and our action officers were backed up by strong teams. Susan and Consul General Rena Bitter helped me coordinate these efforts, but each team implemented its strategy independently, with only high-level direction. We were generously and increasingly supported by colleagues and leaders at the State Department and White House as the visit drew nearer. A series of high-level visits preceded the "Big Visit," and we used each one to advance our goals.

From January onward, Scott Kofmehl, who was then at the National Security Council but had been the Vietnam desk officer at the State Department, helped orchestrate our efforts. Scott was an enterprising and talented diplomat, and he shared my view that we should use the visit to make progress on our biggest challenges. With Scott in the lead, the White House took the robust agenda we had planned and made it even more ambitious, pursuing strategies that would address the toughest issues remaining from the war: dioxin cleanup and a lifting of the ban on U.S. arms sales (specifically, lethal military equipment) to Vietnam that had been imposed in the mid-1960s.

April 5, 2016, was Prime Minister Nguyễn Tấn Dũng's last day in office after ten years, and he asked me to attend a dinner with him and three other Vietnamese leaders. He had told me earlier that he wanted to speak to me before stepping down. I had assumed that with all the turmoil he faced since the Party Congress led to his ouster, he hadn't found the time—but he had.

The prime minister placed me, the only foreigner, in the seat of honor. Although Minister of Public Security Tô Lâm, a Dũng loyalist, ostensibly hosted the dinner, the evening was devoted to Dũng's legacy. Vice Foreign Minister Hà Kim Ngọc and former Trade Minister Trương Đình Tuyển also joined us. Tuyển had steered Dũng through three years of negotiations over the Bilateral Trade Agreement in the late 1990s and five years of negotiations over the Trans-Pacific Partnership (TPP) trade agreement.

Over appetizers, Dũng let me know that he had never before had dinner with a foreign ambassador during his long tenure as prime minister. "During my final night in office, I am dining with you, the ambassador of the United States, because I value Vietnam's relations with your country," he stated.

The prime minister also said, "A closer relationship with the United States will be a key part of my legacy." Vietnam's leaders already knew that President Obama would travel to Vietnam, though the visit had not been announced publicly. "President Obama's visit will be a vital opportunity to cement trust between our countries," Dũng noted.

He urged me to have the president lift the decades-old ban on the sale of arms as an indication of the normalization of security relations and, in his view, as a way to "sweep away the last remaining relic of the war." He said that Vietnam would not immediately make defense purchases from the United States, but "lifting the ban has enormous symbolic importance and will open doors to full cooperation in many areas."

Dũng also hoped that President Obama would "speak with a stronger voice" on the standoff in the South China Sea. "Right now, it's very dangerous," he said, with China continuing to militarize the reefs and islets it occupied in the Spratly Islands. The international community, he urged, "must respond to the U.N. Tribunal on the Law of the Sea's decision in a way that enforces international law."

Most of Dũng's musings, however, were about the TPP. "This trade agreement is a turning point of strategic significance for Vietnam," he said. "The primary value of [Vietnam's membership in the] TPP is to create a strategic partnership between the United States and Vietnam." He commented that the United States would not lose jobs to Vietnam, but rather "jobs will flow from other countries, especially China."

Dũng and Tuyển agreed that Vietnam's goal was to move up the global value chain and take advantage of the TPP to enhance education, innovation, and entrepreneurship. "Vietnam can produce high-value goods, not just textiles, basic goods, and apparel," the prime minister said. He predicted that the National Assembly would ratify the TPP by October. He was off by only a couple of weeks, as Vietnam became the seventh country to ratify the TPP on November 12, 2016.

Tô Lâm agreed with the prime minister that President Obama's visit would deepen Vietnam's security relationship with the United States. Tô Lâm had met recently with a vice president of Microsoft and was eager to step up collaboration on cybersecurity. "We can also broaden our intelligence exchange beyond current channels," he added, indicating that his ministry and the Ministry of National Defense were at last ready for such collaboration. Lâm knew that James Clapper, the U.S. director of national intelligence, would visit Vietnam before the president and wanted me to know that he was prepared to work with the United States on intelligence matters. I replied that a commitment to the TPP would lead to progress in security collaboration, intelligence sharing, and even respect for human rights.

Dũng described his family's suffering during the war. "My father and three uncles were killed," he noted. "I was injured four times, and I still have shrapnel in my leg." Vietnam had 800,000 tons of unexploded ordnance left over from the war, "yet still we have overcome the past, and the Vietnamese people look forward, not back." In this spirit, he suggested that President Obama "make a political commitment to resolve remaining war legacies," specifically by promising to clean up dioxin contamination at the Biên Hòa air base near Hồ Chí Minh City and continuing disability assistance to those affected by Agent Orange.

I framed U.S. concerns about human rights as a choice for Vietnam: would the country continue to imprison peaceful bloggers and activists, or would it take actions that would facilitate Congress's ratification of the TPP and the European Parliament's ratification of the EU-Vietnam free trade agreement? "You can't integrate with the international community only by observing economic norms," I said. "Vietnam has a responsibility to fulfill its human rights commitments as well. You can boost your economy if you do so."

As we ate dessert, Dũng recalled meeting with President Obama in Cambodia in 2012 and the president's decision to invite Vietnam to join the TPP. Dũng asked about Donald Trump's prospects in the 2016 presidential election and then said, "I hope to see Hillary Clinton visit Đà Nẵng for the APEC [Asia-Pacific Economic Cooperation] summit in 2017." He recalled that Clinton had visited Hanoi in 2010, when she was secretary of state, and had "changed the rules" by speaking publicly about the U.S. national interest in freedom of navigation through the South China Sea.

Dũng apparently hoped that he would influence Vietnamese policy for years to come even though he was stepping down from power. He wanted his legacy to include solidifying Vietnam's friendship with the United States, consolidating a proactive approach to territorial disputes in the South China Sea, and, most important, Vietnam's entry into the TPP.

I liked Dũng, and I admired his determination to bring Vietnam into the TPP. He was first and foremost a nationalist, but his view of the world included room for a friendship with the United States, and he was proud of his relationship with U.S. leaders. I was sorry to see him go, yet I had confidence that Vietnam's new prime minister and president also wanted to deepen the country's partnership with the United States.

In spring 2016, the Mekong Delta, a piece of land roughly the size of Denmark or West Virginia, experienced its worst drought in a hundred years. Lack of fresh water and a significant intrusion of saltwater destroyed the livelihoods of two million people in eighteen of Vietnam's provinces. The drought affected the entire delta's rice crop, which accounted for 90 percent of the country's rice exports. A large portion of that rice is purchased by African and other Asian nations, which meant that the drought had a measurable effect on global food security.

Vietnam's environmental experts and scholars said that the drought had been caused by troubles with dams upstream on the Mekong River. They were particularly incensed that because of Chinese dams 1,500 miles upstream, there would not be enough fresh water available in the dry season for farming in the delta, and there would be high levels of salinity intrusion, causing additional damage to Vietnamese agriculture.

During the first three months of 2016's dry season, water released from China's dams reached an all-time low. Then in mid-March, Hanoi officially pleaded with Beijing to release water from its upstream Mekong dams. The Chinese government answered by opening the spillways of the Jinghong dam for more than a month. China's state-run media praised Beijing's actions by airing statements like that of Gu Xiaosong, of the Guangxi Academy of Social Science, who said, "While China and Vietnam face bitter relations due to the South China Sea dispute, the release of water will surely assuage tensions between the two nations."[2] Perhaps, but Thailand exacerbated the crisis by withdrawing enormous amounts of Mekong water to irrigate its crops when domestic reservoirs ran dry.

In April, I brought Secretary of Agriculture Tom Vilsack to the Mekong Delta to see the damage. Alarmed, Vilsack called his friend Janet Napolitano, a former member of President Obama's cabinet and at that time president of the University of California (UC). California was also experiencing a historic drought, and Vilsack wanted UC experts to share the lessons they had learned with Vietnam's experts. The prime minister told us he was grateful for this offer, and Minister of Agriculture and Rural Development Cao Đức Phát sent Vietnamese experts to UC Davis.

Before Vilsack's visit, I had developed a friendship with Phát, a Fulbright alumnus and policy wonk who loved his work and cared deeply about finding solutions that could help Vietnam's farmers—who made up three-fourths of the country's population. I invited Phát to lunch and served him American steak, trying to persuade him to lift restrictions on beef, an important U.S. export. He laughed as he dug into the tender beef, before becoming animated as he turned the discussion to rice.

"A huge portion of Vietnam's greenhouse gas emissions comes from rice farming," Phát told me. "But we have introduced new farming techniques that reduce the amount of water, fertilizer, and pesticides needed to produce each kilo of rice. This saves the farmer money, raises yields, and releases much less methane [a potent greenhouse gas] into the atmosphere." Under Phát's leadership, Vietnam was making progress in developing climate-smart agriculture.

I visited one of the Red River Delta farms that used this method. The farmer who spoke to us was an advertisement for the method's success. She described how much she had saved in fertilizer costs, how much she had reduced her use of pesticides, and how much easier it was to harvest each kilo of rice. Still, according to Phát, changing farmers' habits remained the toughest obstacle to overcome: "Vietnamese have farmed a certain way for generations. And no matter how much we explain to farmers that the new methods will cut costs and boost yields, most resist the change." Phát and his team also tried to persuade rice farmers to reduce their harvests from three to two annually and to introduce salt-tolerant rice.

The April calamity in the Mekong Delta coincided with another environmental disaster in central Vietnam, one caused by a toxic waste spill. A Taiwanese steel plant had dumped toxic chemicals off the coast of Hà Tĩnh province, killing the fish that people depended on for their livelihood.

When Deputy Secretary of State Tony Blinken arrived in late April to prepare for President Obama's upcoming visit, the new Vietnamese government had been in place for about two weeks. I had known Tony for more than thirty years, since we had both worked on the *Harvard Crimson* while in college. Brand-new Vietnamese leaders were dealing with the environmental crises in the Mekong Delta and central Vietnam, as well as citizen protests over environmental issues in major cities. Tony was the right choice for an envoy at a tense moment. He believed in relationships, and the Vietnamese leaders trusted him. Tony had visited Vietnam only a year before and had developed especially good relations with National Assembly Chair Nguyễn Thị Kim Ngân and Deputy Prime Minister and Foreign Minister Phạm Bình Minh.

Tony was faced with a delicate task. In the weeks before President Obama's arrival, the United States wanted to see progress—or at least no backsliding—on human rights. Yet the new government faced pressure from Party leaders to show toughness in dealing with the civil unrest and protests. We received a number of pledges on human rights from the Vietnamese, but I was not sure that they would be honored.

We made quick progress with our plans for the president's visit, but differences over human rights would pose the toughest challenges. Longtime friends of Vietnam recognized how dangerous this was for the relationship and made a strong case for positive action on human rights. Kerry, Senator John McCain, and former Senator Bob Kerrey wrote an op-ed for the *New York Times* in which they said: "Human rights are universal, and we have made clear to the leaders in Hanoi our strong belief that Vietnam will reach its full potential only if and when its people have the right to express themselves freely in the arenas of politics, labor, the media and religion. In our visits to Vietnam, we have been impressed by the eagerness of its citizens to take advantage of technology and to compete in the global labor market. We are convinced that the government in Vietnam has nothing to lose, and much to gain, by trusting its citizens."[3]

On May 18, 2016, I met with a very senior leader and influential Politburo member. It was just the two of us: no interpreters and no staff members. President Obama was arriving in Hanoi in a few days, and we needed to discuss a sensitive matter.

Vietnamese leaders were particularly spooked because of the environmental protests, which by then had spread from Hà Tĩnh province to large cities. The seven-week-old government had partially blocked Facebook to prevent the protests in Hồ Chí Minh City from growing too large. Protestors had been rounded up in the center of Hanoi. This was the first test of the new government, and it was coming on the eve of a visit by the president of the United States.

"There have been riots," the senior leader told me, after everyone else had left the room. "And certain actors have taken advantage of the riots to provoke our citizens. They do not represent the Vietnamese people." He added darkly, "Some say they have the backing of the U.S. government."

"President Obama is coming here to strengthen our partnership," I said. "As the president said to General Secretary Trọng in the Oval Office, the United States respects different political systems. We do not seek to overthrow your government." After a pause, I added, "Each time President Obama travels, he meets with members of civil society. He has done so in

Malaysia, in Cuba, in the Middle East—everywhere. He intends to do so in Vietnam as well. It shows his commitment to inclusive governance."

"This will be very difficult," the leader responded. "But I have an idea. We will propose to you a list of participants."

"Thank you for your consideration," I replied. "However, that would not be suitable. The president will meet with all four of your top leaders. He will show respect to Vietnamese history and culture. You must also show respect to the United States and to its president. You should not try to dictate every conversation he has while in Vietnam. In no other country has the government prevented him from meeting with civil society representatives."

The leader's reluctance continued. I suggested that we might have to postpone President Obama's visit.

"No, please do not cancel the visit," the leader said. "We want your president to come here. We understand that this meeting with civil society representatives is important to President Obama. I will support it. But your president must not meet with anyone who has broken Vietnamese laws. And he must not meet with anyone currently under investigation."

I said I would check with the White House to see if those conditions were acceptable. "You will not interfere?" I asked. "You will let the president speak with these people unimpeded?"

"We will allow the meeting to take place," he replied. But there was a kicker: "You must give us a list of participants in advance."

"After all this time, and all this work together, you still do not trust me?" I asked. "For us to build a real partnership, we must learn to trust each other."

"I trust you," he replied. "But we must know whom the president will meet—to keep everyone safe, including your president."

We shook hands.

Our embassy provided the White House with a list of twenty civil society representatives whom we considered to be edgy, but who had not (yet) been arrested for violating Vietnamese laws. We had no way of knowing which Vietnamese citizens might be currently under investigation—many were—so I could not be certain that we had complied with the leader's request that the president not meet with someone under investigation.

White House staffers decided to invite nine of the twenty people from the list we gave them to a roundtable discussion with President Obama. Our embassy staff members thought that the nine were people who could provide the president with a realistic picture of Vietnam's human rights challenges.

On the day the president arrived, representatives of Vietnam's Foreign Ministry who were in charge of the visit were very nervous. "The president should just 'drop by' a meeting with them," Vietnamese diplomats told us. "The U.S. should be 'selective' about invitees." One senior official warned me that "there should be no incidents" during the president's visit. I wondered how the United States could prevent "incidents." What did that even mean in the Vietnamese context? Did the government expect us to prevent protests?

The Vietnamese, who are always sticklers for protocol, had reasons to worry about the challenges of having the president of the United States visit their country. Vietnam had four top leaders, and the United States had only one. Only with Tony Blinken's intervention had we reached a compromise that showed respect to all four without overwhelming the president's schedule. Vietnamese leaders also resented the massive number of security personnel—and weapons—we brought in to protect the president.

Whenever the American president travels to a foreign country, the U.S. government sends in planeloads of equipment, two armored limousines, and snipers. Each event on the calendar had to be carefully planned and orchestrated, with run-throughs at each site and detailed security and communications plans. For President Obama's trip to Vietnam, our team planned motorcade movements with extreme precision because any delay would upset the entire schedule.

As we headed to Hanoi's Nội Bài Airport to welcome President Obama, I wondered about one logistical question. Sometimes the president invites the ambassador to ride with him in "The Beast," the armored limousine, and sometimes he is too tired or busy to do so.

After I welcomed the president on the tarmac, I was greatly relieved when he signaled to me: "Jump in, Ambassador." The photos I saw later showed a big grin on my face. Facing me in the jump seat was my longtime friend Susan Rice, the president's national security advisor. Opposite the president was Ben Rhodes, the deputy national security advisor. I had differed with Susan during preparations for the General Secretary Trọng's visit to Washington and with Ben during preparations for this visit. But I respected both advisors for their intelligence, savvy, and deep loyalty to the president.

I could tell immediately during our forty-minute ride that President Obama had absorbed all of his briefing papers and much more. He did not need to discuss talking points or the purpose of each meeting. He already knew what he needed to accomplish. Instead he sought a deeper understanding of the broad context in which his visit was taking place.

The president asked questions that ranged from "What changes are taking place in Vietnamese society?" to "What is the citizen's relationship to Vietnamese authorities, especially to the police? What forces drive Vietnam's rapid urbanization? What motivates Vietnam's young people?"

I answered each question as thoughtfully as I could, and I was glad I not only had expertise in Vietnam but also in Indonesia, where the president had spent part of his childhood, so that I could draw a few comparisons. President Obama wanted to dig beneath the surface and achieve as much as possible during this three-day trip.

As we neared the hotel, he asked, "Are you here with your family?"

He was offering an opening, and I took it. "We're a typical American family," I replied. "My husband is black, I'm white, and our children are brown."

The president laughed and said, "You'd make a good Benetton ad." He asked to meet our family, and Clayton and I were happy to oblige.

The first day of the visit went smoothly and without incidents, as President Obama met at length with Vietnam's president, as well as more briefly with the prime minister and Party general secretary, and took a stroll with the National Assembly chair. Especially with President Quang, President Obama engaged in substantive dialogue on every key issue—including human rights. President Obama announced an end to the ban on arms sales, knowing that members of Congress and the human rights community would criticize him for doing so. On the commercial front, VietJet airline purchased a hundred Boeing aircraft and Pratt and Whitney engines, and General Electric made a multibillion-dollar-sale of wind energy equipment. The U.S. Agency for International Development agreed to fund training and exchanges that would help Vietnam meet its TPP commitments. The Vietnamese government agreed to have Peace Corps volunteers come to Vietnam to teach citizens how to speak and read English. Both governments committed to taking practical actions to reduce greenhouse gas emissions and adapt to climate change, including in the Mekong Delta, and expanded their cooperation on global health.

One of the most significant accomplishments of the visit was the U.S. commitment to clean up the dioxin we used when fighting the war in Vietnam. President Obama and President Quang released a joint statement that said

"The United States committed to partnering with Vietnam to make a signifi-cant contribution to the clean-up of dioxin contamination at Bien Hoa Air Base."[4] Leaders on both sides were pleased.

I had been instructed to decline the offer of a state dinner for President Obama, and I had recommended a state lunch instead. A hundred guests were treated to an elaborate meal, but I had no time to eat. As the lunch began, my friend Ginny Foote received a message from the Ministry of Public Secur-ity. The ministry said that I had not provided the list of participants for the next day's meeting between President Obama and civil society representatives. I had given it to an official at the airport the day before, but the list had not reached the ministry's top leaders.

This misunderstanding had made the ministry officials angry. I showed Ginny a copy of the list, which she photographed and sent by text to the min-istry. As President Obama was watching a cultural performance, Ginny and I told Kerry about the potential glitch in our plans.

That evening the celebrity chef Anthony Bourdain hosted President Obama at a simple meal at a restaurant. The two drank beer and slurped *bún chả*, a bowl of grilled pork and noodles that Hanoians love. The entire tab was $6—including two beers for each man. Vietnamese citizens could scarcely believe that a U.S. president would enjoy one of their simplest meals, and they were immensely proud.

On the street outside the restaurant, a crowd gathered and spontaneously welcomed President Obama with genuine warmth. (When Bourdain died by suicide in 2018, Vietnam's social media were full of sad messages. He was viewed as a friend who understood Vietnam's cuisine and therefore something of its soul.)

While the president was eating *bún chả*, the people we had invited to join him for the planned discussion the next day started to disappear. One of them was so afraid of what the police might do to him that he eluded the security services by driving north to Vietnam's border with China. Police picked up another man and drove him to a town two hours away from Hanoi as a way of preventing him from meeting with the president. A third was detained by police. Police pressured the employer of a fourth person to prevent a meeting with the president. A fifth holed up in a hotel and called our embassy to ask for protection.

Furious that Vietnam's police would defy an American president in this clumsy and disrespectful manner, I texted the senior leader I had met with about this a few days earlier, and with whom I thought I had a firm agreement. I found out that he was out of the country. Finally, my embassy team learned that the government considered five of the nine people we had invited to be what it called inciters of trouble.

I called Kerry, who quickly phoned Minh and insisted that the Vietnamese live up to their agreements about the roundtable discussion.

At 2:00 A.M., I located Vietnam's ambassador to the United States and warned him: "Secretary Kerry spoke with the deputy prime minister about the president's roundtable discussion tomorrow and the detention or intimidation of five participants. He expects to receive a response. The two will meet tomorrow morning and then the secretary will advise the president what to say to the press."

In the morning, bleary-eyed from lack of sleep, I joined Kerry in a small meeting with Minh. Kerry was tough and impressive. "In Cuba, the government did not stop President Obama from meeting with members of civil society," the secretary asserted. "Do you want the president to say, publicly, that Vietnam is worse than Cuba?"

Minh blanched. "Let me make some calls," he said.

I was angry with Minh and with the senior leader who had reneged on his commitment. When we were alone, I asked Kerry, "What do you do when someone betrays you?"

Without missing a beat, he replied, "It happened to me yesterday. My advice is: Don't burn bridges. Let them know what went wrong, don't slap them on the back, but don't burn bridges."

After the visit, I repeated Kerry's advice to my staff. "Don't slap them on the back," I repeated, "but don't burn bridges." Throughout his career, Kerry has shown that he follows this advice himself. It's good advice for diplomacy and for life.

The Hanoi police released one of the civil society representatives who had been detained. Our embassy provided a vehicle for another person to travel from his hotel to the meeting place with President Obama. But the person whom the police had taken for a ride was too far away for us to get him back in time. The man who had driven by himself to the Chinese border did not want to return. The person whose employer had been intimidated by the police had decided not to meet with the president.

As we traveled with President Obama in his limo to the roundtable meeting, Rhodes provided an update on what had happened. I thought I had let the president down. I had been sure the Vietnamese would honor their deal with me.

The president didn't blame me for being naive and trusting the Vietnamese. "This is new for them," he said, sounding relaxed. "No leader has ever visited their country and insisted on meeting with civil society. Change will take time."

President Obama met with the remaining six representatives, and they had a dynamic, honest discussion. One of them was my friend Đỗ Nguyễn Mai Khôi, the singer and independent National Assembly candidate. The others were Bình, an LGBT+ advocate; Nguyễn Hồng Oanh, an advocate for the rights of people with disabilities; Pastor Trung, who operates an unlicensed church with drug rehabilitation facilities; Mai Phan Lợi, a journalist and head of a press freedom nongovernmental organization; and Pastor Huy, the leader of a faith community first established by Southern Baptist missionaries in 1962.

Afterward, instead of comparing Vietnam negatively to Cuba, President Obama said to reporters:

> I should note that there were several other activists who were invited who were prevented from coming for various reasons. . . . Although there has been some modest progress and it is our hope that through some of the legal reforms that are being drafted and passed there will be more progress, there are still folks who find it very difficult to assemble and organize peacefully around issues that they care deeply about.
>
> And it's my hope that the government of Vietnam comes to recognize what we've recognized and what so many countries around the world have recognized, and that is that it's very hard to prosper in this modern economy if you haven't fully unleashed the potential of your people. And your people's potential, in part, derives from their ability to express themselves and express new ideas, to try to right wrongs that are taking place in the society. And so it's my hope that, increasingly, the Vietnamese government, seeing the enormous strides that the country is making, has more confidence that its people want to work together but also want to be able to assemble and participate in society in ways that will be good for everybody in the long run.[5]

I asked my staff to contact everyone—those who participated in the roundtable and those who had been prevented from doing so—to find out how they were faring.

The gentleman who had been driven two hours out of Hanoi was back at home and safe, no worse for the experience. Another activist remained

PHOTO 29 Nguyễn Hồng Oanh, President Barack Obama, and Đỗ Nguyễn Mai Khôi, Hanoi, May 2016 (Credit: Associated Press/Carolyn Kaster).

out of town but said that she, too, was safe. The third reported that he had been monitored, but not harassed, after he made clear to the police that he would not meet with President Obama. One activist who participated in the meeting with the president told us that he was invited to "have coffee" with police a few hours after meeting the president. The others reported no problems.

Still, I thought that the president had been too generous to me. I *had* been naive in believing that my deal with the senior leader would hold. I followed Kerry's advice and let the Vietnamese know I would not forget the betrayal. I didn't slap the Vietnamese on the back after the president's visit, nor did I burn bridges.

Too much was at stake in the area of human rights in Vietnam, including reconciliation.

In Hanoi, President Obama spoke to a crowd of 2,200, mostly young people, and quoted heroes from Vietnam's ancient and modern history—including the national hero Lý Thường Kiệt; poet Nguyễn Du; the venerable Thích Nhất Hạnh; and composer Trịnh Công Sơn, often referred to as Vietnam's Bob Dylan. The president reminded the Vietnamese of the long history of ties between Vietnam and the United States: "More than 200 years ago, when our Founding Father, Thomas Jefferson, sought rice for his farm, he looked to the rice of Vietnam, which he said had 'the

PHOTO 30 The author and John Kerry at President Barack Obama's speech to the Vietnamese people, Hanoi, May 2016 (Credit: Virginia Foote).

reputation of being whitest to the eye, best flavored to the taste, and most productive.'"[6]

Instead of dwelling on the war, President Obama referred to Vietnam's 1945 Declaration of Independence, when Hồ Chí Minh deliberately paraphrased America's own Declaration: "All people are created equal. The Creator has endowed them with inviolable rights. Among these rights are the right to life, the right to liberty, and the right to the pursuit of happiness."

President Obama showed an interest in Vietnam's people, history, and culture, and the citizens of Vietnam repaid his respect with genuine affection. He also stressed the value that Americans place on human rights: "When there is freedom of expression and freedom of speech, and when people can share ideas and access the internet and social media without restriction, that fuels the innovation economies need to thrive. . . . When there's freedom of the press—when journalists and bloggers are able to shine a light on injustice or abuse—that holds officials accountable and builds public confidence that the system works."

PHOTO 31 The author, President Barack Obama, and Clayton Bond with Lucy and TABO, Hanoi, May 2016 (Credit: White House/Pete Souza).

He spoke of free elections, freedom of religion, and free assembly. I turned to a senior Vietnamese official a few seats away to gauge his reaction. He nodded and mouthed one word: "Wonderful."

Before the president departed for Hồ Chí Minh City on Air Force One, Clayton and I brought our kids to his hotel. We waited with a few select others for our chance to see the president.

The photographers had set up special lights, and the room was hot. Our one- and two-year-old kids weren't patient, and the moment the president arrived, our son staged a full-on meltdown as only a two-year-old can, thrashing and screaming on the floor. Unfazed, President Obama asked his staff for two gifts, small blue boxes emblazoned with the seal of the president of the United States. When he rattled them (chocolate was inside), our son was transfixed. His tears dried quickly, the president threw his arms around both dads' shoulders, and the photographer snapped a picture.

In that cherished photo, the wetness of our son's eyes is barely visible. He has a gentle smile, brought out not by his parents but by the president of the United States.

Later, I asked the president, "How did you do it?"

"I'm the baby whisperer," he laughed.

I said, "I think being a dad is far harder than being an ambassador."

The president agreed. "Being a dad is harder than being president. But you're in a high-maintenance stage right now," he added. "When the kids get to be six or so, that's when the sweet spot begins. It lasts until around age twelve, and then it gets harder again."

I smiled, happy to receive wise father-to-father advice from President Obama.

In Hồ Chí Minh City, a million people swarmed into the streets to welcome President Obama and watch his motorcade pass by. "In seven and a half years of travel," the president said, "with the possible exception of Tanzania, I have never received a warmer welcome."

President Obama's Hồ Chí Minh City stop highlighted a young, dynamic, and friendly Vietnam. He turned the established order on its head when he interviewed young entrepreneurs who used digital platforms to sell goods. In Asia, it was almost unthinkable for the leader of the free world to ask questions of young businesspeople. Then President Obama answered questions—unscripted—at a gathering of six hundred young Vietnamese, members of his Young Southeast Asian Leaders Initiative.

A woman in her twenties, Suboi, introduced herself as a rapper. Not missing a beat, Obama asked, "Why don't you give me a little rap? Let's see what you got." To encourage her, he added, "Come on. Do you need like a little beat? Badoom, badoom."

Suboi grinned and began to rap a funny song about corruption. "Some people have a lot of money, and big houses, but are they really happy?" she rapped. "It's been a crazy day." She told the president that a lot of people in Vietnam think rapping isn't art and that it's not for women.

Her song and words went viral on social media, helping define the visit's significance. Overseas, television viewers expected to see Vietnamese communists in baggy green uniforms. Instead they saw a hip young female rapper. Modern Vietnam had arrived.

The president also followed up on General Secretary Trọng's commitment in New York to permit a new, autonomous, U.S.-style university to be established in Vietnam. President Obama said: "We're very excited that this fall, the new Fulbright University Vietnam will open in Ho Chi Minh City—this nation's first independent, non-profit university—where there will be full academic freedom and scholarships for those in need. (Applause.) Students, scholars, researchers will focus on public policy and management and business; on engineering and computer science; and liberal arts—everything from the poetry of Nguyen Du, to the philosophy of Phan Chu Trinh, to the mathematics of Ngo Bao Chau."[7]

At his meeting with young Vietnamese in Hồ Chí Minh City, the president reiterated that promise of full academic freedom to the enthusiastic applause of six hundred young Vietnamese. Nguyễn Vũ Tú, a Vietnamese diplomat who was my longtime friend, joined Kerry and me for this event, and I reflected on the years that Tú had devoted to making the Fulbright Economics Teaching Program an effective institution for helping transform Vietnam's economy. Behind the scenes, he was also facilitating the creation of Fulbright University Vietnam.

By this point in the trip, Kerry had received additional verbal commitments regarding the university's autonomous governance and academic freedom. Translating that verbal promise into an operating license and written guarantee took two more years, but another milestone had been reached. Public Affairs Officer Alex Titolo, who stage-managed the president's Hồ Chí Minh City stop, continued shepherding the project to its realization, and he pursued that goal with skill and determination.

Fulbright University Vietnam could shift the paradigm of higher education in Vietnam. It was designed so that students would not just absorb information and facts but learn how to work with the knowledge they acquired. Students did best, the founders of the university believed, when they were the ones who did the thinking and learning, rather than merely being recipients of knowledge.

As a final stop before returning to the United States, President Obama visited the Jade Emperor pagoda. Immediately after the president left, the abbot sealed the temple by closing the main doors. In doing so, he followed the Taoist and Buddhist traditions, with the intent of preserving the president's energy within the temple where it could mingle with other temple entities. He wanted to prevent malicious forces from entering the temple and dissipating the positive energy and the karmic consequence of the president's visit. In Chinese geomancy, negative forces can proceed only in a straight line and cannot penetrate certain barriers, particularly if there are other protective forces within.

Minutes later, a dozen people entered the courtyard and bowed before the temple doors. In traditional times, that is what people did at a temple after an emperor or other powerful person had appeared. In modern Vietnam, such a response had occurred only after the appearance of someone the devotees held in extraordinarily high regard—someone like the Dalai Lama. The worshippers performed the prostrations as a sign of appreciation to the temple entities for interceding in worldly affairs so that President Obama would come to their place of worship.[8]

A few weeks later, a young man visiting the residence asked if I would take a selfie with him, a common occurrence. Later, he wrote to tell me that he had returned to his conservative, rural home province and shared the photo with his father. When he told his father that I was gay, his father replied, "That's not possible. The American ambassador could not be gay."

The young man then showed his father the photo of my family with President Obama. At that moment, the young man wrote, his father began the journey toward acceptance of his own gay son.

During my thirty-year career as a diplomat, I never felt luckier than I did during those three days in May 2016 when President Obama visited Hanoi and Hồ Chí Minh City. Since 1995, when President Clinton established full diplomatic relations between the two countries, the United States had grown steadily more popular in Vietnam.

By the time President Obama visited, 92 percent of Vietnamese—young or old, northern or southern—considered the United States to be their country's closest friend. Bullying from the Chinese government had pushed Vietnam into the U.S. embrace, and President Obama opened his arms to accept a new partner.

13

A New President

●　●　●　●　●　●　●　●　●　●　●　●　●

On July 11, 2016, a month after President Barack Obama's visit, I brought a senior-level Vietnamese delegation aboard the USS *John Stennis*, an aircraft carrier traveling through the East Sea (Vietnam's name for the South China Sea) near the Spratly Islands.

Nothing conveys the sense of awesome power like the experience of visiting an aircraft carrier. Essentially a floating city of more than five thousand people, the *John Stennis* carried around ninety fixed-wing aircraft and helicopters, and we watched many of them take off and land. I recorded a few brief iPhone videos of those noisy takeoffs and landings, including the screech to a halt in two seconds when a plane's tailhook was caught by one of the four arresting wires.

I posted my aircraft carrier videos on Facebook, and more than 800,000 Vietnamese viewed, shared, and "liked" them. Vietnamese leaders were grateful for Defense Secretary Ash Carter's declaration a year before that U.S. ships and planes would continue to "fly, sail, and operate wherever international law allows" in the South China Sea. The people of Vietnam were struck by the U.S. assertion of its might in the sea.

Our trip to the *John Stennis* occurred a day before the announcement of a U.N. tribunal ruling that overwhelmingly favored the Philippines in the 2014 case concerning China's vast claims in the South China Sea. Vietnam had taken significant risks in siding with the Philippines in that case, and the enthusiastic reactions to my short, shaky videos were another indication that the Vietnamese people wanted the United States to remain engaged in the sea.

That same week, China staged its annual maritime military drills in the South China Sea, showing off its new and powerful deepwater naval capabilities and signaling to the world its resolve to maintain dominance there, no matter what judges in The Hague had decided.

In the early nineteenth century, when the United States took its place on the world stage, President James Monroe proclaimed U.S. hegemony in the Western hemisphere. In the beginning of the twentieth century, the Monroe Doctrine referred specifically to keeping European powers out of the Caribbean. As China became increasingly powerful, it appeared to view the South China Sea as its lake, and its territorial claims over the entire sea were akin to establishing a Chinese Monroe Doctrine. During the Obama administration, the United States refrained from taking a position in the disputes over islands in the sea and instead sought a peaceful resolution to them and insisted on freedom of navigation in international waters.

The South China Sea was not the Caribbean: half of the world's seaborne cargo passed through the South China Sea each year. The health of the Japanese and South Korean economies depended on free passage of goods and ships through (and aircraft above) those waters, and those U.S. allies felt particularly vulnerable to China's encroachment. The United States did not accept China's long-term plan for regional hegemony, but it also did not want to provoke a direct conflict with China—especially over disputed islets and features that, by themselves, have no strategic value.

Unfortunately, the 2016 U.N. decision was largely irrelevant. Chinese Foreign Minister Wang Yi rejected the decision outright, stating that the tribunal proceedings were a "political farce staged under legal pretext" and adding that they had been "plotted and manipulated by certain forces outside the region."[1] President Rodrigo Duterte of the Philippines, who had taken power days before the tribunal's ruling, did not push Beijing to honor it. Instead, he cozied up to China and canceled defense agreements with the United States, a longtime ally. Beijing responded with vows to invest billions of dollars in the Philippines. Within the Association of Southeast Asian Nations (ASEAN), Vietnam became increasingly isolated in confronting the Chinese in the East Sea.

Before Duterte's election, Vietnam had let the Philippines take the heat in standing up to China. But the Philippines's about-face meant that Vietnam had to provide leadership within ASEAN for diplomacy involving maritime territorial disputes.

China laid claim to islands and reefs and then dredged up land from the sea bottom, adding up to 3,200 acres of new real estate.[2] The Chinese military built permanent facilities on the reclaimed land, creating islands that were like huge stationary aircraft carriers. These facilities included deepwater ports, intelligence collection systems, aircraft hangers, and long runways that could accommodate military jets.

Vietnam and the United States were aligned in attempting to internationalize the territorial dispute, revive the 2016 tribunal ruling, and deepen the two countries' maritime collaboration. Later, the U.S. Air Force enrolled the first Vietnam Air Defense and Air Force pilots in its pilot training program, a necessary step before Vietnam could receive aircraft from America in the near future. The U.S. assistance was designed to improve Vietnam's ability to patrol its waters by air as well as by sea.

Later in July 2016, the USNS *Mercy*—a thousand-bed, twelve-story floating hospital—returned for a second year in a row to Đà Nẵng. There, a small Vietnamese hospital ship diagnosed patients before sending them to the *Mercy*. U.S. servicemen and women led dive training and English-language training, and they renovated kindergartens and hospitals in Đà Nẵng and nearby. The United States used the *Mercy*'s visit to communicate its intent to remain active and engaged in the South China Sea.

In response to Vietnam's limited ability to monitor what was happening over the horizon in the South China Sea, the U.S. military invested in training that would give the Vietnamese better monitoring capabilities and provided information, navy-to-navy engagement, and a context for U.S. operations to maintain freedom of navigation in the disputed waters.

Back in Hanoi, where we determined the *John Stennis* and *Mercy* visits to have been successful, Evan Morrissey (a very talented diplomat working on security relations) suggested having a U.S. aircraft carrier pay a visit to a Vietnamese port. If that happened, thousands of U.S. servicemen and women would come ashore in Vietnam. While I liked the idea, my first thought was that Vietnamese leaders would refuse the offer as too provocative, given the country's tensions with China.

I turned to our defense attaché, Colonel Tuấn T. Tôn, affectionately known as "T3," and asked if this was even feasible. "I think it would be difficult," he said, "but as you always say, sir, 'nothing is impossible.'" It was a big, hairy, audacious idea. Our political-military team began developing a strategy to make it happen.

The U.S. elections were only a few months away. After a presidential transition, civilian officials change, but most military leaders remain in place. That

212 • Nothing Is Impossible

summer and autumn, I did not raise the idea with the State Department, because I expected its leadership to change dramatically, even if Hillary Clinton became president.

Instead, I set out to convince Pacific Command Commander Admiral Harry Harris that there would be security benefits to having a U.S. aircraft carrier visit Vietnam. Harris is a brilliant strategist, and he embraced the idea and our embassy's approach to implementing it.

The first time I called on Harris in Camp Smith, Hawaii, the Pacific Command headquarters where his top-floor office overlooks Pearl Harbor, he surprised me by placing me at the head of the table.

"I can't sit in your seat," I objected.

"You are my guest," he replied.

Harris knew how to earn and receive respect. He was comfortable in his own skin.

On a bike ride in August 2016, Thảo Nguyễn Griffiths introduced me to one of Hanoi's most colorful artists, Đào Anh Khánh, who had outraged the censors with his enormous sculpted phalluses and many paintings of vaginas. A former policeman, and son of a high-ranking police official, Khánh had begun his career by monitoring the activities of artists in Hanoi to determine whether their work posed a threat to the Communist Party or public morals.

Then Khánh decided to quit his job and the Party, become an artist himself, and start painting full-time. Thảo and I biked to his studio, and Khánh showed us a performance space as well as his plans for a much larger arena in a rural area outside of Hanoi. Khánh's former colleagues on the police force were aware of his notoriety and had dismantled some of his more provocative erotic sculptures. They weren't likely to lose interest in him.

Thảo and I also visited George Burchett's studio on Đặng Thai Mai Street. George was captivated by the story of Bà Triệu, also called Triệu Thị Trinh (her actual given name is unknown). A female warrior in the third century (225–248), Bà Triệu bravely resisted the invading Chinese and is known as Vietnam's first true feminist. According to legend, when Bà Triệu's brother told her that women were not supposed to act in such a way, she replied: "My wish is to ride the tempest, tame the waves, and kill the sharks in the East Sea. I will not resign myself to the usual lot of women who bow their heads and become concubines."[3]

Bà Triệu raised a rebel army and is said to have fought more than thirty battles before she was twenty-one years old. She was supposedly taller than nine feet, with a voice that sounded "like a temple bell." She rode into battle on an elephant, wearing golden armor and carrying a sword in each hand.[4] George was an admirer of female beauty and enjoyed saying that Bà Triệu's breasts extended three feet from her chest and that she threw them over her shoulders when she fought.

George wrote: "Unlike most superheroes of pop culture, Bà Triệu has her roots in her people; she is one of them. The people made her bigger than life as a tribute to her spirit and courage. They gave her an ample bosom in defiance of oppressive Confucian morals. Bà Triệu was strong and free in a society that required women to be weak and submissive. And a society where women are weak and submissive is itself weak and oppressive."[5]

In 248, the Chinese army finally defeated Bà Triệu and, according to legend, she chose to throw herself into a river and drown rather than surrender. Bà Triệu is a national hero in Vietnam and a role model for generations of Vietnamese women. A national holiday honors her bravery, and most Vietnamese cities have a street named after her.

In September, I traveled with colleagues from the U.S. Agency for International Development to the central province of Quảng Nam, where the U.S. government had pledged funds to protect Vietnam's last remaining elephants. When I visited the central highlands twenty years earlier, I had seen many herds of wild elephants. Now the small herd in Quảng Nam was Vietnam's last group of elephants still living in the wild.

On the same September trip, I saw the endangered red-shanked douc langur,[6] a leaf-eating monkey that lives on the Sơn Trà peninsula in Đà Nẵng. Its global population had shrunk to less than two thousand. Even more critically endangered, Delacour's langur lives in a small area in the north, including Cúc Phương National Park. We had posted photos of Delacour's langurs on Facebook when a million or so Vietnamese were following our bicycle trip from Hanoi to Huế, hoping to draw attention to efforts to rescue the species from extinction. Only two hundred of the animals remain in their native habitat. Naturalists told me about similar efforts to save the critically endangered Cát Bà langur, which is found only on Cát Bà Island on the edge of Hạ Long Bay. Only seventy remain, giving the Cát Bà langurs the dubious distinction of being the world's rarest primate species.

When I spoke at a 2017 conference in Boulder, Colorado, I met Bert Covert, who was leading successful efforts to save the douc langurs and other threatened primates. Bert collaborates closely with Vietnamese scientists to conduct fieldwork and educate young Vietnamese anthropologists and biologists who have an interest in biodiversity conservation. Bert was optimistic

PHOTO 32 Douc langur, Đà Nẵng province, June 2018 (Credit: Herbert Covert, Professor of Anthropology, University of Colorado Boulder).

that the conservation efforts, public education, and outreach of these young scholars and activists will be effective, and he reported that his Vietnamese collaborators are working in universities, government research institutes, recently established Vietnamese nongovernmental organizations (NGOs), and international NGOs. Vietnam is among the top fifteen countries in the world for primate diversity, and 88 percent of its primates are threatened.[7]

Bert told me about the work of GreenViet, an NGO established in 2011 by Hà Thăng Long and colleagues in Đà Nẵng. GreenViet leads conservation efforts to save the red-shanked douc langurs through grassroots activities such as workshops on conservation with thousands of school kids each year. Bert believes that successful conservation requires leadership by in-country groups—both governmental and nongovernmental organizations. Scholars at the Hồ Chí Minh City's Southern Institute of Ecology of the Vietnam Academy of Science and Technology are leaders in biodiversity research and conservation in southern Vietnam. Lưu Hồng Trường, director of the institute, oversees a team of young Vietnamese scientists who conduct biodiversity surveys and both basic and applied research, and who have a sincere desire

PHOTO 33 The author with cardboard cutouts of Hillary Clinton and Donald Trump, Hanoi, November 2016 (Credit: U.S. Department of State/Lê Đức Thọ).

to protect nature. They work with local communities to foster sustainable use of natural resources.

The twelve-hour time difference between Vietnam and the U.S. East Coast meant that we watched the 2016 election returns in the morning with coffee and donuts at the American Center in the embassy's annex. Our team spent weeks preparing a guest list for the event that included Communist Party officials, diplomats, journalists, and students. We set up booths decorated in red, white, and blue, and our guests could learn about the Electoral College, cast mock ballots, and have their pictures taken with cardboard cutouts of the presidential candidates.

"Here we explain the role of first ladies," our cheerful community liaison officer told students to lure them to her booth. "And, possibly, the first first gentleman." We brought in a jazz band, and the air buzzed with music and activity.

The weather in Hanoi was wet and overcast, and we hustled VIP guests in through a side door so they wouldn't be rained on while waiting in a long security line. I chatted with diplomats and high-level Vietnamese officials as we watched the returns on wall-mounted television screens. During breaks in the action, I escaped the VIP room and mingled with two hundred students who had joined the party. They were especially excited by the event because their country did not hold elections. "May I take a selfie with you?" was the most common question I heard.

Vietnam's leaders are selected in an opaque process open only to the eighteen-member Politburo, the Communist Party's supreme decision-making body. Our guests—both high- and low-level—admired the United States. They found our messy and unpredictable politics thrilling. They also recognized that the results of our election had real meaning for Vietnam. The political fate of the United States hung in the balance, and so did theirs because the United States was Vietnam's most important partner.

I recalled the 1996 election party hosted by Chargé d'Affaires Desaix Anderson, when he delivered remarks that I had written explaining the mechanics of a U.S. presidential election. Twenty years later, I had asked my embassy team to prepare three speeches: one if Hillary Clinton won; a second if Donald Trump won; and a third if the outcome remained uncertain. I had been on Vice President Al Gore's staff during the 2000 election, and I knew how possible it was that there might not be an immediate, clear-cut victory. The stakes seemed even higher in November 2016.

When it became clear that Donald Trump was going to win in Florida and North Carolina and that Pennsylvania, Wisconsin, and Michigan might also go his way, I knew what I needed to do. I collared my press attaché and said: "The race will soon be over. You must get me to the podium quickly." With television cameras rolling, I stood at the lectern and gave the third speech, explaining that nothing was certain until all the returns came in. "The Electoral College process is uncertain," I ad-libbed, "and it will be some time before Congress formally declares the winner." As ambassador, I had a responsibility to remain publicly neutral and avoid any overt partisanship. Still, I knew how difficult it would be for me to hide my dismay if I had to announce a Trump victory.

When Hillary Clinton served as secretary of state, I had worked for her proudly and thought she represented stability and experience, traits needed in diplomacy. Under pressure from the Democratic Party's populist wing, represented by Vermont Senator Bernie Sanders, Clinton had distanced herself from the Trans-Pacific Partnership (TPP) trade agreement—the highest goal of U.S.-Vietnam relations during my tenure as ambassador. However, I had spoken with Clinton's top foreign policy advisors and felt confident that as president she could find a way to preserve U.S. leadership in Asia and international trade.

I had devoted three decades of my life to that arc of the world between Japan and Pakistan, trying to strengthen America's Asian alliances and build partnerships with key nations such as India, Indonesia, and Vietnam. Early in my career, I could see that America's future would be in Asia, and in my view that prediction had been validated by President Obama's pivot or rebalance toward Asia. I wanted to continue strengthening U.S. ties to Asia, but the election results threatened all that I believed was important.

In stark contrast to Clinton, Trump appeared to be untruthful, undisciplined, and erratic. Although unpredictability can sometimes be useful in diplomacy—at least President Richard Nixon and Secretary of State Henry Kissinger had argued that it was—a Trump presidency looked like it could be a train wreck for the United States, especially overseas. An ambassador is the president's personal representative and, if I remained in this post, I would have to carry out the new president's policies.

As an openly gay man with a spouse who is Black and children of Mexican origin, I rejected Trump's racism and sexism. I believed that Clinton would continue moving along President Obama's path toward creating greater opportunity for all Americans.

I left the election party immediately after my speech and went home to grieve. The next day, I submitted a letter of resignation, effective January 20, 2017. I could not in good conscience serve in a Trump administration, nor did I expect that my services would be wanted.

When one of the embassy team members, a security officer, heard about my decision, he said: "Ambassador, we need your leadership now more than ever. You can't abandon us, or all that you've worked to create will be lost." He had a point. I had devoted many years to overcoming America's troubled past with Vietnam and to building a deep and lasting partnership between the two countries. I felt great loyalty to our embassy team. The State Department had sent a message directing ambassadors to prepare to resign, but I also received a second message saying that the first one was intended for political appointees only. As I was a career ambassador, my resignation was rejected, and I received instructions to remain in place. Perhaps, I thought, it was my duty to stay and do what I could to preserve the U.S.-Vietnam relationship for as long as possible.

Ambassador Dave Shear shared with me the message of a carving in Hanoi's thousand-year-old Temple of Literature, which my friend Leon Fuerth likened to Oxford in the Middle Ages. The plaque reads, "virtue and

PHOTO 34 Carving in the Temple of Literature, Hanoi (Credit: David Shear, Ambassador [ret.]).

talent are the soul of the state." The reference is to the centuries-old Confucian tradition of the so-called remonstrating official. The idea is that a loyalty exists that is greater than that to the emperor, and that loyalty requires officials to speak out when the emperor goes too far.

This message reminded me about the oath I swore to support and defend the U.S. Constitution. I thought perhaps I could serve as a remonstrating official—one who protests wrongful actions—for an appropriate amount of time. I had core beliefs I wanted to uphold. I wanted the young people working for me to know I would defend them. I considered Robert McNamara's admission that, as secretary of defense, he had known we were losing the war in Vietnam but did not say so at the time, and I also thought about other public servants who ignored their core beliefs and allowed terrible things to happen. I did not want to live a life of regret. I wanted to be able to face my children and tell them their papa always tried to do the right thing.

Freelancing is not an option in diplomacy, and I would have to balance my personal ethics with a duty to carry out the policies of America's newly elected officials. I decided to see if I could maintain the trust and momentum we had built in our relationship with Vietnam and support my team, and I would prepare to resign if I was asked to implement policies I could not support.

I met with my team, which represented eighteen U.S. agencies, and reminded them of the oath we had all taken when entering government service. I kept framed on my office wall the oath I swore when I became ambassador as a daily reminder of my commitment to "defend the Constitution of the United States against all enemies, foreign and domestic." U.S. military officers and all presidentially appointed officials had sworn the same oath. Nothing in it refers to loyalty to a president or party; it is only about fealty to the Constitution and people of the United States.

Our embassy team struggled with how to keep U.S.-Vietnam relations moving forward despite the turbulence at home. Vietnam's leaders, pragmatic as always, reached out early and often to members of the incoming administration. In December, Prime Minister Nguyễn Xuân Phúc was the first Southeast Asian leader to speak directly with President-elect Trump, who during his campaign had made his opposition to the TPP clear. I believed that it might still be possible to keep the partnership with Vietnam moving forward in both countries' interest—especially in the area of military-to-military ties—even with the loss of the TPP.

For the holidays, Justice Ruth Bader Ginsburg sent our children a copy of *I Dissent*, a story about how disagreement does not have to be hostile and how people with different views, such as Ginsburg and Justice Antonin Scalia, could still be friends. It was a kids' book but not just for that age group. The last line of the justice's accompanying note to our children referred to the 2016 election: "I will try hard to stay healthy for at least four years ahead." She tried hard indeed.

Thảo took me on another biking trip during the first week of January 2017, this time to visit Giang Văn Minh's temple. A decorated scholar, Minh served as Vietnam's ambassador to China in the seventeenth century. He outsmarted China's emperor, ending Vietnam's annual payment of a heavy gold and silver tribute, and the emperor took revenge by cutting out Minh's tongue and eviscerating him. The emperor then had the diplomat's body cast in silver and returned to Vietnam. The story was a reminder that even in the transition from one U.S. president to another, Vietnam would keep its focus on its powerful northern neighbor—as it had for millennia. It was also a reminder to me that displeasing an emperor can have a price.

Secretary of State John Kerry was in his element as he stood in the prow of the speedboat. It was mid-January 2017, and Kerry remembered each curve of the Bảy Háp River, which flowed through the Mekong Delta, where he had

PHOTO 35 John Kerry and Ed Miller, Cà Mau province, January 2017 (Credit: Associated Press/Alex Brandon).

last been forty-eight years earlier. Kerry was on a mission. Accompanied by Ed Miller, a professor at Dartmouth College and a historian of Vietnam, he wanted to find the spot where he had earned his Silver Star when his Swift Boat crew was ambushed.

On the night of February 28, 1969, Lieutenant Kerry directed the three boats he commanded "to turn to the beach and charge the Viet Cong positions," then he "expertly directed" the boat's fire and coordinated the deployment of the South Vietnamese troops, according to Commander of Naval Forces Vietnam Admiral Elmo Zumwalt, who awarded him the Silver Star.[8] Kerry and his crew were patrolling the Bảy Háp River on a mission to destroy enemy boats, structures, and bunkers when they ran into an ambush. Kerry pursued those who staged the ambush, leaping ashore to pursue and ultimately kill a fleeing Việt Cộng who carried a B-40 grenade launcher. The mission, which sustained no American casualties, succeeded in destroying numerous targets and confiscating a substantial amount of combat supplies.

As we made our way down each turn of the river, past banks dense with foliage, I reflected on those ostensibly successful missions. U.S. leaders had made decisions that sent young men in their teens and twenties to patrol these remote rivers. What could have made those military leaders think that those missions would drive the Việt Cộng out of the Mekong Delta? And how could the young men on boats, speaking no Vietnamese, ever know who was friend and who was foe?

We rounded a bend in the river, and Kerry pointed: "There it is. I know it."

Kerry had visited Cà Mau province in December 2013 and tried to locate the site. But the consulate team had taken him to the place where he had earned the Bronze Star, not the Silver Star. (He also earned three Purple Hearts.) Kerry had earned his Bronze Star by rescuing Green Beret Jim Rassmann from a different tributary of the Bảy Háp River. Injured and under fire, Kerry had crawled out onto the deck of his damaged Swift Boat and pulled Rassmann out of the water.

This time, our team was determined to get to the right spot. A small group from the Hồ Chí Minh City consulate—led by Sean Lindstone, a foreign service officer—worked for weeks on the logistics of this visit, determined to find the precise location of the ambush, and we were confident that they had found it. Miller had conducted detailed research and used 1969-era maps. Over dinner at the Press Club in Hanoi before flying south toward Cà Mau, we spread out the maps. The combination of Kerry's memory and our research had led to the same spot.

Tommy Vallely, Kerry's close friend for almost fifty years, accompanied him on this trip. Tommy and I had collaborated during my tenure on all matters pertaining to Vietnam, and we had planned this trip together. After our Press Club dinner, Tommy told me that Kerry had phoned one of his fellow crew members in the United States as he tried to figure out on Google Maps precisely where they had fought. He wanted to be 100 percent certain of his forty-eight-year-old memories, especially because he did not know if he would visit the Mekong Delta again.

Kerry's close relationship with his crew members from five decades ago was striking. When he lost the presidency by the slimmest of margins in 2004, Kerry spent the evening of election day in Boston with his crew. People who try to brand Kerry as aloof don't know him at all. Loyalty and devotion are among his core attributes.

On the same evening that we pored over maps, I learned that our advance team had made a different discovery that potentially had as much meaning as finding the precise location of the battle.

Sean had spoken with Võ Ban Tâm, a local shrimp farmer at the site of the ambush, who said that as a twenty-two-year-old Việt Cộng guerrilla, he had witnessed the ambush and subsequent killing by Lieutenant Kerry of another Việt Cộng, Ba Thanh. Tâm had been interviewed by a television crew in 2004, but its members had not been able to corroborate his story.

I asked Ben Wilkinson, a Harvard administrator who speaks impeccable Vietnamese, for support. Ben interviewed Tâm and determined that their facts matched: Tâm had seen the 1969 firefight that was so meaningful for Kerry.

After the boat ride, we arranged for Kerry to meet with Tâm, who told Kerry about Thanh, the man he had killed. Tâm said: "He was a good soldier. He knew how to handle a B-40 grenade launcher." Almost five decades after the incident, Kerry at last knew the name, age, and abilities of the man he had killed. Thanh was two years younger than Kerry, and Tâm was a few years younger than Thanh. Tâm and Kerry spoke for a little while, and finally they shook hands. "I'm glad we're both alive," Kerry said.

A dozen years earlier, when Kerry had been a senator, he had given an interview in which he spoke about the man he had killed, whose name he did not yet know: "It was either going to be him or it was going to be us. It was that simple. I don't know why it wasn't us—I mean, to this day. He had a rocket [B-40 grenade launcher] pointed right at our boat. He stood up out of a hole, and none of us saw him until he was standing in front of us, aiming a rocket right at us, and, for whatever reason, he didn't pull the trigger—he turned and ran. . . . If he'd pulled the trigger, we'd all be dead."[9]

During Kerry's 2004 presidential campaign against George W. Bush, an anti-Kerry group calling itself Swift Boat Veterans for Truth circulated a story suggesting that Kerry had shot an unarmed teenage boy in the back—a war crime—and should never have been awarded the Silver Star. This group's attack on Kerry in August 2004 may have given President Bush his narrow victory in November. If the U.S. voter had known in 2004 what we learned in 2017 about those long-ago events, Kerry might have been elected the forty-fourth president of the United States.[10]

The trip to Cà Mau proved that Kerry had told the truth and that the men who sought his defeat in the presidential race had lied. This was Kerry's final trip to Vietnam as secretary of state. It came a week before the inauguration of President Trump, who would roll back many of Kerry's and President Obama's major foreign policy and domestic accomplishments.

As I rode with Kerry in limousines, a military plane, and a speedboat, I could see that he was relaxed and comfortable with all that he had achieved in Vietnam. I felt that he was at ease with what he had accomplished as a veteran, a senator, and America's top diplomat. Yet it was also clear that his work remained unfinished. In the years ahead, he would work vigorously to promoting the use of clean energy—including in Vietnam—and to head off the worst effects of climate change. In November 2020, President-elect Joe Biden named Kerry his special presidential envoy for climate, an incredibly challenging position that would draw on his decades of experience in trying to place the world on a better track.

My focus on January 20, 2017, was not on the inauguration of the forty-fifth U.S. president taking place in Washington, DC. Instead, I gripped a thin metal ladder, leaned in close, and noticed that a cut on my right forearm, caused by a fall the day before, had reopened. Water poured down the bumpy rock wall, and a little blood—mixed with the cold rivulets of water—was running down my arm.

With each step up, I had to kick the flexible ladder away from the wall—forty stories high from its submerged bottom to the top—to wedge my boots into narrow rungs. I didn't particularly want to look down, since the bottom was very far below. However, I had no choice because that was the only way to find the next rung.

In the two days since we entered into Sơn Đoòng, the world's largest cave, heavy, unseasonable rain and ten feet of raging river had submerged the simple bridges we'd used to climb into the cave. That morning, we had found ourselves trapped by fast-rising water with no way to return to the entrance. "We haven't done this before, but there is no other way," said our Yorkshire-born guides, Deb and Howard Limbert. "We're climbing out over the 'Great Wall.'"

We paddled to the wall's base in small, tippy boats. My friend Michael Piro, a Hanoi-based businessman, rode in a leaky boat that rapidly filled with muddy water as he attempted to climb out and seize the swinging ladder. This part of the cave was so vast that Hanoi's tallest skyscraper could fit in it with room to spare.

The lake was a hundred feet deep, and only an hour earlier, when Deb's boat had overturned, we had almost lost the rolled-up ladders in its depths. If her quick reflexes hadn't prevented the ladders from sinking, we might have spent a lot longer in the cave.

One by one, all ten of us heaved ourselves over the first of two summits, soaked and with our hearts pounding. It was the thrill of a lifetime.

Sơn Đoòng's calmer moments were, at times, sublime. We took turns showering, naked, under a rare waterfall. This one had clear water, filtered through limestone, that poured from the cave roof a hundred meters above. Light spilled in from an opening that Deb and Howard called "Watch Out for Dinosaurs."

PHOTO 36 Sơn Đoòng Cave, Quảng Bình province, January 2017 (Credit: Photo by the author).

Geologists have written about Sơn Đoòng's beauty, its stalagmites the size of the Capitol Dome, the 450-million-year-old fossils adorning its walls, and the tunnels formed within the cave. Water has carved out intricate cave pearls and giant sand dunes. In two spots, the roof has collapsed, diverting water from nature's delicate stone sculptures and causing jungles to spill in. The first of these, known as "The Garden of Eden," includes towering rock formations and undulating, fern-covered terraces. Plant, fish, and insect species have been discovered in the cave that don't exist anywhere else on earth.

The environment is harsh and also very fragile. Developers wanted to build a cable car into the cave, which by the time we visited had seen about as many visitors as had ventured into outer space. The cable car would bring eight thousand tourists per day through the six-mile cave. Mass tourism would destroy what is rare and priceless.

We began our journey four days before reaching the Great Wall, which is five and a half miles deep in the cave. It took us a day and a half just to reach the cave entrance, climbing through deep jungle, picking off leeches, fording more than thirty streams, and traversing Hang Én—the world's third-largest cave—just to reach the hidden valley that protects Sơn Đoòng. We slept in tents for three nights, and we would have stayed for a fourth if the rising waters hadn't forced us over the wall.

Maps from what the Vietnamese call the American War showed a disappearing river amid the limestone karst, which to an experienced caver is a sign that something interesting might exist. Hồ Khanh, an intrepid Vietnamese hunter who joined our trek, had felt cool air rising from the cave's mouth in 1990 but had not been able to find it again until 2009. When we visited Sơn Đoòng, the cave had been known to the world for only seven years despite its enormity.

Peter Ryder, a longtime friend who is a real estate developer, and I had managed to assemble a great team of adventurers. Brian Bulloch, a former Marine, periodically did pull-ups in anticipation of our climbs. Michael was such an enthusiastic photographer that he continued filming as his boat sank at the Great Wall's base and he noted calmly, "we're going down." Recent college graduates Lucas Ryder (Peter's son) and Grant Rickon added great energy to our group and were always ready for a challenge.

My friends of more than four decades, Eileen Kim and Mark Asbury, had flown in from California—Eileen having decided at the last minute to join us. My embassy colleague Nick Tyner had been on the bike ride to Huế the year before, which meant that he was already used to being wet and cold. At one moment in the cave he asked me, "do you travel any other way?"

Alex Rosenblatt, a marathon runner and enthusiast of the outdoors, played the guitar each evening, and when we sang, echoes of the music bounced off the cave walls and bats swooped overhead. The guitar bore the signatures of a half-dozen ambassadors who had explored Sơn Đoòng the previous May, while our embassy team was busy preparing to host President Obama. (I added one more signature to the guitar before the trip ended.)

Each day after wrestling with rock, mud, cold, and rain, our kind and generous guides and porters cooked an unthinkable variety of delicious Vietnamese dishes, with rice wine to wash them down. We helped each other over the steep parts, and Bamboo, An, Quân, Tom, Nui, Anh, and Tuấn—our local guides from Phong Nha village—made sure we were safe. Despite the hardships, no one wanted the adventure to end.

If the cable car was built, we would be among the last to see the cave in its pristine beauty. Yet it would be a difficult feat of engineering to anchor the cable car, especially as rocks as big as locomotives were still shifting on the unstable ground around Sơn Đoòng. I hoped that developers would abandon the project as technically infeasible.

Others did more than wonder and hope. My friend Tom Malinowski—assistant secretary of state for democracy, human rights, and labor and the person who took my place on an earlier cave trip just weeks before President Obama arrived in Vietnam—had begun his career as a speechwriter. Seeing an opportunity, he lobbied to include a reference to Sơn Đoòng in the speech the president gave in Hanoi.

"If we're going to ensure the health of our people and the beauty of our planet," the president said to the people of Vietnam, "then development has to be sustainable. Natural wonders like Hạ Long Bay and Sơn Đoòng Cave have to be preserved for our children and our grandchildren."[11]

This was a galvanizing moment for activists who wanted to save Sơn Đoòng. Lê Nguyễn Thiên Hương, an alumna of California State University, Fullerton, had founded a Facebook group, #SaveSơnĐoòng, and took advantage of the moment. The next day when President Obama spoke to six hundred members of the Young Southeast Asian Leaders Initiative in Hồ Chí Minh City, Hương leaped to her feet and offered him a #SaveSơnĐoòng T-shirt and traditional conical hat. She told the president, "Yesterday I literally burst into tears when you mentioned preserving the cave for our children, our grandchildren."

She asked him, "If you have a chance to visit Sơn Đoòng, would you like to do it on foot by trekking, or would you take a cable car?"

I was in the audience next to Kerry and felt a surge of panic because I had not briefed the president on the controversy over the cable car. I should not have worried because this president knew intuitively what to say. "First of all," Obama replied, "I definitely want to go visit the next time I come. And I'm a pretty healthy guy, so I can go on foot. How long is it? Seven days? Okay, I'm good. I can do that."

He continued: "One of the great things about your generation is that you're already much more conscious about the environment than my generation was or previous generations were. And that's really important not only to preserve beautiful sites in our countries, but also because economic development and the well-being and the health of your people and everyone around the world is going to depend on how we deal with some of these environmental issues."

Hương was thrilled. Those of us who cared about Sơn Đoòng Cave knew we had scored big. Hương spoke to the press: "Vietnamese take pride in their beautiful landscapes recognized as the world's natural heritage sites. But they don't take action to protect them."[12]

Soon after my trip to the cave, I joined the six ambassadors who had ventured with Malinowski into Sơn Đoòng in appealing to Nguyễn Ngọc Thiện, Vietnam's minister of culture, sports, and tourism. Writing in our personal capacities, we urged him to recognize Vietnam's responsibility to preserve an extraordinary and unique site (UNESCO had declared the cave a World Heritage Site in 2003).

"We recognize that decisions about the future of Sơn Đoòng Cave are entirely a matter for the Vietnamese government, consulting as necessary with UNESCO given Sơn Đoòng's status as a World Heritage Site," we wrote. "However, as friends of Vietnam, we hope that you will consider carefully the case for preserving Sơn Đoòng in its current state.

"While construction of a cable car may carry short-term economic benefits, we believe that it would also cause significant long-term damage to Vietnam's image and reputation, as well as to the prospects for developing sustainable, environmentally sensitive tourism. Construction of a cable car will change the character of the cave completely and destroy what it has taken nature millions of years to build."[13]

The minister did not take long to reply. Even though he was careful not to rule out eventual development of the cave for mass tourism, he promised to carry out an environmental impact assessment. "Before reporting to the Prime Minister for final decision," he wrote, "the Ministry . . . will consult relevant ministries, the National Heritage Council and especially the World Heritage Centre, IUCN [the International Union for Conservation of Nature, an NGO], and the World Heritage Committee, and find necessary solutions to ensure the full protection of the Outstanding Universal Values of the world heritage."[14]

We had at least bought some time, and I convened the interested parties, including the director Jordan Vogt-Roberts, who had recently filmed *Kong: Skull Island*[15] in Vietnam and was passionate about saving Sơn Đoòng. We decided that our best bet was to play the UNESCO World Heritage Site card. Vietnam took its international commitments seriously and, at that moment, a Vietnamese diplomat was a candidate to chair UNESCO.

Two months later, on May 19, 2017, our efforts seemed to pay off, at least for a time. The World Heritage Committee, which had invested funds and effort to protect Sơn Đoòng, challenged the need to build a road to the site and noted that Hanoi had promised that "construction of the cable car will only be conducted with the endorsement of the World Heritage Committee."[16]

Drawing on an analysis by the World Heritage Centre and IUCN, the committee warned that the provincial government had taken steps indicating that "the project remains under consideration."[17] The committee then requested that Vietnam "permanently cancel plans of [sic] the cable car development."[18]

This declaration from UNESCO succeeded in getting the attention of Vietnam's government, though cable car plans were still being considered. But the diplomats who had intervened at this moment would soon be off to other postings. There was no guarantee that Vietnamese governments would continue to honor UNESCO's request. To save Sơn Đoòng Cave, Vietnamese activists like Huong had to remain vigilant.

In early March 2017, my team and I made our last long bicycle ride. We traveled to Thảo's home province, the rugged Hà Giang at the northernmost tip of Vietnam. This was also the home province of Lieutenant Colonel Jacky Ly, head of the U.S. Office of Defense Cooperation and a key leader in developing the U.S. security relationship with Vietnam.

Jacky was born in Hà Giang, but he and his family had left when he was only a year old to avoid a devastating border war with China. Hà Giang is surrounded on three sides by China and suffered greatly during the twelve-year border war that ended in 1991. Jacky's family made it to the United States twelve years later, and after finishing high school, Jacky joined the U.S. Army as a way of giving back to his adopted country.

On our trip, we inaugurated a secondary school that had been built in Jacky's home village, Phố Bảng, and we walked over to the now peaceful provincial border with China. Jacky had organized donations from a group of Vietnamese Americans to the adjacent village's elementary school, providing the kids with beds to sleep on and proper utensils for eating. It was an emotional visit for Jacky. Earlier, when he had been promoted to lieutenant colonel, I performed the official pinning-on ceremony to affix his new rank insignia to his uniform. I considered it a great personal honor, exceeded only when Jacky later asked me to perform the marriage ceremony during his wedding to another Vietnamese-born American, Angeline. Moments like those were among the high points of my time as ambassador.

In mountainous Hà Giang, our team of hardy bikers scaled Mã Pí Lèng, the province's highest pass, via some of the steepest climbs I have yet experienced. At Mã Pí Lèng's highest point, we were able to look down into Vietnam's dramatic Grand Canyon, carved by the Nho Quế River. There, we met up with a dozen or so teenage boys, who thought it would be fun to ride bikes with the American ambassador. Our team members had fancy bicycles, with lots of gears, but the boys' bikes were basic. Still, they had cycled up the steep road without gears or a backup van. We drank tea and sodas with these kids and talked about their plans for the future. Several wanted to become policemen, and one planned to join the army.

For any bicyclist, the sweet reward after a long, steep climb is a long, fast descent. As we sped into the boys' hometown of Mèo Vạc, I knew that the fun part of my tour in Vietnam had come to an end. The months ahead would be tough, as I tried to represent the United States under a new president whose policies I did not support.

We stopped our bikes at the bottom of the mountain, and a fourteen-year-old boy, who had been shy at first, realized it was time to say so long. Our trip had ended, and he gave me a farewell hug when it was time to leave. Perhaps he sensed that I, too, was sad to say goodbye.

Ditches and Tree Roots

●●●●●●●●●●●●●●

> Both our societies live with ghosts, with memories, and with legacies. With the aftermath.
>
> **DREW GILPIN FAUST**, remarks delivered on March 23, 2017, at the University of Social Sciences and Humanities

In a speech at the University of Social Sciences and Humanities in Hồ Chí Minh City, Drew Gilpin Faust—president of Harvard University, a historian of the American Civil War, and author of *This Republic of Suffering: Death and the American Civil War*—discussed the difficulties in reconciling after that bitter divide: "We continue to struggle over the war's meaning for the nation's abiding racial divisions. Americans still battle over the use of the Confederate flag, the emblem of the would-be white southern nation that fought to preserve black slavery, a symbol that today is seen by most Americans as an affront and an obstacle to racial justice."[1]

Clayton and I hosted a dinner for Faust in Hanoi the night after her speech. As ambassador, I too found myself dealing with the aftermath of a civil war, and I told her about my experiences with members of the Vietnamese American community in Southern California, Texas, Virginia, and Washington State. "Many members of that community have asked me about Biên Hòa Cemetery near Hồ Chí Minh City," I said.

"It's an important place for many," I explained, "because soldiers who fought for South Vietnam are buried there. Properly burying the dead, in their homeland, matters to the Vietnamese, whatever part of the country they come from. After I visited the cemetery, I asked that a U.S.-based NGO be permitted to fund its cleaning and maintenance. My requests have been denied. What should I do?"

Faust said that cemeteries "take on outsized meaning as symbols" and noted how long it took before Southern soldiers were buried at Gettysburg. She recommended that instead of talking about "The Dead," with capital letters, I speak about "honoring people who died." I thought that her idea could be helpful as we continued to pursue reconciliation.

Deputy Foreign Minister Lê Hoài Trung was also at the dinner, and Faust's observations led me to suggest to him that allowing the digging of ditches and the cutting of tree roots to clean up the cemetery and avoid the deterioration of the graves would be meaningful.

A day before her speech at the University of Social Sciences and Humanities, Faust had visited a Vietnamese military cemetery at Ấp Bắc, where a significant battle had taken place, showing what the Việt Cộng could do. On January 2, 1963, a small contingent of North Vietnamese guerrillas mauled a South Vietnamese division, led by an incompetent protégé of President Ngô Đình Diệm. The day after the battle, Neil Sheehan, a *New York Times* reporter, asked Brigadier General Robert York what had happened.[2]

"What the hell's it look like happened, boy?" the general replied. "They got away, that's what happened!"[3]

The battle of Ấp Bắc demonstrated to the Việt Cộng that they could defeat the nominally superior South Vietnamese forces, even though the South was well equipped with up-to-date military hardware and had significant support and funding from the United States. Despite being outnumbered more than five to one, the Việt Cộng had inflicted heavy damage and then melted away, boosting their morale and confidence. Referring to Ấp Bắc, Faust said in her speech, "Created a century after our American Civil War and half a world away, this graveyard represents the same human urgency to honor the dead and their sacrifice."

Faust said that after America's Civil War, the victors ultimately concluded that reconciliation depended upon honoring each human being's dignity, even in death. Biên Hòa Cemetery had become a potent symbol for those on the losing side of Vietnam's civil war. A decision by the victors to allow the cemetery's rehabilitation would therefore be meaningful. I wanted Vietnamese leaders in Hanoi to make this decision, but as ambassador, I had to step gingerly into this fraught and highly emotional territory.

Also in March 2017, I met with President Trần Đại Quang[4] to plan for a visit to the United States by Vietnam's prime minister, Nguyễn Xuân Phúc. I was now acting on behalf of the administration of President Donald Trump, and I told President Quang that Vietnamese compliance with U.N. sanctions on North Korea was a "litmus test" for the new U.S. leaders. Vietnam needed to pass the test if security relations and the overall partnership between the two countries were to continue on their positive trajectory. In my meeting with Quang I also floated the idea of having a U.S. aircraft carrier visit Vietnam. Quang was a poker-faced man, and his reaction was hard to read. Still, I thought he was intrigued by the proposal.

The United States had made clear its unhappiness about North Korean attempts to ship coal illegally to Vietnam. The Vietnamese acted on this and intercepted the shipments. Phúc subsequently ordered a complete freeze on the import of all North Korean coal. He also placed visa restrictions on North Korean workers and expelled individuals affiliated with U.N.-sanctioned entities. From the U.S. perspective, this was a big win.

Hanoi reinforced to North Korean leaders in private communications that their only path to a secure and prosperous future lay in peaceful relations with the United States. As a former U.S. adversary and a Communist nation, Vietnam had special credibility in delivering that message.

Early in 2017, I nominated Nguyễn Ngọc Như Quỳnh, one of the world's most famous bloggers (better known as "Mother Mushroom," from a term of endearment she uses with her daughter), for the State Department's 2017 International Women of Courage Award.

In October, police had arrested Quỳnh, who cofounded the Network of Vietnamese Bloggers and regularly posted anti-Chinese blogs. Her arrest violated Vietnam's international obligations and its own 2013 constitution. Nine ambassadors joined me in protesting the arrest.

When Quỳnh won the State Department's award on March 29, I announced this on Facebook, and hundreds of thousands of Vietnamese responded online. Lê Hải Bình, a ministry of foreign affairs spokesperson, denounced the award "as lacking objectiveness, inappropriate, and not beneficial to developing ties."[5]

Quỳnh's mother, Nguyễn Thị Tuyết Lan, wrote a letter accusing Khánh Hòa province police of harassing and terrorizing her relatives.

"Two of my sisters' families received four summonses to meet with the police for their involvement in Nguyễn Ngọc Như Quỳnh's case," Lan's letter said. "My sisters are not familiar with politics and always try to work hard to make ends meet. They are confused and afraid. . . . When meeting with the police, they were threatened for having complained about seizure of land that was unlawfully seized by the government in 2007. . . . The fact that my sisters were 'summoned,' not 'invited' by the police just because they are Quỳnh's relatives is an abuse of power against citizens who didn't violate the law. This is a form of mental intimidation against Quỳnh's relatives. . . . I am choking with indignation about the actions of Khánh Hòa provincial police against my relatives. I don't know what else they will do to harass and terrorize my family. I beg the Vietnamese community and international community to help my family."[6]

Even some Vietnamese who support the government thought that this action—the harassment of a prisoner's family—was over the top. Võ An Đôn, a human rights attorney, reported that Quỳnh endured terrible conditions: "She subsisted only on a diet of anchovies and spinach soup for the first seven months and was denied both sanitary pads and underwear."[7] Quỳnh's mother heard nothing about Quỳnh's whereabouts or well-being for eight months, until police permitted the two to have a brief reunion in prison only hours before Quỳnh's trial for crimes against the state.

In its first months, the Trump administration attempted to ban Muslims from entering the United States. This ban was challenged in U.S. courts. I had to explain the checks and balances of America's constitution-based system to the Vietnamese, and I tried to reassure them (and myself) that most Americans still welcomed and valued diversity. Many of my State Department colleagues had signed an internal dissent message, objecting to the Muslim ban. Like me, they believed that the United States derived its strength from its diversity. When their message became public, their argument swayed no one in the White House but certainly increased the president's disdain for the State Department.

During the campaign, President Trump had been clear about his opposition to the Trans-Pacific Partnership (TPP) trade agreement, and his administration kept his promise to withdraw the United States from the agreement. This decision affected Vietnam, and I attempted to explain to officials that fundamental U.S. interests remained unchanged, even with a new president. In April, I met with Nguyễn Tấn Dũng, the former prime minister. I knew how much he had risked by pushing for his government to join the TPP, and I wanted to see him face-to-face. The United States, I believed, had drawn Dũng out to the end of a long limb and then cut it off.

Dũng met me in the Government Guest House in Hanoi, and I remarked to embassy colleagues following the discussion that, after a U.S. official had left office, he could never have held such a meeting on government property. Dũng was accompanied by senior Foreign Ministry officials, who dutifully took notes and reported our discussion to their superiors.

I told Dũng that I personally regretted America's withdrawal from the TPP. He explained that his views were also "personal and not official." He hoped that the U.S.-Vietnam Comprehensive Partnership would deepen during the Trump presidency. He urged the United States to "continue to play an active role in maintaining peace and security" in the region and to "ensure freedom of navigation and overflight in the East Sea" (using the Vietnamese name for the South China Sea).

Dũng stressed that Vietnam favored "free trade" and hoped that trade relations with the United States could deepen under the terms negotiated in the TPP, even without the agreement. Without rancor about the Trump administration and with Vietnamese pragmatism, Dũng said he hoped that President Trump would "meet soon" with Prime Minister Phúc and that the president would visit Đà Nẵng for the Asia-Pacific Economic Cooperation (APEC) leaders' week later that year.

I followed up on this meeting with a close advisor to Dũng who had weathered the transition to a new prime minister. This official did not take such a high view of America's withdrawal from the TPP. "We will now abandon the reforms we had promised under the TPP," he told me. "Those who opposed our agreement on workers' rights are delighted. They will keep a Party monopoly on all labor unions. The pressure is off the state-owned enterprises. Reform has stalled."

I did not believe that reform would stop altogether. Other TPP partners thought that the trade agreement might continue even without the United States, resulting in more economic changes. However, the Vietnamese official was correct about the consequences for workers' rights, the most significant TPP accomplishment and a human rights breakthrough. As President Trump continued to stir up racial tensions in America and to clamp down on immigration via his Muslim ban and the construction of a wall on the U.S.-Mexican border, it became increasingly difficult to press the Vietnamese about human rights.

The same Vietnamese official said that Vietnamese business leaders were instead turning toward China and Chinese investment in Vietnam had increased. Vietnamese trade with the United States would also increase, but—in Southeast Asia and beyond—China, not the United States, was setting the rules of trade.

In mid-April, I traveled to Washington, DC, to get a better understanding of what Trump administration officials were thinking and what pitfalls to avoid. I spoke with Andrew Quinn, a friend and colleague who had helped negotiate the TPP and now was serving on the National Economic Council as special assistant to the president for international trade, investment, and development. Drew gave me hope there might be some defenders of trade liberalization in the new administration. However, the day after we met, he was relieved of his White House duties.

The State Department was a mess, unsure of how to please Secretary of State Rex Tillerson or the White House. I found one senior official whose integrity and spirits remained intact. Acting Assistant Secretary for East Asia Susan Thornton was a steady, knowledgeable career diplomat who had earned Tillerson's trust. But Susan told me that she was prepared to step aside if Tillerson or the White House wanted someone else for her position. She urged me, and all the professional diplomats still working on Asia, to keep doing our jobs.

I didn't then understand, though I suspect Susan did, how determined White House Chief Strategist Steve Bannon was to get rid of her. Bannon thought that Susan was too friendly to China, and she eventually left the administration in July 2018.

I called on another friend, Kurt Campbell, who had been assistant secretary of state for East Asia and a close advisor to Hillary Clinton during her campaign. Kurt warned me against saying anything negative about the Trump administration. "They won," he said, "and that's it."

A sense of vindictiveness pervaded the new team. Experienced foreign policy practitioners, especially those who believed in trade liberalization, were not welcome.

One of my Washington meetings, chaired by Senior Advisor to the President Steven Miller, was to discuss how to reverse a long-standing policy that prevented immigrants who entered the United States between the fall of

Saigon in 1975 and the establishment of diplomatic relations in 1995 from being deported to Vietnam. The people subject to deportation orders had fled communism and come to the United States as refugees. Miller showed a particular determination to deport the Vietnamese refugees.

More than eight thousand Vietnamese Americans were accused of crimes and subject to deportation orders. More than seven thousand of them had fled South Vietnam on boats and through the jungle in the years immediately following the war. The majority of those targeted for deportation—sometimes for minor infractions—had sided with the United States during the war, and their loyalty was to the flag of a nation that no longer existed. After the war, the United States had accepted more than eight hundred thousand Vietnamese refugees. These refugees had started new lives in the United States, married and raised children, paid taxes, and established deep roots in their new country. A man who left Vietnam at the end of the war could have spent his entire life loyal to the South and might have fought for a decade or more against the Communist North. Someone who left five or ten years after the war ended would likely have endured the misery of a reeducation camp.

After refusing for decades to repatriate any Vietnamese immigrants, Vietnam had signed an agreement in 2008 that allowed for the repatriation of some but excluded those who had entered the United States before normalization of diplomatic relations in July 1995. Miller wanted to change that. Immigration and Customs Enforcement (ICE) officials advocated for the immediate abrogation of the 2008 agreement. State Department lawyers pushed instead for a unilateral interpretation of the agreement so the Trump administration could try to deport immigrants who had arrived in the United States before 1995. I feared not only that these returning refugees would become human rights cases, but also that this change in policy would upset our economic agenda and harm the ongoing process of reconciliation.

In mid-May, Robert Lighthizer, the new U.S. trade representative, came to Vietnam for an APEC ministerial-level meeting. Lighthizer had a friendly and engaging manner, but his visit was a disaster in terms of substance. The Vietnamese, other APEC country representatives, and the U.S. business community were stunned by the arrogance of his remarks and his willingness to sabotage an international trade agenda in favor of an "America first" approach.

By this time, a visit to the United States and a meeting with President Trump at the White House had been planned for Prime Minister Phúc.

When the prime minister arrived in New York City on May 30, U.S. investors in Vietnam—including the businessman Phil Falcone (my Harvard classmate and one of the biggest U.S. investors in Vietnam) and Kurt Campbell, one of his advisors—welcomed Phúc and his commercial delegation at a star-studded investor gathering at the InterContinental New York Barclay hotel. At the event, incentives and opportunities for doing more business with the United States were highlighted, and Phúc promised that by 2035, 30 percent of Vietnamese citizens would be members of the middle class. He touted Vietnam's reforms and its upgraded credit ratings and pledged that the country would increase its purchases of U.S. exports. American investors were impressed.

I accompanied the prime minister on his flight from New York to Washington. He ambled back to my seat on the plane to ask how he could best engage with President Trump. "Be yourself," I urged him. "Use visual aids, but don't rely too heavily on notes." Maps would be good, too, I suggested.

In time for Phúc's visit, U.S. companies had completed more than $8 billion worth of commercial deals, mostly for high-tech products—including almost $6 billion worth of sales for General Electric. In Washington, the prime minister was joined by Secretary of Commerce Wilbur Ross in a ceremonial signing of the biggest completed deals.

Our meeting with Ross before the signing was particularly unsettling, however. The eighty-one-year-old secretary seemed lost, unable to find his place in his briefing notes or to determine which trade challenges to emphasize. His translator was also hapless, and we had to rely on the prime minister's. Ross focused on obscure agricultural disputes over shrimp, catfish, cheese, and drugs for veterinary medicine, all mentioned in an annex to his briefing paper. These issues were supposed to be the purview of Agriculture Secretary Sonny Perdue. The meeting with Perdue was far more productive, as both leaders enjoyed solving problems.

Phúc's meeting with Lighthizer was also useful, especially because Lighthizer had so recently visited Vietnam. That evening, at a dinner hosted by the U.S. Chamber of Commerce, Lighthizer introduced the prime minister by noting that "our trade deficit presents new challenges and shows us that there is considerable potential to improve further our important trade relationship."

Phúc stated that Vietnam was eager to increase trade with and investments by the United States. "In terms of trade," he said, "it is absolutely realizable for us to increase our trade turnover, thus turning the U.S. into Vietnam's largest trading partner and promoting fair and equal bilateral trade relations. It is Vietnam's desire that the U.S. will facilitate the import of textiles and garments, footwear, seafood, fruits, and other products."

When I was a foreign policy staffer for Vice President Al Gore, I visited the Oval Office a number of times. As ambassador, I accompanied Vietnam's Communist Party leader to his meeting with President Barack Obama. Nothing could have prepared me for the strangeness of President Trump's meeting with Vietnam's prime minister on May 31, 2017.

The Oval Office looked the same. The wall-to-ceiling windows continued to overlook the South Lawn. The famous "Resolute" desk dominated the room. But it didn't feel like the Oval Office I remembered. In President Obama's time, rooms outside the Oval Office buzzed with activity, while the office itself was serene. Now the situation was reversed. The West Wing seemed eerily quiet. Inside the Oval Office, people scurried in and out. Deputy National Security Advisor Dina Powell and a cluster of other advisors huddled around the "Resolute" desk, where Presidents Rutherford Hayes, Franklin Roosevelt, and John Kennedy had governed. No one left to make room for the new arrivals, and the office seemed to get more crowded with each passing moment.

Standing behind a cluster of aides and attempting to get the president's attention, National Security Advisor General H. R. McMaster tried to introduce me to President Trump: "Mr. President, this is our ambassador to Vietnam."

I stared at a stiff helmet of orange hair as the president looked up and said, "You're lucky. That's a good job."

"Yes, sir, I'm very lucky," I said. "I love my job and feel privileged to do it."

"So, who are we meeting?" the president asked.

"The prime minister of Vietnam," McMaster replied.

"What's his name?"

"Nguyễn Xuân Phúc," a senior National Security Council official said. "Rhymes with 'book.'"

"You mean like Fook You?" President Trump asked. "I knew a guy named Fook You. Really. I rented him a restaurant. When he picked up the phone, he answered 'Fook You.' His business went badly. People didn't like that. He lost the restaurant."

All those present laughed dutifully.

"Mr. President," McMaster interrupted, "we only have five minutes for this briefing."

More people slipped in and out. I wondered how anyone could concentrate in all the chaos. After hearing that Vietnam had a trade surplus with the United States and a trade deficit with China, the president interjected: "The Chinese always get great deals. Except with me. I did a great deal in China."

President Trump then instructed Lighthizer to "bring the U.S. trade deficit with Vietnam to zero in four years."

Lighthizer nodded, perhaps not knowing how to reply. It was an impossible task. He then tried to shift the president's focus. "The ambassador [to Vietnam] is trying to finish a deal to build a new embassy," he said. "We can have a groundbreaking ceremony when you visit."

A member of Lighthizer's staff had told me, earnestly, that President Trump liked groundbreaking ceremonies. He enjoyed holding a gold-plated shovel for the photographers.

"I'm visiting?" the president asked, apparently unaware that he had agreed to join an autumn summit of APEC in Vietnam. He then disappeared into another room.

Jared Kushner, the president's son-in-law and a White House advisor, was paying attention to our conversation about building a new embassy in Hanoi. "How much will it cost?" Kushner asked. I replied that the U.S. embassy in Beijing cost more than $1 billion. A new embassy in Hanoi might be built for less—perhaps half as much, depending on the cost of the land.

"$500 million?" Kushner seemed surprised. "That's a lot. Why are we spending so much? If we're going to give them that, we should get something back."

I wondered if he understood that we were trying to build a new embassy for the United States and not for Vietnam. "Our current leased space is dilapidated," I told him. "It was supposed to be temporary twenty-two years ago. It's not safe. A truck bomb could drive right up to it and blow us up in a moment. Like in Benghazi."

Kushner had already formed an opinion. "If they're going to get that [embassy]," he said, "We need something in return. Tell them we'll build it if they bring our trade deficit to zero."

I repeated my argument about security for American citizens, but Kushner's dark eyes had shifted elsewhere. He was no longer listening.

Ushered out of the Oval Office, I stood in the hallway and chatted with Vice President Mike Pence. He had just returned from Jakarta, Indonesia, where he had addressed the Association of Southeast Asian Nations. I told Pence that Vietnam had received his speech warmly. Smiling, his blue eyes focused on mine, the vice president demonstrated an uncanny ability to make me feel like I was the most important person in the world.

We waited while President Trump and Prime Minister Phúc met in the Oval Office "one-on-one"—with interpreters and about a hundred television and print journalists. President Trump noted that the United States has "a major trade deficit with Vietnam, which will hopefully balance out in a short period of time. We expect to be able to do that."

The prime minister showed the president a map of the South China Sea as a reminder that China's behavior concerned Vietnam most of all.

The president and prime minister then moved to the Cabinet Room, where the vice president, cabinet members, and I joined them. President Trump again urged Prime Minister Phúc to reduce Vietnam's trade deficit with the United States from $32 billion to zero in four years. He also encouraged Vietnam to ratchet up its pressure on North Korea, and he asked that Vietnam accelerate its acceptance of Vietnamese refugees subject to deportation orders. I knew the source of the third request: I had seen Miller slip in and whisper into the president's ear just as he was heading to the Cabinet Room.

It was left to the prime minister of Communist Vietnam to extol the virtues of free and fair trade. He said that trade "leads to growth and jobs. Our two economies are more complementary than competitive."

President Trump spoke again about trade deficits and said, "we must make more progress before the APEC summit." The president told the prime minister that Saudi Arabia had placed orders worth $450 billion during the president's recent visit there. "Jared [Kushner] and Rex [Tillerson] worked really hard," he said. The message was clear: presidential visits came with a price tag.

When McMaster suggested that "an aircraft carrier visit would be historic and an important symbol," the prime minister replied carefully that Vietnam "appreciated the initiative to bring an aircraft carrier. When we have the capability, we'll receive it." He added, "We are not yet in a position to do so."

Vietnamese leaders needed first to gauge the Chinese reaction before committing to a date for an aircraft carrier visit.[8] In a joint statement released following the prime minister's White House visit, the Vietnamese said only that the two leaders had "looked into the possibility of a visit to a Vietnamese port by a United States aircraft carrier."[9]

As President Trump walked Prime Minister Phúc out of the West Wing, the group ran into Marc Kasowitz, one of the president's lawyers. Kasowitz also represented Falcone. In December 2016, Kasowitz and Falcone had arranged for President-elect Trump to speak by phone with the Vietnamese prime minister.

Kasowitz grinned when he saw the prime minister. He appeared to have been waiting outside to show that he had access to the West Wing and therefore "juice" with the current president. Surprised to see him, the prime minister smiled, his head tilted to one side.

"You know him?" the president asked, and the prime minister acknowledged that he did. Kasowitz shook my hand vigorously. "You know him, too?" the president asked me. I nodded.

After the December 2016 phone call, I had written to my bosses in the Obama administration's State Department, concerned that such a call, arranged by Falcone, showed Vietnam's prime minister that access to the new U.S. president could be bought.[10] I never received a reply.

After a January 12, 2017, meeting in Hanoi with Kasowitz, Falcone, and a gaggle of New York real estate lawyers associated with President Trump, an embassy colleague and I had compared notes. "I feel like I need to take a shower," she said. I, too, wanted to scrub away the scent of corruption.

Before meeting me, Kasowitz had asked a friend, "What leverage do we have over the ambassador? What do we need to give him to bring him onto our side?" My friend explained patiently that any U.S. ambassador has a responsibility to help American businesses succeed. No leverage or quid pro quo was needed for me to do my job.

The day after Prime Minister Phúc's Oval Office visit, the United States withdrew from the Paris Accord on climate change. When President Trump announced that he would pull out of the climate change agreement, a colleague I admired resigned from his post as acting ambassador in Beijing. I wondered whether it was time for me to step down. Vietnam was among the five countries that will suffer most immediately from rising sea levels. I had spent more than two years arguing that Vietnam should wean itself from its dependence on Chinese coal. The United States devoted much of its assistance budget in Vietnam to addressing climate change mitigation and adaptation efforts.

Ironically, President Trump's and Prime Minister Phúc's joint statement after their meeting included a U.S. commitment to continue collaboration on climate change, and the U.S. Agency for International Development (USAID) received a boost in its budget for climate mitigation and adaptation measures in Vietnam. When I asked at the National Security Council if the president would approve the joint statement with the climate change commitment, I learned that the president did not read such statements.

In June, Miller dispatched a team from ICE to urge the Vietnamese to accept more deported Vietnam war refugees. This team did not consider State Department officials in Hanoi to be sufficiently enthusiastic about the new deportation policy. I was stunned by the missionary zeal of the ICE team members, who—echoing President Trump's remarks when he launched his presidential campaign—declared that all the refugees subject to final deportation orders were "either murderers or rapists." I knew that this claim was untrue. Some of those refugees had been arrested for driving under the influence of alcohol, stealing, or lesser crimes. Deeply worried about this policy and its potential impacts, I wondered how to convey to the Vietnamese that America had not lost its way. I thought that U.S. immigration policies were becoming increasingly racist, vindictive, and un-American.

At a U.S. Independence Day celebration in Hồ Chí Minh City, I told the crowd that the United States was "a nation of people from every imaginable background, and we are so proud of that diversity. This certainly includes Vietnamese Americans, who contribute so much to the richness, productivity, and beauty of our country. Our values speak to who we are as a people. And they drive us to continue to forge ahead and create a better future."

For me, that was America's promise—not the attempt to create a nation guided by racism and fear. A few days later, I wrote a cable to Tillerson objecting to Miller's policy on deportation. I said that the administration's approach to deportations would jeopardize President Trump's other goals for U.S. relations with Vietnam, including reducing the trade deficit, strengthening military relations, and coping with regional threats to peace such as those emanating from North Korea.

I wrote to my family members to prepare them for the possibility that I would be relieved of my duties. Any day, I thought, I might receive an order to pack up and head home.

In July 2017, the USS *Coronado* and USNS *Savor* visited Cam Ranh International Port, for a joint activity with the Vietnam People's Navy. Cam Ranh Bay had been a refuge for U.S. Navy ships during the war, and in recent decades, it had been the Asian port of choice for Russian ships.

Japan also sent a ship, the J.S. *Sazanami*, and Umeda Kumio, the Japanese ambassador to Vietnam, invited my team and me to come on board that vessel. Japanese sailors on the *Sazanami*'s deck performed a smart welcoming ceremony with colorful, sharp sabers. Then we joined Japan's ambassador and the ship's commanding officers—along with Rear Admiral Donald Gabrielson, commander of U.S. Task Force 73—for a meal of sushi, sashimi, and ramen. I was reminded that the United States had been at war with Japan when my father was a child, and when I was a child the United States had waged war against North Vietnam from this spot. Now our three nations are allies and partners.

That summer, the United States also provided Vietnam with a first tranche of fast coastal patrol boats. I was honored to hand over to Vietnam's Coast Guard the first six (of twenty-four) forty-five-foot high-speed patrol boats called "Metal Sharks" in Quảng Nam province. In contrast to military materials and equipment that the Russians provided, the U.S. package included better equipment and spare parts, a fully operational maintenance facility, a state-of-the-art training facility, and extensive joint training—a testament of the U.S. commitment to Vietnam.

During President Obama's 2016 visit, he had fully normalized defense ties between the United States and Vietnam by lifting the long-standing ban on the sale to Vietnam of U.S. arms. President Obama had done this knowing that his action would invite criticism, especially from human rights groups. That ban had been a symbolic obstacle to security cooperation with Vietnam, and its removal allowed us to go forward with a plan that had been in the works since early in my tenure: to transfer the U.S. Coast Guard cutter *Morgenthau* to Vietnam.

In August 2017, I climbed aboard the *Morgenthau* at the Coast Guard's Honolulu base to see its Vietnamese naval captain and crew training side by side with American Coast Guard sailors who knew the ship inside and out.

For many decades, Vietnam's military received weapons, training, and other support from Russia. By the time I became ambassador, the Vietnamese had spent $4 billion—a large portion of the country's annual defense budget—on Kilo-class submarines but had received no training or maintenance as part of the purchase.

When Vietnam bought military hardware from Moscow, the Vietnamese government also had to set aside at least 5 percent of the budget to take care of bribes and kickbacks. In contrast, U.S. companies adhered to the Foreign Corrupt Practices Act of 1977, which imposes enormous fines and jail time on executives who pay bribes. One U.S. defense company lost a multimillion-dollar deal with the Vietnamese Navy because it would not pay the $2 million in bribes demanded to seal the deal. Russian (and other) military equipment providers had no such worries.

Our embassy team knew that to get Vietnam to lessen its dependence on Russia, we had to demonstrate American reliability and show that U.S. equipment was higher quality and a better deal in the long run. That began with the *Morgenthau*, a cutter with a proud history. The late John Rexford, a friend since his diplomatic service in Indonesia, wrote to me when he learned of the transfer: "From 1970 to 1971 the *Morgenthau* served in Vietnam, a participant in the U.S. Navy's Operation Market Time . . . I am confident she will serve Vietnam well for many years to come. When I first boarded her in 1976 as part of the Gold Eagle Crew, the *Morgenthau* sank in the dry dock in Baltimore. We had to remove and rebuild every electric motor and clean all diesels—a big mess!—and we did this in 30 days. We were able to recover her and kept on schedule, sailing to the North Atlantic to protect for the first time America's 200-mile fishing zone."[11]

Transferring the *Morgenthau* to Vietnam was a complex operation, involving three months of pretransfer training, then five months of posttransfer training, and finally two months of transit to Vietnam. The ship—the largest in Vietnam's fleet—arrived in Vietnam in October 2017.

Before that, it had taken two years of planning to create conditions where it was possible for Vietnam to accept the U.S. offer. The embassy's indefatigable political-military team—led by Colonel Tuấn T. Tôn and Lieutenant Colonel Jacky Ly, my cycling friend and colleague born in Hà Giang—stayed close to Vietnam's military leaders until a formal request was made. This request for a ship required Politburo approval, because Vietnam's leaders always wanted to know how China would react before taking such a big step. Vietnam's leaders also needed to gauge Russia's reaction, as Moscow did not want to lose its coveted position of providing Vietnam with its weaponry.

Giving the *Morgenthau* to Vietnam helped show that the United States was a reliable security partner. Pacific Commander Admiral Harry Harris and Defense Department leaders saw this as part of a strategic investment in a high-profile security partnership in the South China Sea, an area of great concern to the U.S. Navy. They also viewed the Hamilton class cutter as a sustainable platform for cooperation with Vietnam's Coast Guard, with which the United States had for years engaged in joint security activities.

The *Morgenthau*, renamed CSB 8020, became Vietnam's flagship, patrolling the South China Sea and serving as a proud symbol of the U.S.-Vietnam security cooperation. Prime Minister Phúc expressed appreciation for the cutter during his meeting with President Trump and told him that Vietnam was interested in "acquiring more defense equipment from the U.S., including additional Coast Guard cutters." By the time we provided the *Morgenthau* to Vietnam, the United States had already given the Vietnamese Coast Guard the six fast coastal patrol boats and engaged in multiple naval exchanges, including eight annual humanitarian visits to Vietnam as part of the Pacific Partnership, a masterful tool for engagement by the U.S. Navy. These activities helped build trust between the two countries and their confidence in each other, as well as enabling the USS *Carl Vinson*'s 2018 visit.

When I visited Hawaii in August 2017, Harris invited Bill Hagerty (the incoming U.S. ambassador to Japan), his wife, and me to a barbecue reception at Harris's home on a naval base at Pearl Harbor. At the beginning of the meal, Harris introduced his guests to the noncommissioned officers and enlisted sailors who had prepared our food. He knew their names and their hometowns. The troops admired Harris, and they knew he cared for them and had their backs.

I asked Harris to support our embassy's plan to have an aircraft carrier visit a Vietnamese port. I also asked Admiral Scott Swift, commander of the U.S. Pacific Fleet, for his support. Then I continued to work on persuading the Vietnamese leaders. I had raised the idea with President Quang, and U.S. officials had urged Prime Minister Phúc to consider it during his White House visit. Tôn and I knew that we still had more work to do if we wanted our plan to be implemented.

The same month, Vietnam opened a seven-story peacekeeping training facility funded by the United States,[12] which would enable Vietnam to train not only its own troops at the national Peacekeeping Center but also those of other Southeast Asian nations. Days later, Vietnam's Military Hospital 175 celebrated its completion of a U.S. training and equipment program for peacekeeping. The United States was not the only country providing support. Australia agreed to transport Vietnamese troops to South Sudan; and China, Japan, and South Korea also participated in peacekeeper training efforts.

This effort was a manifestation of what Vice Foreign Minister Hà Kim Ngọc had said in 2015, when he exhorted the United States and Vietnam to "move beyond bilateral cooperation to regional and global collaboration." It led to Vietnam's deployment in 2016 of a medical mission and Level II field hospital to South Sudan, which had been in the works for three years. Vietnam, a country that had suffered from centuries of war, had engaged in its first deployment of a unit of international peacekeepers.

On August 23, 2017, Health and Human Services Secretary Tom Price visited Hồ Chí Minh City, where he joined Health Minister Nguyễn Thị Kim Tiến in opening an emergency operations center (EOC) that linked the

Pasteur Institute and its talented public health officials directly to the U.S. Centers for Disease Control and Prevention (CDC) in Atlanta, Georgia, and another EOC that the United States had helped create in Hanoi. The CDC had had two decades of on-the-ground collaboration with Vietnamese public health institutions and had established a high degree of credibility and trust with Vietnamese health officials. Price's visit demonstrated how deep U.S.-Vietnam public health collaboration had become.

The EOCs in Vietnam's north and south, and a later one established in central Vietnam, were jointly operated by the Ministry of Health and the U.S. CDC, and the centers enhanced CDC-trained epidemiologists' ability to report in real time epidemic surveillance information to Hanoi and to CDC headquarters. A health partnership had grown since Mike Linnan served as the U.S. embassy's first health attaché, under Ambassador Pete Peterson. Public health was one of the first areas of collaboration between the two countries after full diplomatic relations had been established. Mike represented the CDC for five years at the embassy in Hanoi and then started the Hanoi School of Public Health. By the time Price visited, Vietnam had invested heavily in its health care system, with public health expenditures per capita increasing 9 percent per year between 2000 and 2016.[13]

Since the 1970s, the CDC has acted internationally to protect health in the United States. This task demands that the CDC have warning systems in place to alert public health officials to emerging infectious disease problems elsewhere in the world. Many diseases originate in Southeast Asia and China, and the CDC's global health security programs in Vietnam and elsewhere have grown and been strengthened.

The EOCs were used by epidemiologists during the COVID-19 pandemic, and Vietnam's sharing of public health information with the World Health Organization and CDC served the country well. Vietnam had learned the lessons of the Severe Acute Respiratory Syndrome (SARS) epidemic in 2003, H1N1 (swine flu) in 2009, and the Middle East Respiratory Syndrome epidemic in 2015. When COVID-19 hit, Vietnam's leaders acted swiftly and decisively, quickly ramping up temperature screening, investing in contact tracing and testing capabilities, imposing targeted lockdowns, and issuing frequent communications to the Vietnamese people about the seriousness of the pandemic.

We had much work to do to prepare for President Trump's visit to Vietnam in November, and I used that visit to slow down Miller's deportations plans. (Yes, the "deep state" was at work.) I sent more internal messages arguing that a showdown over deportations would hinder the success of the trip.

Following my instructions, I warned a senior Vietnamese diplomat that if Vietnam did not receive more deported refugees more quickly, the administration was considering punitive measures, including the elimination of port courtesies. "Port courtesies" meant that senior Vietnamese officials had simpler entry into the United States, and that they were not frisked at the airport. The official laughed and said simply, "If there are no port courtesies, no Vietnamese officials will visit." Vietnam would not tolerate disrespect. The official knew that without any visits of Vietnamese officials to the United States in the months leading up to a presidential visit to Vietnam, it would be impossible for the United States to advance its diplomatic goals.

On September 12, I sent a second message directly to Tillerson:

> The United States' history in Southeast Asia has made certain removals particularly sensitive, and we are concerned that our interagency partners may recommend penalties more quickly than we will be able to move past those sensitivities. The cases of concern—more than 8000 for Vietnam and 4500 for Laos—often involve those who entered the United States as refugees in the aftermath of the Indochina conflict. In many cases, they are individuals who fought against the current regimes in Vietnam and Laos and their immediate families. In the case of Vietnam, there is a longstanding Agreement in place to accept returning nationals who left after the 1995 normalization of relations; Laos has shown willingness to accept Lao nationals who entered the United States on documents issued by the Lao Peoples' Democratic Republic.[14]

I sent copies to McMaster at the White House and to senior officials at the Departments of State, Defense, and Homeland Security. I noted separately to State Department and White House officials that if the United States cut off port courtesies, we could expect a bumpy visit by President Trump to the November APEC summit.

Admiral Swift championed the idea of an aircraft carrier visit to Vietnam. On October 6, 2017, he visited Vietnam and included a side trip to the Bạch Đằng River, near Hải Phòng in northern Vietnam. It was there that Vietnam's great military heroes—Ngô Quyền, Lê Đại Hành, and Trần Hưng Đạo—had defeated northern aggressors by sinking stakes into the mud, using the weight of their adversaries for self-impalement. Swift viewed one of the original iron-tipped stakes. He understood that honoring these generals from past centuries would help bring about a decision to tighten Vietnam's security ties with the United States in the present. A month later, when President

Trump visited Hanoi, President Quang agreed to a plan for the first visit by a U.S. aircraft carrier to a Vietnamese port since the war. Swift's visit to the Bạch Đằng River and the respect it showed to Vietnamese military traditions led to that breakthrough.

On October 24, I met with the chairman of the People's Committee of Bình Dương province. We spoke of U.S. investments in his fast-growing province, as well as of taxes, power shortages, and other issues that mattered to U.S. companies there. Then we turned to the matter that had truly brought me to his province.

I repeated the request I had made to Vice Minister Trung at dinner with President Faust many months before. "I request permission for American citizens to finance digging ditches and cutting tree roots in Biên Hòa Cemetery," I said. "No flags, no symbols, no politics. Just digging ditches and cutting tree roots."

The chairman thanked me for sharing my "personal concerns" and said that he would consider the practical suggestions about improving maintenance, so that more families could pay their respects at Biên Hòa Cemetery. "Of course, I will have to consult with Hanoi," he added.

He did not say no.

Knowing it was unlikely that I would be able to visit Hồ Chí Minh City again as ambassador, I also paid a farewell call on former President Trương Tấn Sang. A former teacher, he always seemed pleased to speak with me in Vietnamese. In our discussion, I focused on the puzzle of reconciliation. Sang was optimistic, noting that Vietnam now had the confidence to welcome even those Vietnamese Americans who were most critical of the regime. "I understand that the government has increased public access to the Biên Hòa Cemetery," he told me. "It would be good for volunteer organizations to restore the graves of 'our brothers' who died fighting."

On October 27, I visited the cemetery with Nguyễn Đạc Thành, president of the Orange County, California–based Vietnamese American Foundation. We lit incense to honor the deceased South Vietnamese soldiers. Thanh reported that about 8,000 of the 12,000–18,000 soldiers' graves had been restored through quiet efforts, and 2,000 of those had been restored in the previous year. He said that immediate practical needs included drainage, tree cutting, road improvements, and lawn mowers, all of which awaited Vietnamese government approval.

I didn't hear from the chairman of Bình Dương's People's Committee until a few months later. The prime minister had asked the Foreign Ministry, working with the province, to facilitate the renovation of Biên Hòa

Cemetery by the Vietnamese American Foundation. The foundation was given permission to dig ditches and cut tree roots, and more than two hundred big trees had already been cut down. No one had lost face. Honor would be shown not to "the Dead," but to people who had died.

Reconciliation could proceed a little further.

On the same October trip, I visited another site in Biên Hòa, the former U.S. air base that was the country's worst dioxin hot spot. There, Senior Lieutenant General Nguyễn Chí Vịnh told me that Vietnam wished to hold a bilateral event during the upcoming APEC summit to highlight the successful dioxin remediation at the Đà Nẵng airport.[15]

Unfortunately, we had not succeeded in securing assistance funding, and cleaning up the last and largest "hot spot" at Biên Hòa would cost between $137 million and $1.4 billion. For planning purposes, we agreed with the Vietnamese on $390 million as a compromise, because technologies that cost less than that would leave the problem unresolved, but obtaining $1.4 billion was impossible.

The compromise amount would wipe out USAID's entire budget for East Asia in a given year, so I proposed a deal in which USAID would pay $150 million, the Defense Department would match that amount, and Vietnam and other international donors would make up the difference. I told Vietnam's government that I did not think the U.S. contribution would exceed $300 million and suggested that we jointly seek support from other governments. At least we had identified the cost and scope of the task.

In early 2016, Senator John McCain, chairman of the Armed Services Committee, had vetoed the effort to spend any Department of Defense funds for what he viewed as a humanitarian effort. Eventually, he was persuaded that addressing this war legacy would open up possibilities for security collaboration with Vietnam. With his support, my team and I had made another run at the Defense Department. That attempt prompted department lawyers to say that such an arrangement would open up the U.S. military to further claims from other combat zones. I pointed out that cleaning up Đà Nẵng had not resulted in any further claims.

In 2017, Tillerson's State Department canceled President Obama's 2016 commitment to cleaning up dioxin. When I objected, I received instructions to cease and desist, and the Defense Department also told us to give up. I did not, and neither did the members of my team. I pushed for a commitment to cleaning up dioxin as a deliverable for President Trump's November visit to Vietnam. Two months before the visit I wrote in a cable, "resolving dioxin as a legacy of the war is essential to the future of our defense ties with Vietnam." When I went to Biên Hòa, we were still at an impasse over funding.

Senior Lieutenant General Vịnh proposed that having Vietnam and the United States sign a memorandum of intent on dioxin remediation at Biên Hòa would lead to greater financial support from international partners and the Vietnamese government. Vịnh reviewed various remediation plans in detail, stressing that implementation would occur only after the United States made a concrete commitment. Vịnh reinforced what I had come to understand: dealing honestly with the past, by taking the lead in cleaning up Agent Orange, was key to carving out a different future for the United States and Vietnam.

Vịnh and I reviewed detailed maps of the areas around the air base with the highest levels of dioxin, and I reported to the State and Defense Departments and the White House that the dioxin had "migrated off-base, and potentially exposed 120,000 individuals living near the base perimeter." I added that "studies have demonstrated elevated levels of dioxin in blood and breast milk of surrounding residents."

A creek at the west end of the Biên Hòa air base carried water from the base to a nearby river. Colleagues told me that the creek contained highly concentrated dioxin. Kids played in the mud by the creek. Their parents fished from the river, and those fish had most likely absorbed toxic chemicals.

Seventy-five families lived along the creek. As I peered into their homes and watched children the ages of my own kids run and play, I wanted to scream: "Get away from here. You are in danger." We had failed those families. The effects of dioxin would pass from generation to generation. The bureaucratic delays we encountered in trying to fund the cleanup had real-life results: those families were condemned.

I thought it was important to pay respects to the North Vietnamese soldiers at Biên Hòa Cemetery as I had to the South Vietnamese soldiers. Six months earlier, U.S. veterans Bob Connor and Martin Strones had helped locate a mass burial site of Việt Cộng and North Vietnamese soldiers on Biên Hòa air base. Vietnam's government had identified the remains of seventy-two soldiers, sixty-six of whom still had living relatives. At a small shrine, I joined Vietnamese military officials and Consul General Mary Tarnowka to light incense to honor the deceased soldiers.

In mid-October, I learned that by October 27, my family and I would have to move out of the ambassador's residence and into a hotel to make room for President Trump's delegation, which would arrive in early November. On the twenty-seventh, while I was visiting Biên Hòa Cemetery, my successor was recommended by the Senate Foreign Relations Committee and confirmed by the full Senate. There is almost always a gap between a committee vote on confirmation and the vote of the full Senate—but not this time. Forty-eight hours later, the State Department sent me plane tickets and instructions to depart immediately. We had expected to leave our home and Vietnam after the president's visit, which I had considered my duty to support, but the Trump administration had other plans. We packed quickly and said a few hurried farewells. On November 4, 2017, we were hustled out of Hanoi with our two- and three-year-old children. My successor arrived a few hours after we departed.

I had been asked to leave Vietnam, but I could have remained at the State Department. I was on a short list for another ambassadorship and had been offered a position as diplomat in residence at the University of California, Los Angeles. However, by the summer of 2017, I had concluded that I could not work for the Trump administration any longer and could better serve my country from outside government, by helping to build a new, innovative university in Vietnam. On November 9, I resigned from the State Department after thirty years of public service.

President Trump gave a speech in Đà Nẵng for the APEC leaders' summit on November 10, and he told the world that the era of U.S. leadership on trade liberalization had ended. At a business summit, in a venue overlooking the South China Sea, the president said that the United States could no longer tolerate chronic trade abuses and would insist on fair and equal policies. He said that the United States was ready to make a bilateral deal with any country in the Indo-Pacific region, but only on the basis of mutual respect and mutual benefit.

"When the United States enters into a trading relationship with other countries or other peoples," the president continued, "we will, from now on, expect that our partners will faithfully follow the rules." He added, "We expect that markets will be open to an equal degree on both sides and that private industry, not government planners, will direct investment." He offered a "renewed partnership" that would promote shared prosperity and security.[16]

Lighthizer amplified the president's comments by saying that the United States would not hesitate to use its huge "economic leverage" to force other countries to change their behavior: "The president spoke loud and clear: the era of trade compromised by massive state intervention, subsidies, closed markets and mercantilism is ending." He added, "free, fair and reciprocal trade that leads to market outcomes and greater prosperity is on the horizon."[17]

President Trump's trade agenda focused almost exclusively on trade deficits in manufactured goods. He spoke of an "Indo-Pacific dream," which on the surface seemed to be an inclusive vision—but that dream was undercut by a fixation on "America first" and on a bilateral approach to trade. More broadly, the president rejected regional approaches to diplomacy and flatly opposed globalism.[18]

By contrast, China's President Xi Jinping in his speech at the APEC leaders' summit endorsed regionalism and globalization as "beneficial to all."[19] Observers, who had wanted to support the U.S. president, greeted his speech with silence, and then warmly applauded remarks by Xi.

The TPP could have provided the United States with tremendous leverage in its strategic and economic competition with China. It would have anchored America's economic future in the opportunities of a dynamic and growing Asia. It would have allowed the United States, instead of China, to continue setting the global rules of trade. But President Trump, a self-styled negotiator, threw away his strongest leverage for dealing with China when he abandoned the TPP.

Vietnam had a right to feel abandoned as well. After taking great risks to ensure Vietnam's inclusion in the trade agreement, Prime Minister Dũng found himself isolated and, for a variety of reasons, lost his job. His successor tried to reason with the new U.S. president, but he did not take the bold steps needed to address the growing trade imbalance with the United States. The TPP could have helped right that imbalance, if the United States had held onto its strongest trade tool. China, the clear winner in America's abandonment of the TPP, moved swiftly into the leadership vacuum.

Epilogue

● ● ● ● ● ● ● ● ● ● ● ● ● ●

Reconciliation

My thirty years as a diplomat gave me the great privilege of serving the United States of America—a cause far greater than myself. My resignation in 2017 came with mixed emotions, as I joined other senior Foreign Service officers in heading for the exit.

We all had our own reasons for departing, but many of my friends and colleagues shared a deep concern that the policy direction of the administration of President Donald Trump was diminishing America's role in the world. I knew I could not implement some of those policies while also following my own principles.

Most important, abandoning the Trans-Pacific Partnership (TPP) trade agreement was a self-inflicted wound that undermined America's strength in Asia. America gave the playing field over to leaders who do not share our values, and we left American jobs there, too. In addition, other departing Foreign Service officers and I mourned the U.S. abdication of responsibility regarding climate change, especially in 2017, when the storms were so immense that previously each would have been considered so big that its like would occur only every five hundred years.

I spent many years attempting to strengthen ties between Vietnam and the United States. I felt protective of that relationship and didn't want mistakes to damage it. The embassy team shared my commitment to serving the United States and building a positive new relationship with a former enemy.

PHOTO 37 Lucy, the author, TABO, and Clayton Bond at the retirement ceremony, Washington, DC, December 2017 (Credit: U.S. Department of State).

The State Department held a retirement ceremony for me in December 2017 in the Treaty Room outside the secretary of state's office, with a portrait of Thomas Jefferson looking on. Deputy Assistant Secretary Constance Dierman acknowledged the sacrifice involved in service, including the sacrifices that families make, while Clayton stood at my side and our children rode on our shoulders. My friend and mentor of twenty-six years, Ambassador Cameron Hume, spoke with passion and eloquence and then presented an American flag to Clayton. I was happy to have the opportunity to reflect on three decades of public service as I stood in front of the flags of the countries where I had served as a junior, mid-level, or senior officer. I urged my Foreign Service colleagues who attended the ceremony to remain firm in their determination to uphold the oath we had all sworn to "defend the Constitution against all enemies, foreign and domestic."

America's involvement in Vietnam caused terrible suffering on all sides. To reconcile with Vietnam, the United States first tried to achieve the fullest possible accounting of those we had lost during the war. Vietnamese leaders supported that goal because of their own interest in economic development, and for twenty-five years they helped Americans find the remains of people missing in action (MIAs), bringing closure to many U.S. families. Vietnam's losses during the war are measured in the millions, and only in recent years was closure for their families made a priority. It is essential for reconciliation.

In January 2017, Bob Connor, who served as a sergeant with the U.S. Air Force Security Services in Vietnam in 1967–1968, was helping his grand-daughter with a school project on the Vietnam War when he saw on Google Earth the location of a battle that took place on the Biên Hòa air base while he was on guard duty there. "Significant battle took place here at the start of the Tet Offensive '68," Connor wrote in a note he left on Google Earth. "Those VC [Việt Cộng] killed had to be buried in a mass grave at the end of the runway."[1]

Ten days later, Connor heard from Chế Trung Hiểu, a seventy-year-old veteran of the North Vietnamese People's Army, who, according to Connor, was "very excited to hear about the grave because they knew nothing about it."[2] During the day-long battle in 1968, the Việt Cộng lost 150 men who were buried on the base, 424 who were buried outside its eastern perimeter, and another 673 who were buried just outside its northeastern perimeter.

Connor reached out to his commanding officer, Colonel Martin Strones, who had counted the bodies as they were piled into the mass grave on the base. The two traveled to Hồ Chí Minh City, where someone Hiểu had iden-tified as "the colonel" came to their hotel in full uniform and saluted Strones and Connor. The Americans returned the salute. The four men drove in a caravan to Biên Hòa, but the battle location was covered with fully grown rubber trees. Disappointed, the Americans returned home after a week with-out finding the mass grave.

Three weeks later, the Vietnamese found the grave only twenty yards from where Strones had suggested they dig. They discovered seventy-two sets of remains and, using DNA and other methods of analysis, identified thirty individuals. Military and provincial officials organized a reburial on July 12, 2017, which Strones and Connor joined via video teleconference. The Amer-icans met some of the 1,500 Vietnamese citizens from twenty-three provinces who attended the ceremony.

Connor was in his mid-seventies and had a wife, Dianne, who was ill, but he continued this work and contacted more than forty U.S. veterans. Some of those he reached out to wanted to be helpful, but others did not want to be reminded of the past. Only one was angry about the effort to locate the dead Vietnamese. "Let those stinking commies lay where they are," he wrote Connor. "I won the nation's 5th highest award for heroism . . . and killed as many of those commies as I could."[3] Many U.S. veterans feel hostility toward or want nothing to do with Vietnam. Many choose not to speak about their experiences there.

Connor and Richard Magner, a former Cobra helicopter pilot in Vietnam, pressed on, locating additional mass graves in the country. Their information could lead to the recovery of the remains of as many as 8,000 soldiers, bringing closure to more than 25,000 living family members. As of this writing, they are researching battles and grave sites that involve at least 1,800 additional missing Việt Cộng or North Vietnamese soldiers.

Connor's volunteer efforts also led to information about U.S. soldiers who were buried by the Việt Cộng as they headed north with their prisoners of war (POWs). That information has been turned over to the Defense POW/MIA Accounting Agency (DPAA), leading more American families to closure. A number of former Việt Cộng are now engaged in the effort, following up on Connor's leads and providing information in return on potential grave sites involving four U.S. Army and three U.S. Air Force servicemen. Details are passed onto the DPAA.

Recognizing the significance of Connor's volunteer effort, the U.S. government took a long-overdue step. In December 2019, Defense Secretary Mark Esper agreed that the U.S. military could assist in the effort led by the U.S. Agency for International Development (USAID) to help the Vietnamese recover their lost, including support for Vietnamese laboratories in expanding the country's capacity for DNA analysis.[4]

Connor's efforts, and those of his U.S. veteran colleagues, involved recognizing the shared humanity of those lost on both sides, many of whom had families who needed to know what had happened to a loved one. Helping Vietnamese families achieve closure also represents a determination to be honest about the past, and it contributes greatly to reconciliation between Vietnam and the United States.

Vietnamese Americans find their way to reconciliation more readily when both countries are honest about the past. Many of these people suffered terrible losses during the war and want nothing to do with today's Vietnam. Some, especially members of the younger generation, want to know or even help the people of their homeland. A 2004 resolution passed by the Politburo pledged that the Vietnamese government would not discriminate against people based on their history, and since then limitations on visa requirements, investment, and real estate ownership have been lifted further. However, many Vietnamese Americans see these steps as in Vietnam's self-interest and seek more concrete gestures that their concerns—about human rights, honoring the dead, and personal safety while traveling—will be addressed.

Older Vietnamese military leaders remain suspicious that reconciliation and bridge-building efforts could undermine Vietnam's Communist Party. But these concerns are fading with time. The Vietnamese diaspora—consisting of two million people, who as a group are increasingly prosperous and politically active—will determine how quickly ties grow between businesses in Vietnam and those in the United States, as well as how many travelers move and how much student exchange occurs between the two countries. Members of the diaspora will set the pace of reconciliation between people. The Vietnamese government can help accelerate that pace through simple gestures such as allowing the graves of southern soldiers to be maintained, so their memories will not be dishonored. As I said to Vice Minister of Foreign Affairs Lê Hoài Trung during the dinner for Drew Faust, the president of Harvard University, in March 2017: "No flags, no symbols, no politics. Just let them dig ditches and cut tree roots."

Being honest about the lingering effects of dioxin is also essential if the United States hopes to build a lasting security relationship with Vietnam. When President Barack Obama visited Vietnam in 2016, he made commitments to clean up dioxin on the Biên Hòa air base, but my team and I could not obtain funding to fulfill that pledge. However, in 2018 the Department of Defense at last agreed to pay $150 million, 40 percent of the projected cost of the cleanup, with USAID paying another 40 percent. The determination of Tim Rieser, an advisor to Senator Patrick Leahy, paid off, with Vietnam promising to make up the difference and a possible contribution by Japan—exactly the proposal we had made eighteen months before.

In spring 2019, the project began with the relocation of seventy-five families from their dioxin-soaked neighborhood downstream from Biên Hòa. For many victims, it was too late to avert tragedy. The deformities caused by dioxin exposure are horrific and are carried from generation to generation.

Between 2007 and 2021, Congress appropriated nearly $390 million for Agent Orange in Vietnam, one-fourth of it for disability assistance and three-fourths for air base cleanup. A significant advancement occurred in April 2019 when Senator Leahy led a delegation of eight senators to Vietnam. In Biên Hòa they witnessed the signing of a memorandum of intent between USAID and the Ministry of National Defense for a five-year, $65 million disabilities assistance program.

The Biên Hòa cleanup aims to keep future lives intact, but the Vietnamese public worries also about how to help the many individuals whose lives have already been deeply damaged by dioxin. In 2020, Vietnamese donated $16 million in mostly small individual gifts to the Vietnam Association of Victims of Agent Orange for direct assistance to people disabled by the effects of dioxin. Congress appropriated $13 million for USAID disability assistance the same year.

As Chuck Searcy, a veteran and activist, wrote, "The U.S. government is now willing to accept, along with many medical researchers and scientists, the likelihood that dioxin contamination from Agent Orange used during the war, and residual toxins still present in the environment, caused some of the medical and health problems affecting even the current generation of Vietnamese children today. Maybe recognition of that responsibility will encourage the United States to do more to help families in Vietnam who have struggled long and against great difficulties to live lives with some semblance of normality."[5]

Some 200,000 Vietnamese have signed a petition supporting French citizen Trân Tô Nga in her lawsuit against the chemical companies in a French court. Long-serving Vietnamese diplomat Tôn Nữ Thị Ninh has observed, "Just make sure the American government doesn't push it [Agent Orange] off to the side of the road, but the same [is true] for our officials. They tend to want to make it easier to talk about trade and economic cooperation. I think that the expectations will come from [our] society, the pressure . . . the public will keep on them."[6] Ultimately, the United States needs to make good with the Vietnamese people on Agent Orange.

The Trump administration's racially based immigration policy toward Vietnamese refugees ignored America's wartime past. I did not receive any reply from Secretary of State Rex Tillerson to my two messages regarding the matter of Vietnamese deportations until November 2017, a few weeks after I had resigned from government service. Tillerson wrote that "the status quo on repatriation cannot continue" and that Vietnam needed to take back more deportees.[7]

Remembering the lesson of Defense Secretary Robert McNamara, who did not reveal his misgivings about the war even after leaving his government position, I decided after my resignation that my duty as a remonstrating official was to speak out publicly, because few people knew the deportations were taking place. On April 2, 2018, the *Foreign Service Journal* published my views about the policy of deportations.[8] As a result, national media outlets began reporting on the administration's policy, noting that those deported included Amerasians and members of ethnic minority groups who had supported the United States and South Vietnam in the fight against the North Vietnamese.

In 1988, President Ronald Reagan had signed into law the American Homecoming Act (also known as the Amerasian Homecoming Act), which gave preferential immigration status to children in Vietnam fathered by American servicemen. These children—with one parent Vietnamese and the other White or Black—suffered from discrimination in Vietnam, and after they fled to the United States, they faced discrimination again. Now, it seemed that the United States was turning its back on them a third time. A friend who is a Vietnam veteran commented on President Trump's deportation policy, describing it as "odious in the whole, but especially so in the case of Amerasians."[9]

A man facing deportation sent me a photo of his Vietnamese American wife and their two children, who would be without their husband and father after he was deported to Vietnam. He wrote: "At the age of 5, I was forced to leave my family behind [in Vietnam]. Living in the United States at a young age without parents or true guidance, I've made mistakes. That was more than 18 years ago. Now, the Trump Administration wants to force me to separate from my wife and kids. This is even worse than being separated from my original family 40 years ago."

I learned about Tuấn, a Vietnamese American living in San Jose, California, who as a teenager had served three years in prison for stealing a car. Eighteen years later, he had married and was raising two children. He had opened a supermarket that had grown to employ forty-five other people, and he paid $500,000 per year in taxes. By 2018, he had spent two years in detention at the hands of Immigration and Customs Enforcement (ICE), and the policies of President Trump's administration meant that he would be deported to a country where he no longer had any ties.

On April 26, 2018, attorneys filed a class action suit in the U.S. District Court for the Central District of California on behalf of the deportees. Lawyers in the suit cited my comments protesting the administration's policy. In mid-June, ICE sent a letter to the court indicating that it would no longer pursue the deportations of individuals who had arrived in the United States before 1995. I hoped that the courts would halt the administration's deportations, but it was only a short reprieve.

In September, veteran journalist Scott Martelle published an editorial in the *Los Angeles Times* decrying the deportations: "In its insatiable quest to rid the U.S. of immigrants, the Trump administration has been rounding up

Vietnamese refugees who have been in the country for more than a quarter of a century and trying to send them back to Vietnam—despite a formal bilateral agreement that refugees who arrived here prior to the 1995 normalization of relations between the two countries would not be sent home."[10]

In that autumn's midterm elections, twenty-four Vietnamese Americans ran for state senator, city council member, the California State Assembly, sheriff, or Westminster mayor in Orange County, California. Their campaign signs dominated street corners in Little Saigon. Four Republican members of Congress from Southern California who were aligned with President Trump's administration on immigration lost narrowly to Democratic challengers. Given the large number of Vietnamese American voters in each of their districts, the administration's deportations policy likely played a role in the Republicans' defeat.

I wondered if the administration would see how unpopular the policy had become and cease pursuing deportations. But it was soon clear that the reprieve had been only for the midterm elections, and the administration quickly resumed pressuring the Hanoi government to accept more deportees.

On December 13, 2018, twenty-six members of Congress wrote to President Trump, Secretary of State Mike Pompeo, and Secretary of Homeland Security Kirstjen Nielsen, expressing concerns about the Department of Homeland Security's intention to renegotiate the terms of the 2008 memorandum of understanding between Vietnam and the United States.[11]

On December 15, former Secretary of State John Kerry called the deportations "despicable" on Twitter, writing: "After so many—from George H. W. Bush to John McCain and Bill Clinton—worked for years to heal this open wound and put a war behind us—they're turning their backs on people who fled and many who fought by our side. For what possible gain?"[12]

As the public debate continued, it moved into the political realm, where I believe it belonged. The American people and their elected representatives should make decisions about this issue, instead of having Senior Advisor to the President Steven Miller pursue his agenda in secret. I believed that it was my duty to bring the matter to the attention of Congress and the public. As Julian Bond taught my husband and me, "It is . . . the highest duty of a citizen to seek to correct his government when he thinks it is mistaken."[13]

Some U.S. courts are sympathetic to the plight of these refugees from the Vietnam War. Others are not, and many deportations have occurred. I had not thought that America was a nation that would turn its back on those who had fought side by side with U.S. soldiers—or on the children of our soldiers, just because they were born in Vietnam.

In 1996, Eon Productions asked for permission from Vietnamese authorities to shoot its James Bond film *Tomorrow Never Dies*[14] in Hạ Long Bay, but the Vietnamese government created so many obstacles that the director, Roger Spottiswoode, and the producers decided to shoot in Thailand instead. The film grossed $333 million and was seen all over the world. Bond movies attract tourists to the spots where they are filmed, and this was a missed opportunity whose costs went far beyond what was immediately lost in local production expenses.

In 2016, when another Hollywood director, Jordan Vogt-Roberts, asked to film *Kong: Skull Island* in three locations in Vietnam, the government in Hanoi encouraged him to do so and offered him support. Officials in Quảng Ninh (which includes Hạ Long Bay), Quảng Bình and Ninh Bình provinces made the filmmakers, cast, and crew feel welcome.

At a press conference attended by more than a hundred journalists, Vogt-Roberts said, "When we got out of the car [in Ninh Bình], we immediately saw a stunningly beautiful sight that we thought was not real. It was magical." He continued: "Colours and shades of the mountain ranges will make audience [sic] say 'wow' when they are seen. We fell in love with this place."[15] The press and people of Vietnam appreciated his respect and love for the country.

Tom Hiddleston, a heartthrob actor in the film, said at the same press conference: "I have wanted to visit Vietnam since I was a teenager. I had a visa to visit during my summer vacation. Our trip was postponed because I was cast in my first film. But now I can fulfill my dream of seeing Vietnam." Crowds of young women waited outside Hanoi's Metropole Hotel, hoping to get a glimpse of Hiddleston.

Samuel L. Jackson, the highest paid actor in the business, laughed about his young costars, Hiddleston and Brie Larson, receiving so much attention. It helped, too, that Larson won the Academy Award for best actress for *Room*[16] a few weeks later. She flew from Vietnam to accept the award and flew back immediately afterward to continue filming.

I visited the set in Ninh Bình to talk with the producers, director, and cast. They loved their time in Vietnam. Jackson told *Southeast Asia Globe* that "of all the fantastical locations he has worked" in over his forty-year career, Vietnam was his favorite.[17] Vogt-Roberts and the producers persuaded the Vietnamese to allow special helicopters—American ones—film some of the

PHOTO 38 Samuel L. Jackson and the author, Ninh Bình province, February 2016
(Credit: U.S. Department of State/Pope Thrower).

shots in Hạ Long Bay. These shots are like none ever seen before. It was an
audacious request: the last time American helicopters had flown over Vietnam, it was to drop napalm on villages. Vietnam had come a long way in
twenty years.

Between *Tomorrow Never Dies* and *Kong* much had changed, with
increases in the openness of Vietnamese leaders and the willingness of Americans to show respect to Vietnam. When Americans showed respect, as
President Obama did by welcoming General Secretary Nguyễn Phú Trọng
to the Oval Office, doors opened wider.

President Obama's pursuit of the TPP included strong conditions for workers'
rights. Vietnam's leaders, including Trọng, wanted TPP membership for their
country and were prepared to sign the strongest human rights agreement in
the country's history. President Obama's assertion that adherence to human
rights "is just who we are" did not deter the Vietnamese from joining the TPP.

Under President Trump, the United States withdrew from the TPP and
grew quiet on human rights. European nations—using negotiations over
a European Union–Vietnam free trade agreement—filled the void and

continued to apply pressure to Hanoi. On April 5, 2018, Nguyễn Văn Đài, Lê Thu Hà, and four other activists were given lengthy jail sentences for conducting activities aimed at overthrowing the state. Đài was sentenced to fifteen years in prison and five years of house arrest, and Hà was sentenced to nine years in prison. Vietnamese police had never allowed Đài to see the Bible I had given him. Two months later, in June, Đài and Hà were released from prison. Đài and his wife, Vũ Minh Khánh, moved to Germany to live in exile. The free trade agreement entered into force in July 2020.

In October 2018, after two years of protests by the international community, Vietnam released Nguyễn Ngọc Như Quỳnh ("Mother Mushroom"), who had won the State Department's 2017 International Women of Courage Award, from prison and sent her immediately into exile. Arriving in Houston, Texas, with her elderly mother and two small children, Quỳnh told supporters that she would "never keep silent" in her fight for democracy in Vietnam.

Vietnam had not yet broken from its pattern of arresting dissidents and sending them into exile. The country's leaders wanted to have free trade, innovation, and openness, but they also wanted to control what Vietnamese citizens could say and think. The tension between those two goals is likely to persist.

If the United States again makes human rights a policy priority, then using the leverage that trade provides could make a difference in Vietnam. We can influence human rights in Vietnam somewhat by simultaneously showing respect for a different political system and insisting that Vietnam respect what is important to Americans. This will continue to be a difficult challenge.

When the aircraft carrier USS *Carl Vinson* pulled up to the coastal city of Đà Nẵng in March 2018, it was the first port call by a U.S. aircraft carrier since the Vietnam War ended. Many observers saw the strategic significance of the visit as a signal to China, but it was also a sign of faith between former foes. "It's a pretty big and historic step, since a carrier has not been here for 40 years," said Rear Admiral John V. Fuller, the commander of the *Carl Vinson* strike group, whose father had served in Vietnam.[18]

Đà Nẵng had been a major staging post for the American war effort in Vietnam. When the *Carl Vinson*'s 5,500 sailors came ashore, they were the largest contingent of American soldiers on Vietnamese soil since 1975. During its four-day port call, the *Carl Vinson*'s personnel visited two centers for Vietnamese children with disabilities—many of whom were presumed to be suffering from the consequences of Agent Orange.[19] With this acknowledgment of dioxin's harmful effects, the aircraft carrier's port visit included honesty about the past.

The *Carl Vinson* visit was also a result of Vice Foreign Minister Hà Kim Ngọc's recommendation that the two countries collaborate on matters of regional and global significance. The aircraft carrier had been deployed for a month in the South China Sea, which half the world's seaborne cargo passes through each year. Having the *Carl Vinson* in Đà Nẵng was a powerful signal to China to rethink its bullying posture, and the visit highlighted U.S.-Vietnam collaboration on a key regional challenge: peace and freedom of navigation in the South China Sea. In the Indo-Pacific region, room still exists for the United States to deepen collaboration not only with the members of the Association of Southeast Asian Nations but also with India. As China became more aggressive in the Indian Ocean, New Delhi responded by sending its ships into international waters in the South China Sea.[20]

North Korea continues to threaten the United States and its Asian allies. Vietnam had maintained a cordial relationship with North Korea for many years, and President Trump's administration saw an opportunity for Hanoi to serve as a bridge to Pyongyang. In February 2019, President Trump and Kim Jong Un, North Korea's leader, met in Hanoi's Metropole Hotel. Like his father, Kim Jong Un preferred to travel by armored train, and Vietnam's capital is fewer than two thousand miles from Pyongyang. Kim's grandfather, Kim Il Sung, had visited Vietnam in 1958, and the younger Kim often sought to draw comparisons between himself and his grandfather.

Vietnam could show North Korea the benefits that might flow from making peace with the United States. Aiming his remarks at the North Koreans, Secretary of State Mike Pompeo pointedly noted before the summit that U.S. bilateral trade with Vietnam had grown 8,000 percent in two decades and American companies had poured billions of dollars of investments into Vietnam. Pompeo said: "The fact that we're co-operating—and not fighting—is proof that when a country decides to create a brighter future for itself alongside the United States, we follow through on American promises. The miracle could be your miracle."[21]

Pyongyang had sent air force personnel to assist the North Vietnamese in achieving victory over the U.S.-backed South Vietnamese Army. Vietnam and the United States used to "point a gun and knife at each other," Kim Euikyeom, a spokesperson for South Korea, said about the choice of host nation for the summit.[22]

In the end, President Trump walked out of the Hanoi summit, and Kim ordered the execution of officials involved with it. According to National Security Advisor John Bolton, this proved that "making a mistake in North Korean foreign policy could be fatal not only to your career but to yourself."[23] The summit accomplished nothing that would contribute to peace on the Korean peninsula, but Vietnam had shown that it would collaborate with the United States on regional and global challenges and that it could play in the big diplomatic leagues.

Growth in education ties between the United States and Vietnam surged as relations between the countries (and Vietnam's economy) flourished. Fulbright University Vietnam is the latest symbol of this educational collaboration. The U.S. and Vietnamese governments supported its creation, promising that it would become a world-class Vietnamese university based on U.S. academic principles, and that it could transform the lives of young people, address the pressing needs of Vietnamese society, and possibly shift the paradigm of higher education in Vietnam. By creating a new undergraduate program, Fulbright has been able to pursue the most up-to-date innovations and cutting-edge pedagogy. Fulbright students do more than obtain information—they learn how to work with that knowledge. Fulbright also celebrates the key traditions of U.S. higher education: open inquiry, meritocracy, rigorous research, and critical analysis.

Fulbright's historical connection with the John F. Kennedy School of Government at Harvard University and its lineage as successor to the Fulbright Economics Teaching Program gave it a strong foundation to collaborate with leading universities in Vietnam, the United States, and other countries. The United States had created important international universities in the past, including Tsinghua University in China, American University in Cairo, and American University in Beirut. These institutions succeeded largely because they were not viewed as transplants of a U.S. university but rather independent institutions with deep roots in their home countries.

Fulbright's first chief academic officer, Ryan Derby-Talbot, said that a key goal was to provide students with a safe space to fail, in which they could try new things, innovate, and take risks. This approach was radical in the context of Vietnam's Confucian culture, where failure is frowned upon.

In 2018, I delivered a number of high school graduation speeches in Hồ Chí Minh City. I spoke to graduates who had been born in the Year of the Dragon—who, according to Vietnamese tradition, were expected to be ambitious and natural leaders.

"Even the ambitious, energetic leaders born in the Year of the Dragon must be willing to accept the occasional setback," I told the students. "After a setback or a failure, you have to dust yourself off and move on. You may find that something will happen that is even better than what you had been aiming for. Resilience in the face of failure is a useful quality, especially when pursuing what I believe matters in life: love and purpose."[24]

China's control of upstream dams on the Mekong River has led many Vietnamese leaders to view the Mekong as their second front—the South China Sea being the first—in Vietnam's ongoing conflict with its neighbor to the north. In July 2019, the lower Mekong experienced the lowest water levels ever recorded, probably due to reduced water outflow from upper Mekong dams, including the Xayaburi Dam, and less rainfall than usual. Already suffering from coastal erosion and shrinking because life-giving sediment was caught behind Chinese dams, the delta experienced drought and increased salinity. To feed themselves and their families, farmers reacted by bringing up more water from underground aquifers. This causes other problems because when this water is removed from underground—its presence there adds buoyancy to the land above—gravity causes the land to sink. The delta is now sinking at a rate of half an inch per year. Some areas with the highest amounts of groundwater extraction are sinking at a rate of one inch per year. Melting ice caps and glaciers are causing the sea around the delta to rise at about one-tenth of an inch per year, but land subsidence is occurring at a greater magnitude and with more immediate impact than sea level rise.

The Mekong Delta produces 70 percent of Vietnam's aquaculture products, but a by-product of aquaculture is animal waste that harms the environment. To make up for losses in rice crops and shrimp farming, the government encourages the farming of high-value fruits and vegetables.

The Mekong is not the only river system vulnerable to climate change. The deltas of Asia's big rivers—including the Mekong, the Brahmaputra (which flows through Tibet, India, and Bangladesh), the Yangtze and Yellow Rivers in China, and the Red River (flowing from China's Yunnan province through northern Vietnam)—are all threatened by a combination of flooding, rising sea levels, and the large populations living in the fertile deltas. The United States faces similar issues in its Mississippi, Sacramento, and Columbia Rivers' deltas.

Preserving the ecological balance of critical river systems—and sharing lessons on how to do it—is another opportunity for the United States and

Vietnam to develop habits of cooperation and collaboration, which would further build trust between the two nations.

Asia's fastest-growing economies—among them China, India, and Vietnam—are the most in need of hydropower dams (and other relatively clean sources of energy). These three nations depend heavily on coal, and as a result, dirty air in China and India has drawn much global attention. Air pollution in major Asian cities is already associated with more than 500,000 premature deaths per year.[25] Unfortunately, Vietnam is now vying with the two Asian giants to produce the most toxic levels of air pollution.

Vietnamese citizens are well aware of the immediate effects of air pollution on human health, and that has alerted them to the dangers of relying on coal and other fossil fuels. Hanoi's energy planners had intended to build more than fifty additional coal plants by 2020, but the Vietnamese people began to say, "not in my backyard."[26] Fearful of more environmental protests like those in spring 2016, the government in Hanoi started exploring alternatives.

Shifting from coal and oil to renewable sources of energy will take time. Vietnam has offshore sources of natural gas that can fuel its growth for decades. And shifting to cleaner energy sources will matter for the globe. The World Resources Institute estimates that energy consumption is the source of 73 percent of human-caused greenhouse gas emissions, and Vietnam in recent years has joined the list of countries responsible for significant emissions due to its growing demand for energy.[27]

In January 2019, former Secretary of State John Kerry told Vietnam's leaders that burning coal carries external costs, including damage to human health. He noted that the state-owned entity responsible for meeting Vietnam's insatiable energy demands, Electricity Vietnam, favors the use of coal. "EVN stands for Electricity Vietnam, not Coal Vietnam," Kerry said.[28] This was consistent with what he had said often in Vietnam about sustainable technologies and the need for immediate action to address climate change.

An architect of the Paris Agreement, Kerry has a long history of climate change diplomacy, and his credibility in Vietnam was high. He developed a proposal that included private-sector financing for the use of wind and solar power, along with transmission lines that would boost energy efficiency. It also called for using Vietnam's hydropower more effectively and tapping into a domestic natural gas field. Kerry made a compelling case that financing could be obtained to reduce the need for cheap coal plants backed by Chinese banks and built by Chinese companies.

Kerry recommended to Prime Minister Nguyễn Xuân Phúc and other Politburo members, who knew and trusted him, that they get rid of pricing policies that favored coal versus alternative sources of energy. Noting that natural gas produces 50–60 percent less carbon dioxide than even the cleanest coal does, he urged Vietnam's leaders to pursue policy changes to permit natural gas to play a bigger part of Vietnam's energy mix.

"Vietnam has not yet opened its energy sector to competition," Kerry said, "in contrast to how much it has opened other sectors." He added: "Opening to competition will create a faster path to energy production and transmission, which Vietnam needs badly. Vietnam should allow a pilot project with a truly commercial structure. Then watch how fast the private sector will respond and investment will flow in."

Vietnam's leaders listened to Kerry. Vietnam's Power Development Plan for 2011–2020 had relied heavily on coal to meet the country's rapidly increasing energy needs. But in February 2020, the Politburo issued Resolution 55, which shifted the emphasis from coal to renewable energy, liquefied natural gas (LNG), and energy efficiency and battery storage technologies,[29] as well as diversifying Vietnam's trading partners to include the United States, Russia, the Gulf States, and Australia. Instead of relying on huge investments in coal-fired plants, Vietnam had discovered that its solar and wind power capacity had increased exponentially.[30] Although coal was not dead, Vietnam seemed to recognize that it posed not only environmental but also security risks, by increasing Vietnam's dependence on China.

Greater reliance on renewable energy, LNG, and energy efficiency could cause Vietnam to exceed its commitments in the 2015 Paris Agreement. Leaders in Vietnam came to regard renewables as optimal not only because they reduce greenhouse gas emissions but also because the time from signing a commercial deal to producing energy is faster than with other energy sources, and they do not require imports of primary energy.

The United States and Vietnam both recorded their first cases of COVID-19 in late January 2020. Even with an 870-mile porous border with China and a population of a hundred million, during the next sixteen months Vietnam managed to keep its number of COVID cases to less than 5,000, with only 39 deaths. The International Monetary Fund hailed Vietnam's success in containing COVID as a "roadmap for other developing countries."[31] By contrast, in the same time period the United States suffered more than 33 million cases and more than 590,000 deaths, more than ten times the number of American lives lost in the Vietnam war.

Vietnam learned many of its public health techniques and the scientific and technical capabilities for containing COVID through collaborations with the United States that began in the early years of reconciliation, when Pete Peterson was ambassador. Public health collaboration deepened when President George W. Bush decided to make Vietnam a focus of his administration's efforts to combat HIV/AIDS in 2004 by including it as the only Asian country in the President's Emergency Plan for AIDS Relief.

Outside of China, Vietnam probably acted faster than any other country to curb the spread of COVID. "Its first risk assessment exercise was conducted in early January—soon after cases in China started being reported," according to Kidong Park, the World Health Organization's representative to Vietnam.[32] In February and March 2020, the Steering Committee on the Prevention and Control of COVID-19, led by Deputy Prime Minister Vũ Đức Đam, took a series of quick steps to prevent the disease from spreading in Vietnam, including suspending all flights to and from China, Hong Kong, or Taiwan. Controls on arrivals from abroad tightened steadily, and by mid-March, Vietnam no longer issued visitor visas and placed travelers from highly infected countries in quarantine. At one point, nearly eighty thousand people suspected of having been exposed to the virus were in strict quarantine at home or in government-run facilities such as military barracks or university dormitories. By March 21, all of Vietnam's borders had been sealed, schools had been closed, masks were required in public, large events had been canceled, and a general shutdown had been imposed.

A hard-working, data-driven leader, Đam framed the pandemic as an enemy, issuing public service announcements warning that the virus is "threatening the human race" and that "we have entered a war." Everyone is now a "soldier," Đam said.[33] Vietnam mobilized a small army of doctors, nurses, and health care professionals. The country even mobilized artists. Trần Duy Trúc, a seventy-six-year-old painter who had spent his life making propaganda art, turned to designing posters to encourage the public fight against coronavirus. One of his designs included a mother helping her daughter put on a mask while urging people to wash their hands. "Artists can be seen as fighters," Trúc said, "They have to draw their best pictures to make people understand and help them win against this enemy."[34] If any country can win a war against a powerful enemy, it is Vietnam.

Overseeing the effort, Đam ensured that Vietnam began testing early, using low-cost test kits developed by Vietnamese scientists. The country also undertook extensive contact tracing, with the Army and grassroots Party networks performing much of the legwork. Given its low case numbers,

Vietnam used testing to identify clusters of cases and prevent wider transmission. When community transmission was detected (even if in just one case), the government reacted quickly with contact tracing, commune-level lockdowns, and widespread local testing to ensure that no cases were missed. Vietnam performed more tests per confirmed case than any other country in the world by a long shot—even though testing per capita remained relatively low.[35]

As a result, Vietnam curbed the pandemic more effectively than any other Southeast Asian country. It was then able to lift most of its containment measures in May and begin reviving the nation's economy. The success of public health efforts put Vietnam in a position to reemphasize its attractiveness for supply chains. The process of competing with or even supplanting China as the favorite target for foreign direct investment was already well under way before the pandemic.

In May, Vietnam Airlines' brand-new Boeing 787 flew nonstop from Hanoi to San Francisco, the first such direct flight in history. The initial flights during the pandemic were to bring Vietnamese citizens home, but when regular flights resume, they will widen the aperture of exchange, allowing more tourists, students, investors, and family members to pass back and forth between the United States and Vietnam.

In July 2018, I was surprised to learn from the Ministry of Foreign Affairs that President Trần Đại Quang had conferred upon me Vietnam's highest honor for a foreign citizen, the Order of Friendship. By then, it was well known that I was not popular with President Trump's administration for having spoken out against some of his policies. I wondered why the Vietnamese government would take the risk of angering Washington. My friend Thảo Nguyễn Griffiths said the answer was easy. "Vietnam values a 'friend in need,'" she said. I had been a friend to Vietnam in both good times and tough ones, according to Thảo.

The award was presented on behalf of the ailing president by Vice Minister Trung, who called me "a true friend of Vietnamese people" and noted that I was "the first U.S. ambassador to Vietnam to receive the Order of Friendship."

Trung described what we had accomplished together during my three-year term: visits by General Secretary Trọng to the White House in July 2015, by President Obama to Vietnam in May 2016, by Prime Minister Nguyễn Xuân Phúc to the White House in May 2017, and by President Donald Trump to Vietnam in November 2017.

PHOTO 39 Deputy Foreign Minister Lê Hoài Trung bestows the Order of Friendship on the author, Hanoi, July 2018 (Credit: The Gioi & Vietnam/Trần Anh Tuấn).

Trung catalogued improvements in economic and trade cooperation, in "education-training, people-to-people contact, resolving war legacies, particularly in putting forward the dioxin detoxification project in Đà Nẵng Airport." He added, "We are very happy to see that this project has been a great success and that both sides are working together to implement a similar project in Biên Hòa Airport." Dioxin clean-up was difficult and expensive, but critical if the relationship between the United States and Vietnam was to move forward.

Trung said that the Vietnamese people will "always remember you, an ambassador looking so relatable in the traditional Vietnamese outfit, going to market to buy a peach blossom tree for Tết, or even freeing fishes on Kitchen God Day. People from different provinces still recall with fond memories the images of you cycling across Vietnam."

Trung quoted the well-known Vietnamese poet Chế Lan Viên: "The land we stay in is but itself, the land we leave our soul becomes." He closed by saying, "Wherever you go and in whatever position you might hold, you still hold dear in your heart our country and people."

Military dominance alone will not build the strong alliances and partnerships that the United States needs in the Indo-Pacific. Those partnerships provide

PHOTO 40 The author, TABO, Lucy and Clayton Bond wearing traditional Vietnamese clothing to celebrate Tết, Hanoi, February 2017 (Credit: U.S. Department of State/Lê Đức Thọ).

real, tangible benefits to the United States. Strong partnerships—not just with Vietnam, but also with India, Indonesia, Thailand, Japan, the Republic of Korea, Singapore, and other countries in the region—provide jobs to Americans, contribute to regional stability, and help us address global challenges to human health, the environment, and international security.

When the United States commits to these partnerships, it facilitates commercial deals worth hundreds of billions of dollars and boosts educational exchanges, creating or supporting hundreds of thousands of jobs in the United States. Strengthening alliances or forming security partnerships with countries that share our interest in open sea lanes helps the United States uphold international law. Partnerships create a more prosperous and safer America.

When the United States shows respect and builds trust, it can build relationships that enable friends and partners to pursue shared interests together. After thirty years in Asia and twenty-five years in and out of Vietnam, I know with certainty that building such relationships is the only way to make America even greater.

My time in Vietnam had come full circle. Together with my colleagues in Hanoi, we had shown respect for Vietnam's history, language, and mythology. We had pushed to the limit the possibilities for chronicling the truths of the "American War." Together with my embassy team and the people and leaders of Vietnam, we had progressed further down the road toward reconciliation.

Acknowledgments

I wish first to thank someone who helped me when I served twice as a diplomat in Vietnam and again with his kind and generous assistance as I wrote this book. Former Secretary of State John Kerry gave me the privilege of a lifetime by letting me serve as his representative, and President Barack Obama's, in Vietnam. Having been a lieutenant, senator, and secretary, and now a presidential envoy, John Kerry compounded that honor by writing a thoughtful foreword to *Nothing Is Impossible*. For his decades of service to our nation, his unwavering determination to bring about U.S.-Vietnamese reconciliation, his dedication to diplomacy, and his commitment to preserving this planet for future generations, John Kerry is a hero. He and Teresa Heinz Kerry are also my friends, and for that I am deeply grateful.

I received unstinting support from former diplomatic colleagues, whose memories were often more accurate than my own. Chris Abrams, the late Desaix Anderson, Bill Bach, Rena Bitter, Brett Blackshaw, Jillian Bonnardeaux, Bùi Thế Giang, Jan Cordell, Bryan Dalton, Mike Eiland, Michael Kidwell, Scott Kofmehl, Mark Lambert, Jacky Ly, Ken Moorefield, David Muehlke, Nguyễn Vũ Tú, Pete Peterson, Jeannette Pina, John Rexford, Charles Sellers, Laura Stone, Susan Sutton, Alex Titolo, and Tuấn T. Tôn wanted to tell the story of America's reconciliation with Vietnam as accurately as possible. Each of them answered my questions patiently, though I often contacted them at inconvenient times, and they reviewed drafts of this book and shared my enthusiasm for the project. To the extent that this account truly reflects what transpired between two former enemies, now friends, over the past twenty-five years, these colleagues and friends are the reason. I am responsible for any mistakes.

This is a book about reconciliation between people, not just governments. I am equally grateful to friends outside of government who gave of their time and dipped into deep wells of memory to help bring this book to life. I relied heavily on the memories and files of friends whom I admire, including Charles Bailey, George Black, Bob Connor, Bert Covert, Ken Crouse, Mike DeGregorio, Brian Eyler, Virginia Foote, Thảo Nguyễn Griffiths, Chris Helzer, and Bob Schiffer. All of them share a love of Vietnam and a commitment to telling the truth.

I don't see how it would be possible to stick with a three-year book project unless the writer feels a strong compulsion to finish it and receives encouragement and prodding along the way. I am very grateful for the inspiration, especially at early stages, that I received from Skip Boyce, Don Fehr, Alison Osius, Fred Rich, Quách Cảnh Toàn, and Bạch Tông. I thank Rutgers University Press, and especially Jasper Chang, for believing that this was a story worth telling. Thanks also to Sherry Gerstein and meticulous copy-editor Jeanne Ferris at Westchester Publishing Services. And I am proud of my collaboration with Henry Ferris, a brilliant editor, who took sluggish or murky prose and made it clear and alive.

I would not have learned what I needed to know as a diplomat without years of patient teaching and coaching by two remarkable friends and mentors, Leon Fuerth and Cameron Hume. I was blessed to work for wonderful bosses, including Ambassadors Tom Hubbard, Ravic Huso, the late Darryl Johnson, Scot Marciel, Nick Platt, Nancy Powell, and Linda Thomas-Greenfield; Secretary of State Madeleine Albright; Vice President Al Gore; and President Bill Clinton. I received kind and generous reassurance as I pursued my dream job from Dan Baer, Bill Burns, Tom Countryman, Glynn Davies, Rose Gottemoeller, Maria Otero, and Uzra Zeya. And I am forever grateful for the support of President Barack Obama and Senator John McCain. Thanks to all for the opportunities you gave me.

Learning Vietnamese was hard. From 1995 to 1996, Cô Hiền, Thầy Độ, and Thầy Duy showed great patience in teaching me the language; in 2014, Cô Hà and Cô Hạnh made language learning fun again; and while I was ambassador, Cô Chung further enhanced my cultural understanding as she helped me improve my Vietnamese. I am grateful to my driver, Anh Minh, who was strict about pronunciation as I practiced my remarks en route to events. He never lost his focus on the road. Each of you opened a door to my engaging deeply with Vietnam.

To my children, Theodore Alan (TABO) and Lucile Elizabeth Bond-Osius, I hope that this book illuminates a little about your early years, as you learned to walk and eat and speak in the wonderful nation of Vietnam. You received love from many people, including your grandmother, Nancy Osius Zimmerman, who traveled across the ocean twice to be with our family. Your granny, Claudette Davis Bond, and grandpa, Alan Bond; aunts Meg, Sarah, Lisa, Debra, Alison, Melinda, Lucy, and Grace; and your generous godparents Alicia, Becky, Chris, David, Eileen, Gil, Melba, and Sam all proved what Hillary Clinton told us—that it takes a village. The late Julian Bond and his wife, Pam Horowitz, taught Clayton and me what it means to bring love and purpose together in a marriage. To my husband, Clayton, you are the reason that nothing is impossible for our family, because of your love for us and your commitment to what is right and true. I can never thank you enough.

Notes

Preface

1   PBS NewsHour, "Meet Bicycle Diplomat Ted Osius, America's Modern Ambassador to Vietnam," May 20, 2016, https://www.pbs.org/newshour/show/meet-bicycle-diplomat-ted-osius-americas-modern-ambassador-to-vietnam.
2   Ken Burns and Lynn Novick, dir., *The Vietnam War* (Walpole, NH: Florentine Films, 2017), https://www.pbs.org/kenburns/the-vietnam-war/.

Chapter 1   An Improbable Friendship

1   John McCain and Mark Salter, *Faith of My Fathers* (New York: Random House, 1999), 349.
2   John Kerry, *Every Day is Extra* (New York: Simon and Schuster, 2018), 109.
3   "Vietnam Veterans against the War: Statement by John Kerry to the Senate Committee of Foreign Relations April 23, 1971," https://faculty.etsu.edu/history/documents/vietvetswar.htm.
4   As reported by Ken Moorefield, an eyewitness. On April 25, 1975, the U.S. Defense Department reported that 21,000 South Vietnamese officials, American agency local employees, and their families had been evacuated by the airlift. William Bach, email to the author, April 14, 2020.
5   Quoted in Stanley Karnow, *Vietnam: A History* (New York: Viking Press, 1983), 667.
6   Doug Potratz, "Last Marine to Die in Vietnam," Fall of Saigon Marines Association, accessed March 4, 2021, https://fallofsaigon.org/iframe.php?id=6.
7   Sue Holland, "A Note about Corporal Charles McMahon," Fall of Saigon Marines Association, accessed March 4, 2021, https://fallofsaigon.org/iframe.php?id=13.
8   Quoted in George J. Church, "Saigon: The Final Ten Days," *Time*, April 24, 1995, 11, http://content.time.com/time/subscriber/article/0,33009,982844-11,00.html.
9   John J. Valdez, "The Last to Leave," Fall of Saigon Marines Association, accessed March 4, 2021, https://fallofsaigon.org/iframe.php?id=1.

10 Quoted in Sean Wilentz, "John McCain," Encyclopaedia Britannica, accessed March 5, 2021, https://www.britannica.com/biography/John-McCain.

11 The United States, the Soviet Union, China, France, and Britain negotiated with the Vietnamese-backed government of Prime Minister Hun Sen and three rebel groups, including the Khmer Rouge, until an agreement was reached in October 1991.

Chapter 2   A Time to Heal and a Time to Build

1 George Packer, *Our Man: Richard Holbrooke and the End of the American Century* (New York: Alfred A. Knopf, 2019), 177.

2 Quoted in Steven Greenhouse, "Senate Urges End to U.S. Embargo against Vietnam," *New York Times*, January 28, 1994, https://www.nytimes.com/1994/01/28/world/senate-urges-end-to-us-embargo-against-vietnam.html.

3 Quoted in Seth Mydans, "Opening to Vietnam: In California," *New York Times*, July 12, 1995, https://www.nytimes.com/1995/07/12/world/opening-vietnam-california-for-many-those-who-fled-vietnam-day-sadness-anger.html.

4 Quoted in Mydans, "Opening to Vietnam."

5 Quoted in Alison Mitchell, "U.S. Grants Vietnam Full Ties; Time for Healing, Clinton Says," *New York Times*, July 12, 1995, https://www.nytimes.com/1995/07/12/world/opening-vietnam-overview-us-grants-vietnam-full-ties-time-for-healing-clinton.html.

6 Ann Mills Griffiths, email to the author, August 4, 2020.

7 Jan Scruggs, "The Time Is Now," *New York Daily News*, July 11, 1995.

8 David Varney, "It's Too Soon to Give In," *New York Daily News*, July 11, 1995.

9 According to a *USA Today*/CNN/Gallup poll cited in "A New Era," *USA Today*, July 11, 1995.

10 John McCain, "Restoration of Diplomatic Relations with Vietnam," Cong. Rec., Vol. 141, No. 111 (July 11, 1995), https://www.govinfo.gov/content/pkg/CREC-1995-07-11/html/CREC-1995-07-11-pt1-PgS9723-3.htm.

11 McCain, "Restoration of Diplomatic Relations," S9723.

12 Years later, Desaix (b. February 12, 1936; d. February 12, 2021) lent Clayton and me a painting he had done of Hạ Long Bay for our Art in Embassies exhibition at the ambassador's residence. We chose as our exhibition's theme "Toward A More Perfect Union," inspired by President Barack Obama's second inaugural address—in which he spoke of what truly makes America great: our founding creed that all of us are created equal and our "never-ending journey to bridge the meaning of those words with the realities of our time." Clayton and I selected photographs and paintings by American artists that illustrated that theme, such as Will Barnet and Are Berge's paintings of families of different ethnicities, Consuelo Canada's photograph of white and black hands, a photograph of Martin Luther King Jr., and Warren Leffler's photograph of a gay rights demonstration in New York City. Thousands of people saw these works during the three years we lived in the residence, as well as Rick Rocamora's photo titled "God Bless America," a portrait of new U.S. citizens (men from the Philippines who had fought with the United States in World War II and waited fifty years for citizenship), and Peter Steinhauer's photo of a woman from the H'mong Hoa minority group. We purchased two Catherine Karnow photos to round out the exhibition.

Since 1963, the State Department's Art in Embassies program has created temporary exhibitions of original works of art by American artists all around the world. Proposed by President John Kennedy and supported by Congress, the program is a partnership between the federal government and the American arts community. Secretary of State Dean Rusk (in office 1961–1969) said, "I am proud of the art in embassies program, both because it represents important aspects of our national culture and because it is a cooperative enterprise which blends the ideas and energies of government and private citizens and organizations interested in the visual arts." (Quoted in "Art in Embassies," OBO/OPS/ART, U.S. Department of State, https://ininet.org/united-states-department-of-state-art-in-embassies-program -obo.html.) Secretary of State John Kerry said: "Extending our reach, amplifying our voice, and demonstrating our inclusiveness are strategic imperatives for America. Art in Embassies cultivates relationships that transcend boundaries, building trust, mutual respect and understanding among peoples. It is a fulcrum of America's global leadership as we continue to work for freedom, human rights and peace around the world." (Quoted in "Art in Embassies Program 2016/17," https:// guyberube.com/art-in-embassies-program/.) Frequently exhibitions focus on connections between U.S. culture and that of the host country. Our exhibition fostered discussions about diversity and inclusion.

13 Kurt Campbell, "Press Roundtable," February 2, 2012, https://photos.state.gov /libraries/hochiminh/174995/pr/Hanoi-120202-Campbell-Media.pdf.

14 Daniel Fern, "Vietnam on Two Wheels," *State Magazine*, February 1998, https://1997-2001.state.gov/publications/statemag/statemag_feb98/pom.html

15 Thomas W. Lippman, "Former POW Nominated Ambassador to Vietnam," *Washington Post*, May 24, 1996, https://www.washingtonpost.com/archive/politics /1996/05/24/former-pow-nominated-ambassador-to-vietnam/c5ab18ab-9c9c-456d -9af3-1349274f763c/.

Chapter 3 The Story of Pete Peterson

1 Quoted in "Veteran and Former POW Returns to Vietnam as Envoy," *Wall Street Journal*, May 12, 1997, https://www.wsj.com/articles/SB863375051547748000.

2 Sandy Banisky, "U.S. Envoy Was Hanoi's 'Guest' Nominee," *Baltimore Sun*, June 4, 1996, https://www.baltimoresun.com/news/bs-xpm-1996-06-04-1996156008-story .html.

3 Quế was imprisoned in 1978–1988, 1990–1998, 2003–2005, and briefly in 2011 on state security charges related to his activism.

4 Reed Tucker, "Almost Everything You Thought about the Famed Fall of Saigon Photo Isn't True," *New York Post*, April 23, 2019, https://nypost.com/2019/04/23 /new-book-reveals-truth-behind-this-famed-fall-of-saigon-photo/.

5 Bringing the tools of trade to Vietnam proved difficult. For the Overseas Private Investment Corporation (OPIC) to support U.S. business in Vietnam, it first needed to make a determination about labor conditions. American labor unions, led by the AFL-CIO, had forced OPIC to cease its operations in South Korea and Saudi Arabia because of those countries' labor rights violations, and the AFL-CIO initially refused to engage in Vietnam. Both right- and left-leaning members of Congress were trying to defund OPIC, which in 1997 operated in only one Communist country, Poland (where Solidarity was an effective and successful labor union).

There were a few champions within organized labor who were willing to engage with Vietnam. AFL-CIO President John Sweeney admired Ambassador

Peterson and had a good relationship with Bob Schiffer, OPIC's vice president for investment development. Barbara Shailor, in charge of international programs at AFL-CIO, was interested in Vietnam.

In April 1997, Treasury Secretary Robert Rubin returned from a trip to Vietnam during which he had signed an agreement requiring the Hanoi government to repay the debt owed by the former Saigon regime. This was a bitter pill for Vietnam, but the White House explained that Congress would accept nothing less. Rubin declared that Vietnam, not Russia, was the future. During a follow-up meeting that included Sandy Kristof, Asia director at the National Security Council; a representative of the Export-Import bank; OPIC's Mildred Callear; and Bob Boorstin, Rubin's senior advisor, Schiffer proposed sending a labor delegation to Vietnam. Rubin was skeptical but gave the idea his blessing. Schiffer and Shailor obtained Sweeney's approval for an advance visit to Vietnam by Dennis Rivera's deputy (Rivera, an AFL-CIO national board member and head of the New York Service Employees International Union, was a New Yorker who had been active in the antiwar movement).

As labor attaché, I was control officer for a second labor delegation that was led by the AFL-CIO's Phil Fishman, staffed by Schiffer and Ginny Foote, and included Owen Hernstadt from the International Association of Machinists and Aerospace Workers; George Korpious, an OPIC Board member; the Department of Labor's Betsy White; and Rivera. The delegation returned to the United States with a positive report on workers' rights. As a result, the AFL-CIO supported OPIC's engagement in Vietnam, Sweeney agreed not to oppose the Bilateral Trade Agreement with Vietnam in Congress, and Congress renewed funding for OPIC.

6   David Lamb, "Job Opportunity or Exploitation?," *Los Angeles Times*, April 18, 1999, https://www.latimes.com/archives/la-xpm-1999-apr-18-fi-28567-story.html,

7   Lamb, "Job Opportunity or Exploitation?"

8   Some of the Nike representatives ran into strong resistance from the Taiwanese and Korean managers of the factories where Nike produced shoes. Brad Figel, a Nike employee who had convinced Knight that reform was needed, also persuaded him to set up a micro-loan program with the Women's Union and provide night school for Nike employees. Schiffer arranged for the U.S. surgeon general to visit some of Nike's factories, as well as Chris Matthews, a journalist who visited factories without the approval of Nike executives. When Matthews returned to Washington, he mentioned his Nike factory visits on his show in a positive light. Increased transparency resulted in Nike realizing both that not everyone who visited the company's factories was going to criticize it and that hearing from U.S. student groups, NGOs, and others could be a learning process for Nike and for its factories about consumer and international expectations of acceptable labor practices. From 1999 through 2002, Nike hosted thousands of American visitors to its factories. Foote brought several Congressional staff delegations to the factories. In early 1999, the *Los Angeles Times* journalist David Lamb interviewed a twenty-seven-year-old worker and concluded that "a job at Nike would seem a prize not much shy of hitting the lottery" (Lamb, "Job Opportunity or Exploitation?"). That transparency changed the narrative for Nike, and its lessons remain relevant today.

Senior Vietnamese leaders also became interested in Nike and its practices. Nike hosted General Võ Nguyên Giáp and former Party General Secretary Lê Khả Phiêu, who came away impressed. Their exposure to Nike and the practices of U.S. companies may have shaped their view of economic integration and the importance of job creation for exports. They were impressed to see twenty thousand people with good jobs, good food in the canteen, and access to on-site medical clinics in modern factories where once there had been rice paddies or military bases. These experiences likely reaffirmed that these leaders were taking Vietnam in the right direction.

9   Larry Berman, *Perfect Spy: The Incredible Double Life of Pham Xuan An* (New York: HarperCollins, 2007), 220.

10 Viet Thanh Nguyen, "The Great Vietnam War Novel Was Not Written by an American," *New York Times*, May 2, 2017, https://www.nytimes.com/2017/05/02 /opinion/vietnam-war-novel-was-not-written-by-an-american.html.

11 Michael was born July 2, 1957, and died July 21, 2018.

12 Ginny Foote, email to the author, July 27, 1999.

13 Mark McDonald, "U.S., Hanoi Seal Historic Trade Pact," *Mercury News,* July 25, 1999.

14 McDonald, "U.S., Hanoi Seal Historic Trade Pact."

15 The final issue to be resolved was the percentage of Vietnam's telecommunications industry that U.S. companies could own. China's entry into the WTO was under negotiation at the same time, and both Vietnam and the United States were limited in their flexibility because of what was happening in the parallel China negotiations. The United States wanted to push Vietnam to accept more generous terms to increase pressure on China. In the end, the United States backed down.

16 "A New Vietnam Pact," *Wall Street Journal*, July 21, 2000, https://www.wsj.com /articles/SB964144116206882205.

17 "A New Vietnam Pact."

18 Quoted in "Full Text of US President Bill Clinton's Speech in Vietnam," *Le Viêt Nam, aujourd'hui* [The Vietnam News], Agence France Presse, November 17, 2000, http://patrick.guenin2.free.fr/cantho/vnnews/bclint14.htm.

19 "Full Text of US President Bill Clinton's Speech in Vietnam."

20 According to a source who participated in the meeting.

21 "Full Text of US President Bill Clinton's Speech in Vietnam."

22 Email from Pete Peterson to author, August 3, 2020.

Chapter 4   David and Goliath

1   Desaix Anderson, *United States–Vietnam Reconciliation: Through War to a Strategic Partnership* (Washington: New Academia, 2021), 219.

2   Anderson, *United States–Vietnam Reconciliation*, 1.

3   Leon S. Fuerth, email to the author, September 15, 2016.

4   Douglas Martin, "Henry A. Prunier, 91, U.S. Soldier Who Trained Vietnamese Troops, Dies," *New York Times*, April 17, 2013, https://www.nytimes.com/2013/04 /18/world/asia/henry-a-prunier-army-operative-who-helped-trained-vietnamese -troops-dies-at-91.html.

5   History.com Editors, "Vietnam Declares Its Independence from France," A&E Television Networks, https://www.history.com/this-day-in-history/vietnam -independence-proclaimed.

6   Letter from Ho Chi Minh to President Harry S. Truman, February 28, 1946, Washington and Pacific Coast Field Station Files, 1942–1945, Records of the Office of Strategic Services, 1919–2002, National Archives Catalog, National Archives at College Park, https://catalog.archives.gov/id/305263.

7   Theodore H. White, *In Search of History: A Personal Adventure* (New York: Warner Books, 1978), 396.

8   The *Pentagon Papers* put it this way: "U.S. assistance, which began modestly with $10 million in 1950, reached $1,063 million in fiscal year 1954, at which time it accounted for 78% of the cost of the French war burden. The major portion of the increase came in the last year of the war, following the presentation in 1953 of the Navarre Plan, which called for the enlargement of Franco-Vietnamese forces and a dynamic strategy to recapture the initiative and pave the way for victory by 1955. The optimistic endorsement of the Navarre Plan by Lt. General John W. O'Daniel, head of the MAAG in Indochina, as being capable of turning the tide and leading to a decisive victory over the Viet Minh contributed to Washington's agreement to substantially raise the level of assistance. But equally important, the Navarre Plan, by being a concrete proposal which held out the promise of ending the long war, put France in a position to pressure the United States for more funds to underwrite the training and equipping of nine additional French battalions and a number of new Vietnamese units." (https://www.mtholyoke.edu/acad/intrel/pentagon/pent6.htm.)

9   Bernard B. Fall, "Dienbienphu: Battle to Remember," *New York Times*, May 3, 1964, https://www.nytimes.com/1964/05/03/archives/dienbienphu-battle-to-remember.html.

10 Stanley Karnow, "Ho Chi Minh," *Time*, April 13, 1998, http://content.time.com/time/magazine/article/0,9171,988162,00.html.

11 Quoted in Karnow, "Ho Chi Minh."

12 White, *In Search of History*, 406.

13 Leon S. Fuerth, email to the author, September 15, 2016.

14 Anderson, *United States–Vietnam Reconciliation*, 1.

15 Stanley Karnow, *Vietnam: A History* (New York: Viking Press, 1983), 287.

16 Quoted in *Vietnam: A History*, 321.

17 Chester L. Cooper, "Pilgrimage to Hanoi," *Washington Post*, June 29, 1997, https://www.washingtonpost.com/archive/opinions/1997/06/29/pilgrimage-to-hanoi/70dbd42ae-4ba9-46d8-946e-93a54f82c4eb/.

18 Cooper, "Pilgrimage to Hanoi."

19 Errol Morris, dir., *The Fog of War* (New York: Sony Pictures Classics, 2003).

20 Hannah Beech, "U.S. Aircraft Carrier Heads to Vietnam, with a Message for China," *New York Times*, March 4, 2018.

21 Nguyễn Thị Lan Anh writes, "China took control of Scarborough Shoal in 2012. It further extended its sovereignty claims to include submerged features, such as James Shoal, in 2014. Beijing built artificial features in the Spratlys from 2014 to 2016. On maritime rights and jurisdiction specifically, China deployed oil rigs, conducted seismic surveys, intimidated fishermen and rammed fishing vessels, exercised water cannons, harassed oil exploration and exploitation activities of other littoral states, challenged freedom of navigation and flight operations in the area, etc. The purpose of all of these activities is to control the navigation routes, seabed and air space of the South China Sea as well as the resources in the water within the nine-dash line" ("The 'Four-Sha' Claim: Signaling a Post Covid-19 Global Order," *Maritime Issues*, April 29, 2020, 7, http://www.maritimeissues.com/uploaded/The%20%E2%80%9CFour-Sha%E2%80%9D%20Claim_Signalling%20a%20Post%20Covid-19%20Global%20Order.)

Chapter 5   The Legacies of War

1   Irene Ohler and Đỗ Thùy Duong, *Bà Triệu's 21st Century Daughters: Stories of Remarkable Vietnamese Women* (Hanoi: Women's Publishing House, 2016), 45.

2   Ohler and Đỗ, *Bà Triệu's 21st Century Daughters*, 43.

3   Ambassador Douglas B. "Pete" Peterson, "U.S.-Vietnam Relations: The BTA and Normalization's End," speech to the Asia Society, St. Regis Hotel, Washington, DC, March 9, 2001, quoted in "Remarks as Prepared for Delivery Distributed by the Office of International Information Programs," *The Washington File,* U.S. Department of State.

4   Peterson, "U.S.-Vietnam Relations."

5   Quoted in Le Ke Son and Charles R. Bailey, *From Enemies to Partners: Vietnam, the U.S. and Agent Orange* (Chicago: G. Anton, 2017), 148.

6   Quoted in Le and Bailey, *From Enemies to Partners,* 97.

7   Tim Rieser, "The U.S.-Vietnam Relationship and War Legacies: 25 Years into Normalization," Stimson Center, July 15, 2020, video, https://www.stimson.org /event/the-u-s-vietnam-relationship-and-war-legacies-25-years-into-normalization/.

8   Quoted in Le and Bailey, *From Enemies to Partners,* 153–154.

9   Scientific name: *Orcaella brevirostris.*

10 "Ne Win," *Economist,* December 14, 2002, https://www.economist.com/obituary /2002/12/12/ne-win.

11 Scientific name: *Pangasianodon gigas.*

12 Occasionally one is caught. The species is on the critically endangered list of the International Union for Conservation of Nature (https://www.iucnredlist.org /species/15944/5324699).

13 Brian Eyler, *Last Days of the Mighty Mekong* (London: Zed Books, 2019), 21. Eyler's scholarship informs this chapter.

14 According to Eyler, international civil society groups and local ones in Cambodia, Vietnam, and Thailand have organized campaigns and protests against dam construction. In 2014, the World Wide Fund for Nature (WWF) launched a "Say No to Don Sahong Dam" campaign, citing the dam's potential impact on the food security of millions of people in the Mekong region. "More than a quarter of a million people around the world are sending a strong and clear message to Mega First. Stop Don Sahong dam or risk the dubious honor of precipitating the extinction of a species," said WWF former country director Chhith Samath in a 2014 online statement. He continued, "Don Sahong dam is a dangerous experiment and Mega First is gambling with the livelihoods of millions" (quoted in Eyler, *Last Days of the Mighty Mekong,* 88). See also Richard Cronin and Courtney Weatherby, "Letters from the Mekong: Time for a New Narrative on Mekong Hydropower," Stimson Center, October 2015, https://www.stimson.org/wp-content/files/file -attachments/Letters_from_the_Mekong_Oct_2015.pdf.

15 Emerging Infectious Diseases: Asian SARS Outbreak Challenged International and National Responses," General Accounting Office, April 2004, 33, https://www .gao.gov/assets/gao-04-564.pdf.

16 In January 2003, Chinese officials played down the numbers of people infected by SARS and the disease's geographic range within the country. Guangdong provincial authorities did not report the epidemic to Beijing until February 8. Three days later, Beijing disclosed that more than three hundred people had been infected by a mystery illness in Guangdong since mid-November 2002. In March, Beijing health

officials began sharing data with a WHO team but delayed the team's visit to Guangdong. Still fearful of creating a widespread panic that might cause economic damage, Beijing tightly controlled media coverage of the epidemic and instructed doctors not to speak to foreign or domestic reporters.

17 In November 2002, Foshan City in China's Guangdong province recorded the first SARS cases. In February 2003, a doctor from Guangzhou, Guangdong's capital, carried the disease to Hong Kong and infected fellow travelers in the Metropole Hotel. From there, the disease dug into Hong Kong and spread via travelers first to Singapore, Vietnam, and Canada, and then to twenty-four more countries. Although not proven, it seemed that so-called super-infectors spread the disease with particular efficiency. One woman traveled from Hong Kong to Singapore, triggering a chain reaction that infected fifty family members, friends, and close contacts, as well as fifty-six health care workers. Her parents were among those who perished.

18 World Health Organization, "SARS Outbreak Contained Worldwide," news release, July 5, 2003, https://www.who.int/news/item/05-07-2003-sars-outbreak-contained-worldwide.

19 I described this phenomenon as it played out in U.S. partnerships with India and Indonesia. See Ted Osius, "Global Swing States: Deepening Partnerships with India and Indonesia," *Asia Policy*, no. 17 (2014): 67–92, www.jstor.org/stable/24905256.

Chapter 6   Think Unthinkable Thoughts

1 J. William Fulbright. "Foreign Policy—Old Myths and New Realities," Speech in the U.S. Senate, March 25, 1964, *Kentucky Law Journal* 53, no. 1, article 2, 33, https://uknowledge.uky.edu/klj/vol53/iss1/2.

2 A few intrepid American scholars headed to Vietnam at the same time that Vietnamese began studying in the United States. As a Luce scholar at Vietnam's National Economics University in 1997, Eddy Malesky learned Vietnamese, econometrics, and survey design. After traveling through the provinces and seeing the different speeds of development, Malesky wrote his PhD thesis at Duke University on Vietnamese provincial governments' differing approaches to economic reform. Back in Vietnam, he played tennis with Jonathan Stromseth, director of the Asia Foundation, and they exchanged ideas about provincial governance. The trio of Malesky, Stromseth, and Đậu Anh Tuấn (legal director of Vietnam's Chamber of Commerce and Industry) met in a Hanoi *bia hơi* (a local beer joint) and came up with the idea of the Provincial Competitiveness Index (PCI) survey. After a trial run in 2004 in forty-five provinces, they received U.S. Agency for International Development funding to cover all sixty-three provinces in 2005.

Provincial leaders, who were forced for the first time to defend their economic performance, paid serious attention to the PCI, which soon affected the levels of revenue they received from Hanoi—and their promotions. Malesky, Stromseth, and Tuấn learned a lesson about what works and what doesn't in economic development. "Stop trying to tell people what to do," Malesky realized. "Instead, give them the resources to understand their problems, and they'll find solutions." Vietnam had the raw materials for reform, including high literacy rates, hardworking citizens, and a real commitment to reform.

Starting in 2005, the PCI surveyed 10,000 private businesses annually, and Malesky and Tuấn presented the results to Vietnam's highest-ranking provincial leaders and elite businesses. To perform well on the PCI, a province needed to have:

(1) low entry costs for starting up a business; (2) easy access to land and secure business premises; (3) a transparent business environment and equitable business information; (4) minimal informal charges; (5) limits on how long bureaucratic procedures and inspections could take; (6) limited crowding out of private activity resulting from policy biases toward state-owned enterprises; (7) proactive and creative provincial leaders, who could solve problems for companies; (8) developed and high-quality business support services; (9) sound labor training policies; and (10) fair and effective legal procedures for dispute resolution.

Along with the FETP, the PCI promoted a virtuous cycle, one in which provincial officials could be rewarded with promotions for creating the conditions for prosperity. Those whose provinces stagnated economically found that their careers also stagnated.

3   Hillary Clinton, "America's Pacific Century," *Foreign Policy*, October 11, 2011, https://foreignpolicy.com/2011/10/11/americas-pacific-century/.

4   Barack Obama, "Remarks to the Australian Parliament, Parliament House, Canberra, Australia, November 17, 2011," https://obamawhitehouse.archives.gov /the-press-office/2011/11/17/remarks-president-obama-australian-parliament.

5   John Kerry, "Remarks at a Working Lunch with Vietnamese President Truong Tan Sang," July 24, 2013, https://2009-2017.state.gov/secretary/remarks/2013/07 /212378.htm.

6   Soon after I arrived in Hanoi, the text on the monument was revised. When McCain visited, I brought him and the other senators traveling with him to see the clean, improved monument. The Vietnamese pejorative prefix "*Tên*" before McCain's name had been replaced with "*phi cong*" or "pilot." McCain's name was spelled correctly. The repairs had been done quietly, with no fanfare. I learned that Nghị had instructed that the changes be made. Prior to Nghi's meeting with McCain, the marker had read: "NGÀY 26-10-1967 TẠI HỒ TRÚC BẠCH QUÂN VÀ DÂN THỦ ĐÔ HÀ NỘI BẮT SỐNG TÊN JOHN SNEY MA CAN THIẾU TÁ KHÔNG QUÂN MỸ LÁI CHIẾC MÁY BAY A4 BỊ BẮN RƠI TẠI NHÀ MÁY ĐIỆN YÊN PHỤ. ĐÂY LÀ MỘT TRONG 10 CHIẾC MÁY BAY BỊ BẮN RƠI CÙNG NGÀY." Translated, this said: "On 26 October 1967 at Truc Bach Lake, Hanoi's people and armed forces captured USAF Major John Sney Ma Can [*sic*] who flew the A-4 aircraft shot down at the Yen Phu power plant. His was one of ten planes shot down that day."

In early 2015, it was revised to read: "NGÀY 26-10-1967, TẠI HỒ TRÚC BẠCH QUÂN VÀ DÂN THỦ ĐÔ HÀ NỘI BẮT SỐNG PHI CÔNG JOHN SIDNEY McCAIN THIẾU TÁ KHÔNG QUÂN THUỘC LỰC LƯỢNG HẢI QUÂN HOA KỲ ĐÃ LÁI CHIẾC MÁY BAY A4 BỊ BẮN RƠI TẠI NHÀ MÁY ĐIỆN YÊN PHỤ. ĐÂY LÀ MỘT TRONG 10 CHIẾC MÁY BAY BỊ BẮN RƠI CÙNG NGÀY." Translated, this says: "On 26 October 1967 at Trúc Bạch Lake, Hanoi's people and armed forces captured U.S. Naval Air Force Lieutenant Commander John Sidney McCain who flew the A-4 aircraft shot down at the Yen Phu power plant. His was one of ten planes shot down that day."

The differences are: (1) the correct spelling of McCain's name; (2) the correct identification of his rank and military branch; and (3) dropping TÊN from TÊN PHI CÔNG, which makes the text becomes more formal and fair. TÊN is a classifier for despicable individuals such as enemies, thieves, robbers, cheaters, and rapists. The Vietnamese language has a group of classifiers that have built-in positive or negative connotations, which can be added or dropped to express the speaker's attitude toward the subject modified by the classifier. After TÊN was dropped, the text was no longer marred by the speaker's bias against the subject. This subtle difference is relevant to a native speaker. There are jokes about Vietnamese who tried to impress their French bosses by punishing the Vietnamese subordinates who used derogatory classifiers to address those same French bosses. As the classifier didn't translate at all, the nonnative speaker finds the punishment puzzling.

7   Ted Osius, "Statement of Ted Osius at Senate Committee on Foreign Relations," June 17, 2014, https://vn.usembassy.gov/statement-of-ted-osius-at-senate-committee-on-foreign-relations/.

8   President Barack Obama, letter to the author, November 18, 2014.

9   John Kerry, "Joint Press Availability with Vietnamese Deputy Prime Minister and Foreign Minister Pham Binh Minh," Government Guest House, Hanoi, Vietnam, December 16, 2013, https://2009-2017.state.gov/secretary/remarks/2013/12/218747.htm.

10 The source for this quotation and subsequent quotations in this chapter can be found in "Remarks at Swearing-In Ceremony for U.S. Ambassador to Vietnam Ted Osius III," December 10, 2014, https://2009-2017.state.gov/secretary/remarks/2014/12/234941.htm.

Chapter 7   Diplomacy from a Bicycle Seat

1   "President Receives US, Panamanian, Qatar Ambassadors," The Socialist Republic of Vietnam Online Newspaper of the Government, December 16, 2014, http://news.chinhphu.vn/Home/President-receives-US-Panamanian-Qatar-Ambassadors/201412/23324.vgp.

2   George Packer tells a different story in *Our Man: Richard Holbrooke and the End of the American Century* (New York: Alfred A. Knopf, 2019). According to Packer, Albright tolerated Holbrooke in her old job, and the fourteen-month delay between Holbrooke's nomination and his confirmation resulted from a series of investigations.

3   President Barack Obama, letter to the author, November 18, 2014.

4   "5 mục tiêu chính của đại sứ Mỹ Ted Osius," Tuổi Trẻ, December 25, 2014, https://tuoitre.vn/5-muc-tieu-chinh-cua-dai-su-my-ted-osius-690114.htm.

5   Nancy Pelosi, Democratic Leader, letter to the author, April 30, 2015.

Chapter 8   Châu, Khiết, and the Students of Vietnam

1   Quoted in "Preservation of Royal Altars at World Heritage Site—Triệu Tổ Temple, Huế Imperial City Supported by the U.S. Ambassador's Fund for Cultural Preservation," Hue Monuments Conservation Centre, updated March 14, 2014, http://hueworldheritage.org.vn/TTBTDTCDH.aspx?TieuDeID=96&TinTucID=1258&l=en.

2   Quoted in "US Ambassador Visits Hue's Temple to Grant Preservation Funding," February 7, 2015, Thanh Nien News, http://www.thanhniennews.com/arts-culture/us-ambassador-visits-hues-temple-to-grant-preservation-funding-38515.html.

3   "Ancient Temple in Hue Receives Facelift," April 29, 2016, VNA, https://en.vietnamplus.vn/ancient-temple-in-hue-receives-facelift/92584.vnp.

4   "Unveiling Ceremony the Restoration and Preservation of Trieu To Temple—Front Building, Hue Imperial City, Vietnam Supported by the U.S. Ambassador's Fund

for Cultural Preservation," April 27, 2016, http://hueworldheritage.org.vn
/TTBTDTCDH.aspx?TieuDeID=131&TinTucID=2486&l=en-title=UNESCO.

5 Courtney Marsh, dir., *Chau, Beyond the Lines* (Los Angeles: Cynasty Films, 2015).

6 Email from the author to Assistant Secretary of State for East Asian and Pacific
Affairs Danny Russel, Deputy Assistant Secretary of State for East Asian and
Pacific Affairs Scot Marciel, and National Security Council Senior Director for
Asian Affairs Daniel Kritenbrink, January 8, 2016.

7 George Black, "The Victims of Agent Orange the U.S. Has Never Acknowledged,"
New York Times Magazine, March 16, 2021, https://www.nytimes.com/2021/03/16
/magazine/laos-agent-orange-vietnam-war.html

8 Michael Crow, letter to Thomas J. Vallely, a copy of which Crow gave to the author,
December 2, 2015.

9 World Bank Group and Ministry of Planning and Investment of Vietnam, *Vietnam
2035: Toward Prosperity, Creativity, Equity, and Democracy* (Washington: World
Bank, 2016), xxvii. https://www.worldbank.org/en/news/infographic/2016/02/23
/vietnam-2035-toward-prosperity-creativity-equity-and-democracy or https://
openknowledge.worldbank.org/handle/10986/23724.

10 The authors wrote: "As Vietnamese citizens become more prosperous, they will
want to participate more effectively in governance to influence policy choices. They
will also want the economic, social, and political freedoms that citizens enjoy in
more advanced societies" (World Bank Group and Ministry of Planning and
Investment of Vietnam, *Vietnam 2035*, 61). Party leaders rejected the report's call for
more democratic governance.

Chapter 9   China and the Trans-Pacific Partnership

1 Ken Crouse, email to the author, April 20, 2020.

2 McCain, *Faith of My Fathers*, 230.

3 Họp báo với Đại sứ Ted Osius, American Center, Ho Chi Minh City, January 18,
2015, https://vn.usembassy.gov/vi/press-roundtable-with-ambassador-ted-osius-vi/

4 Ash Carter, "Remarks on the Next Phase of the U.S. Rebalance to the Asia-Pacific,"
Department of Defense, April 6, 2015, https://www.defense.gov/Newsroom
/Speeches/Speech/Article/606660/remarks-on-the-next-phase-of-the-us-rebalance
-to-the-asia-pacific-mccain-instit/.

5 Quoted in Prashanth Parameswaran, "TPP as Important as Another Aircraft
Carrier: US Defense Secretary," The Diplomat, April 8, 2015, https://thediplomat
.com/2015/04/tpp-as-important-as-another-aircraft-carrier-us-defense-secretary/.

6 Freedom House, "Freedom on the Net 2017: Vietnam Key Developments June 1,
2016–May 21, 2017," accessed May 3, 2021, https://freedomhouse.org/country
/vietnam/freedom-net/2017

7 To her credit, Rice told me after the meeting took place: "You were right to push for
this. I'm glad it took place." A confident leader can adjust her views and continue to
learn.

8 Ash Carter, "A Regional Security Architecture Where Everyone Rises," Remarks as
delivered at the International Institute for Strategic Studies Shangri-La Dialogue,
May 30, 2015, Singapore. https://www.defense.gov/Newsroom/Speeches/Speech
/Article/606676/iiss-shangri-la-dialogue-a-regional-security-architecture-where
-everyone-rises/

Chapter 10   The Communist Party

1   Ted Osius, "Twenty Years of Diplomatic Relations with Vietnam—And What Comes Next," Spring 2015, *American Ambassadors Review*, https://www .americanambassadors.org/publications/ambassadors-review/spring-2015/twenty -years-of-diplomatic-relations-with-vietnam-and-what-comes-next.

2   Bill Clinton, "Remarks at the U.S. Embassy's Twentieth Anniversary July 4 Celebration," July 2, 2015, https://vn.usembassy.gov/remarks-by-former-president -bill-clinton-at-the-twentieth-anniversary-july-4-celebration/.

3   Antony Blinken, "A Strategic Opportunity to Advance U.S.-Vietnam Relations," July 6, 2015, *Foggy Bottom* (blog), https://medium.com/foggy-bottom/a-strategic -opportunity-to-advance-u-s-vietnam-relations-421bd8bbbc01.

4   Rory Kennedy, dir., *Last Days in Vietnam* (New York: Moxie Firecracker Films, 2014).

5   Ambassador Michael B. G. Froman, Minister of Industry and Trade Vu Huy Hoang, exchange of letters, February 4, 2016, 2. https://ustr.gov/sites/default/files /TPP-Final-Text-Labour-US-VN-Plan-for-Enhancement-of-Trade-and-Labour -Relations.pdf

6   For example, the analyst Nguyễn Khắc Giang describes Trọng, whose third term as general secretary of the Communist Party began in January 2021, as the most powerful Vietnamese leader since Lê Duẩn ("Succession Politics and Authoritarian Resilience in Vietnam," *Southeast Asian Affairs,* vol. 2020 no. 1, 2020, 411–426, https://muse.jhu.edu/article/754758).

Chapter 11   The Notorious RBG

1   The Constitution of the Socialist Republic of Vietnam, Article 3. https://vietnamnews .vn/politics-laws/250222/the-constitution-of-the-socialist-republic-of-viet-nam.html

2   Ted Osius, "Ambassador Osius's Remarks at CSIS-CSSD Conference on U.S.-Vietnam Relations Opening Session," U.S. Embassy and Consulate in Vietnam, January 14, 2016, https://vn.usembassy.gov/speeches20160114amb-osius-remarks-at -csis-cssd-conference/.

3   Ambassador Hugh Borrowman, email exchange with the author, February 24, 2016

4   Ambassador David Devine, email exchange with the author, February 25, 2016

5   As quoted in "Mai Khoi," Safe Stories About Arresting Music, https://www .safeseries.no/copy-of-artists-bio-nor

6   Adam Bemma, "The Singer Raising Her Voice against Vietnam's New Cyber-Law," Al Jazeera, January 1, 2019, https://www.aljazeera.com/news/2018/12/singer-raising -voice-vietnam-cyber-law-181231002449253.html.

7   Bemma, "The Singer Raising Her Voice against Vietnam's New Cyber-Law."

8   Reginald Chua and Carey Zesiger, "Vietnam Hovers at the Edge of Cyberspace and Hesitates," *Wall Street Journal*, September 12, 1996.

9   Quoted in "Thủ tướng Dũng: Không thể cấm mạng xã hội (Prime Minister Dung: Cannot Ban Social Networks)," BBC, January 15, 2015, https://www.bbc.com /vietnamese/vietnam/2015/01/150115_pmdung_social_media; and quoted in Associated Press, "Vietnamese Leader Says Banning Social Media Sites Impossible," Federal News Network, January 16, 2015, https://federalnewsnetwork.com /technology-main/2015/01/vietnamese-leader-says-banning-social-media-sites -impossible/.

10   More than half of Vietnam's population has access to the internet, and 84 percent own a smartphone. Every week, Vietnamese spend 24.7 hours online, second only to Singapore in Southeast Asia. See Nguyen Khac Giang, "The Digital Economy Era Has Arrived," *Saigon Times*, February 3, 2019, https://english.thesaigontimes.vn /65837/the-digital-economy-era-has-arrived.html.

11   Ted Osius, "U.S. Ambassador Ted Osius' Speech at Ho Chi Minh National Academy of Politics," U.S. Embassy and Consulate in Vietnam, September 27, 2016, https://vn.usembassy.gov/20160927-ambassador-speech-hochiminh-national -academy-politics/.

12   Mai Khoi, "How Facebook Is Damaging Freedom of Expression in Vietnam," *Washington Post*, October 2, 2018, https://www.washingtonpost.com/news/global -opinions/wp/2018/10/02/how-facebook-is-damaging-freedom-of-expression-in -vietnam/.

13   Barack Obama, Inaugural Address, United States Capitol, January 21, 2013, Washington, https://obamawhitehouse.archives.gov/the-press-office/2013/01/21 /inaugural-address-president-barack-obama

14   Quoted in "Statement from HRC President Chad Griffin on the Passing of Julian Bond," Human Rights Campaign, August 16, 2015, https://www.hrc.org/press /statement-from-hrc-president-chad-griffin-on-the-passing-of-julian-bond.

Chapter 12   A New Journey

1   While our joint endeavors changed over time, our basic goals remained the same and are described in Chapter 7 of this book. We succeeded in advancing twelve joint endeavors for President Obama's visit: (1) conclude negotiations for the Trans-Pacific Partnership (TPP) trade agreement; (2) deepen security cooperation; (3) establish the Fulbright University Vietnam and strengthen education cooperation; (4) increase respect for human rights and the rule of law; (5) deepen commercial ties, especially in aviation and infrastructure; (6) clean up dioxin hot spots; (7) boost collaboration in energy, especially clean energy; (8) reduce wildlife trafficking; (9) establish the Peace Corps in Vietnam; (10) boost health collaboration, including establishing emergency operations centers and increasing Vietnam's capacity to address antimicrobial resistance; (11) strengthen law enforcement collaboration, especially in cybersecurity; and (12) promote entrepreneurship. (Earlier, we had used carrots and sticks to persuade the Vietnamese to grant long-term visas to American visitors.) While two other endeavors could not be completed during my tenure, my successor, Ambassador Daniel Kritenbrink pursued them: initiate direct flights between the United States and Vietnam and build a new U.S. embassy. Although we signed an agreement in principle to bring Peace Corps volunteers to Vietnam to teach English, carrying the agreement out proved difficult, so that endeavor languished until 2020, when Kritenbrink revived the initiative and concluded an implementing agreement.

2   Quoted in Kou Jie, "China Opens Water Supply to Drought-Stricken Mekong Countries," *Global Times*, March 16, 2016, https://www.globaltimes.cn/content /974022.shtml.

3   John Kerry, John McCain, and Bob Kerrey, "Lessons and Hopes in Vietnam," *New York Times*, May 24, 2016.

4   Office of the Press Secretary, "Joint Statement: Between the United States of America and the Socialist Republic of Vietnam," The White House, May 23, 2016,

https://obamawhitehouse.archives.gov/the-press-office/2016/05/23/joint-statement
-between-united-states-america-and-socialist-republic

5 Barack Obama, "Remarks by President Obama after Meeting with Vietnamese
   Civil Society Leaders," White House, May 24, 2016, https://obamawhitehouse
   .archives.gov/the-press-office/2016/05/24/remarks-president-obama-after-meeting
   -vietnamese-civil-society-leaders.

6 Barack Obama, "Remarks by President Obama in Address to the People of
   Vietnam," White House, May 24, 2016, https://obamawhitehouse.archives.gov/the
   -press-office/2016/05/24/remarks-president-obama-address-people-vietnam.

7 Obama, "Remarks by President Obama in Address to the People of Vietnam."

8 My consulate colleague Franc Shelton related this story to me.

Chapter 13 A New President

1 Chinese Foreign Minister Wang Yi, "Remarks on the Award of the So-called
   Arbitral Tribunal in the South China Sea Arbitration," Embassy of the People's
   Republic of China in the United States, July 12, 2016. http://www.china-embassy
   .org/eng/zt/abc123/t1380241.htm

2 Associated Press, "China Has Reclaimed 3,200 Acres in the South China Sea, Says
   Pentagon," May 13, 2016, *Guardian*, https://www.theguardian.com/world/2016
   /may/13/pentagon-report-china-reclaimed-3200-acres-south-china-sea.

3 Irene Ohler and Đỗ Thùy Dương. *Bà Triệu's 21st Century Daughters: Stories of
   Remarkable Vietnamese Women* (Hanoi: Women's Publishing House, 2016), 5.

4 Ohler and Đỗ, *Bà Triệu's 21st Century Daughters*, 5.

5 George Burchett, "Viet Nam's Wonder Woman an Immortal Force," *Vietnam News*,
   July 23, 2017.

6 Scientific name: *Pygathrix nemaeus*. Delacour's langur is *Trachypithecus delacouri*,
   and the Cát Bà langur is *T. poliocephalus*.

7 Herbert H. Covert, Hoang Minh Duc, Le Kha Quyet, Andie Ang, Amy Harrison-
   Levine, and Tran Van Bang, "Primates of Vietnam: Conservation in a Rapidly
   Developing Country," *Anthropology Now* 9, no. 2 (2017): 27–44. https://www
   .tandfonline.com/doi/abs/10.1080/19428200.2017.1337353.

8 Silver Star Citation—John Kerry (1969). https://en.wikisource.org/wiki/Silver
   _Star_Citation_-_John_Kerry.

9 Quoted in James Carroll, "A Friendship That Ended the War," *New Yorker*,
   October 13, 1996, https://www.newyorker.com/magazine/1996/10/21/a-friendship
   -that-ended-the-war.

10 Carol Morello, "Back on the Mekong Delta, John Kerry Meets a Man Who Once
   Tried to Kill Him and Finds Exoneration," *Washington Post*, January 14, 2017,
   https://www.washingtonpost.com/world/back-on-the-mekong-delta-john-kerry
   -finds-a-man-who-once-tried-to-kill-him-and-exoneration/2017/01/14/89ae82a0
   -d9ce-11e6-a0e6-d502d6751bc8_story.html.

11 Barack Obama, "Remarks by President Obama in Address to the People of
   Vietnam," White House, May 24, 2016, https://obamawhitehouse.archives.gov/the
   -press-office/2016/05/24/remarks-president-obama-address-people-vietnam.

12 Quoted in Minh Thu, "For the Love of the Caves," *Vietnam News*, August 7, 2016.

13 Letter from ambassadors Giles Lever (UK), Cecilia Piccioni (Italy), the author,
   Martin Klepetko (Czech Republic), Camilla Mellander (Sweden), Claudio

Gutierrez (Argentina) and Tom Malinowski to Nguyễn Ngọc Thiện, minister of culture, sports and tourism, February 16, 2017.

14 Minister Nguyễn Ngọc Thiện, letter to the embassies of the United Kingdom, Italy, United States, Czech Republic, Sweden, and Argentina, the Vietnamese foreign ministry and the office of the prime minister, March 3, 2017.

15 Jordan Vogt-Roberts, dir., *Kong: Skull Island* (Burbank, CA: Legendary Pictures, 2017).

16 World Heritage Committee, "Item 7B of the Provisional Agenda: State of Conservation of Properties Inscribed on the World Heritage List," May 19, 2017, 76, http://whc.unesco.org/archive/2017/whc17-41com-7B-en.pdf.

17 World Heritage Committee, "Item 7B of the Provisional Agenda," 77.

18 World Heritage Committee, "Item 7B of the Provisional Agenda," 77

Chapter 14   Ditches and Tree Roots

1 Drew Gilpin Faust, "Aftermath: War, Memory and History," Ho Chi Minh City University of Social Sciences and Humanities, Vietnam, March 23, 2017, https://www.harvard.edu/president/speeches-faust/2017/aftermath-war-memory-and-history/

2 Neil Sheehan's *A Bright Shining Lie: John Paul Vann and America in Vietnam* gives a detailed account of the battle of Ấp Bắc, when the South Vietnamese army suffered a humiliating defeat at the hands of the Việt Cộng.

3 Quoted in William P. Head, "The March to Oblivion: The Defeat at Ap Hamlet and the Americanization of the Vietnam War," *Journal of Third World Studies* 31, no. 2 (2014): 72, www.jstor.org/stable/45195058. Accessed April 13, 2021.

4 Quang was born on October 12, 1956, and died on September 21, 2018.

5 "Người Phát ngôn Bộ Ngoại giao: Việt Nam luôn bảo vệ, thúc đẩy các quyền cơ bản của người dân," Communist Party of Vietnam Online Newspaper, March 30, 2017, https://dangcongsan.vn/thoi-su/nguoi-phat-ngon-bo-ngoai-giao-viet-nam-luon-bao-ve-thuc-day-cac-quyen-co-ban-cua-nguoi-dan-432286.html

6 Nguyễn Thị Tuyết Lan, "Tố cáo: Công an An ninh điều tra tỉnh Khánh Hòa sách nhiễu và khủng bố người thân của blogger Mẹ Nấm—Nguyễn Ngọc Như Quỳnh," *Dân Làm Báo*, April 9, 2017, https://danlambaovn.blogspot.com/2017/04/to-cao-cong-an-ninh-ieu-tra-tinh-khanh.html.

7 Quoted in "Mother Mushroom: How Vietnam Locked Up Its Most Famous Blogger," Guardian, July 9, 2017, https://www.theguardian.com/global-development/2017/jul/09/mother-mushroom-how-vietnam-locked-up-its-most-famous-blogger.

8 Since then, the visit of an aircraft carrier has become an almost regular event. In March 2018, the USS *Carl Vinson* pulled up to the coastal city of Đà Nẵng, marking the first time since the Vietnam War that an aircraft carrier from the U.S. Navy had visited Vietnam. Two years later, the USS *Theodore Roosevelt* visited Đà Nẵng, respecting Vietnam's rule that foreign navies make no more than one port visit per year.

9 Gerhard Peters and John T. Woolley, "Joint Statement—Enhancing the Comprehensive Partnership Between the United States of America and the Socialist Republic of Vietnam," The American Presidency Project, May 31, 2017, https://www.presidency.ucsb.edu/documents/joint-statement-enhancing-the-comprehensive-partnership-between-the-united-states-america

10 Although I was personally fond of Phil Falcone, I worried that securities fraud charges by the Securities and Exchange Commission—and Falcone's

acknowledgment that he and his firm had broken securities law—meant that a businessman of questionable reputation was facilitating the first contact between President Trump and Vietnam's prime minister.

11 John Rexford, email to the author, May 26, 2017.

12 The United States partially funded the training facility. The United States also provided equipment, including a Level II field hospital, which can provide advanced life support, basic surgery and intensive care, as required for Vietnam to participate in a United Nations peacekeeping mission in South Sudan. See Ted Osius, "Ambassador Osius's Remarks at the Vietnam Peacekeeping Center's S5 Building Dedication," U.S. Embassy and Consulate in Vietnam, August 28, 2017, https://vn .usembassy.gov/ambassador-osius-remarks-vietnam-peacekeeping-centers-s5 -building-dedication/.

13 Hui Sin Teo, Sarah Bales, Caryn Bredenkamp, and Jewelwayne Salcedo Cain, "The Future of Health Financing in Vietnam: Ensuring Sufficiency, Efficiency, and Sustainability," World Bank, Washington, 2019, https://openknowledge.worldbank .org/handle/10986/32187.

14 Author's personal files, September 12, 2017.

15 Under Secretary of State Thomas Shannon represented the United States at that event.

16 President Donald Trump, "Remarks at APEC CEO Summit," Da Nang, Vietnam, November 10, https://asean.usmission.gov/remarks-president-trump-apec-ceo -summit-da-nang-vietnam/

17 Quoted in Vicki Needham, "Lighthizer Vows to Pursue Trump's 'American First' Trade Agenda," Hill, November 10, 2017, https://thehill.com/policy/finance /359800-lighthizer-vows-to-pursue-trumps-america-first-trade-agenda.

18 Don Emmerson, quoted in "The Nelson Report," email from Chris Nelson to the author, November 10, 2017.

19 "Full Text of Chinese President Xi's Address at APEC CEO Summit," XinhuaNet, November 11, 2017, http://www.xinhuanet.com/english/2017-11/11/c_136743492.htm.

Epilogue

1 Quoted in Stephanie Farr, "A Grave Mission back to Vietnam," *Philadelphia Inquirer*, September 20, 2017, https://www.inquirer.com/news/inq/how-google -earth-search-led-veteran-back-vietnam-track-down-mass-graves-20170920.html.

2 Quoted in Farr, "A Grave Mission back to Vietnam."

3 Quoted in Bob Connor, email to the author, May 3, 2020.

4 Ambassador Daniel Kritenbrink, "Transcript: The U.S.-Vietnam Relationship and War Legacies: 25 Years into Normalization," Stimson Center, July 15, 2020, https://www.stimson.org/wp-content/uploads/2020/07/July-15-Transcript_The -US-Vietnam-Relationship-and-War-Legacies.pdf. On a visit to Vietnam, Defense Secretary Esper also stated that "the United States will provide the Vietnam Coast Guard a second high-endurance cutter" in 2020. See Mark T. Esper, "Secretary of Defense Mark T. Esper Remarks at the Diplomatic Academy of Vietnam," U.S. Embassy and Consulate in Vietnam, November 20, 2019, https://vn.usembassy.gov /secretary-of-defense-mark-t-esper-remarks-at-diplomatic-academy-of-vietnam/.

5 Chuck Searcy, email to the author, March 11, 2018.

6 Quoted in Le and Bailey, *From Enemies to Partners,* 13

7 U.S. Secretary of State Rex Tillerson, unclassified message to the author, November 14, 2017.

8   Ted Osius, "Respect, Trust and Partnership: Keeping Diplomacy on Course in Troubling Times," *Foreign Service Journal*, April 2018, https://www.afsa.org/respect -trust-and-partnership-keeping-diplomacy-course-troubling-times.

9   Mike Eiland, Facebook comment on the author's page, April 20, 2018.

10 Scott Martelle, "Now Trump Is Targeting Vietnamese Refugees," *Los Angeles Times*, September 5, 2018.

11 The December 13, 2018, letter to President Trump stated, "We write to express our deep concern about the Department of Homeland Security's (DHS) intention to renegotiate the terms of the 2008 memorandum of understanding (MOU) between Vietnam and the United States.

"This longstanding agreement, which was signed by the U.S. and Vietnamese governments in 2008 under President George W. Bush, did not outline a bilateral agreement regarding the deportation of any Vietnamese citizens who arrived in the United States before July 12, 1995, as this was subject to previous legal positions of the two countries. [Article 2, Para. 2]

"Even for those who came to the U.S. after July 12, 1995, the agreement promises to 'take into account the humanitarian aspect, family unity and circumstances' of each person being considered for repatriation and to carry out repatriation 'in an orderly and safe way, and with respect for the individual human dignity of the person repatriated.' [Article 2, Para. 1, 3]

"The terms of this agreement recognize the complex history between the two countries and the dire circumstances under which hundreds of thousands of Vietnamese fled to the U.S. to seek refuge from political persecution in the aftermath of the Vietnam War. Many of those who fled were South Vietnamese who had fought alongside or otherwise supported the U.S. government during the war.

"Upon their arrival in the U.S., Vietnamese refugees, many of them young children or teenagers, were resettled in struggling neighborhoods without support or resources to cope with significant trauma from the war. As a result, some made mistakes that funneled them into the criminal justice system. However, these refugees have completed their time and are now positively contributing to their communities. These individuals and their families are Americans who are not familiar with the country they fled from.

"Since 2008, the MOU has not been renegotiated. It has allowed families to stay together and enabled individuals not only to rebuild their lives but also to make a difference in their communities.

"We strongly oppose any renegotiation of the MOU that strips the current protections afforded to Vietnamese refugees, including the exclusion from the agreement of pre-1995 immigrants and the humanitarian considerations provided to all others.

"We further urge you to honor the humanitarian spirit and intention embodied in the current agreement. To do otherwise would send thousands of Vietnamese refugees back to a country they fled years ago, tear apart thousands of families, and significantly disrupt immigrant and refugee communities in the U.S."

The following members of Congress signed the letter: Alan Lowenthal; J. Luis Correa; Judy Chu; Pramila Jayapal; Zoe Lofgren; Al Green; Anna G. Eshoo; Barbara Lee; Brad Sherman; Donald S. Beyer, Jr.; Eliot Engel; Gerald E. Connolly; Jan Schakowsky; Jimmy Gomez; Adam Smith; Juan Vargas; Peter Welch; Ro Khanna; Ruben Gallego; Scott Peters; Stephanie Murphy; Rick Larsen; Cedric L. Richmond; Frank Pallone, Jr.; Jimmy Panetta; and Mark Pocan.

12 John Kerry (@JohnKerry), "Despicable. After so many—from George H.W. Bush
    to John McCain and Bill Clinton—worked for years to heal this open wound and
    put a war behind us," Twitter, December 14, 2018, https://twitter.com/johnkerry
    /status/1073291681267662848?lang=en

13 Quoted in Michael G. Long, ed., *Race Man: Julian Bond Selected Works, 1960–2015*
    (San Francisco: City Lights Books, 2020), 39. Bond was defending Martin Luther
    King Jr.'s right to free speech and opposition to the Vietnam War.

14 Roger Spottiswoode, dir., *Tomorrow Never Dies* (London: Eon Productions, 1997).

15 Quoted in "New King Kong Begins Filming in Vietnam," Vietnamnet, Febru-
    ary 22, 2016, http://english.vietnamnet.vn/fms/art-entertainment/151501/new-king
    -kong-begins-filming-in-viet-nam.html

16 Lenny Abrahamson, dir., *Room* (New York: Filmnation Entertainment, 2015).

17 Quoted in Angela Dawson, "The Big Interview: Samuel L. Jackson on His New-
    found Love of Vietnam," *Southeast Asia Globe,* February 7, 2017, https://
    southeastasiaglobe.com/samuel-l-jackson-vietnam/.

18 Quoted in Hannah Beech, "U.S. Aircraft Carrier Heads to Vietnam, with a
    Message for China," *New York Times*, March 4, 2018.

19 One of the two centers, run by the Đà Nẵng branch of the Vietnam Association of
    Victims of Agent Orange (VAVA), was built with a $250,000 donation from
    Patricia Lanza, a Westchester County, New York, philanthropist whom the U.S.
    Fund for UNICEF brought to Đà Nẵng in 2008 in collaboration with Charles
    Bailey. Nguyễn Thị Hiền, then director of the Đà Nẵng branch, made her pitch, and
    Lanza asked her assistant for her checkbook and wrote out a check for the full
    amount on the spot. This story shows how the serendipitous (and fortuitous)
    relationship between the U.S. government and American philanthropy helped
    begin to address the Agent Orange legacy.

20 As Indian ambassador to Vietnam Preeti Saran told the author in August 2015,
    Vietnam and India have enjoyed smooth and fruitful relations for more than
    seventy years. Their relationship is "like a clear, cloudless sky," she said, with few
    difficulties and numerous opportunities to act based on mutual interest.

21 Quoted in David Brunnstrom, "Pompeo Urges North Korea's Kim to Follow
    Vietnam's Example," Reuters, July 8, 2018, https://www.reuters.com/article/us
    -northkorea-usa-vietnam/pompeo-urges-north-koreas-kim-to-follow-vietnams
    -example-idUSKBN1JYoDS.

22 Quoted in Patricia Zengerle and David Brunnstrom, "Trump Says to Meet North
    Korea's Kim in Vietnam in Late February," Reuters, February 5, 2018, https://www
    .reuters.com/article/us-usa-northkorea/trump-says-to-meet-north-koreas-kim-in
    -vietnam-in-late-february-idUSKCN1PVo34?feedType=RSS&feedName
    =worldNews.

23 John Bolton, *The Room Where It Happened: A White House Memoir* (New York:
    Simon and Schuster, 2020), 301.

24 "International School of Ho Chi Minh City Graduation Ceremony—Class of
    2018," ISHCMC, June 1, 2018, https://www.youtube.com/watch?v=_3iyxx8yIZQ

25 Rajat Nag, "Asia's Challenges: Beyond the Fast Lane, Ensuring Inclusive and Green
    Growth," presentation at the Center for Strategic and International Studies,
    Washington, DC, March 20, 2012, 22.

26 More than 42,000 megawatts of new coal capacity are under development,
    according to a report by environmental groups. See Amy Harder, "Inside John
    Kerry's Shadow Diplomacy on Climate Change," Axios, April 8, 2019, https://www

.axios.com/john-kerry-vietnam-diplomacy-climate-change-5912b5f6-27aa-474b
-b129-56180427f821.html.

27 Mengpin Ge and Johannes Friedrich, "4 Charts Explain Greenhouse Gas Emissions
    by Countries and Sectors," World Resources Institute, https://www.wri.org/blog
    /2020/02/greenhouse-gas-emissions-by-country-sector

28 John Kerry, "Address to Vietnam Economic Forum," January 11, 2018, author's notes.

29 "Vietnam's Politburo Issues Resolution on Orientation of New National Energy
    Development Strategy to 2030 with a Vision to 2045," Baker McKenzie, Febru-
    ary 27, 2020, https://www.bakermckenzie.com/en/insight/publications/2020/02
    /vietnam-national-energy-development-strategy.

30 While coal did not meet its target in the Power Development Plan (PDP) VII,
    covering 2011–2020, renewables surpassed their targets multiple times. PDP VII
    had forecast an increase in renewable capacity from about 135 to 850 megawatts
    (MW) by 2020. The total installed and grid-connected solar capacity by the end of
    2019 reached 5.4 gigawatts (GW). This increased renewables' share of generation
    capacity from 0.4 percent in 2015 to 9.6 percent in 2019. By comparison, during the
    entire ten-year planning period for PDP VII, Vietnam added 6,700 MW of coal
    and thermal energy. Politburo Resolution 55 on Vietnam's energy development
    strategy bridges a gap between PDP VII, which focused on coal, and PDP VIII,
    which covers the period from 2021-2030, and will offer a greater role for renewables,
    battery storage, energy efficiency, and LNG. The data are from Minh Ha-Duong,
    "Decentralized Renewable Energy Broke Vietnam's Power Planning Logic," *Tia
    Sang*, March 25, 2021. See also: Julia Nguyen, "Vietnam's Solar Industry: Bright
    Prospects for Investors," Vietnam Briefing, March 8, 2020, https://www.vietnam
    -briefing.com/news/vietnams-solar-industry-bright-prospects-investors.html/; and
    "Stuck in the Pipeline: Vietnam's Coal Projects Stall While Renewables Surge,"
    Market Forces, August 2019, https://www.marketforces.org.au/stuck-in-the-pipeline
    -vietnams-coal-projects-stall-while-renewables-surge/.

31 Era Dabla-Norris, Anne-Marie Gulde-Wolf, and Francois Painchaud, "Vietnam's
    Success in Containing COVID-19 Offers Roadmap for Other Developing Coun-
    tries," IMF News, June 29, 2020, https://www.imf.org/en/News/Articles/2020/06
    /29/na062920-vietnams-success-in-containing-covid19-offers-roadmap-for-other
    -developing-countries.

32 Quoted in Max Walden, "How Has Vietnam, a Developing Nation in South-East
    Asia, Done So Well to Combat Coronavirus?," ABC News, May 12, 2020, https://
    www.abc.net.au/news/2020-05-13/coronavirus-vietnam-no-deaths-success-in-south
    -east-asia/12237314.

33 Quoted in Patrick Winn, "Is Vietnam the Coronavirus-Fighting Champ of the
    World?" The World, May 7, 2020, https://www.pri.org/stories/2020-05-07/vietnam
    -coronavirus-fighting-champ-world.

34 Quoted in Michael Tatarski and Patrick Sawer, "Life after Lockdown: Vietnam
    Reopens Tentatively after Zero Deaths," *Telegraph*, May 2, 2020, https://www
    .telegraph.co.uk/news/2020/05/02/life-lockdownvietnam-reopens-tentatively-zero
    -deaths/

35 Todd Pollack et al, "Emerging COVID-19 Success Story: Vietnam's Commitment
    to Containment," Exemplars in Global Health, accessed March 15, 2021, https://
    www.exemplars.health/emerging-topics/epidemic-preparedness-and-response/covid
    -19/vietnam.

Bibliography

The bibliography contains only authored books. Other sources are cited in the notes only.

Anderson, Desaix. *An American in Hanoi: America's Reconciliation with Vietnam.* White Plains, NY: EastBridge, 2002.
———. *United States-Vietnam Reconciliation: Through War to a Strategic Partnership.* Washington: New Academia Publishing, 2021.
Berman, Larry. *Perfect Spy: The Incredible Double Life of Pham Xuan An.* New York: HarperCollins, 2007.
Bolton, John. *The Room Where It Happened: A White House Memoir.* New York: Simon and Schuster, 2020.
Bowden, Mark. *Hue 1968: A Turning Point of the American War in Vietnam.* New York: Atlantic Monthly Press, 2017.
Campbell, Kurt M. *The Pivot: The Future of American Statecraft in Asia.* New York: Hachette Book Group, 2016.
Crow, Michael M., and William B. Dabars. *Designing the New American University.* Baltimore, MD: Johns Hopkins University Press, 2015.
Eyler, Brian. *Last Days of the Mighty Mekong.* London: Zed Books, 2019.
Faust, Drew Gilpin. *This Republic of Suffering: Death and the American Civil War.* New York: Alfred A. Knopf, 2012.
Hayton, Bill. *Vietnam: Rising Dragon.* London: Yale University Press, 2010.
Karnow, Stanley. *Vietnam: A History.* New York: Viking Press, 1983.
Kerry, John. *Every Day Is Extra.* New York: Simon and Schuster, 2018.
Lamb, David. *Vietnam, Now: A Reporter Returns.* New York: PublicAffairs, 2002.
Le, Ke Sơn, and Charles R. Bailey. *From Enemies to Partners: Vietnam, the U.S. and Agent Orange.* Chicago: G. Anton, 2017.
Long, Michael G., ed. *Race Man: Julian Bond Selected Works, 1960–2015.* San Francisco: City Lights Books, 2020.
McCain, John, with Mark Salter. *Faith of My Fathers.* New York: Random House, 1999.

McNamara, Robert, with Brian VanDeMark. *In Retrospect: The Tragedy and Lessons of Vietnam.* New York: Times Books, 1995.

Nguyễn, Thanh Việt. *The Refugees.* London: Corsair, 2017.

———. *The Sympathizer.* New York: Grove Press, 2015.

Ohler, Irene, and Đỗ Thùy Dương. *Bà Triệu's 21st Century Daughters: Stories of Remarkable Vietnamese Women.* Hanoi: Women's Publishing House, 2016.

Packer, George. *Our Man: Richard Holbrooke and the End of the American Century.* New York: Alfred A. Knopf, 2019.

Phạm, Andrew X. *Catfish and Mandala: A Two-Wheeled Voyage through the Landscape and Memory of Vietnam.* New York: Farrar, Straus and Giroux, 1999.

White, Theodore H. *In Search of History: A Personal Adventure.* New York: Warner Books, 1978.

World Bank and Ministry of Planning and Investment of Vietnam. *Vietnam 2035: Toward Prosperity, Creativity, Equity, and Democracy.* Washington, DC: World Bank, 2016.

Index

Note: Vietnamese names are indexed by surname with a cross-reference from the first name, in accordance with how names are written and how Vietnamese people are typically known. Vietnamese names written in the Western style are inverted and indexed by surname. Photographs are indicated by page numbers in italics.

About the Author

TED OSIUS was a diplomat for thirty years. He served from 2014 to 2017 as U.S. ambassador to Vietnam, a country he has known and loved since 1996. Only the second openly gay career diplomat in U.S. history to have achieved the rank of ambassador, Osius went to Vietnam with his husband and children.